Abject Loyalty

James H. Murphy

Abject Loyalty

Nationalism and Monarchy in Ireland

During the Reign of Queen Victoria

The Catholic University of America Press

Washington, D.C.

Library of Congress Cataloging-in-Publication Data

Murphy, James H.

Abject loyalty : nationalism and monarchy in Ireland during
the reign of Queen Victoria / James H. Murphy.

p.   cm.

Includes bibliographical references and index.

ISBN 0-8132-1076-3 (alk. paper)

1. Ireland—Politics and government—1837–1901.

2. Nationalism—Ireland—History—19th century.

3. Monarchy—Ireland—History—19th century.   I. Title.

DA950 .M94   2001

941.5081—dc21

00-047462

For Stina Ericsson, Richard Nash,

Richard & Patricia McDonnell,

and Luke & Nora Healy.

Contents

Acknowledgments

I wish to acknowledge, with much gratitude, the gracious permission of Her Majesty Queen Elizabeth II to use material from the Royal Archives, Windsor Castle, in this book. I am also grateful to the Council of Trustees of the National Library of Ireland for permission to quote from the Larcom Papers.

The staff of the Royal Archives and of the Royal Photographic Collection were unfailingly kind and helpful to me. In particular, Lady de Bellaigue and Pamela M. Clark, registrar and deputy registrar, respectively, of the Royal Archives, gave me every assistance in my work there. Elaine and Claude Tonna-Barthet, Conrad and Gráinne Murphy, and Tony Brennan very kindly accommodated me during my various research trips to Windsor and London. Dr. D. A. Beirne and Miriam Flanagan, of All Hallows College, Dublin, were also very helpful in facilitating my research work.

Professor R. V. Comerford and Dr. Margaret Kelleher, both of the National University of Ireland, Maynooth, each read my text at an early stage and made most helpful suggestions, for which I am deeply grateful. I would also like to thank the following individuals who helped my work in various ways: Professor Walter L. Arnstein of the University of Illinois at Urbana-Champaign, Deborah Hill Bornheimer of Boston, Professor D. George Boyce of University College Swansea, Professor Terry Eagleton of the University of Oxford, Professor John D. Fair of Georgia State University, Professor Tom Garvin of University College Dublin, Dr. Patrick Maume of the Queen's University of Belfast, and Dr. Alan O'Day of the University of North London. Finally, I am grateful to the staffs of the Bodleian Library, the British Library, the National Library of Ireland, the National Archives of Ireland, and the libraries of Columbia University, New York University, All Hallows College Dublin, Trinity College Dublin, and University College Dublin.

JHM

Introduction

Nationalist Ireland and British Monarchy

This is an account of the significance of monarchy in nineteenth- and, indeed, twentieth-century Ireland, but particularly during the reign of Queen Victoria. It weaves together two strands, one largely private, the other largely public. The first is the story of the interaction of the British monarchy with Ireland, especially during Queen Victoria's sixty-three-and-a-half-year reign. It is the story of Queen Victoria's occasional public actions, such as royal visits, but mostly of her private views—many of them in their bluntness closer to those of the Victorian middle classes than to those of wily politicians—and attempts to influence government policy. Some of this story is already known, though it has never been completely told before. Its sources are archival, principally the four thousands documents that constitute Queen Victoria's correspondence relating to Ireland and which, together with her journal, are preserved in the royal archives at Windsor Castle.

The second strand is the story of the public reaction in nationalist Ireland to monarchy, or to the perception of monarchy, and of the insight that it gives us as to how people regarded monarchy and its role. It is the story of the response of individuals and crowds to royal visits, and of the discourse on the monarchy employed by nationalist politicians and journalists. Of course a picture of the public mood at any given time is not so easy to reconstruct as are the views of political leaders but it can be inferred from the actions of those leaders as they seek to react to and shape it.

The sources for this second strand are more public than those for the first and can be found in books, open letters, and in public and parliamentary speeches. Above all, newspapers provide a rich source for this story. In the following account over fifty newspapers and journals are cited, though there is special reliance on a thorough reading of the *Freeman's Journal* for the period. This was Ireland's premier daily nationalist paper and ran to over twenty thousand editions during the reign of Queen Victoria.

This second story has never really been told before. Perhaps the reason is that it has been thought a story not worth telling. It is presumed that Irish nationalists were hostile to the British monarchy. And, indeed, by the time of Irish independence in 1922, there was an official and settled antipathy toward the monarchy both among the new governing class and among large portions of the Irish population. The route to such antipathy, however, is long and tangled. It is the subject of this book.

Why is it, for example, that Queen Victoria, whose power under the British constitution was limited in the extreme, is still derided in Irish nationalist mythology as the Famine Queen, indifferent to, if not actually responsible for, the deaths of millions in Ireland in the 1840s, when the British politicians who actually devised and implemented government policy at the time are for the most part forgotten? The beginnings of an answer lie in a rather obvious psychological observation: one only needs to feel antipathy toward that which is a threat.

The perhaps startling reality is that the British monarchy, inasmuch as it was perceived as a threat by nationalists in nineteenth-century Ireland, was not a threat because it had any political power but because it was popular in Ireland and because it was seen to symbolize a future for Ireland as a contented part of the United Kingdom that was anathema to nationalists.

❖

In 1801 Ireland became part of the United Kingdom of Great Britain and Ireland. Four bishops and twenty-eight representative peers from Ireland were admitted to the House of Lords in London and one hundred Irish Members of Parliament (MPs) were elected to the House of Commons. Hitherto Ireland had been a separate kingdom and there had been an Irish Parliament, under the control of the so-called Protestant ascendancy, the governing class in Ireland, though its powers were limited by statues such as Poynings's Law (1494) and the Declaratory Act (1720). In 1782, in the wake of the British defeat in North America, Ireland had gained a measure of independence from the government in London and the latter's representatives in the Irish executive in Dublin Castle. The threat of revolutionary France and the Irish rebellion of 1798, however, convinced the London government that the time had come to take Ireland more directly under its control.

Wales had long since been attached to England and the kingdoms of Scotland and England, joined dynastically since 1603, had already formed a parliamentary union in 1707. With the coming into force of the Act of Union (1800), the islands of Britain and Ireland formed a legislative union, though a residual Irish executive continued to exist at Dublin Castle and, as nationalists were often to point out, for most of the nineteenth century Ireland was subject to what was generally known as coercion, emergency legislation to counteract systemic lawlessness of an agrarian or political nature which reduced an individual's rights to the ordinary, due process of law.

Three kingdoms had been joined together to form the United Kingdom but how many countries or nations existed within the new dispensation and how did the continuing separateness of their existence relate to a shared sense of British identity? It was only really in the 1880s that the Liberal Party under Gladstone came to something like the view that there were four nations within the kingdom, each with its own particular needs. At the other end of the scale was the view that the kingdom was essentially England and that Ireland, Scotland, and Wales were, like Yorkshire or Devon and Cornwall, merely regions of a greater England.[1] Thus in 1857 the Sheffield MP J. A. Roebuck confidently told the House of Commons that "Ireland is a part—an integral part of England, governed as England is, suffering under no political or natural misfortune. . . . She is not and ought not to be considered an independent country."[2]

The construction of a sense of British identity, however, consisted in more than a simple attempt at the Anglicization of the Celtic fringes.[3] It

1. See D. G. Boyce, "The Marginal Britons: The Irish," in Robert Colls and Philip Dodd, eds., *Englishness: Politics and Culture, 1880–1920* (London: Croom Helm, 1986), 231. "It was instinctive for the English to regard the terms English and British as virtually synonymous. . . . The Irish were not a distinct nation. . . . If Ireland was different, so then was Yorkshire; regionalism was not nationalism; and any threat that seemed about to elevate regionalism into something more sinister—any threat like O'Connell's monster meetings of Irish Roman Catholics—was met with firmness and, if need be, with force to prevent, as Sir Robert peel put it in 1843, the dissolution of the empire." See also Hugh Kearney, *The British Isles: A History of Four Nations* (Cambridge: Cambridge University Press, 1989), passim.

2. 7 July 1857, *Parliamentary Debates*, 3d Series, vol. 146 (19 June–17 July 1857), col. 1049.

3. See Linda Colley, "Britishness and Otherness: An Argument," in Michael O'Dea and Kevin Whelan, eds., *Nations and Nationalism: France, Britain, Ireland, and the Eighteenth-Century Context*, Studies in Voltaire and the Eighteenth Century 335 (Oxford: Voltaire Foundation,

had been forged in the eighteenth century after the formation of Great Britain from England and Scotland. Indeed, it is instructive to reflect on the fact that, after the formation of the United Kingdom of Great Britain and Ireland in 1801, "British" came to be used as the adjective for the national identity of the new United Kingdom.

Britain was an invented nation that did not suppress older national identities but created a new overarching national identity. It was forged by three factors: a common Protestant culture, the need to coalesce against foreign threats in a series of wars between 1689 and 1815, and the promise of prosperity that the existence of the growing British Empire overseas held out.[4] Catholic France was a threat on all three fronts: religious, military, and imperial. It was the enemy that helped Britain to become galvanized into a coherent nation.[5]

All of this made it hard for Ireland to become assimilated to British identity, particularly with the growth of Catholic nationalism in Ireland under Daniel O'Connell from the 1820s onward.[6] And yet there was a determination in Britain that Ireland could never be allowed internal autonomy, much less independence. There were two reasons for this. The first, as politicians from Sir Robert Peel to Lord Randolph Churchill argued, was that if Ireland was granted self-rule it would lead to the breakup of the British Empire. If Ireland, then why not India? This argument became an idée fixe in British political thinking to such an extent that it could survive the granting of a large measure of self-rule to other parts of the British

---

1995), 66. "Britishness was not just imposed from the centre, nor can it be understood solely or even mainly as the result of an English cultural or economic colonisation of the so-called Celtic fringe. The extent of such anglicisation has, to begin with, often been exaggerated."

4. Linda Colley, "Britishness and Otherness," 66 and 75, and *Britons: Forging the Nation, 1707–1837* (New Haven, Conn.: Yale University Press, 1992), 367.

5. Colley, *Britons*, 368. "A powerful and persistently threatening France became the haunting embodiment of that Catholic Other which Britons had been taught to fear since the Reformation in the sixteenth century."

6. Colley, "Britishness and Otherness," 76. "From the British and not just the Irish side—Ireland could seldom be accommodated within the framework of the United Kingdom, was often the poor relation. It was the ideal jumping off point for a French invasion, and both its Protestant and Catholic dissidents traditionally looked to France for aid. . . . Ireland's relationship with the empire was always a deeply ambiguous one. How could it not be when London so persistently treated the country in a way it never treated Scotland and Wales, as a colony rather than an integral part of a truly united kingdom?"

Empire such as Canada, a case to which Irish nationalists were not slow to point. The second reason had to do with the mythology of British greatness which had reached its zenith in the defeat of Napoleon. As this occurred after the Act of Union, it was felt that it must somehow have been dependent on it.[7]

If Ireland did not fit naturally into the United Kingdom's constitutional consensus, then it could not be allowed to change that consensus no matter how much tension was created thereby. Questioning the constitution was not an open political issue; therefore, it was a sign of disloyalty. The constitutional settlement of the United Kingdom thus in time became a contentious settlement, at least as far as Ireland was concerned, with those elements that supported the settlement, including the London political establishment and the Crown, engaging themselves in a long-term struggle for ideological convergence for their view of the permanence of the constitution against the centrifugal forces of Irish nationalism.

Irish nationalists sometimes argued that the queen was still the queen of the kingdom of Ireland. For them the throne was separable from the then constitutional position of Ireland in the United Kingdom. Throughout her reign, however, Queen Victoria and much of the British political establishment saw her throne on the contrary as being inseparable from the constitutional settlement of the United Kingdom, to the extent that even an Irish Parliament subordinate to that of the United Kingdom would not be tolerated. The Crown thus identified itself with the United Kingdom though this was ultimately to the detriment of its credibility with Irish nationalists.

To Queen Victoria all Irish nationalists who called for self-government were implicitly rebels, without political legitimacy. To an increasing number of Irish nationalists, as time went on, the Crown was not seen as an impartial constitutional institution, as it largely became in Britain by the end of the nineteenth century. It was a partisan political force. The difference lay in conflicting perspectives on what could be counted as legitimate political goals. The struggle over Ireland and the monarchy's role within it was thus highly ideological.

Indeed, the role of the Crown in the struggle against nationalism was to increase in importance in Ireland in the course of the nineteenth century.

7. Boyce, "Marginal Britons," 234. "To break up the United Kingdom would be to unpick the seams of British history and undermine the basis of British power."

In the 1870s the rise of the Irish Parliamentary Party and parliamentary reform spelt the end of the influence of metropolitan British political parties in nationalist Ireland. The Irish Liberals were virtually eclipsed and the
Conservatives could win few seats outside Protestant and pro-union Ulster. The Crown was the last hope for the union settlement in nationalist
Ireland.

✦

The monarchy itself was by no means a static or even a stable institution during the eighteenth and nineteenth centuries. With the death of the
last Protestant Stuart, Queen Anne, in 1714, the British Crown was passed
to the electoral princes of Hanover, who formed one of the two branches
of the House of Brunswick.[8] Their chief virtue was their Protestantism.
Into the nineteenth century, there continued to be a strong link between
dynastic allegiance and religious affiliation.[9]

In spite of a period of popularity at the time of King George III's gold-
en jubilee in 1809,[10] the monarchy was not an institution that was held in
high esteem when Queen Victoria came to the throne in 1837.[11] The Regency morality of her uncles was condemned. Her family's German connections, augmented by her marriage to Prince Albert of Saxe-Coburg and
Gotha, made the monarchy seem un-English, and in a utilitarian age, the
ceremonial of monarchy seemed redundant.

By the middle of Queen Victoria's reign the monarchy was no longer
seen as politically partisan, thanks to the counsel of the astute Albert, and
had lost most of its remaining political power, thanks to the queen's protracted withdrawal from public life following his death.[12] By the end of

---

8. The other branch was that of the dukes of Brunswick, to which George IV's wife,
Caroline of Brunswick, belonged. Both branches were united in the later nineteenth century. British sovereigns remained rulers of Hanover until the accession of Queen Victoria in
1837. As a woman she was not allowed to succeed in Hanover, which passed to her uncle
the duke of Cumberland. In the settlement following the Napoleonic Wars Hanover was
raised to the status of a kingdom, though it was later forcibly absorbed by Prussia. Its last
king, the blind George V, died in exile.

9. See J. C. D. Clark, *English Society, 1688–1832: Ideology, Social Structure, and Political Practice
during the Ancien Regime* (Cambridge: Cambridge University Press, 1985), 196–97.

10. Colley, *Britons*, 217.

11. Richard Williams, *The Contentious Crown: Public Discussion of the British Monarchy in the
Reign of Queen Victoria* (Brookfield, Vt.: Ashgate, 1997), 4.

12. Williams, *The Contentious Crown*, 115.

her reign the monarchy had become the symbol both of British national identity and of British imperial greatness and the focus of patriotism and renewed national ceremonial.[13]

There were several reasons for this. One was that W. E. Gladstone, in spite of his personal difficulties with Queen Victoria, sought to promote veneration for the monarchy not only as a counter to the short-lived English republican movement of the early 1870s but also as the basis for a new sense of British national identity.[14] "Both Gladstone and Disraeli arrived at this strategy in response to the creation of a large urban electorate in 1867; a consensual image of the nation was needed if the politics of class were to be avoided."[15]

A second reason involved the modification of the notion of patriotism. In England the language of patriotism had long been associated with popular rights and radical protest against the state. Beginning with Lord Palmerston and Benjamin Disraeli the language of patriotism began to move across the political spectrum until by the time of the eastern crisis of 1877–1888, it had become the vocabulary of conservatism. By the end of the century this conservative patriotism had become the social norm and had come to be symbolized in loyalty to the Crown.[16] Thus in Britain the monarchy was in a far more secure position at the end of Queen Victoria's reign than it had been at the beginning. But some of the very factors that had strengthened it in Britain were to weaken it in Ireland.

Nineteenth-century Irish nationalism was a complex phenomenon. Terms such as "nationalist" itself were widely used in the later part of the nineteenth century, less so in the earlier part. For the sake of convenience in this discussion, "nationalism" and "nationalist" will be used to denote a

13. David Cannadine, "The Context, Performance, and Meaning of Ritual: The British Monarchy and the 'Invention of Tradition' c 1820–1977," in Eric Hobsbaum and Terence Ranger, eds., *The Invention of Tradition* (Cambridge: Cambridge University Press, 1983), 101–64.

14. Freda Harcourt, "Gladstone, Monarchism, and the 'New Imperialism,' 1868–74," *Journal of Imperial and Commonwealth History* 14, no. 1 (October 1985): 20–51.

15. Williams, *The Contentious Crown*, 209.

16. See Hugh Cunningham, "The Language of Patriotism," *History Workshop* 12 (Autumn 1981): 23–24, and "The Conservative Party and Patriotism," in Robert Colls and Philip Dodd, eds., *Englishness, Politics, and Culture, 1880–1920* (London: Croom Helm, 1986), 283–307.

particular broad tradition of Irish politics during the whole of the century.

Nationalists varied widely on how they saw Ireland's future, depending
on whether they saw the nation in pragmatic terms or in terms of tran-
scendent romanticism. However, four main schools of thought were
prominent: (1) reform within the United Kingdom, (2) an Irish mode of
government and society within the United Kingdom, (3) some form of autonomy together with a continuing connection with Britain, and (4) a
completely independent republic.

At the mildest end of nationalism some would have been content with
social, religious, and economic reforms within the United Kingdom. They
would thus have welcomed the agendas of meliorist British governments,
both Liberal and Tory, who wanted to achieve "justice for Ireland." Others
sought to achieve an Ireland with its own distinctive way of life and institutions, an Ireland run according to Irish ideas. This was the position that
Scotland, with its own distinctive legal, religious, and educational systems,
had achieved in the United Kingdom. For a majority, though, Ireland required a significant degree of internal self-government if it was to flourish
as a nation.[17]

Clearly the idea of Ireland as a nation and of what that might entail politically was by no means a fixed or settled matter. It is of interest that
many of the slogans connected with the concept of the nation leave the
possibilities open. "Ireland a Nation" was a common slogan. "A Nation
Once Again" was the title of a popular song. Both omit a verb and therefore encompass, in the case of the first, for example, a variety of meanings:
Ireland *is* a nation, Ireland *will be* a nation, Ireland *ought to be* a nation. The
concept of the nation, therefore, had hermeneutical, programmatic, and
heuristic aspects to it. It was a way of explaining the present, urging a way
to the future, and testing how that future might be achieved.

During the course of the nineteenth century the call of most Irish nationalists for "repeal" (of the Act of Union) or for "home rule" was for
the establishment of internal Irish autonomy through the restoration of
"Grattan's parliament," the "Queen, Lords, and Commons" of Ireland as it
had been before the Act of Union. Of course, an Irish House of Com-

---

17. See R. V. Comerford, *Fenians in Context* (Dublin: Woflhound, 1985), 31–32. For Comerford the principal division of opinion in nineteenth-century Irish nationalism was between those who sought self-government and those who sought "an Ireland with its own
distinctive life and institutions."

mons, elected by an enfranchised Catholic majority, would have been a very different institution from the Commons of ascendancy days and one not likely to appeal to the Protestant minority in Ireland—though this was an issue that few nationalists cared to address. The call for the restoration of "Grattan's parliament" was thus in many ways merely a slogan. When it came to it, as with the Liberal plans for home rule in 1886 and 1893, an Irish Parliament subordinate to that at Westminster would have been acceptable to most nationalists.[18]

Throughout the nineteenth century the monarchy was often spoken of as the "golden link" or "golden bridge" between Britain and Ireland. Yet it meant different things on either side of the Irish Sea. With the decline in the actual powers of the monarchy, self-appointed constitutional expects such as Walter Bagehot, whose *The English Constitution* was published in 1867, backed the view that the role of the monarchy was to provide an emotional focus to mitigate divisions in society.

For British politicians, therefore, the golden bridge of the monarchy was a means whereby the Irish might become reconciled to their position within the United Kingdom. For Irish nationalist politicians, the golden bridge could provide a continuing symbolic link with Britain that might, to an extent, disguise the high degree of autonomy that they hoped to have gained.

Most Irish nationalists were monarchists, therefore, of either the enthusiastic or the grudging but realistic varieties. This ought not to come as a surprise. In the nineteenth century the vast majority of countries were monarchies of one form or another. International relations were relations between monarchs, a fact that gave Queen Victoria a greater influence than her domestic constitutional position warranted. In the age of nationalism, subjecthood was still as viable a form of political identity for the individual as membership in a nation, and the two were in principle by no means incompatible. Monarchy seemed the natural form of government and it had the blessing of the Catholic Church—a fact of great significance in Ireland, where the overwhelming majority of nationalists were Catholics.[19]

18. For Alan O'Day, in *Irish Home Rule, 1867–1921* (Manchester: Manchester University Press, 1998), passim, there was a division among the advocates of home rule between those who sought self-government on moral grounds, to heal Ireland's internal divisions, and those who sought it on material grounds, to enhance Irish prosperity.

19. See Tom Garvin, *1922: The Birth of Irish Democracy* (Dublin: Gill and Macmillan, 1996), 11. "It was not until well into the nineteenth century that republican ideas of a sort gained a firm hold in the minds of a proportion of the Catholic majority in the country. Prior to

Fiction provides examples of often complex attitudes toward monarchy. The views of Mrs. O'Kelly, in Rosa Mulholland's novel *Marcella Grace*, combine an enthusiastic monarchism with an Irish patriotism, for example, in a manner that ought to cause little surprise, as she is a Catholic landlord:

"I pay my respects periodically to the viceroy of my queen. Neither do I forget to patronise the home manufactures of my country; only this day I expect a parcel of rich tabinet, woven in Dublin, to make me a castle train. My *modiste* wished me to have it of Lyons velvet, but I said 'no, not unless it can be made for me in Ireland.'"[20]

More remarkable is *A Royal Democrat: A Sensational Irish Novel*, by the radical Alice Milligan. At first sight it seems to tilt against monarchy, telling the story of a Prince of Wales who is shipwrecked in Ireland and prefers to live anonymously as an Irish nationalist rather than succeed to the throne. Even among advanced nationalists though he encounters the continuing allure of monarchy, as in this exchange with Nola, the young woman he ends up marrying, who is to visit London:

"You will see the young Queen drive out in the afternoon; but I forgot you are a democrat and take no delight in staring at Royalty."
    "Oh, I have a good deal of womanly curiosity still, in spite of my principles and I confess that I should like very much to see Queen Frederika. She is beautiful, they say; but perhaps that is the usual flattery which great people receive."[21]

Startlingly, the novel ends with the now widowed Nola becoming "the dearest friend and constant companion" of the queen in a fantasy that reveals a deep-seated, nationalist desire to be embraced by monarchy rather than to reject it.[22]

    Though in theory accepting of the monarchy, many nationalists became in practice increasingly anti-monarchical in temperament. In the case of a few, such as the republican Maud Gonne, this was for ideological reasons. In the case of the many, however, it was a logical political response to the anti-nationalist function that the monarchy was seen to be playing, albeit a response that in time became ingrained and visceral.

then, most Irish Catholics were probably monarchists in their political thinking such as it was."
    20. *Irish Monthly* 13 (1885): 57.
    21. Alice L. Milligan, *A Royal Democrat: A Sensational Novel* (1890; Dublin: M. H. Gill, 1892), 126.
    22. Milligan, *A Royal Democrat*, 288.

Nor ought temperamental anti-monarchism to be necessarily equated with espoused republicanism. Some of the most virulent anti-monarchists of the 1880s, for example, were the young Turks of the Irish Parliamentary Party, William O'Brien, Tim Healy, and the Redmond brothers, who officially supported the continuance of the monarchy in Ireland. The views on the monarchy of the ageing Fenian, and official republican, John O'Leary, seemed benign by contrast. For him, Queen Victoria was "a highly respectable foreign lady" who "symbolized that British rule which was hateful to my soul" but who could not help being "the English Queen of Ireland."[23]

Republicanism was the preference of only a minority in Ireland and was most enthusiastically espoused by Irish people who had links with some of the world's few republics such as the United States of America and France, though the latter might best be termed a "serial republic." There were republicans, such as John Mitchel, for whom an Irish republic entailed a radical change in the order of society. But they were relatively few in number.

In the context of nineteenth-century Irish politics, republicanism mostly stood not so much for a particular vision of society as for a particular version of Ireland's relationship with Britain: total separation. It was a relationship in which the last link, golden or otherwise, had been broken and as such it was not accounted by the majority as a very realistic option. For the sake of the coherence of its empire, Britain would never allow this. In any event, Britain was the dominant world power. As its nearest neighbor Ireland could never hope to live in isolation from it.[24]

It is not possible to gauge scientifically what ordinary people in nineteenth-century nationalist Ireland thought of the monarchy. But it may be possible to construe their views to an extent from the public discourse of their political leaders.[25] However, the connection between the culture of

23. John O'Leary, *Recollections of a Fenian and Fenianism*, 2 vols. (London: Downey, 1898), 2:131.

24. See O'Day, *Irish Home Rule*, 6. "Republicans might dream of an unambiguous break, but they usually failed to address the matter of Ireland's place within a British-dominated North Atlantic imperium."

25. See Williams, *The Contentious Crown*, 2. "I cannot pretend to be making an analysis of national public opinion, except in so far as newspapers and speech-makers reflect and shape the opinions of readers and audiences."

official political discourse and the opinions of ordinary people is a complex one. To a degree each reflects the other. To a degree each forms the other.

What politicians can say in public is determined both by a sensitivity to their constituency in the broad sense and by the constraints of what it is allowable to say in public at any given time. Politicians who offended against the views of those they sought to represent were often subject to an immediate rebuke in an age of public meetings and processions, before the era of the television studio and the need for opinion polls. Thus in July 1883, when nationalist politicians cooperated with Liberals and Tories in a trade exhibition in Cork that opened with the singing of "God Save the Queen," there was a significant public boycott of the event.[26]

Until the 1870s the political culture that constrained Irish politicians worked in favor of monarchy, thereafter it worked against it. In April 1869 Daniel O'Sullivan, the mayor of Cork, made semiprivate remarks insulting to the royal family that were subsequently reported in the newspapers. Enmeshed as they were in the general political culture of the United Kingdom at the time, Irish politicians found themselves supporting the British outrage at his remarks. By the early 1880s the self-assertiveness of nationalist politicians had grown to such an extent that insults about the royal family were almost de rigeur for those who wanted to advance their political careers in Ireland.

As for the views of ordinary people, they not only influenced politicians but were also influenced by them.[27] This was especially so concerning enthusiasm for the monarchy. The nationalist political class came to deride popular support for the monarchy as the result either of a sense of colonial inferiority, which they termed "flunkeyism," or as the phoney result of direct pressure from the landlord and higher commercial classes, which were Protestant and pro-union, on the lower ranks of society. And once nationalism had decisively set its face against the monarchy in the early decades of the twentieth century, individuals could express support for the monarchy only at the cost of having their Irishness questioned. Yet interest in the monarchy continued and continues to exist, as evidenced in recent

26. *Freeman's Journal*, 4 July 1883; hereafter cited as *FJ.*

27. Williams, *Contentious Crown*, 2. "Politicians and their literary protagonists attempted to influence opinion on the great issues through the reproduction in print of speeches, through the publication of pamphlets and, above all, through the newspapers." Williams's study is of Britain but his remarks apply also to Ireland.

decades by the large number of Irish television viewers of royal weddings and funerals. It remains an unresolved issue.

※

For most of the nineteenth century elections of MPs in Ireland, as in Britain, were rather imperfect affairs from the point of view of modern democracy. Until 1872 electors voted in public and were subject to pressure and bribery. The Catholic Relief Act of 1829 allowed Catholics to sit as MPs but reduced the number of electors in the process. Gradual parliamentary reform occurred by means of legislation in 1832, 1850, 1868, 1884, and 1885, which redrew constituency boundaries and progressively reduced property qualifications for voting, though universal male and partial female voting rights were not conceded until 1918.

In such circumstances public meetings, banquets, and processions were of enormous importance. Such meetings could have a number of ostensible purposes: to listen to speeches, to agree on resolutions, to draw up memorials, to make pledges, to greet returned heroes or bid farewell to departing ones, to bury the recently deceased or to memorialize the venerable dead. But their real purposes included gauging public support, assuring allegiance, pressurizing authority, and securing a mandate for action.

There were five major forces in nineteenth-century nationalist Ireland that were capable to attracting support, or at least significant support from different sectors of the public, as evidenced by attendance at mass gatherings: physical-force activism, religion, land agitation, constitutional politics[28] and monarchy. There were of course other minor movements that attracted mass support, but they tended to fall within the ambit of one of the five major forces. Thus Father Mathew's Temperance Movement of the 1840s came to an extent under Daniel O'Connell's spell and many of the cultural, language, and sporting movements that sprang up toward the end of the century were infiltrated by the Irish Republican Brotherhood.

28. In this context the term "constitutional" is the term conventionally used to connote politics that employed all legal means open to it and did not have recourse to violence. It thus indicates a mode of political activity. Inasmuch as such politics was often directed at securing political autonomy for Ireland, it was often depicted by members of the political establishment in Britain as being rebellious, disloyal, or unconstitutional, as indicated in the discussion slightly earlier in this chapter. For them only that which supported the existing constitutional settlement was properly "constitutional." The use of the term in this second sense indicates an object of political activity, that is, the bolstering of the union. Where the term is used in this book the context should be sufficient to indicate which of the two uses for the term is intended.

Though it often had a political dimension and links with constitutional politics, physical-force political activism was primarily a covert and often a piecemeal activity. Public support for those involved in rebellions or outrages and for their motives, if not always for their actions, was demonstrated by mass turnouts at funerals, most famously for that of Terence Bellew MacManus in 1861, and in attendance at amnesty meetings for those convicted of participating in rebellions or outrages. The campaign for the amnesty of Fenian prisoners in the late 1860s and early 1870s is a good example of the latter.

Public demonstrations of support for religion and land agitation followed a surprisingly similar pattern. For the most part, nationalists were Catholics and increasingly committed ones at that as the nineteenth century wore on. Whereas there were occasional mass gatherings, often for episcopal or papal jubilees, support for religion was most obviously demonstrated by regular attendance at the local church. Similarly, though the "land war" of the 1880s was punctuated by mass meetings, the strength of the movement lay in and was demonstrated by a commitment to local means of agitation, such as boycotting.

Quite obviously largely constitutional politics movements relied heavily on the effects of the mass meeting, from the "monster" meetings of O'Connell's Repeal Association in the 1840s to the great public meetings, often associated with elections in a more enfranchised age, of the Irish Party in the 1880s. One of the reasons why constitutional political leaders in nationalist Ireland were so nervous concerning the monarchy was because support for it was demonstrated in essentially similar ways. Royal visits occasioned great gatherings of people along the routes of royal processions which could be compared with numbers attending nationalist political meetings. And there is no doubt that hundreds of thousands of people did turn out to see royal visitors to Ireland. It is often asserted, for example, and probably not without justification, that one million people saw Queen Victoria during the course of her 1853 visit to Dublin.[29]

Given the large numbers turning out for royal visits, two related questions arise. What was the disposition of the crowds and what was the significance of their disposition? Though nationalist politicians often tried to

---

29. The one million figure is claimed, for example, in the entry on Queen Victoria in Leslie Stephen and Sir Sydney Lee, ed., *The Dictionary of National Biography* (London: Smith Elder, 1909), 22 (Supplement):1304; hereafter cited as *DNB*.

play down the level of enthusiasm, few seriously disputed that on most royal visits the crowds were enthusiastic. One of those who did was John O'Leary who nearly fifty years afterward claimed to recall that on her 1849 visit Queen Victoria "was received with considerable curiosity, and, as far as one could judge a total absence of all other feelings. She passed down the broadest street in Dublin, or perhaps in Europe, amid a gaping crowd, but, as far as I could see or hear, without a single cheer or other sign of sympathetic interest. And her Majesty did not like her position, if one were to judge by her looks and no wonder either."[30] O'Leary's account is contradicted by all contemporary accounts of the 1849 visit, which report enormous enthusiasm on the part of the crowds.

Another way of gauging the existence of widespread enthusiasm is through English sources. Referring to Queen Victoria's entry into Dublin on her 1900 visit, her assistant private secretary, Frederick Ponsonby, he noted that there was some booing at two points on the route. Nonetheless, he wrote of it that "[a]lthough I had seen many visits of this kind, nothing had ever approached the enthusiasm and even frenzy displayed by the people of Dublin."[31] In 1903 the enthusiasm in Queenstown for Edward VII at the conclusion of his first visit to Ireland as king was so great that one subsequent commentator remarked, "And these are the people whom some call disloyal."[32]

Such reactions were not the sole province of those who wanted to see the monarchy popular in Ireland and might be expected to overstate enthusiasm. Of crucial significance therefore is English opinion opposed to royal visits to Ireland which, by criticizing the popular welcome for royalty, acknowledged its reality. Thus for Lord Byron in "The Irish Avatar" the enthusiastic reception accorded to George IV, "the Messiah of royalty," in Ireland in 1821 was the cause of

> My contempt for a nation so servile, though sore,
> Which though trod like the worm will not turn upon power.[33]

---

30. O'Leary, *Fenianism*, 2:61.

31. Frederick Ponsonby, *Recollections of Three Reigns* (London: Eyre and Spottiswood, 1951), 63.

32. Quoted in Sidney Lee, *King Edward VII: A Biography*, 2 vols. (London: Macmillan, 1927), 2:167.

33. Lord Byron, *The Poetical Works of Lord Byron* (London: John Murray, 1876), 575, quoted in *United Ireland*, 14 March 1885.

And for Richard Monckton Milnes the huge welcome that Queen Victoria received in Ireland in 1849 was "idolatrous and utterly unworthy of a free, not to say ill-used, nation."[34]

The question as to what such enthusiasm signified is a more complex one. A common English, and sometimes Irish, explanation was that the Irish were natural monarchists and, being Celtic and thus supposedly emotional, prone to enthusiasm for the royal family. "The [Irish] people are more easily moved to loyalty for the Queen and royal family than the English or Scotch," Lord Spencer told Gladstone in 1885.[35] Four years later an English MP complained to the House of Commons that Irish MPs had not helped English Radicals to oppose increased royal grants. However, he went on, "I am not surprised at this because chivalric devotion to persons and great respect for hereditary rank have been, and still are, more powerful factors with the Irish race than they are with ourselves."[36]

Some nationalists claimed conveniently that the crowds that welcomed royal visitors were merely the representatives of a distinct, nonnationalist minority. Thus when Victoria's second son, Prince Alfred, Duke of Edinburgh, visited Dublin in 1884, *United Ireland* claimed that he had been greeted by "the few flunkeys who are always to be found in Dublin" whereas "the vast bulk of the people" ignored him.[37]

The less settling truth was probably that those who greeted royal visitors were often the same people who supported home rule, and even the Fenians. Some may have been interested in mass gatherings of a variety of political complexions as a form of entertainment.[38] Others may simply have been unself-consciously capable of sustaining several sorts of allegiances simultaneously. In April 1868, for example, the viceroy, Lord Abercorn, told Queen Victoria that former Fenians had been seen cheering the Prince and Princess of Wales on their recent visit.[39]

34. Quoted in *DNB*, 22 (Supplement):1298.

35. Lord Spencer to W. E. Gladstone, 26 January 1885, in Gladstone Papers (hereafter cited as GP), Add MSS 44312 ff 1–8, in Peter Gordon, *The Red Earl. Papers of the Fifth Earl Spencer*, vol. 1 (1835–1885) (Northampton: Northampton Records Society, 1981), no. 386, p. 291.

36. 25 July 1889, E. H. Pickersgill, *Parliamentary Debates*, 3d Series, vol. 338 (10 July–21 August 1889), col. 1333.

37. *United Ireland*, 6 September 1884.

38. R. V. Comerford (*Fenians*, 79) writes that many people attended the funeral of Terence Bellew MacManus in 1861 "because it was a spectacle and an excuse for ovating."

39. RA D 24/34, Lord Abercorn to Queen Victoria, 25 April 1868. This was a judgment with which the Fenians themselves agreed. When the Prince of Wales visited in 1865 the

No doubt the fickleness of the populace was an unsettling thought for nationalist leaders and was the principal cause of their growing hostility toward the monarchy. In truth, however, support for the monarchy was less deeply rooted than support for nationalism, as Queen Victoria herself noted in 1897 in the wake of the enthusiastic reception that the recent visit of the duke and duchess of York had occasioned, "It was the same on the occasion of our three visits there, but alas, it did not produce a lasting effect, and the Queen feels that this may still be the case."[40]

And yet the reception of royal visitors was a key preoccupation for nationalist leaders to the extent that they often felt it necessary to engage in a hermeneutics of royal occasions in order to explain, or explain away, popular enthusiasm. In his *The Last Conquest of Ireland (Perhaps)* John Mitchel assesses Queen Victoria's 1849 visit which, due to his transportation to Tasmania, he had not personally witnessed.

In the course of only two paragraphs Mitchel offers four explanations for the warmth of her reception. The first is that it was the doing of "the great army of persons, who, in Ireland, are paid to be loyal, [and] were expected to get up the appearance of rejoicing." The second is "the natural courtesy of the people" which prevented them from protesting against the visit. The third is "the Viceroy's precautions against any show of disaffection." And the fourth is the people's expectation, false as it turned out, that a lack of protest might bring clemency for those recently convicted and transported on account of the brief 1848 rebellion.[41] The cheering crowds were thus acting in a fashion that showed that they were simultaneously venal, instinctively respectful, cowed by the threat of force, and pursuing a shrewd political calculation.

If nationalist leaders were unwilling easily to accept that royal visitors were popular in Ireland and were perplexed by their own attempts to account for the reception of the population, there are perhaps three further personal factors that help to make royal popularity in Ireland comprehensible. The first was the fame—"celebrity" in today's terms—of the ruling family of what was in the nineteenth century the world's greatest empire.

Fenian newspaper, the *Irish People*, admitted that "[t]he men who would not unwillingly see a Prince hung or beheaded might on a gala day receive the same Prince with acclamations" (*Irish People*, 13 May 1865).

40. RA D 43/39, Queen Victoria to Lord Cadogan, 3 September 1897, in Lee, *Edward VII*, vol. 1, p. 245.

41. John Mitchel, *The Last Conquest of Ireland (Perhaps)* (London: Burns Oates and Washbourne, n.d.), 215–16.

Second, there was the glamor of younger royal visitors. This was still an advantage to the thirty-year-old Queen Victoria in 1849 and was certainly an advantage to the Princess of Wales in 1868 and to Princess Louise in 1871.

The final factor had to do with what was perceived as the personal disposition of royal visitors in favor of Ireland. If the Crown as an institution was set in favor of the union, perhaps the wearer of the crown might be better disposed to a change that might favor nationalist Ireland. This was rarely the case, but Irish Catholic nationalists persisted in fantasizing otherwise, a practice that was possible only because of the very limited information which the wider public had of what members of the royal family actually thought about Ireland.

All this meant that the popularity of the Crown in Ireland was more a matter of the personal popularity of individual members of the royal family than it was in Britain, a fact confirmed by the widely reported story of what an old woman in the crowd had shouted to Queen Victoria about her children on her arrival in Kingstown in 1849: "Ah, Queen, dear, make one of them Prince Patrick and Ireland will die for you!"[42] It was advice that Victoria took, naming her third son Arthur William Patrick Albert.

George IV's welcome in 1821 was partly due to the fact that it was believed, on the evidence of his earlier life, that he supported what was rather dramatically known as Catholic Emancipation, a relief measure that would allow Catholics to take their seats as MPs. In fact, he was by the beginning of his reign adamantly opposed to it. "Lord Melbourne," wrote young Queen Victoria of the views on the visit of her first prime minister, "said that George IV was in a very awkward position when he was in Ireland, for that whole country was in a ferment of enthusiasm believing the King to be for the Catholic Emancipation, whereas in his heart he was against it."[43]

At the other end of the century Edward VII was wrongly believed to be in favor of home rule[44] and was frequently rumored to be contemplating conversion to Catholicism. And at the beginning of her own reign Queen Victoria was also wrongly thought not to be personally opposed to repeal of the union. Ironically, too, in the early 1890s during the controversy sur-

42. Stanley Weintraub, *Victoria* (1987; London: John Murray, 1996), 205.

43. RA Queen Victoria's Journal: 21 February 1838, hereafter cited as QVJ, in Viscount Esher, *The Girlhood of Queen Victoria: A Selection of Queen Victoria's Diaries, 1832–1840*, 2 vols. (London: John Murray, 1912), 1:288.

44. Lee, *Edward VII*, 2:162. "The persistent rumour that King Edward differed from his mother in his views of Home Rule had little justification, at any rate when he ascended the throne."

rounding Gladstone's second home rule bill, which Queen Victoria opposed, the Irish public were reassured by the publication of the biography of a former archbishop of Canterbury. It revealed the role that the queen had played in a rather similar crisis in the 1860s, one that had resulted in an outcome satisfactory to nationalism. Irish nationalist opinion was thus reassured.

※

In the most general sense of the word the politics of nineteenth-century Ireland can be seen in terms of the major forces in Irish life—physical-force activism, religion, land agitation, constitutional politics, and monarchy—moving away from conflict and coming into a variety of alignments. In the 1830s and 1840s O'Connell, for whom physical-force activism was always anathema, tried unsuccessfully to recruit monarchy for Irish nationalism and for repeal of the union. In the 1860s there was a clash between Fenianism and the Catholic Church.

By the 1880s, however, constitutional politics, physical-force activism, land agitation, and Catholicism had all more or less merged into a nationalist accommodation, if not always a nationalist consensus. The Land League and the Irish Parliamentary Party were intimately connected with each other. The "new departure" initiative of the late 1870s was an attempt to garner support for constitutional politics from at least some sections of the physical force tradition. Finally, in 1884 there was agreement between the Catholic bishops and the Irish Parliamentary Party whereby the latter agreed to press Catholic claims in education.

Monarchy alone remained as a Trojan horse of unionism within the nationalist polity. It was opposed both because nationalist politicians feared its influence might indeed reconcile Irish people to the union and because enthusiasm for monarchy in Ireland was used to feed a British discourse that saw Ireland as a country that could be appeased by concessions short of home rule and that did not take nationalist demands seriously.

These were the reasons for the often virulent nature of nationalist opposition to monarchy and for the extremes of emotion that it evoked. It was the enemy within that had to be turned into the much more manageable enemy without. It had to be excised from the "common myths and historic memories"[45] of the Irish nation.

45. Anthony D. Smith, in *National Identity* (London: Penguin Books, 1991), 5, argues that five factors contribute to the entrenching of national identity: (1) a homeland, (2) common myths and historic memories, (3) common, nonpublic culture, (4) common legal rights and duties, and (5) a common economy with territorial mobility.

British opinion, too, had to be made to see that Ireland was not a contented part of the United Kingdom; insulting the monarchy was the most public and yet the safest and easiest way to do so. Ironically, though, this was a fact also recognized by British governments who at times almost seemed relieved that nationalists were blowing off steam against the monarchy rather than opposing the state in more active ways. In 1872 Lord Spencer wrote to Queen Victoria, in a rather insensitive manner given her devotion to the memory of her late husband, that he was at least consoled that "such childish tricks" as the recent attack on the statue of Prince Albert in Dublin indicated that "no grave acts of rebellion or armed force are contemplated."[46]

The relationship between nationalism and monarchy in nineteenth-century Ireland took place in the context of the then institutions of Irish and British government. At the head of the Irish government was the lord lieutenant general and governor general of Ireland, known as the lord lieutenant or the viceroy, who lived in the Vice Regal Lodge in Phoenix Park and presided at the court of Dublin Castle where, like the queen in London, he received loyal addresses, held dinners and balls, and presided at *levees*, at which gentlemen were presented to him, and *drawing rooms*, at which ladies were presented to him.

The lord lieutenant was always a peer. Since 1767 holders of the office had been required to reside in Ireland. He was both the personal representative of the sovereign and a member of the executive government of the United Kingdom. Lords lieutenant were thus not impartial administrators of the law, they were party political appointees. When a government fell the lord lieutenant went too.

It was a system unique in the British Empire and was always considered potentially damaging to the monarchy. A viceroy was not simply a representative of the monarchy, he was virtually a substitute for the monarch.[47] All the more dangerous, then, that, as an anachronistic hangover from the eighteenth century when the Crown and the executive were more closely aligned, Ireland's viceroy should be associated with partisan politics.

The lord lieutenant was assisted by a chief secretary who was also a par-

46. RA D 27/104, Lord Spencer to Queen Victoria, 10 June 1872.
47. In the latter part of the century India became the only other part of the empire to have a viceroy; all other territories had governors.

ty politician. Beneath him was the under-secretary, the nonpolitical permanent head of the Irish civil service. Neither the lord lieutenant nor the chief secretary were automatically members of the London cabinet. Sometimes one was, sometimes the other, and sometimes neither. Occasionally both belonged to the cabinet. In 1885 Lord Ashbourne was appointed to the cabinet in his capacity as lord chancellor of Ireland.

It is often asserted that as the nineteenth century wore on the lord lieutenancy became more ceremonial and that real political power came to rest with the chief secretary. However, as late as 1882 Lord Spencer was appointed as lord lieutenant for the second time with a strong executive mandate and a seat in the cabinet. Queen Victoria corresponded and had meetings about Ireland on a regular basis not only with the prime minister and the lord lieutenant but also with the home secretary who, especially in the earlier part of her reign, often had the responsibility of introducing legislation for Ireland into Parliament. In the latter part of her reign home secretaries were still being consulted about Ireland, though now mostly about Irish-inspired outrages in Britain.

Nationalist leaders in nineteenth-century Ireland, in spite of having majority support, were in political opposition within the United Kingdom. They did not have their hands on the levers of state power. Until 1898 even much of local government was still in the hands of the nonrepresentative grand juries. The 1840 Municipal Corporations Act, however, opened the way for growing Catholic nationalist influence in a reduced number of town boroughs and in Dublin.

As early as 1836 the future prominent Tory Sir James Graham warned the House of Commons that once municipal reform was granted the O'Connellites would gain control over the Corporation of Dublin and turn it into "a Parliament assembled in College-green without the nuisance of a secondary hereditary chamber."[48] In spite of the great stage-managed debate that O'Connell had held in the Dublin Corporation in early 1843 on the repeal of the union, the reformed corporation never quite became a parliament. However, it did become the most important public forum in Ireland for the expression of nationalist views. More than that, though, it was a forum whose very constitution brought it into significant and immediate contact with monarchy.

---

48. 8 March 1836, *Parliamentary Debates*, 3d Series, vol. 32 (8 March–20 April 1836), col. 64.

For modern ceremonial heads of state, including constitutional monarchs, the principal value of most public appearances is to encourage local communities and socially beneficial activities. In nineteenth-century Britain and Ireland, the chief purpose served by royal public activity was the eliciting of expressions of loyalty to the monarchy and thus to the state. Attendance at levees and drawing rooms was an expected gesture of allegiance by the nobility, gentry, and upper reaches of the middle class. The general populace was expected to express its loyalty by cheering royal processions. Public bodies such as churches, educational institutions, and corporations were expected to furnish loyal addresses not only on royal visits but also on occasions such as the birth or death of members of the royal family.

The annually elected head of the Dublin Corporation was called the "lord mayor." He was expected to greet ceremonially incoming lords lieutenant by laying the mace and civic sword at the viceroy's feet and by offering him the city keys. Each year he held a banquet at the Mansion House for the lord lieutenant which enabled the viceroy to meet the Dublin establishment. Three toasts were made at it, one to the monarch, another to the other members of the royal family, and a third to "the lord lieutenant and prosperity to Ireland."

The position of lord mayor of Dublin was also a very senior position within the United Kingdom when it came to royal ceremonial. Together with the lord mayor and the Corporation of London and the Lord Provost and Corporation of Edinburgh, the lord mayor and Corporation of Dublin had the right of personal audience with the monarch for the purpose of presenting loyal addresses and, just as important, petitions.[49]

Equally, there was an expectation that they would do so. Whether or not they ought to do so on particular occasions was one cause of tension for Liberal and later nationalist members of the Corporation, with the dwindling number of Dublin Tories consistently arguing that, as the Corporation existed only as the result of a royal charter, it was inconsistent for it not to be respectful to royalty.

One of the difficulties caused by the personal nature of the lord lieutenant's representational role was that it theoretically rendered visits from

---

49. It was only late in the century that the title of lord mayor was conferred on the mayors of other cities. On occasions when addresses from London, Dublin, and Edinburgh were presented, the lord mayor of London took precedence. A dispute over whether Edinburgh or Dublin came next was settled by each taking it in turns to have precedence.

the actual monarch and members of the royal family unnecessary. This did not in practice inhibit royal visits, but it was true that royal visits were few and far between. The absence of palpable monarchy from Ireland for long periods, for which Queen Victoria was much criticized in Britain, then its sudden presence, had the effect of bringing latent and sometimes dormant ideological conflicts into a heightened tension and eliciting a reaction. Thus beginning in the 1860s a discernible, if not always neatly defined, tendency emerged whereby royal occasions provoked counterassertions of nationalist identity and discontent.[50] This tendency grew in intensity in two phases, the first in the late 1870s and early 1880s and the second in the late 1890s, with changes in society and generational shifts in nationalist and republican leadership. Sometimes indeed reaction against the monarchy had the effect of pushing nationalism forward, as with the galvanizing celebrations of the 1798 rebellion in 1898 that were a response to the celebrations of the queen's Diamond Jubilee in 1897.

To an increasing extent, then, nationalism began to find self-definition in what at times came close to being a dialectic of opposition to monarchy. This was a process that included the envisioning of nationalist leaders as countermonarchs. Daniel O'Connell preferred the Enlightenment title of "Liberator" but was widely hailed as the uncrowned king of Ireland. In time the same title was used of Parnell, whom Queen Victoria once tellingly referred to as a "Pretender."[51] Nationalist leadership was thus in some ways a refashioned monarchical leadership, a construction that lasted well into modern times with Éamon de Valera being known as the "Chief" and Charles Haughey as the "Boss."

Self-definition in opposition to monarchy was a process that reached its culmination in the Civil War of the early 1920s, following the Anglo-Irish Treaty. It was fought over the issue of the parliamentary oath of allegiance to the king; antipathy to monarchy had by then become the only irreducible element in ideological Irish republicanism.

50. A similar pattern is discernible in other countries and in more recent times. The highly successful tour of South Africa undertaken by King George VI and Queen Elizabeth, after World War II, was quickly followed by the victory of the Afrikaner National Party. Queen Elizabeth II's visit to Australia for its bicentenary in 1988 was followed by the beginnings of the Australian republican movement.

51. RA D 30/85, Queen Victoria to Lord Granville, 29 January 1881, in Queen Victoria, *Letters of Queen Victoria,* 2d series, ed. George Earle Buckle, vol. 3 (1879–1885) (London: John Murray, 1928), 186.

In spite of continuing covert monarchism, the failure or rather the defeat of monarchy in nationalist Ireland has been so great as to seem inevitable in retrospect. Yet this was not so. Monarchy might have succeeded in Ireland had circumstances been different. In nineteenth-century England there was a good deal of radical and socialist opposition to the monarchy, from whose tone Irish nationalist leaders probably learned much, and there was even an organized republican movement in the early 1870s. Yet in time opposition to the monarchy faded away.

In this context it is worth reflecting on the lessons of other countries. Ireland had less reason to dislike the Hanoverian or Brunswick monarchy than did the American colonies in the 1770s, where George III became the political scapegoat for the disaffection of the rebelling colonists, or indeed than Scotland, which saw the bloody culmination of the conflict between Jacobites and Hanoverians in 1745 and its aftermath in the clearance of the highlands by George II's son, "Butcher" Cumberland.

The monarchy too has been relatively successful in countries that have posed an equal if not greater challenge than Ireland. Over more than two hundred years the Brunswick—now Windsor—monarchy has been part of an evolving polity that has managed the remarkable feat of containing Anglophone and Francophone populations in one country, Canada. It is a country moreover that historically has had more than its own fair share of sectarian tensions between Orange and Irish Catholic factions.

The dual monarchy of Austria-Hungary has long since vanished, as has the monarchical union that held Norway and Sweden together. Belgium, however, is continuing testimony to the ability of the "golden link" of a monarchy to hold together two very distinct linguistic and cultural regions, albeit where there is something approaching parity between them. This, though, was not the case with Britain and Ireland.

CHAPTER ONE

"The Messiah of Royalty"

Ireland and Brunswick During the Early Union, 1801–1837

The Brunswick monarchy found itself at the beginning of the union, and especially after the end of the Napoleonic Wars, in a position of considerable security in Ireland. This was not because of any special strength on its part so much as because the two principal enemies it had faced in the eighteenth century, Jacobitism and Jacobinism, were no longer a threat.

From the late seventeenth to the mid-eighteenth century the hopes of many in Ireland rested in the Jacobite cause, the return of the Stuart monarchy, whose Catholicism had cost it the throne in 1688. The exiled Stuarts rose to mythic status in Gaelic literature, becoming the focus of traditions of the rightful king and of the leader of Irish exiles. Thus James II "assumed the mantle of the archetypal ideal Irish king who was destined to return from exile and save his people."[1]

However, with the failure of Bonnie Prince Charlie's campaign in 1745

---

1. Breandán Ó Buachalla, "James Our True King: The Ideology of Irish Royalism in the Seventeenth Century," in D. G. Boyce, Robert Eccleshall, and Vincent Geoghegan, eds., *Political Thought in Ireland since the Sixteenth Century* (London: Routledge, 1993), 30. Professor Ó Buachalla continues, "By removing himself from the Irish scene, James merely cemented his position in Irish ideology. Abroad he—and his descendants—could be identified with causes they never espoused; attributes they never possessed could be effortlessly applied to them."

Jacobitism ceased to be a realistic political programme.[2] By the beginning of the nineteenth century the last of the Stuarts was dead and so was Irish Jacobitism.[3] If Jacobitism experienced a gradual demise, Jacobinism in its Irish form, a republicanism inspired by Enlightenment ideas and French revolutionary practice, came to a cataclysmic end in the bloody rebellion of 1798. Though the hierarchical conservatism of Jacobitism seemed far removed from the egalitarianism of Jacobism, the two movements were not unrelated or that dissimilar in the Irish context because both sought the overthrow of the existing order of society.[4]

The leadership of the United Irishmen, the focus for the revolutionary movement in the 1790s, espoused republican and secular ideals. However, in practice, the membership of the movement mostly sought "popular self-government and economic liberation from England"; for them, the movement's "nationalism and formal republicanism were the means to attain these ends rather than ends in themselves."[5] In addition, the movement found itself engaged in sectarian conflict, in alliance with peasant agrarian groups, which "debased the purity of the republican and liberal coinage and contributed to the desecularization of the movement."[6] All this meant that "the United Irishmen failed to leave deep ideological footprints in the sand. Their brand of liberal republicanism failed to survive the rebellion of 1798."[7]

2. See C. D. A. Leighton, *Catholicism in a Protestant Kingdom* (London: Macmillan, 1994), 56.

3. In his discussion of the residual legacy of Jacobitism, however, Tom Garvin, in *1922: The Birth of Irish Democracy* (Dublin: Gill and Macmillan, 1996), 11, sees calls for the crowning of de Valera as king of Ireland in the 1920s as signs that "under the veneer of modern Irish republicanism it is sometimes possible to detect echoes of this older, almost dreamy but clearly monarchist style of thought."

4. Breandán Ó Buachalla, "Irish Jacobitism and Irish Nationalism: The Literary Evidence," in Michael O'Dea and Kevin Whelan, eds., *Nations and Nationalism: France, Britain, Ireland, and the Eighteenth-Century Context*, Studies in Voltaire and the Eighteenth Century 335 (Oxford: Voltaire Foundation, 1995), 114.

5. Nancy J. Curtin, *The United Irishmen: Popular Politics in Ulster and Dublin, 1791–98* (Oxford: Clarendon Press, 1994), 35.

6. Curtin, *The United Irishmen*, 284.

7. Curtin, *The United Irishmen*, 286. Professor Curtin goes on, "They proved unable to construct a secular political culture which emphasized civic rights and duties and was capable of withstanding the heavy resurgence of sectarianism in Ireland from the late 1790s, a resurgence to which the United Irishmen contributed." See too Garvin, *1922*, 11: "It was not until well into the nineteenth century that republican ideas of a sort gained a firm hold in the minds of a proportion of the Catholic majority in the country. Prior to then, most Irish Catholics were probably monarchists in their political thinking, such as it was."

At the end of the nineteenth century and of Queen Victoria's reign British commentators were fond of characterizing the kingdom over which she reigned as "a crowned republic," that is, as a state in which citizens had the rights and freedoms of a democratic republic while being presided over by a constitutional, limited monarchy. The beginning of the century, however, saw one of the last great acts of royal power, when George III refused to countenance Catholic emancipation on the grounds that it offended against his coronation oath to uphold Protestantism. It led to the resignation of the prime minister, William Pitt the younger, who had promised Catholics that the union of Ireland with Britain would be accompanied by such a reform. It also began the alienation of Irish Catholics from the new constitutional settlement, which many of them had actually welcomed, and gave eventual impetus to their turn toward the idea of an Irish nation as their political salvation.

The Catholic question, the debate over the civil status of Catholics, had been an issue since the middle of the eighteenth century. Could Catholics be trusted with the rights and privileges of other subjects? Charles O'Conor was the principal early Irish advocate of the removal of civil disabilities against Catholics. His view of the Brunswick monarchy was a positive one. He hoped that it would be favorable to the removal of the penal laws.[8] Protestations of loyalty and respectful requests for reform followed, and the Catholic Relief Acts of 1778, 1782, and 1782–1783 removed many of the anti-popery penal laws, though by the 1790s elements of the Catholic Committee, founded by O'Conor in 1760 to press for change, had become linked with the United Irishmen.

In the first decades of the nineteenth century the strategy of campaigners for the final reform, so-called Catholic emancipation, consisted in the formation of Catholic committees and boards, though these were periodically suppressed by the government, to petition Parliament, and in the introduction into Parliament of Catholic relief bills by sympathetic members, such as the ageing Henry Grattan.

An early setback occurred with the death in July 1806 of Charles James Fox, an advocate of emancipation. Several years later splits and divisions began to develop on the Catholic side over whether as a quid pro quo for Catholics being allowed to become members of Parliament the British government ought to have a veto over the appointment of Catholic bishops.

8. Leighton, *Catholicism*, 122.

For reasons of international diplomacy the papacy was inclined for a time toward accepting some form of veto. However, such a veto was adamantly opposed by Daniel O'Connell, an increasingly important campaigner on emancipation.

King George III had for several decades been prone to bouts of illness that reduced his capacity to govern. In 1811 the Prince of Wales and future George IV was appointed prince regent with all his father's authority. It was widely expected that he would support Catholic emancipation, not least because his father had opposed it. He had often expressed support for emancipation. He had been a friend of Fox and had had a number of Catholic mistresses.[9]

The prince regent had six brothers who were, in order of seniority by age, the dukes of York, Clarence (the future William IV), Kent (father of Queen Victoria), Cumberland (king of Hanover from 1837), Sussex, and Cambridge. With the death of the regent's heir and only child, Princess Charlotte, in 1817, his brothers' significance increased. Between them they had fathered a large number of children. However, these were the result either of nonmarital partnerships or of marriages that were not officially recognized because of the draconian legal restrictions applying to the marriages of members of the royal family. The premature end of the regent's line led to a race among his brothers to marry approved German princesses and produce royal heirs.

Of the six brothers, who as males took precedence over George III's daughters, Kent and especially Sussex were strongly in favor of Catholic emancipation. In 1813 Sussex made a speech in favour of emancipation at a dinner of the Friends of Civil and Constitutional Liberty. As a result he was attacked in a pamphlet for "conspicuously placing himself at the head of a tavern meeting whose object was to subvert the Constitution."[10] Kent, who was present at the meeting, also came in for criticism.

"High were the hopes of the Catholics of Ireland when the late Princess Charlotte filled the position of heiress to the throne."[11] They were less impressed by the "grand old duke of York" who was next in line be-

9. Thomas Bartlett, *The Fall and Rise of the Irish Nation: The Catholic Question, 1690–1830* (Dublin: Gill and Macmillan, 1992), 302.

10. An Orangeman, *An Address to the Duke of Sussex* (London, 1813), quoted in Hereward Senior, *Orangeism in Ireland and Britain, 1795–1836* (London: Routledge and Kegan Paul, 1966), 167.

11. *FJ*, 10 February 1852.

cause both he and his brother Cumberland were strongly opposed to emancipation. In 1807 the Whig cabinet resigned when George III refused to allow a bill to enable Catholics to become senior officers in the army. The new government under the duke of Portland encouraged petitions against the reform to counter those in favor. Cumberland, as chancellor of Dublin University, urged both the university and the Dublin Corporation to submit petitions.[12] In March 1821 an emancipation bill was passed by the Commons but was defeated in the Lords with the help of Cumberland and York.

The prince regent was influenced by Cumberland to change his mind on the subject of emancipation. In 1813 he opposed Grattan's Catholic relief bill.[13] By this time too the regent had come to hate Daniel O'Connell who had referred to "the fatal witchery" of the anti-Catholic influence exercised on the regent by his current mistress, Lady Hertford.[14] Yet O'Connell knew that alienating the regent and future king served no good purpose, so he used the visit of the recently crowned King George IV to Ireland in August 1821, the first visit by a monarch in nearly one hundred and thirty years, as an occasion to demonstrate a fulsome loyalty.

George IV's visit to Dublin was part of a postcoronation tour that also took him to Hanover and to Scotland, where with characteristic flamboyance he entered Edinburgh wearing full Highland dress. The coronation itself, on 19 July, in London had been an extravagant occasion and was marked in Dublin by the illumination of the city. However, an element of tragic farce attended George's ascent to the throne.

In June 1820 his wife, Caroline of Brunswick, from whom he had been long separated, returned to England to some public acclaim. George was determined that she should not enjoy the status of queen and so he had the government initiate an arcane parliamentary procedure to divorce her from him and deprive her of regal status. It resulted in a process that for all practical purposes was a trial before the House of Lords. This proceeded to a minute investigation of her sexual conduct.

12. Senior, *Orangeism*, 164–68.

13. Senior, *Orangeism*, 166.

14. Oliver MacDonagh, *O'Connell: The Life of Daniel O'Connell, 1775–1847* (London: Weidenfeld and Nicolson, 1991), 111. By this time, too, O'Connell had become a lifelong enemy of Sir Robert Peel, with whom he nearly fought a duel in 1815.

At her trial Caroline was represented by Henry Brougham, on whom she was officially entitled to bestow the title "queen's attorney-general." Ireland had its own law officers and, even though the appointment would have been a redundant one because no trial of the queen was being contemplated there, Daniel O'Connell toyed with the idea of seeking to be appointed as the queen's Irish attorney-general.[15] Years later he was to deny it,[16] but it may have been that he saw it as a way of being appointed as a king's counsel, the senior of the two ranks of barrister from which he was still excluded as a Catholic.

The trial of Queen Caroline collapsed in November 1820 and her popularity again increased. In order to cause George further discomfort, she appeared at Westminster Abbey on his coronation day, demanded to be crowned queen, and had to be shut out. Nor was the king able to forget her during his visit to Ireland, for shortly after the coronation Caroline fell into a terminal illness.

King George embarked on the royal yacht at Portsmouth on 29 July. By 9 August he was in Holyhead, where he was held up for several days by bad weather. Caroline died on 7 August; news of her death reached George just before he set sail for Dublin. In the days before the telegraph and the train the timing of travel was imprecise. As one of the principal events of the king's visit was to be his formal entry into the city, and as no one in Dublin knew exactly when he would arrive, it was decided that his actual arrival would be informal and that his formal entry would take place on 17 August. He arrived at the port of Howth on Sunday, 12 August, his fifty-ninth birthday, and proceeded directly to the Vice Regal Lodge. This was just as well as, relieved and disturbed by Caroline's death, he was drunk on arrival. In "The Irish Avatar" Byron is sarcastic about the juxtaposition of the death of Caroline and the Irish visit, using conventional imagery of the marriage of monarch and people to stinging effect:

> Ere the daughter of Brunswick is cold in her grave,
> And her ashes still float to their home o'er the tide,
> Lo! George the triumphant speeds over the wave,
> To the long-cherish'd isle which he loved like his—bride![17]

15. MacDonagh, *O'Connell,* 171.

16. *FJ,* 8 July 1840. O'Connell had written to the *Leeds Mercury* to deny he had ever been Queen Caroline's lawyer.

17. Byron, *Poetical Works,* 576.

George put on no great show of grief in Dublin. However, in London there was considerable sympathy for the dead queen. The *Times* claimed that "thousands—we may say millions—of eyes will be suffused in tears." Caroline was eventually to be buried in Brunswick. However, on 14 August her supporters arranged for an elaborate funeral procession of her remains through London. The government tried to intervene to limit the scope of the procession. Several people were killed in clashes between troops and Caroline's supporters.

In his peaceful Irish capital George continued, except for a mourning arm band, as if nothing was amiss. He made his formal entrance on Friday, 17 August, processing down Sackville Street and thence to Dublin Castle. His appearance was especially geared to the spectacle of the occasion and his clothes proportioned theatrically with a view to how they would appear to the distant spectator. "His Majesty was dressed in a full military uniform, decorated with the Order and Ribbon of St Patrick. His hat was ornamented with a rosette, composed of Shamrock of more than twice the size of a military cockade."[18] Over the next two weeks he reviewed troops, held a levee and a drawing room in Dublin Castle, attended an installation ceremony of the Knights of St Patrick, and held a ball; he also went to church and visited the theater. At the levee O'Connell was presented to the king, who muttered "God damn him" audible enough for O'Connell to hear him.[19]

The king spent 24–27 August at Slane Castle, County Meath. Its owner, Lord Conyngham, was lord steward of the king's household throughout George's reign. Lady Conyngham was the king's last mistress. In spite of the popular rhyme that King George and Lady Conyngham spent their time in Slane

> Quaffing their claret, then mingling their lips,
> Or tickling the fat about each other's hips[20]

their relationship was probably more about companionship than passion. In 1838 Queen Victoria's first prime minister, Lord Melbourne, had a discussion with his teenage sovereign about her uncle's mistresses, Mrs. Fitzherbert, Lady Jersey, Lady Hertford, and Lady Conyngham. "The last

18. *FJ,* 18 August 1821.
19. RA QVJ, 21 February 1838, in Esher, *Girlhood,* 1:288.
20. Quoted in Christopher Hibbert, *George IV Regent and King, 1811–1830* (London: Allen Lane, 1973), 215.

named I observed was very good-natured," wrote the queen in her journal, "Lord Melbourne said, 'She was the most good-natured, but the most rapacious; she got the most money from him.'"[21]

Before the end of his stay George visited public buildings and institutions in Dublin and made trips to the Curragh of Kildare and to Powerscourt House in Wicklow. He left from Dunleary, which he renamed Kingstown, on Monday, 3 September. An unabashed O'Connell presented the departing monarch with a laurel crown.[22]

The public reception of the king in Ireland was ecstatic. The Irish were reported to be "out of their wits with joy."[23] Henry Hobhouse, under secretary at the Home Department, believed that "nothing could have gone off better than the King's visit to Ireland."[24] "Were you here you would imagine Ireland to be the richest country in the world, such exertions have these poor people made to testify their attachment to George the Fourth," wrote General Barnard to his sister-in-law.[25]

The attention of monarchy had a remarkable effect on unlikely individuals, at least in the short term. As S. H. Burke wrote, "I was a rebel to old King George in '98 but by God I'd die a hundred deaths for his son, because he is a real King and asks us how we are."[26] And the visit contributed to the return of the former United Irishmen leader, Lord Cloncurry, to the political establishment. Noting the "strange madness" that overcame the populace, he himself ended up inviting the king to his house as a "pledge of sincerity."[27]

The London *Times* was amazed by reports that the usually unpopular Lord Castlereagh (then Lord Londonderry), Irish chief secretary during the critical years 1798–1801 and thus "the reputed author of their [Irish] grievances," had been "cheered and applauded" during the royal visit. It

21. RA QVJ, 30 April 1838, in Esher, *Girlhood*, 1:315.

22. See Hibbert, *Regent and King*, 221, and Judith Hill, *Irish Public Sculpture: A History* (Dublin: Four Courts, 1998), 77.

23. Hibbert, *Regent and King*, 221.

24. A. Aspinall, ed., *The Diary of Henry Hobhouse, 1820–1827* (London: Home and Van Thal, 1947), 74, quoted in Hibbert, *Regent and King*, 221.

25. General Sir Andrew Barnard to Lady Anne Barnard, 24 August 1821, in Anthony Powell, ed., *The Barnard Letters, 1778–1824*, 2 vols. (London: Duckworth, 1928), 2:298.

26. S. Hubert Burke, *Ireland Sixty Years Ago* (1885), quoted in Joanna Richardson, *George IV: A Portrait* (London: Sidgwick and Jackson, 1966), 94.

27. Lord Cloncurry, *Personal Recollections* (1849), 277, quoted in Hibbert, *Regent and King*, 210.

was a sign that the Irish were "at once the most credulous and most forgiving of mankind."[28]

No doubt the reception of the king had something to do with hopes for emancipation. No doubt, too, it had something to do with spectacle and with the recent rise in Britain's place in the world as perhaps the greatest power in Europe and, with the collapse of the Spanish, Portuguese, and original French overseas empires, as certainly the greatest world power. For Daniel O'Connell, it was a lesson in the power of monarchy and its capacity to destabilize political oppositions. It was also a more personal lesson too in the power of public gatherings and of the grand public style for the man who was for the next twenty-five years to fill the role of agitator first for emancipation and then for repeal, marshalling vast political gatherings and promoting the cult of his own personal role for political ends.

For the moment it was back to ordinary politics over the question of emancipation for O'Connell. In 1822 the duke of Wellington's elder brother, Lord Wellesley, was appointed as lord lieutenant. He was in favor of Catholic emancipation and, indeed, married an American Catholic in 1825. His influence was balanced, however, by the appointment of the ultra-Tory Henry Gouldbourn as chief secretary.

O'Connell's address of welcome to Wellesley referred to him as the representative of "the kindly disposition of our beloved Sovereign."[29] Yet when Wellesley failed to reply to O'Connell's call that he suppress a demonstration in Dublin on 12 July by the Protestant Orange Order, it led to a cooling off of O'Connell's hopes for the new lord lieutenant. Wellesley did ban a similar demonstration at the statue of William III on 4 November. This in turn led to a riot at the Theatre Royal on 14 December when Wellesley's box was pelted by Orangemen with fruit, a bottle, and some wood.

The insult to the lord lieutenant opened the way for O'Connell to score a propaganda victory over the Orangemen and ultra-Tories, using a strategy that he would rely on to a considerable degree during Queen Victoria's reign. He expressed outrage at the treatment of the king's representative and in doing so sought to show that he was the true loyalist to the Crown

28. *Times*, 22 August 1821.

29. John O'Connell, ed., *The Select Speeches of Daniel O'Connell*, 2 vols. (Dublin, 1854), 2:139, quoted in MacDonagh, *O'Connell*, 178.

and that those who had insulted the lord lieutenant were the disloyal ones. His plan was to reverse the ideological polarities and—as he told his wife—to have Catholics "admitted to be the only genuine loyalists."[30]

※

The period from 1823 marked a new departure for O'Connell. In May of that year the Irish Catholic Association was founded and the next year began collecting one penny per week Catholic rent from ordinary enthusiasts, an act that turned it into a movement with mass support. Initially, its agenda was a broad one of Catholic grievances against, among other things, the legally enforced payment of tithes by Catholics to the Protestant clergy of the Established Church in Ireland. Inevitably, though, emancipation became its principal focus.[31]

By March 1825 the government was so fearful of the Association that it suppressed it. However, with an even-handedness that indicated that the British Tory government no longer wished simply to be identified with Irish Tory interests, the Orange Order was suppressed at the same time. O'Connell traveled to London, where he was rapturously received in Whig political circles. A Catholic relief bill was passed by the Commons but was defeated in the Lords on 18 May with the help of the duke of York. In July the Association was refounded with a name change to get around its legal suppression.

The next two years were frustrating ones for O'Connell, marked by some progress but also several false dawns. In 1827 a Protestant supporter of emancipation defeated an ultra-ascendancy candidate in Waterford. In early 1828 death and illness seemed to come to O'Connell's aid. On 5 January York died, leaving his less ideological brother Clarence heir to the throne. On 15 February Lord Liverpool, the long-serving Tory prime minister whose policy was to try to avoid tackling Catholic emancipation, had a stroke. However, his pro-emancipation successor George Canning died after only four months in office.

January 1828 saw the coming to power of the double act of the duke of Wellington and Sir Robert Peel that was to dominate Tory politics for

30. Daniel O'Connell to Mary O'Connell, 21 December 1822, in M. R. O'Connell, ed., *The Correspondence of Daniel O'Connell*, vol. 2 (1815–1823) (Dublin: Blackwater, 1973), no. 982, p. 413.

31. The following account of the campaign for emancipation is based on MacDonagh, *O'Connell*, and on Hibbert, *Regent and King*.

twenty years, with Wellington on this occasion as prime minister and Peel as home secretary. Both were adamantly opposed to emancipation, though in April legal disabilities against dissenters were repealed and on 12 May the Commons passed the annual motion for Catholic relief by six votes.

O'Connell's real triumph came in July when he was himself elected as Member of Parliament (MP) for Clare. The prospect of his being turned away from the Commons because of his religion caused the government to reconsider. The issue could no longer be avoided and so on 1 August 1828 Wellington sent the king a memorandum in favor of emancipation, arguing that it was now a political necessity. Though Clarence and the Conynghams supported the measure, George was being steeled in his opposition by Cumberland and succeeded in having the pro-emancipation Lord Anglesey removed as lord lieutenant. Meanwhile in Ireland supporters of the Orange movement set up the tellingly named Brunswick Constitution Club of Ireland to oppose the reform.

On 28 February 1829 Wellington confronted the king at Windsor. Four days later he and Peel met the king and, when they still could not persuade him, they resigned. Later that day George wrote to Wellington, pleading with him to return and finally agreeing to Catholic emancipation. The measure became law on 13 April. It contrived to take back with one hand what it had offered with the other, for it contained a provision that effectively disenfranchised many existing Catholic voters. The king took to referring to Wellington as "King Arthur," to O'Connell as "the king of Ireland," and to himself as the "canon of Windsor."[32] As an assessment of the realpolitik it was not far off the mark.

What was at stake in emancipation was the very foundations of the Protestant British constitution.[33] It brought about a change of equal if not greater importance to that of the parliamentary reform of 1832. Yet if

32. Lionel G. Robinson, ed., *Letters of Dorothea, Princess Lieven, during Her Residence in London, 1812–32* (1902), 187, quoted in Hibbert, *Regent and King*, 310.

33. J. D. C. Clark, *English Society, 1688–1832: Ideology, Social Structure, and Political Practice during the Ancien Regime* (Cambridge: Cambridge University Press, 1985), 409: "The years 1800–32 witnessed, then, not so much the progressive advance of a liberal mood shared by all as the gradual numerical erosion of a social, religious and political hegemony from without, and a final and sudden betrayal from within. In that process parliamentary reform played a subordinate part. . . . Throughout the first decades of the nineteenth-century, Emancipation and Repeal took a great, and a growing, precedence over Reform: Catholic and Protestant Dissent counted for much, democracy for little."

emancipation opened up the prospect of a nonsectarian political culture in Great Britain, ironically it had the opposite effect in Ireland.

In the secularizing discourse of contemporary Ireland O'Connell is now sometimes portrayed as a regressive figure for his promotion of an Irish nationalism whose central feature was Catholicism. A nation, however, often finds initial definition through the common grievances of its population with the power that rules it. The nations of South America thus formed themselves in the contours of the colonial system of imperial Spain because individuals from South America were not allowed to hold office beyond the confines of their own colonial province. Their grievance at the limitations on their mobility created a set of shared grievances with those who had to endure the same geographical limitations and from those grievances nations were born.[34]

If the nation that emerged in early-nineteenth-century Ireland was a Catholic nation, it was thanks in part to the rulers of the United Kingdom, including many members of the house of Brunswick, who for three decades helped to exclude Catholics from an equal participation in its political life.

By the 1840s when the diligent Prince Albert came to systematize his wife's papers, it was only natural for him to entitle the series that dealt with Ireland "Papers concerning the policy towards Ireland and the Roman Catholics."[35] The struggle over emancipation helped to lead to the removal of religion from politics in Britain but to its entrenchment in politics in Ireland.

For the next eighteen years the central issue in the monarchy's relations with Ireland concerned policy toward Daniel O'Connell. He was now an MP and a senior figure in British politics, the first Catholic in well over a century to be so. How was he to be treated?

George IV died in 1830 and his brother, the duke of Clarence, ruled as William IV for the next seven years. He never visited Ireland during his reign but in 1831 he did ennoble his eldest, nonroyal son, George Fitz-Clarence, with the title earl of Munster.

William greatly disliked O'Connell, who began to agitate for repeal of

34. See Benedict Anderson, *Imagined Communities: Reflections on the Origin and Spread of Nationalism* (1981; London: Verso, 1983), 47–65.

35. RA D 14.

the union in 1830 and who after the 1832 election led a group of thirty-nine repealers in the Commons. It was the custom for the monarch to appear in the House of Lords at the beginning and end of each session of Parliament to address both houses in a speech from the throne prepared by the government. William's speech on 3 February 1834 contained a statement of opposition to repeal that was unusually personal in tone:

> I have seen with feelings of deep regret and just indignation, the continuance of attempts to excite the people of that country [Ireland] to demand a Repeal of the Legislative Union. This bond of our national strength and safety I have already declared my fixed and unalterable resolution under the blessing of Divine Providence to maintain inviolate by all the means in my power.[36]

It was clearly aimed at O'Connell's repeal agitation, denying it constitutional legitimacy and typically linking the union with the vitality of the British nation.

The previous year William had shown how similar he was in his dealings with Ireland to his father and brother in his opposition to the Irish Church Temporalities Act, a measure to rationalize the Established Church in Ireland by abolishing ten of its bishoprics. He opposed it on the same grounds his father and brother had used to oppose emancipation, that is, as contrary to his coronation oath to uphold the Protestant faith. His crisis of conscience provoked a sarcastic response from Sir Robert Peel: "I no more believe that it is a violation of the Coronation Oath to unite [the diocese of+] Clonfert to a neighbouring see, than that it was a violation of it to make or sever a union of parishes."[37] The measure became law.

Ironically, on his death William was portrayed in nationalist Ireland as having been more favorable to Ireland than either his brother or his father. "George the Third spurned—George the Fourth betrayed us [over emancipation]. William the good alone gave us noble promise."[38]

This judgment, however, reflects a particular turn in political events. In March 1835 O'Connell had entered into an informal agreement, the Lichfield House Compact, with the Whigs, under Lord Melbourne, who were on the verge of taking office, in order to secure reform in such areas as municipal government and tithes.

36. 4 February 1834, *Parliamentary Debates*, 3d Series, vol. 21 (4 February–10 March 1834), col. 4.

37. Sir Robet Peel to Henry Goulburn, 26 April 1833, in Charles Stuart Parker, ed., *Sir Robert Peel from His Private Papers,* 3 vols. (London: John Murray, 1899), 2:220.

38. *FJ*, 23 June 1837.

It was an arrangement over which William IV had had no control. Indeed, his own earlier attempts to sustain the Tories in power had failed and had provoked O'Connell to form an Irish anti-Tory association that enhanced his links with the Whigs. During the six subsequent years of Whig rule O'Connell went so far as to play down talk of repeal and to tell Melbourne that they should seek to make "Ireland an efficient and useful portion of the empire, by conciliating her people to British rule."[39] Meanwhile the king's failure to influence the shape of the government was a sign of the waning political influence of the monarchy in the face of a more popularly mandated House of Commons.

William's other concern with O'Connell was with how he was to be treated personally. At that time offering political or judicial office was considered a perfectly legitimate way of gaining the support of potential political allies; indeed, several of O'Connell's supporters took office under the Whigs in this manner. The problem with O'Connell himself was that, as Melbourne told Lord John Russell in 1834, "his abilities and powers are such as to give him naturally a claim to the highest offices in the State and a large share in the government of the country."[40]

For William IV, however, it was unacceptable even to invite O'Connell to dinner, and when the lord lieutenant, Lord Mulgrave, did precisely this in 1835 William was not pleased. Melbourne explained that Mulgrave was only extending to O'Connell the courtesy of an invitation to dine at Vice Regal Lodge that was extended to all MPs visiting Dublin, and that it was not a prelude to making O'Connell a privy counsellor and thus a senior member of the political establishment.[41] William replied that he did not understand how it was possible for the lord lieutenant to entertain O'Connell at dinner when only a few years before a government, of which Melbourne was a member, had had him denounce O'Connell as "a disturber of the peace" in a speech from the throne.[42] The answer was that times had changed and that O'Connell and the government were now allies.

39. Daniel O'Connell to Lord Melbourne, 10 May 1838, in Lloyd C. Sanders, *Lord Melbourne's Papers* (London: Longmans, Green, 1889), 372.

40. Lord Melbourne to Lord John Russell, 23 August 1834, in Sanders, *Melbourne*, 209–10.

41. Lord Melbourne to King William IV, 19 October 1835, in Sanders, *Melbourne*, 297. The privy council was the formal group of advisers to the monarch, of which the cabinet was in theory merely a subcommittee. It consisted of senior members of the political and judicial establishment.

42. King William IV to Lord Melbourne, 20 October 1835, in Sanders, *Melbourne*, 372.

One of the results of the death of Princess Charlotte was the rapid marriage of the duke of Kent to Princess Victoire of Saxe-Coburg Saalfield. He died in 1820 but not before they had had a daughter, Alexandrina Victoria. For many years it was by no means certain that Princess Victoria would eventually succeed to the throne because it was considered possible that William IV's wife, Queen Adelaide, might produce an heir. As it was, Victoria did become queen of the British dominions in 1837 but, because of differing succession laws, not of Hanover, which went to her uncle Cumberland.

Victoria spent her childhood at Kensington Palace with her mother, the duchess of Kent. In some ways it could be considered an Irish childhood, as many of the children and young people she met were of Irish extraction. She knew the younger Conynhams from visiting George IV at Windsor Castle. An Irishman, Robert Stephen, fell in love with her half-sister Feodora.[43] And at Kensington she was in constant contact with the children of her mother's adviser, Sir John Conroy, whose family came from County Roscommon.

By the mid-1830s it looked more certain that Victoria would succeed. Conroy arranged for her to undertake a series of royal progresses through England, thus effectively inventing the royal tour. In 1833 he planned to take her to Ireland "via Plymouth to Cork, to visit Killarney, the capital, the Giant's Causeway in the north, after which to cross to Liverpool."[44] He was still hoping to do so in 1836, but William IV, jealous of the princess's popularity, vetoed it. For Conroy, "the King and His family have lost a golden moment, to tie to a very interesting Heiress Presumptive, the feelings of the Irish Nation, for in coming times, it would have been well to have left no stone unturned to draw the countries closer together."[45]

Conroy and the duchess of Kent thought that once Victoria came to the throne they would be a dominant influence. In this they were wrong. Victoria immediately proved to be her own person. Conroy failed to gain the Irish peerage he coveted. However, before her accession others feared their influence and worked against it. One of the issues centered round who

43. Katherine Hudson, *A Royal Conflict* (London: Hodder and Stoughton, 1994), 67.

44. Sir John Conroy to Lord Durham, 30 June 1833, Lambton Papers, Lambton Park, quoted in Hudson, *Conflict*, 90.

45. Sir John Conroy to Lord Durham, 21 July 1833, Lambton Papers, quoted in Hudson, *Conflict*, 90.

would become regent if Victoria came to the throne before her eighteenth birthday. In the late 1820s the duke of Wellington supported the candidature of the duchess as regent, in case of the early death of Clarence, over that of Cumberland for whom he had little regard.

Many years later, in September 1878, Queen Victoria received a letter from Conroy's daughter-in-law who claimed that Cumberland had been "seized with the terrible temptation to remove the only life that stood between him and the throne." The queen noted in the margin, "He never showed the slightest symptom of this." Mrs Conroy then went on to claim that Cumberland had planned to have George IV transfer the control of Princess Victoria from the duchess of Kent and Conroy to him in order to poison her or kill her by neglect. "Utterly false" was the queen's comment.[46]

These allegations about Cumberland, though probably not true, are more comprehensible when seen as part of a much larger issue that centered on the role of the Orange Order in British politics in the first third of the nineteenth century. The order had been founded in 1795 as a result of sectarian factionalism in Ulster. It linked the peasantry with the Protestant ascendancy and was useful to the government in the 1790s. It helped in the suppression of the 1798 rebellion and was against the Act of Union on the grounds that the government intended to accompany it with Catholic emancipation.

By the early nineteenth century "the idea of a popular movement strongly opposed to Catholic emancipation was undoubtedly attractive to ultra tory peers and even to the dukes of York and Cumberland."[47] The Orange Order began to spread in the British aristocracy and British army. In 1813 York became a member. In 1820 he was asked to become grand master of the British lodges of the order. At first he demurred on the grounds of the legality of the organization. However, in February 1821 he agreed. On 21 June 1821 Sir John Newport raised the question of York's involvement in Parliament. The next day York resigned, telling the deputy grand master that the government law officers had advised him that the movement was illegal.[48]

The office of British grand master was not filled again until York's

46. Mrs. Henry Conroy to Queen Victoria, September 1878, quoted in Cecil Woodham-Smith, *Queen Victoria: Her Life and Times* (London: Hamish Hamilton, 1972), 434–35.

47. Senior, *Orangeism*, 159.

48. Senior, *Orangeism*, 166–67, 172–195.

death, when his brother Cumberland assumed the role. There were three hundred British lodges and six thousand members.[49] Cumberland did not confine his activities to Britain alone, however. He began to take an active interest in Orange affairs in Ireland and signed warrants that some Irish Orangemen took as a greater authority than those of the lord lieutenant.

In 1832 a number of Orange peers had Cumberland write a letter to Irish Orangemen urging them not to march in their accustomed demonstrations that year for fear of the government's introducing an anti-processions act. When some Ulster county grand masters kept the letter from their members the parades went ahead and the act was duly passed. The incident is illustrative of the position of power that was accruing to Cumberland.[50]

Throughout 1833 there was an active campaign to extend Orange influence with Tories in Britain through the efforts of William Blennerhasset Fairman. Cumberland encouraged William IV to resist changes to the Established Church in Ireland in 1833 and 1834. It was little wonder, then, that when the Whigs came to power under Melbourne in 1835 they instituted an enquiry into what they feared had the potential of becoming a threat to the state itself. There was particular concern over the existence of Orange lodges within the British army. Anger over this development erupted in the House of Commons on 4 August 1835 when Joseph Hume moved a resolution to make Orangeism illegal. The next day Cumberland claimed that he did not know of the existence of lodges in the army and that he had signed in ignorance batches of blank warrants for military lodges. Hume had been scathing over this issue:

If any man was placed at the bar for an offence and said that he was ignorant that it was against he law, the reply would be that he ought to have known the law. It was also the duty of the Duke of Cumberland to make himself acquainted with the state of the law as regarded these associations. It was no excuse for a man who sent a firebrand through the country that he did not know the uses to which it might be applied.[51]

Another damning piece of evidence consisted in the wording of a petition submitted to Cumberland at a meeting of the Grand Lodge of En-

49. Senior, *Orangeism*, 230.

50. Senior, *Orangeism*, 246–47.

51. 4 August 1835, *Parliamentary Debates*, 3d Series, vol. 30 (3 August–10 September 1835), col. 67.

gland. It began with the words, "May it please your Royal Highness. We, your dutiful subjects." The Dublin *Freeman's Journal* fulminated:

Your dutiful subjects! The dutiful subjects not of the King but of the King's junior brother, the Duke, the virtuous Duke of Cumberland! These miscreants talk a prodigious deal about the divided allegiance of Catholics . . . but where is the instance to be produced of Catholics themselves acknowledging by word or deed the truth of that foul charge? No, no the divided allegiance belongs to the Orangeman; and he is his own accuser. And to whom does the Orangeman yield this treasonable fealty? To the brother of an aged and childless king and to the uncle of an heiress presumptive. England had better take care lest she be plunged into a war of succession. . . . [I]t appears that the laws are trampled under foot . . . and that the allegiance of the troops, and of divers others of the subjects of the realm, is undermined by him whose niece, an infant, stands between his ambition and the throne.[52]

A modified Commons resolution was moved on 11 August. Several days later William IV announced that all secret societies would be suppressed in the army. On 27 August Cumberland voided all Orange military warrants but made no move to resign as grand master or to dissolve the order.

The next year Hume and his ally, William Molesworth, used the fact that Fairman had refused to hand over certain letters to the investigating committee and had subsequently disappeared as evidence for an allegation that Cumberland had plotted a coup through the Orange Lodges against Princess Victoria, who was thought to be under Whig influence.

Though probably untrue, the allegation increased the difficulties facing Cumberland and the Orange Order. On 23 February 1836 Hume proposed the dismissal of all Orangemen who held civil or military office. Lord John Russell took up the matter and asked the king to suppress all secret societies. On 25 February King William indicated that measures would be taken against the Orange Order. Seeing the writing on the wall, Cumberland dissolved the British lodges. Two months later the Grand Lodge of Ireland also voluntarily disbanded.[53]

All of this formed the backdrop to the accession of Queen Victoria in 1837 on the death of William IV. It was greeted with great enthusiasm and relief in nationalist Ireland. Her father had been "one of the steadiest and most consistent friends of Ireland . . . Ireland looks up to her with inde-

52. *FJ*, 8 August 1835.
53. Senior, *Orangeism*, 268–73.

scribable delight."[54] For one thing and by her very existence alone, Victoria had saved the country from the reign of Cumberland, who was now King Ernest of Hanover.

"What have we not escaped by the removal of the Duke of Cumberland," opined one of O'Connell's supporters at a meeting of O'Connell's General Association on 30 June. For another, Victoria "has come to the throne in despite of the Orangemen (cheers). If they could she would not now be Queen of England (cheers) . . . the loyal subjects of the empire would now be wading, perhaps, through blood to place the crown on the head of Victoria." As for Cumberland, he "is now a despotic King—a station to which, no doubt, his feelings will do credit—may he long enjoy it (cheers)—and may we long enjoy his absence (cheers)."[55] The *Freeman's Journal* hoped that Cumberland would "propagate in Hanover the genuine principles of unadulterated Orangeism, and disseminate the demoniac system of the congregated ruffians."[56]

54. *FJ,* 23 June 1837.
55. Speeches of Finn and Doheny, reported in *FJ,* 1 July 1837.
56. *FJ,* 26 June 1837.

CHAPTER TWO

"Darling Little Queen"

Gender and O'Connell's Monarchy, 1837–1847

The London *Times*'s accounts of the rejoicing in Dublin at Queen Victoria's accession were mischievous. There was no mourning for William IV. Instead, "thanksgivings are offered up from the Popish altars, that our young Queen is inclined to embrace the old religion of her forebearers, and, immediately, of her uncle Leopold [king of the Belgians], and her mother the Duchess of Kent who has long been a secret but trusty believer." Victoria was "already made a saint by the Romish priests of Ireland."[1] There may, however, have been an element of truth in the reports. The coming of a new monarch was a time for fantasies as well as for realistic hopes and expectations.

On 21 June 1837 the new queen's accession was proclaimed at St. James's Palace in London. "The crowd cheered vociferously, and prominent in the throng was Daniel O'Connell, who waved his hat with conspicuous energy."[2] In private O'Connell was equally pleased: "Lord Melbourne's government, *aided by the Court,* will be all powerful."[3] He saw Victoria as a partisan ally rather than as a dispassionate constitutional monarch. She was "in excellent hands,"[4] was committed to change, and was therefore, in the older

1. Reported in *FJ,* 3 July 1837.

2. Sidney Lee, *Queen Victoria: A Biography* (London: Smith, Elder, 1902), 51.

3. Daniel O'Connell to P. V. Fitzpatrick, 13 June 1837, in Maurice R. O'Connell, ed., *The Correspondence of Daniel O'Connell,* vol. 6 (1837–40) (Dublin: Blackwater: n.d.), no. 2411, p. 48.

4. Daniel O'Connell to P. V. Fitzpatrick, 9 June 1837, in O'Connell, *Correspondence,* vol. 6, no. 2409, p. 47.

sense of the word, "our patriotic Queen."[5] He at once set about giving her an education in Irish matters. Earlier in the year he had wanted to make an address to her on her coming of age.[6] Now he wrote a pamphlet for her entitled "Ireland and the Irish," which he tried to persuade Lord Durham to give her.[7]

For O'Connell, the defeat of Cumberland and Orangeism and the accession of the pro-Whig Victoria was a golden opportunity to try once more to shift the ideological markers of loyalty. If he could show that repealers and Whigs were the new monarch's true loyalists and the Tories her enemies, then perhaps his agenda of reform for Ireland and repeal of the union might succeed.

A letter from O'Connell dated 28 June 1835 was read at the General Association on 30 June:

It being now certain that the young Queen—whom may God bless—places full confidence in that ministry which was the first during six centuries to desire honestly and faithfully to serve the people of Ireland—we must all, with one accord, rally round the throne of the Queen, and in support of her Majesty's government.[8]

A general election was compulsory on the accession of a new monarch. O'Connell announced the formation of a new anti-Tory grouping which he called "The Friends of the Queen" to fight the election in Ireland. "We have on the throne a monarch educated to cherish the rights and liberties of all the people. . . . Ireland is now ready to amalgamate with the entire empire," promised O'Connell ambiguously. "We are prepared for full and perpetual conciliation."

Meanwhile the government was also using the new queen in a partisan fashion. A letter from Lord John Russell to the lord lieutenant, Lord Normanby, which gave the queen's endorsement for Whig policy in Ireland,

5. Daniel O'Connell to Alexander Sherlock, 25 July 1837, in O'Connell, *Correspondence*, vol. 6, no. 2441, p. 74.

6. Daniel O'Connell to Richard Barrett, 21 April 1837, quoted in O'Connell, *Correspondence*, vol. 6, no. 2397, p. 32.

7. Daniel O'Connell to Lord Durham, c. 12 July 1837, and Lord Durham to Daniel O'Connell, 18 July 1837, in O'Connell, *Correspondence*, vol. 6, nos. 2431 and 2438, pp. 63 and 70. Victoria had already read some Irish history and in 1837 Melbourne recommended that she read O'Driscol's *Ireland* (RA QVJ, 9 February 1837 and 24 January 1838, in Esher, *Girlhood*, 1:185 and 263).

8. Reported in *FJ*, 1 July 1837.

was published. According to the letter, the queen hoped to see her Irish subjects "in the full enjoyment of that civil and political Equality to which by recent statues they are fully entitled."[9]

During the election O'Connell continued to beat his own loyalist drum. He denounced a meeting held at Ludgate Hill coffeehouse in London of a group, under the royal printer Spottiswood, that wanted to fund elections against the Whigs, as a conspiracy against the queen.[10] In the outcome Melbourne continued in government but Whigs and radicals in Britain lost ground, though Irish anti-Tories gained ground and took seventy-one of the hundred and five seats.[11]

Victoria's first actual encounter with O'Connell came at a levee in St. James's Palace on 24 February 1838. "The Queen has expressed a wish to see me. She is determined to conciliate Ireland. I will, of course, attend the next levee, and perhaps some good to Ireland may be the consequence."[12] Victoria was equally excited but for less political reasons. For the young queen, O'Connell was a famous and fascinating public figure:

At about a ¼ p. 2 I went into the Throne room for the levee with my Ladies &c., and all the Household and the Ministers being in the room. The only person who I was very anxious to see and whom I was much interested to have seen, was *O'Connell,* who was presented, and of course, as everybody does when they are presented kissed hands. He was in a full wig as one of the Queen's Councillors in Ireland, and not in the brown Brutus wig he generally wears. He is very tall, rather large, has a remarkable good-humoured countenance, small features, small clever blue eyes, and very like his caricatures; there were likewise two of his sons, Morgan and John O'Connell; his son-in-law Mr Fitzsimon, and his nephew John Morgan O'Connell.[13]

She wrote an account of the levee to her uncle, King Leopold, telling him that it had been "quite a treat" for her to see O'Connell but adding with a note that indicated as much caution as praise that O'Connell had

9. RP [Russell Papers] 2E, Lord John Russell to Lord Mulgrave, draft 18 July 1837, in J. Prest, *Lord John Russell* (London, Macmillan: 1972), 117.

10. Richard Davis, *Revolutionary Imperialist: William Smith O'Brien* (Dublin: Lilliput, 1998), 102.

11. MacDonagh, *O'Connell,* 442.

12. Daniel O'Connell to P. V. Fitzpatrick, 15 February 1838, in W. J. Fitzpatrick, ed., *Correspondence of Daniel O'Connell the Liberator,* 2 vols. (London: John Murray, 1888), 2:123.

13. RA QVJ, 21 February 1838, in Esher, *Girlhood,* 1:286–87.

"been behaving very well this year."[14] O'Connell's view of the queen continued to be unreservedly positive:

I do verily believe that she has the noble ambition of making her reign celebrated by the pure and perfect pacification of Ireland. We never had a sovereign before her present Majesty who was not an actual enemy of the Irish people; the change is propitious and should be cherished.[15]

He attended the coronation in London on 28 June 1838 and joined with the other members of the Commons in cheering the queen nine times.[16] In Dublin it was a wet day but "without compulsion or intimidation the whole town was illuminated."[17]

Victoria continued to enjoy seeing O'Connell until things turned sour in 1843. He presented addresses to her on a number of occasions in 1842 in his capacity as lord mayor of Dublin. On 9 April that year he appeared before the queen-this time with his Brutus wig; she recorded that he was dressed in "a crimson robe with a collar and white bows attached to each shoulder—a white wand in his hand. He read the Address and I was much pleased to hear him. He has a fine deep voice and an impressive manner and behaved with much dignity. He has a strong Irish brogue."[18]

On that occasion the Dublin Corporation had been congratulating the queen on the birth of the Prince of Wales. Almost three months later O'Connell was back again to congratulate her on her escape from the second of the seven attempts that would be made on her life during her reign. This time King Leopold and Queen Louise of the Belgians looked on from a gallery. O'Connell was, after all, an internationally revered statesman. Queen Louise was especially interested to see O'Connell "who was quite agitated. He had his priest with him and she was much struck with the heartiness and the affectionate tone of the address from Dublin."[19]

Lord Melbourne consulted the queen on two sensitive issues concerning Ireland in 1838. The first concerned a proposal to give O'Connell the senior Irish judicial position of master of the rolls. The cabinet favored

14. RA Y 89/4, Queen Victoria to King Leopold of the Belgians, 22 February 1838.

15. Daniel O'Connell to Nicholas Maher, 23 October 1838, in Fitzpatrick, *Correspondence*, 2:156.

16. Lee, *Victoria*, 90.   17. *FJ*, 29 June 1838.

18. RA QVJ, 9 April 1842.   19. RA QVJ, 29 June 1842.

the appointment but Melbourne himself was against it on the grounds that it would cause a clamor: "I know nothing worse than a clamour."[20] Perhaps he hoped that the queen might oppose the appointment and give him the chance to reverse the cabinet's decision. If so, it explains the queen's account of their discussion of the matter. "He then asked me twice over 'Have you any particular feeling about it?' I said none whatever, and therefore it is left to Ministers to offer it, or not, as they may think fit."[21] In the event O'Connell refused the post.

The second issue concerned the government of Ireland and the appointment of a new lord lieutenant. As a result of the Lichfield House Compact, Ireland enjoyed a period of benign rule under Lord Mulgrave (later known as Lord Normanby) as lord lieutenant, Lord Morpeth (later known as Lord Carlisle) as chief secretary, and Thomas Drummond as under secretary.

Toward the end of 1838 it became clear that Normanby wanted to leave office. Melbourne told the queen that Normanby had become too touchy about his dignity in opposing an investigation into the state of crime in Ireland.[22] Nonetheless, "Lord M. said 'All the Irish members are in despair at Normanby's leaving Ireland,' which I can quite understand."[23]

Normanby planned to have himself replaced by the queen's uncle, the duke of Sussex, as an apolitical lord lieutenant. In October 1838 Melbourne initially warned the queen that "it would be extremely dangerous."[24] A few days later he wrote to her officially suggesting it but distancing himself from the project:

If Ireland should be vacant there is a strong feeling amongst many that it would be nice to name the Duke of Sussex. It is said that it would be popular in Ireland, that the name of the Royal Family would do good there, and that it would afford O'Connell a pretext and opportunity for giving up his new scheme of agitation. It is also added that the Duke would suffer himself to be guided on all essential matters by the advice of the Chief Secretary and that he would content himself with discharging the ceremonial duties.[25]

20. Quoted in Philip Ziegler, *Melbourne* (London: Collins, 1976), 279.

21. RA QVJ, 11 June 1838, in Esher, *Girlhood*, 1:349.

22. RA QVJ, 20 March 1839, in Esher, *Girlhood*, 2:131–32.

23. RA QVJ, 11 February 1839, in Esher, *Girlhood*, 2:119.

24. RA QVJ, 22 October 1838, in Esher, *Girlhood*, 2:60.

25. Lord Melbourne to Queen Victoria, 15 October 1838, in Queen Victoria, *Letters of Queen Victoria*, first series, ed. A. C. Benson and Viscount Esher, vol. 1 (1837–43) (London: John Murray, 1907), 165.

O'Connell's "new scheme of agitation" was his foundation of the Precursor Society of Ireland on 18 August 1838. It was a way of putting pressure on the Whigs, with whom he was becoming impatient. He announced that it was his last effort to win concessions for Ireland before resuming active agitation for repeal, though he was later to back off from direct confrontation.[26] As for the Sussex scheme, in the end nothing came of it except that Sussex, who wanted the position, proved "in the highest degree discontented at being informed decisively that there is no intention of sending him to Ireland."[27] By the end of Queen Victoria's reign there had been discussion about the appointment of eight members of her family to the office of lord lieutenant or as official royal representative in Ireland, all of which came to nothing.[28]

The year 1839 was one marked by two serious mistakes on the part of Queen Victoria. She was blamed for her lack of kindness to the gravely ill Lady Flora Hastings, who died on 5 July 1839. Victoria had wrongly suspected Hastings, an unmarried woman and a member of her household, of being pregnant.

The other mistake, the so-called Bedchamber Plot, was more political but also involved the queen's household. Melbourne lost the confidence of the Commons in early May 1839 over a revolt in Jamaica. After he resigned, it was expected that Peel, whom Victoria then disliked, would assume office as Tory prime minister. She was required by convention to change the political complexion of the ladies of her household on a change in government but refused to do so. The debacle of the queen's questionable constitutional behavior resulted in the return to power of Melbourne and to the queen's deep unpopularity with Tories.

26. MacDonagh, *O'Connell*, 458–60, 464: "On 2 September 1839 . . . he dissolved the Precursor Society, replacing it by a Reform Registry Association in which Irish whigs and liberals could participate."

27. Lord Melbourne to Queen Victoria, 21 December 1838, in Benson and Esher, *Letters*, first series, 1:175–76.

28. As well as Sussex in 1838, they were: Queen Victoria's cousin, the duke of Cambridge, in 1852; her sons, the Prince of Wales and the duke of Connaught, in the early 1870s; her son-in-law, Lord Lorne (later duke of Argyll), in 1880; her grandsons, the dukes of Clarence and York, in 1889 and 1891, respectively; and her grandson-in-law, the duke of Fife in 1889. King Edward VII similarly considered the appointment of his brother, the duke of Connaught, and of his son, George, Prince of Wales (formerly duke of York).

The thought of Peel as prime minister was received with alarm in nationalist Ireland. "First of all he will probably advise the Queen to declare war on Ireland."[29] O'Connell wrote an open letter to the people of Ireland on the coming "calamity" of Peel. However, he had continued hopes of the partisanship of the queen:

Let our allegiance to the amiable and exalted personage who wears the crown of these realms be as affectionate as it ever shall be unbroken. She at least has performed her part well and nobly. She supported the friends of Ireland as long as the dissensions and follies that broke out amongst the Reform party permitted her to do so. It is delightful to think that in our youthful Sovereign the people of Ireland have a friend who does not want the inclination—for she, alas! has not the power—to serve them effectually.[30]

The return of Melbourne and the ousting of the Tories delighted O'Connell. "Hurrah for the darling little Queen! Peel is out; Melbourne in again. . . . She has shown great firmness and excellent heart."[31] Nor had he a desire to see any change in the queen's circumstances that might deflect her from her current course. "The Queen is full of intellect. She may not marry for years, as she wishes to enjoy *her* power."[32] Indeed, he wanted to drive home the victory and to consolidate the division between the Tories and the Crown by having the queen visit Ireland:

I am strongly of opinion that the Queen ought to be solicited to go to Ireland this summer. It would be a *brain-blow* to the Orange faction to have the popular party well received at Court and their own leaders treated with the indifference they so highly merit.[33]

The reaction to the ousting of Peel in the nationalist press in Ireland was equally enthusiastic. "Again and again we pray 'God bless the Queen.' 'May she live for ever!' and live for ever she will in the grateful affections of a loyal and devoted and generous and confiding people."[34] The Tories had been "cruel and ungenerous" in attempting "to foist their creatures into the palace of the Queen."[35]

29. *FJ*, 11 May 1839.   30. *FJ*, 11 May 1839.
31. Daniel O'Connell to P. V. Fitzpatrick, 10 May 1839, in O'Connell, *Correspondence*, vol. 6, no. 2618, p. 242.
32. Daniel O'Connell to P. V. Fitzpatrick, 5 August 1839, in O'Connell, *Correspondence*, vol. 6, no. 2643, p. 263.
33. Daniel O'Connell to P. V. Fitzpatrick, 26 May 1839, in O'Connell, *Correspondence*, vol. 6, no. 2624, p. 248.
34. *FJ*, 13 May 1839.   35. *FJ*, 14 May 1839.

The *Times* took to referring to the restored Whig government, sarcastically, as "the O'Connell cabinet."[36] However, throughout England supporters of the Melbourne government had held meetings to thank the queen. The *Freeman's Journal* called for Irish illuminations and public demonstrations of thanks on 24 May, the queen's birthday.[37] O'Connell's Dublin demonstration was held on 23 May. The *Dublin Evening Mail* criticized the change to the anniversary date of the 1798 rebellion. "This demonstration is no homage to the Queen—it is the triumph of a party. It celebrates no principle of loyalty—it is the apotheosis of treason."[38] Opposition to the demonstration from Irish Tories grew in intensity, so finally O'Connell's Precursor Society issued an advertisement asking people not to illuminate their houses because "the disaffected and disloyal faction in this City, who are the violent enemies of the Queen and the people, have determined to create riot and disturbances."[39] Two hundred police were on duty at the meeting, which was held in front of the Custom House and went off peacefully. Lord Cloncurry took the chair and there were calls for municipal and franchise reform.[40] "The vast assembly then separated peacefully, after giving three cheers for the Queen and Mr O'Connell."[41]

O'Connell was, in his own mind, at once the leader of the Irish people, or at least of the nationalists, and the humble servant of the queen. He was careful during this period, in spite of popular acclaim, to avoid the use of language that might make it appear that he was somehow Ireland's monarch. Yet, important as his protestations of loyalty to the queen were to his project in Britain, he wanted to make it clear that he was in an unrivaled position of eminence in Ireland.

The strategy that he began to adopt to do this was to parallel—or even burlesque—his discourse of loyalty, in which he was in an inferior position to the queen, with a discourse of gender, in which he overshadowed and patronized her. Just before the Dublin demonstration he told the Precursor Society:

It seems to me that by a special dispensation of Providence she [Queen Victoria] is placed as a maternal protection to the people at large amid the strides which democratic movements have latterly given. She has done nothing [in refusing to

36. *Times*, 23 May 1839.

37. *FJ*, 20 May 1829.

38. *FJ*, 23 May 1839.

39. *FJ*, 23 May 1939.

40. MacDonagh, *O'Connell*, 462.

41. *FJ*, 24 May 1839.

change the members of her household], however, but what the most affectionate of our females—those most endeared to us by every tie, would do—clinging with that affectionate fondness to those who have in early years contributed to their infant and childish amusements. . . . I am a father, and know well the soothing love of parental affection; I am a grandfather, having a second race of females bounding about me—and all I ask is, may their hearts resemble, in purity of thought and generosity of feeling, in affectionate attachment to those who cherished and watched over them, that of their sovereign.[42]

Victoria begins this passage in the conventional guise of the queen who is the mother of her people. But she is soon turned into a child controlled by emotion rather than by reason. O'Connell then subtly inserts himself into the scene as a wise grandfather. O'Connell returned to the same position of patriarchal superiority in his speech at Bandon that welcomed the queen's engagement with "ludicrous hyperboles of joy."[43] "I am a father and a grandfather, and in the face of Heaven I pray with as much honesty and fervency for Queen Victoria as I do for any one of my own progeny."[44] Several years later he was to say even more explicitly, "I feel towards her the tenderness of a parent."[45]

The mythology of O'Connell as the queen's father or grandfather took root among some sections of the peasantry in a rather literal fashion. By 1843 Lord Monteagle was writing of people who thought that O'Connell was about to marry the queen's mother, the duchess of Kent.[46] This would literally have made O'Connell the queen's stepfather. It was probably only a striking coincidence, though, that in 1847 O'Connell's body was brought back to Ireland on a ship called *The Duchess of Kent.* [47]

❖

On 23 November 1839 the English privy council met to announce the engagement of Victoria to her cousin, Prince Albert of Saxe-Coburg and Gotha. Controversy at once erupted over Albert's religion and the lack of any mention of his Protestantism in the official announcement. Was he in fact a "pauper Papist and princely adventurer"[48] or was the omission deliberately designed to assuage "Irish papists and their nominees at the [privy]

42. *FJ,* 22 May 1839.   43. Lee, *Victoria,* 110.
44. *FJ,* 9 December 1839.   45. *FJ,* 30 August 1843.
46. RA M52/26, Lord Mounteagle to Sir Fitz-Roy Somerset, [late 1843].
47. *FJ,* 3 August 1847.
48. *Times,* reported in *FJ,* 28 November 1839.

council board"?[49] The queen had indeed recently admitted Catholics to membership in the privy council, and "all that is truculent, bigoted and sanguinary in England is arranged against the Queen on account of her good will towards Ireland."[50]

As for the question of Albert's own religion, there was no truth to the rumor of his being Catholic but it was true that the Coburg family was pragmatic when it came to religion and its dynastic advantage. It was one of the three Ernestine branches of the Wettin family. The Albertine branch of the family in Saxony proper had been Catholic kings of Poland and one of them had even been the last Catholic electoral-archbishop of Trier. Closer to home Albert's uncle, Leopold, was king of the Catholic Belgians, and his cousin, Ferdinand, was king consort of the Catholic Portuguese. All of this added fuel to the issue of religion. The London *Times* warned its readers that "[t]he Irish papers in the interest of Mr O'Connell point exultingly to the fact that the family of Prince Albert comprehends professors of the Roman Catholic faith."[51]

O'Connell's own affection for the queen now extended to the royal couple. "Prince Albert is a fine-looking young man with a very manly countenance. I got a smile from her and a civil bow from him yesterday."[52] On 9 December 1839 at Bandon O'Connell once more linked attacking the Tories with defending the queen:

The moment I heard of the daring and audacious menaces of the Tories towards the Sovereign, I promulgated through the press my feelings of detestation and my determination on the matter (cheers, "yes, we read them sir"). Oh if I be not greatly mistaken I'd get in one day 500,000 brave Irishmen to defend the life, the honour, and the person of the beloved young lady by whom England's throne is now filled (exulting and protracted cheers). Let every man in the vast and multitudinous assembly stretched out before me who is loyal to the Queen and would defend her to the last lift up his right hand (the entire assembly responded to the

49. *Times*, reported in *FJ*, 27 November 1839.

50. *FJ*, 4 December 1839.

51. *Times*, 10 December 1839.

52. Daniel O'Connell to P. V. Fitzpatrick, 20 February 1840, in O'Connell, *Correspondence*, vol. 6, no. 2688, p. 309. See also Daniel O'Connell to P. V. Fitzpatrick, 28 January 1841, in O'Connell, *Correspondence*, vol. 7, no. 2804, p. 14. "We have been just up with the address to the Queen. There were very few of the members in attendance. We had therefore a much better view of the dear little lady. She is looking well, and read the answer most sweetly. Prince Albert is really a handsome young man."

appeal). There are hearts in those hands. I tell you that if necessity required there would be swords in them! (awful cheering).[53]

Victoria herself was unimpressed and dismissed the performance as "a violent speech of O'Connell's . . . announcing war on the Tories."[54] However, it caused a sensation in Ireland. The continuing "abuse of an innocent Sovereign" over the Bedchamber episode, the attacks on the Irish people "because their unrequited loyalty has passed into a proverb which augurs badly for the cause of Tory treason," and "the brutal calumnies on Mr O'Connell" all showed "the real state of the Conservative camp."[55]

But the Tories were not about to let the matter of Albert's religion drop. The duke of Wellington moved an amendment to the address at the opening of the parliamentary session to have the word "Protestant" inserted concerning Albert. Melbourne eventually agreed to it in order to avoid more trouble. It was not much of a victory for the Tories, however, who were widely thought to have overreacted to the issue. Victoria noted the view that "the Duke of Wellington had made a sad mistake by moving that the word *Protestant* be put into the address and saying it was left out to please O'Connell!!"[56]

The incident and the debate a few days later on financial provision for Prince Albert allowed O'Connell to appear once more as the ultraloyalist. He told the Commons that his constituents had "instructed him to give his support to the Sovereign in every way. Yes, they had instructed him to vote for this grant, and they felt too that if the Tories had prevailed at court they would offer no opposition to the grant."[57]

The royal marriage took place on 10 February. Much of Dublin was illuminated in celebration. By contrast, in Londonderry, the Apprentice Boys, an association of Protestants much like the Orange Order, attacked the procession celebrating the marriage: "[T]he lads who were carrying the banner [of Victoria and Albert] were kicked and abused in the most barbarous manner—the portrait of her Majesty was torn into atoms and trampled into the gutters."[58]

53. *FJ*, 9 December 1839.

54. RA QVJ, 26 December 1839, in Esher, *Girlhood*, 2:286.

55. *FJ*, 17 December 1839.

56. RA QVJ, 16 January 1840, in Esher, *Girlhood*, 2:297.

57. 27 January 1840, *Parliamentary Debates*, 3d Series, vol. 51 (16 January–6 February 1840), col. 624.

58. *Belfast Weekly Vindicator*, reported in *FJ*, 17 February 1840.

The politicization of Victoria's engagement and wedding was a sign of the continuing rancor over the events of May 1839. It lasted well into 1840. By November, when Vicky, the first child of the marriage, was born, a regency act was already in place that laid down that, in the event of Victoria's death, Albert might act as regent for any offspring of their marriage so long as he remained in England and did not marry a Catholic. There had been some concern in nationalist Ireland that King Ernest of Hanover or the duke of Cambridge might have been named as regent in waiting. As it was, the nomination of Albert marked the beginnings of a partial rapprochement between the court and the Tories.

When the birth came it was received with rejoicing in Ireland. Daniel Murray, Catholic archbishop of Dublin, told the clergy of his diocese that "our most gracious Queen has, through the blessing of God, given birth to an heir to the throne of this great empire." O'Connell's son John told a meeting on 23 November that "she had presented the three countries with a pledge that they shall have a successor to inherit the virtues that so eminently distinguish her Majesty (tremendous cheering)." Even more to the point, "this happy event had placed a barrier between them and despotism."[59]

The despotism in question was that of the king of Hanover, who had returned to haunt Irish Catholic imaginations after the first assassination attempt on the queen by Edward Oxford on Constitution Hill in London on 10 June 1840. Had Oxford succeeded, Hanover would have been king, as O'Connell pointed out in an open letter to the people of Ireland on 13 June, going so far as to hint at a Tory plot behind the attempt. Now at least, with the birth of Vicky, Hanover was only second in line to the throne.

⁂

In March 1840 it looked as though Parliament might pass a new restriction on the Irish franchise. O'Connell's mind began to turn toward popular agitation once more. On 15 April he founded the "Loyal National Association for Full and Prompt Justice or Repeal" at a meeting in the Corn Exchange, Dublin. Among its explicit commitments were loyalty and a prohibition on violence.[60] On 13 July, sensing that the Whigs had not much time left in government, he changed the name to the "Loyal National Re-

59. *FJ*, 24 November 1840.
60. *FJ*, 16 April 1840.

peal Association," though he did not seriously begin agitation for repeal until the autumn of 1842.[61]

For O'Connell, "a local parliament is the inherent and ineffaceable right of subjects of the Crown of England, wherever they are located in sufficient numbers to exercise that right."[62] For his opponents at Westminster, he was supporting demands "which no one knew better than himself meant the dismemberment of the Empire, by threats that if they were not granted England would fear to go to war with anyone!"[63]

In launching the Repeal Association O'Connell was again at pains to stress his loyalty both personally to Queen Victoria and to the institution of monarchy itself:

I am convinced that there was no Sovereign of the house of Brunswick ever before a friend of Ireland. Repeal and not separation is not [sic] the word. I respect the golden link of the crown which bi for ever Ireland and England together. I would rather perish than see the connection between the two countries broken or our allegiance to the throne in the slightest degree lessened by our demand; that we do not want but the representation of our own parliament—the House of Lords as if the union statue had never been passed—the Commons representing the people possessed of universal suffrage. We want to achieve that by peaceful and loyal means.[64]

The speech was a balancing act. His call for universal suffrage was radical. It was one of the demands of the Chartists in Britain. The acceptance of a Tory Irish House of Lords and the enthusiasm for the queen balanced it. The meeting ended with three cheers for the queen, O'Connell, and the repeal of the union. Joining the Repeal Association involved an oath of allegiance to the queen and wearing a button with the harp and crown and the slogans "God Save the Queen" and "Repeal of the Union."

There was a general election in the summer of 1841 that returned a large Tory majority. By that time anyway O'Connell's alliance with the Whigs was at an end. To the *Freeman's Journal* it appeared that Tories, Whigs, and radicals were equally opposed to Ireland and "all that was beneficent in the wishes of the Queen."[65] When Parliament resumed the Whigs were soon

61. MacDonagh, *O'Connell*, 467–69, 492.

62. M. F. Cusack, ed., *The Speeches and Public Letters of the Liberator*, 2 vols. (Dublin: McGlashan and Gill, 1875), 2:294.

63. Theodore Martin, *The Life of His Royal Highness the Prince Consort*, 5 vols. (London: Smith, Elder, 1875), 1:80.

64. *FJ*, 14 July 1840.

65. *FJ*, 14 July 1841.

replaced by a Tory government under Peel, who with time developed a warm relationship with Victoria and Albert.

During his first year in office Peel thought O'Connell a spent force and did not bother much with Ireland. When Ireland returned to the political agenda Peel adopted a stick-and-carrot policy, being firm in resisting repeal while granting other concessions. More than that he attempted, in subtle and not-so- subtle ways, to engage in an ideological battle with O'Connell over loyalty to the monarchy. He sought to manipulate the political discourse so that Toryism and support for the union might be seen as true loyalty and nationalism and support for repeal as disloyalty. In this he largely succeeded, but not for the ends he intended. Imagining that loyalty to the Crown was the stronger political force, he must have hoped that detaching nationalism from loyalty would weaken Irish nationalism. In fact, it weakened Irish loyalty.

Wherever possible Peel tried to drive a wedge between Irish nationalists and the monarchy. An early opportunity came with the birth on 9 November 1841 of Victoria's second child, Prince Albert Edward, known to his family and the public as Bertie, who was quickly created Prince of Wales and would eventually reign as Edward VII.

O'Connell had just entered office as lord mayor of Dublin, becoming the first Catholic since 1688 to hold the post. He was quick to welcome the news of the prince's birth. "He did sincerely hope that the young Prince before he came to the throne, which was his undoubted right, would be sent to Ireland as the Viceroy of his excellent mother, and that he would in that capacity open the parliament in College-green." However, he may still have been nervous concerning the reaction of Dublin Tories to his assumption of the lord mayoralty on the reformed corporation, and so he did not order an illumination of the city to celebrate the birth of the prince as might have been expected. In a somewhat defensive speech to the Repeal Association he explained that this was lest "those who wished to disturb the public peace would take advantage of such an illumination and that serious consequences might follow." Nonetheless, "there was not a Repealer in Ireland who did not cheerfully wish him [the infant prince] long life, good health and every prosperity which should attend a monarch." And he proposed that the Association present an address of congratulations to the queen "which would contain no paltry flattery, but emanate from the sincerity of the heart."[66]

66. *FJ*, 16 November 1841.

It was the custom that on the birth of a male heir to the throne a baronetcy—a hereditary honor that included the title "sir"—be conferred on the lord mayors of London and Dublin. The honor was duly awarded to the London lord mayor but not to O'Connell. It caused indignation on O'Connell's behalf in Ireland but also a questioning of the value of such awards:

What title could add dignity to his name? What could add rank or influence to his position? The foremost man in this country—second to none in the dominions of Great Britain—no heraldic honour, no titular distinction could give eclat to his name, or increase the fame which is not only national, but European. We can well understand, therefore, how Daniel O'Connell can despise the paltry attempt of the Tory Premier to subtract from him position by withholding from him the offer of a baronetcy. . . . For the Lord Mayor himself, we question not he would, with all ardour of loyalty, and all his submission to the Queen, at once and decisively, decline the honour. But still we say, it should have been offered him.[67]

In late November 1841 O'Connell mounted a strong attack on the Tory government but was careful to add that it did not "lessen his allegiance or diminish his respect and attachment to the admirable young Queen. . . . She had evinced a more honest hearted and friendly disposition towards this country than any British monarch that had preceded her."[68] O'Connell and his supporters were now trying to distinguish between loyalty to the queen and support of the government. He himself continued to believe privately that the queen was a pro-Irish partisan. In February 1842 he claimed that she had deliberately "slurred over the speech [from the throne] as if she was repeating an unwelcome lesson."[69]

The *Freeman's Journal* went to some pains to draw a distinction between Britain and Ireland, on the one hand, and Russia, on the other. In the latter a despotic monarchy was allied with a despotic aristocracy against the people, whereas in the former a potentially despotic Tory aristocracy was frustrated by the monarch and the constitution.[70]

Elsewhere it was less sanguine about the queen's checking power and she appeared in the guise of a victim of the government. The Tories were "the party who now govern the Queen and People of these realms for the bene-

67. *FJ*, 18 April 1842.
68. *FJ*, 24 November 1841.
69. Daniel O'Connell to P. V. Fitzpatrick, February 1842, in O'Connell, *Correspondence*, vol. 7, no. 2940, p. 133.
70. *FJ*, 24 August 1842.

fit and at the bidding of the Aristocracy." And the appointment of the king of Hanover's old associate Colonel Fairman as governor of Trinidad was a sign of "the powerless monarch of the kingdom not alone compelled to obey the political dictation of a set of ministers whom she distrusts and disapproves, but openly coerced to delegate her royal power and authority over one of her distant provinces to a man" once suspected of treason.[71]

❖

O'Connell began 1843 by dedicating the first part of his history of Ireland to the queen, though the reaction in the nationalist press was cooler and less effusive, at least as far as the queen was concerned:

"This book is humbly inscribed to Her Most Gracious Majesty the Queen of Great Britain and Ireland." Yes, and "of Ireland." Such are the words of the great champion of Ireland's legislative independence. Such is the language of him who has done more in this broad land to make her name and reign revered than could be accomplished by a hundred ministers. Such is the language of him who while he gives the Sovereign all the honour which to her of right belongs, never forgets that the dignity of the freeman is best evinced by courtesy short but comprehensive— that flattery and subservience only need many words to hide their nakedness of spirit, and that few syllables convey the heart felt homage of the independent.[72]

O'Connell announced that 1843 would be the year in which repeal was achieved. His agitation and pressure on the government took the form of holding nearly fifty vast "monster" meetings, many of which he addressed himself, during the course of the spring and summer. Though estimates of crowd sizes are impossible to verify, it was certainly not untypical for crowds of many hundreds of thousands to turn out to individual meetings.

Loyalty to the Crown and allegiance to O'Connell were prominent features of the mise en scène of the monster meetings. For example, when O'Connell arrived in Dundalk for the meeting on 30 June he was met with a triumphal arch inscribed with "The Queen, O'Connell agus Erin go bragh." Another arch had representations of Queen Victoria and Prince Albert but a legend addressed to O'Connell: "Ireland's Moses, who crushed our foes, welcome to Dundalk."[73]

71. *FJ,* 9 March 1843.   72. *FJ,* 17 February 1843.
73. *FJ,* 1 July 1843.

❖

The government was deeply alarmed by the repeal agitation. It was anxious about the possibility of a rebellion, though in some ways frustrated that the peaceful manner in which the meetings took place did not allow a ready opportunity for suppression. "You can hardly overrate the gravity of the present moment. The peaceable demeanour of the assembled multitudes is one of the most alarming symptoms," Sir Edward Sugden told Peel on 28 May 1843, with no apparent irony.[74]

On 6 May 1843 the lord lieutenant Lord de Grey wrote to London warning of the dangers of the agitation. "When O'Connell states that he has been addressing 70,000; 80,000; 120,000; more; the world believes him. . . . A building has been commenced to hold 3,000 persons and is announced as the future House of Commons. . . . Is this a state of things that can be allowed to go on?"[75] Two regiments of cavalry had already been dispatched to Dublin from England and two regiments of infantry were on their way. However, on 8 May the cabinet decided that no extraordinary measures could be taken until violence had broken out.[76]

To soothe the anxieties of the Orange wing of the Tory Party it was decided that a solemn pronouncement against repeal would be made in Parliament on 9 May. Peel told de Grey that "the duke in the Lords and I in the Commons shall to-night declare our intentions to preserve inviolate the Union and to use all the authority of the Government to support it."[77]

Peel watched in the Lords as the Orange leader Lord Roden asked Wellington a question that gave him the procedural opportunity to make the declaration. In replying he referred to the episode in 1834 when the then government had had a willing William IV declare against repeal in the government-written speech from the throne. Wellington made specific reference not to William's speech but to a joint address of Parliament in reply, as evidence that it was the settled will of Parliament that repeal not be granted.[78]

Ironically, Wellington, who in private was highly exercised about repeal,

74. Sir Edward Sugden to Sir Robert Peel, 28 May 1843, in C. S. Parker, ed., *Sir Robert Peel from His Private Papers*, 3 vols. (London: John Murray, 1899), 3:49.

75. Lord de Grey to Sir Robert Peel, 6 May 1843, in Parker, *Peel*, 3:46–47.

76. Norman Gash, *Sir Robert Peel: The Life of Sir Robert Peel after 1830* (London: Longman, 1972), 402–3.

77. Sir Robert Peel to Lord de Grey, 9 May 1843, in Parker, *Peel*, 3:47–48.

78. 9 May 1843, *Parliamentary Debates*, 3d Series, vol. 69 (9 May–15 June 1843), cols. 1–9.

had made a relatively restrained statement as Tory leader in the Lords. Peel, who had pursued a policy of moderation, thought it wise to use the language of condemnation.[79] When it came to his turn in the Commons to make the declaration in reply to a question from Roden's son, Lord Jocelyn, he quoted William IV's "just indignation" speech itself. He then went on to say that "on the part of her Majesty, I am authorised to repeat the declaration made by King William"[80] against repeal. Several days later he added that the queen also adhered to the part of the king's declaration that promised improvement and reform for Ireland.[81]

In fact, Peel was deceiving Parliament. He had not obtained any permission in advance from the queen about making the solemn declaration on her behalf. He wrote to her sheepishly the next day seeking retrospective approval: "Sir Robert Peel . . . trusts Your Majesty will not disapprove of his having repeated on behalf of Your Majesty the declaration made by King William."[82]

Victoria herself seems not to have been too worried about the events in Parliament concerning Ireland and appears to have raised no great objection to Peel's use of her name. On 9 May she "wrote a few lines to Sir Robert Peel." On 18 May she met him but they talked of India and the Canada Corn Law Bill. It was only on 21 May that her thoughts turned to Ireland when she received letters "giving an alarming account of the Repeal agitation and its extension to the Constabulary Force."[83]

Peel's statement was of dubious constitutional probity; indeed, questions were asked in the Commons on 19 May as to whether it was in order.[84] William IV's speech had been, whatever his own private views, a speech from the throne. Peel's statement purported to represent the queen's private views, and was therefore improper. However, it suited his purposes very well. It was a clear indication that the queen was personally out of sympathy with the Irish nationalists. Peel had wanted all along to discredit O'Connell's protestations that the queen was sympathetic to Irish nationalists and an unwilling prisoner of Tory policy.

In the Irish press there was an attempt to minimize the significance of

79. Gash, *Peel*, 404.

80. 9 May 1843, *Parliamentary Debates*, 3d Series, vol. 69 (9 May–15 June 1843), cols. 23–24.

81. 15 May 1843, *Parliamentary Debates*, 3d Series, vol. 69 (9 May–15 June 1843), col. 332.

82. RA A 14/51, Sir Robert Peel to Queen Victoria, 10 May 1843.

83. RA QVJ, 9, 18, and 21 May 1843.

84. *Times*, 20 May 1843.

what had happened and to deny that what had been expressed really was the personal opinion of the queen, for "the British constitution recognises as its deepest mystery that the *private opinion of the Sovereign can never be known*".[85]

The authorised declaration of her Majesty that she will maintain the union between the two countries is only what might have been expected. The opinions of the minister are always the opinions of the monarch. In this case, then, Peel but re-echoed himself; and when her gracious Majesty has other and more prudent advisers she will no doubt think more favourably of her long-misgoverned kingdom of Ireland than to refuse her sanction to that which alone can, and alone *will* make her Irish subjects happy and content.[86]

"I don't believe a word of it," was O'Connell's public pronouncement on the purported views of the queen.[87] Once more he presented the queen as the prisoner of the Tories. "How dare Peel make such use of her name. . . . [T]hey have got the Sovereign in their power and they have the audacity to attempt to make the Irish people believe that their Sovereign is adverse to them." He then went on to point to the long-term danger of Peel's strategy for the monarchy in Ireland. "I know of no man so great a separatist as he who insidiously attempts to alienate our feelings of allegiance and endeavours to sever the link of affection by which we in Ireland are bound to our still beloved Queen."[88]

Peel's statements over the two weeks following his initial declaration were taken as a sign that he was backtracking slightly. Nationalists claimed that he was beginning to eat his own words.[89] However, matters took a new and unexpected turn on 25 May when *Saunders's News-Letter* published a letter, dated 22 May, written on behalf of the Irish lord chancellor, Sir Edward Sugden, the politically appointed head of the judiciary, to Lord Ffrench, a supporter of repeal, dismissing him from the magistracy. Ffrench had presided at repeal meetings but he was now told that "such meetings are not in the spirit of the constitution and may become dangerous to the safety of the state" and "may tend towards violence." As a result, Ffrench, O'Connell, and eight others were to be dismissed as magistrates. "To allow such persons any longer to remain in the commission of

85. *Nation*, 3 June 1843.   86. *FJ*, 12 May 1843.
87. *FJ*, 12 May 1843.   88. *FJ* 16 May 1843.
89. *FJ*, 30 May 1843: "The minister has been obliged to eat his own declaration, that the Queen was opposed to the prayers of her Irish subjects."

the peace would be to afford the power of the Crown to the carrying of a measure which her Majesty has, like her predecessor, expressed her determination to prevent."[90]

In some ways Sugden was merely pushing the logic of Peel's strategy of denying constitutional legitimacy to repeal demands a stage or two further. But Sugden's actions pushed it too far politically. There were grumblings in Parliament and there was a spate of resignations from the magistracy in sympathy with those who had been dismissed. Peel and the government found themselves having to defend Sugden in public while being privately furious with him.

"I think it better to undeceive Sugden and to let him know and feel that his letter to Lord Ffrench is not the most perfect and unexceptionable performance the world ever saw," wrote the home secretary, Sir James Graham, to Peel.[91] Peel did so, telling Sugden that he had made a mistake in saying that the queen was determined "to prevent the Repeal of the Union," whereas the declaration had spoken of her determination "to maintain the Union as the bond of connection between the two countries." He expected the opposition to pick up on minor points such as this. "Instead of their coming forward, as we should have done, in oblivion of party differences, to aid the Crown in the maintenance of the Union, we must expect every little technical objection that astute men can urge for the purpose of throwing difficulties in the way."[92]

Yet the whole saga had raised more than mere technical issues. Graham bore the brunt in the Commons. Had there been any reports of breaches of the peace at repeal meetings? Had Sugden acted on specific instructions from the government or merely because he had read reports of the declaration against repeal? Graham's obfuscation in reply was that Sugden had been acting under general instructions to discourage opposition to the union.[93]

In the Lords criticism focused once more on the solemn declaration that had been Sugden's pretext for action. Lord Campbell granted that it may have indeed conveyed "the sentiments of their gracious Sovereign," but that it "was an irregular proceeding in a constitutional point of view,

90. *FJ*, 26 May 1843.

91. Sir James Graham to Sir Robert Peel, 1 June 1843, in Parker, *Peel*, 3:51.

92. Sir Robert Peel to Sir Edward Sugden, 1 June 1843, in Parker, *Peel*, 3:51–52.

93. 26, 29 May 1843, *Parliamentary Debates*, 3d Series, lxix (9 May–15 June 1843), cols. 983–84, 986.

introducing the personal opinions of the Sovereign with respect to subjects on which the public were divided." Lord Cottenham agreed and took
the criticism forward to Sugden for saying that the queen rather than the
queen's government was against repeal.[94] Campbell too rounded on Sugden
and argued that the logic of his letter was that repeal meetings had only
been rendered illegal by the declaration in Parliament. If so, why were the
magistrates dismissed for attending repeal meetings before the declaration?[95]

Sugden also received a letter from O'Connell, who wondered how the
twenty "multitudinous meetings" which to date had taken place could have
"an inevitable tendency to outrage" without having ever produced a single
outrage, and then sarcastically remarked that the answer "is not within the
comprehension of a mere Irish lawyer." As for the solemn declaration that
the queen personally opposed repeal, he noted: "You must know . . . that it
is utterly unfounded in fact" but merely likely "to expose her to the hatred
(if that were possible) of her brave, loyal and attached people of Ireland."[96]

Though she had not consented to the solemn declaration in advance
Queen Victoria was certainly supportive of the government's policy. Prince
Albert wrote to Graham that his reports from Ireland "have given to the
Queen and myself much pain as the crisis seems to draw nearer every day
in which the poor deluded people will have to pay for the wickedness of
their misleaders." Later he refers to the repealers as "the enimy [*sic*]."[97] In
early June Victoria told her Uncle Leopold that "the news from Ireland
continues to be very alarming."[98] The *Times* warned its readers that Ireland
was on the verge of rebellion and that repealers were "almost avowedly the
enemies of the Crown."[99]

Ironically, Lord Roden was dismissed from the magistracy in 1849 after
Orangemen killed thirty Catholics at Dolly's Brae on his estate; meanwhile,

94. 30 May 1843, *Parliamentary Debates*, 3d Series, vol. 69 (9 May–15 June 1843), cols. 1077,
1087.

95. *FJ,* 2 June 1843.

96. Daniel O'Connell to Sir Edward Sugden, 27 May 1843, in quoted in Parker, *Peel*,
3:50.

97. RA M 51/147, Prince Albert to Sir James Graham, 26 May 1843.

98. Queen Victoria to King Leopold, 6 June 1843, in Benson and Esher, *Letters*, first series, 1:603.

99. Reported in *FJ,* 10 June 1843.

O'Connell and the other dismissed magistrates had been restored to the magistracy in August 1846 by Sugden's successor.[100] However, O'Connell's version of Queen Victoria as the pro-Irish Whig who was the unwilling prisoner of the Tories had never been true. Over the next few months appeared the first signs that this fantasy was now beginning to crumble not only in the minds of the Irish public but also in his own mind.

In some ways O'Connell himself continued to speak of the queen in the same old way, not least because he feared to do otherwise would be to invited government suppression of the movement. At Tara on 15 August he told the crowd, "The Queen distrusts them [Peel and his ministers] because she knows them too well to entertain other feelings towards them (cheers)."[101] On 22 August he told the Repeal Association that "the connexion between Great Britain and Ireland, by means of the power, authority and prerogatives of the Crown will be perpetual and incapable of severance or separation." But he went on to urge the queen to lead a constitutional revolt against the United Kingdom: "[I]t was for her Majesty but to say the word and her faithful and devoted people of Ireland were once more in the enjoyment of what had been justly described as 'the natural rights of a nation.'"[102]

In late August Queen Victoria appeared in the House of Lords to deliver the speech from the throne at the end of the parliamentary session. It repeated a determination to maintain the union and was most pointed in its condemnation of repeal agitation:

I have observed with the deepest concern the persevering efforts which are made to stir up Discontent and Disaffection among my Subjects in Ireland and to Excite them to Demand a Repeal of the Legislative Union. . . . I feel assured that those of my faithful Subjects who have influence and authority in Ireland will discourage, to the utmost of their Power, a system of pernicious Agitation, which Disturbs the Industry and Retards the Improvement of that Country, and excites feelings of mutual Distrust and Animosity between different classes of my People.[103]

The *Freeman's Journal*, clinging to the imprisoned partisan view of the queen, told its readers that "[w]here, therefore, we now perceive a mitigat-

---

100. *FJ*, 17 August 1846.   101. *FJ*, 16 August 1843.
102. *FJ*, 23 August 1843.
103. 24 August 1843, *Parliamentary Debates*, 3d Series, vol. 71 (31 July–24 August 1843), col. 1009.

ed spirit in the speech her Majesty has now delivered from the throne, we are able to recognise therein her graciousness, while, in whatever is antagonistic to Irish interests, we detect the unmitigable hostility of her servants [the government]."[104] Two days later and still on the subject of the speech, however, a new view of the queen was emerging in the paper: she was no longer the partisan but now the ingénue deceived by the government. Peel "has the audacious courage to deceive our gracious Queen and make her the unwitting means of pronouncing such a fallacy."[105] Shortly afterward the *Nation* took up the same theme, albeit in a modified and more favorable form to the queen:

We believe that it was owing to her that the Speech contained no lying promises with regard to Ireland. She may be deceived by spurious arguments and willed into wrong conclusions; but her character would be a mockery if she allowed herself to be made the instrument of palpable delusions—if she spoke words of royal facts which she must know would never be fulfilled.[106]

O'Connell himself was unrestrained in his criticism of the speech. He recalled that he had described William IV's 1834 speech against him as "base, brutal and bloody." This present speech, he told the Repeal Association on 29 August, in which "the minister [Peel] makes the Queen scold me," was "the excess of stupidity, and impudence." He protested that he was criticizing the speech and not the queen, indeed, that rescuing her from Peel was now one of the additional objectives of the repeal agitation and that "in no other part of her dominions is she so popular [as] in Ireland." But he also said that the government having the queen speak the speech in person, rather than by a commission, was like dragging her "on the chariot wheels of their [the government's] triumph."[107]

O'Connell's criticisms of the speech were injudicious. The Irish law officers thought them seditious.[108] Just over a month later O'Connell was to take part in an injudicious ceremony, at the Mullaghmast monster meeting on 1 October. A deputation, headed by John Hogan, the sculptor, and Henry MacManus, the painter, presented O'Connell with "The Irish National Cap." It was a cap of green velvet, lined and turned up with blue velvet in "the form of the 'old Milesian crown'; to which is added a wreath of shamrocks interwoven with a white band, thus rendering it national, and,

104. *FJ*, 26 August 1843.   105. *FJ*, 28 August 1843.
106. *Nation*, 2 September 1843.   107. *FJ*, 30 August 1843.
108. MacDonagh, *O'Connell*, 521.

therefore, peculiarly adapted to meet the present feelings of the Irish people."[109] Years later Charles Gavan Duffy, no great supporter of the cult of
O'Connell, was to claim that it was "simply a cap of Irish materials and
manufacture." It was merely "*a* national cap, shaped *like* the old 'Milesian
Crown' [emphasis added]."[110] But it was clearly more than this. The uncrowned king was having his coronation, as a contemporary report made
clear: "Mr O'Connell then rose uncovered and Mr Hogan placed the cap
on his head amidst enthusiastic cheers."[111] It was his first formal acceptance of the role of countermonarch, though, having had a burlesque coronation, it was to be nearly two more years before he would preside at a burlesque court.

The government was preparing to intervene with force to suppress the
repeal movement. Wellington wanted to go to Ireland to calm the situation. The acerbic Graham told Peel that Wellington "believes that the
winds and the waves will obey him, and that in his presence there will be a
great calm. If there were a rebellion, his iron hand would crush it. I doubt
very much whether his preventive measures would be of a soothing character."[112] On 7 October Dublin Castle banned the monster meeting that
O'Connell had planned for 8 October at Clontarf, near the city. O'Connell, fearful of violence, complied and canceled the meeting. The next
night he told a banquet at the Rotundo that "[w]e know that the Queen
had nothing to do with the trick of yesterday." As all repeal meetings did,
the banquet ended with the singing of "God Save the Queen."[113] On 10
October O'Connell and other leaders of the repeal movement were arrested; they were to face trial for conspiracy. In Britain the political establishment, unwilling to recognize that they had been forced to suppress
a political movement, persisted in seeing O'Connell as the organizer of a
potential rebellion. "For a long time he seems really to have laboured under the delusion that he was King of Ireland, leader of a physical force capable of overawing the united kingdom."[114] The government had saved
"the Monarchy from the slow fever of unresisted sedition."[115] If allowed,

109. *FJ,* 2 October 1843.
110. C. G. Duffy, *Young Ireland: A Fragment of Irish History, 1840–45,* 3 vols. (London: T.
Fisher Unwin, 1896), 1:170.
111. *FJ,* 2 October 1843.
112. Sir James Graham to Sir Robert Peel, 6 September 1843, in Parker, *Peel,* 3:63.
113. *FJ,* 10 October 1843.
114. *Times,* 14 October 1843.
115. *Times,* 16 October 1843.

repeal would "despoil the Queen's domestic territory—splinter the Crown—which would undermine and crush the throne—which would expose her Majesty to insults and outrage from all quarters of the earth and ocean, and would leave England stripped of her vitality."[116]

Peel and Graham had kept Victoria and Albert informed as the crisis reached its culmination. Banning the Clontarf meeting had been about "prohibiting the mutiny in the streets of Dublin this afternoon."[117] Like many people in Britain, the royal couple's principal emotion concerning O'Connell was fear. Queen Victoria told her Uncle Leopold, "The case against him is *very* strong, the lawyers say."[118] Prince Albert also approved of the arrest and anticipated a swift trial of O'Connell as the government's first step against "this fearful agitator." Indeed, he advocated stronger measures:

The result will show whether the ordinary law is sufficient to protect the state from the risk of anarchy or *not*, and in the latter case make it clear to every well disposed person, that it is desirable that the Gov[t] should be entrusted with some extraordinary power, if it is to be held responsible for the peace of the country. The *extreme* forebearance evinced by the gov[t] hitherto will strengthen its claim for additional support.[119]

If Victoria and Albert had seen themselves as partisans it would undoubtedly have been as partisans for the government cause. For example, the queen and prince had hoped that when the new royal yacht called *Victoria and Albert* became available in the summer of 1843, they might visit Ireland. Repeal agitation prevented it, however.[120] Instead they traveled to meet Louis Philippe, king of the French, and visited Eu on 4 September.

There had been fears in London that France might seek to intervene in Ireland. Peel told Victoria that nineteen Frenchmen had attended the monster meeting on Tara Hill in August and had been "in communication with Mr. O'Connell."[121] Victoria interpreted O'Connell's public criticism of Louis Philippe, subsequent to her successful visit to France, as pique. She

116. *Times,* reported in *FJ* 29 November 1843.

117. RA M 52/3, Sir James Graham to Prince Albert, 8 October 1843.

118. Queen Victoria to King Leopold of the Belgians, 17 October 1843, in Benson and Esher, *Letters,* first series, 1:621.

119. RA M 52/2, Prince Albert to Sir James Graham, 8 October 1843.

120. Stanley Weintraub, *Albert Uncrowned King* (London: John Murray, 1997), 147.

121. RA A15/52, Sir Robert Peel to Queen Victoria, 19 August 1843.

told her Uncle Leopold; "You will have seen how O'Connell abused the King; it is all because our visit to Eu has put an end to any hopes of assistance from France, which he pretended there would be."[122]

❖

The trial of O'Connell and the others did not begin until 14 January 1844. It took place before a "packed" jury. Nationalist feeling was running high. The *Freeman's Journal* objected to the lord mayor offering the New Year's banquet toast to the lord lieutenant, "the hero of Clontarf," as he represented the prime minister as much as the queen. "Loyalty, then, to her gracious Majesty did not require that this official, more than Sir Robert Peel or any other official, should be toasted at the civic feast."[123] On 11 January the Dublin Corporation drew up a memorial to the queen with a plea to stop the trial from going ahead because it was "calculated to renew sectarian jealousy and animosity in Ireland."[124] Two days later an "aggregate" meeting petitioned the queen against the striking off of Catholics from the jury panel for the trial.[125]

O'Connell was found guilty on 10 February. His conviction resulted in a fine and a sentence of one year in Richmond prison, Dublin, beginning on 30 May. The home secretary wrote to the queen, "Sir James Graham presumes to offer his humble congratulations to Your Majesty on this triumph of justice and of law over a conspiracy so dangerous and so artfully conducted."[126]

After his conviction O'Connell proceeded to London, where he was cheered in the Commons by the opposition. On 12 March he was guest of honor at a banquet at the Covent Garden Theatre. Graham wrote to Prince Albert about it, wondering whether the royal patent for the theater might be withdrawn as punishment.[127]

On 8 April O'Connell was guest of honor at a banquet in Cork. It was attended by the mayor and corporation of Waterford. On their way home their steamer was boarded by sailors from a royal naval vessel who removed

122. Queen Victoria to King Leopold, 17 October 1843, in Benson and Esher, *Letters*, first series, 1:621.

123. *FJ*, 2 January 1844.

124. *FJ*, 20 January 1844.

125. *FJ*, 24 January 1844.

126. RA B 8/42, Sir James Graham to Queen Victoria, 12 February 1844.

127. RA M 52/75, Sir James Graham to Prince Albert, 1 March 1844.

the green flag with the word "Repeal" on it from the helm. The *Freeman's Journal* objected to the fact that "this insult to the national colour" had been done in "the name of the Queen of Ireland."[128]

After O'Connell's incarceration there was some talk of a royal pardon but repealers objected to this because it would still have been an assertion that the conviction was just.[129] The Dublin Corporation again memorialized the queen, and William Smith O'Brien drew up a "National Declaration" on behalf of the Repeal Association to "have the Queen undeceived upon the state of Ireland."[130]

The appeal of O'Connell and the others against the conviction loomed in the autumn. Stories circulated that the queen might visit Ireland in early October and, the appeal having failed, extend "an act of royal grace in their favour" and pardon them.[131] However, the appeal did not fail. The House of Lords reversed the decision of the court on 6 September. The next day Dublin was in a tumult of celebration. Graham had to inform the queen that "there was a triumphal procession thro' the streets of Dublin: Mr O'Connell was elevated in a car drawn by eight horses, the concourse of People was immense."[132] Peel made sure to tell Victoria which way each judge in the Lords had voted.[133]

The queen's popularity began to dip in Ireland in 1844, at least in the columns of the principal nationalist newspaper, the *Freeman's Journal*, whose proprietor Dr. John Gray had been one of O'Connell's codefendants. Instead of deference to royalty there were now references to English newspapers offering "incense to Victoria" and to the day when "Victoria might resume the proud title of her ignoble ancestors and sit as Queen of the Emerald Isle."[134] Her speech from the throne at the beginning of the 1845 session of Parliament was devoted to "the pathetic and absorbing subject of the festivities in which the several despots of Europe revelled during their welcome stay at the royal court of England." This was little consolation to the poorly off industrial workers and miners who "cannot fail to read in them evidence of the deep sympathy which her Majesty and her ministers entertain for their conditions."[135]

128. *FJ*, 12, 13 April 1844.   129. *FJ*, 3 June 1844.

130. *FJ*, 7, 20 June 1844.

131. *Globe*, 23 August 1844, reported in *FJ*, 26 August 1844.

132. RA B 8/154, Sir James Graham to Queen Victoria, 8 September 1844.

133. RA A 16/117, Sir Robert Peel to Queen Victoria, 4 September 1844.

134. *FJ*, 31 October and 4 November 1844.

135. *FJ*, 6 February 1845.

❖

The autumn of 1844 had begun with a judicial triumph for O'Connell. But things were to become more difficult for him as Peel turned from a policy of coercion to one of reform in Ireland. During the course of the next year Peel was to propose several measures of reform that would cause dissension within Catholic and nationalist Ireland and problems for O'Connell. They are summed up in the subtitle given by Prince Albert to the first file in Queen Victoria's papers specifically devoted to Ireland: "The Bequests Act, Maynooth Grant and Irish Colleges Bill."[136] Prince Albert himself accepted the need for reform in Ireland in private.[137]

The first measure, then, was the Charitable Bequests Act, which sought to enable people to make donations to religious causes more easily. The bill was opposed by O'Connell; John MacHale, archbishop of Tuam; and Paul Cullen, then a prominent Irish cleric in Rome but eventually to be cardinal archbishop of Dublin. However, Daniel Murray, William Crolly, and Cornelius Denvir who were respectively the Catholic archbishops of Armagh and Dublin and the bishop of Down and Connor accepted positions on the Charitable Bequests Board alongside Protestant bishops of the Established Church.[138]

Peel told the queen that these were "all men of moderate, habitual principles—not participants of agitation or Repeal," and that it was a very positive sign that they had accepted given "the critical state of the public mind following Mr O'Connell's Liberation."[139] He hoped that "the union of the Primate of the Established Church and the Roman Catholic Primate on the same commission will serve as an Example to others—and will have a tendency to diminish Religious Strife and Rancour in Ireland."[140]

Peel was anxious until the last moment about the composition of the board. Great significance was attached to the official announcement, in the *Dublin Gazette* on 18 December, of the appointment of its membership by the queen. It was the first time since the penal laws of the eighteenth cen-

---

136. RA D 14.

137. Weintraub, *Albert*, 160. Hunting at Bagshot with the Duke of Bedford Albert spoke of "the long course of misgovernment [in Ireland], and the necessity of doing something."

138. MacDonagh, *O'Connell*, 541–42.

139. RA A 16/121, Sir Robert Peel to Queen Victoria, 22 September 1844.

140. RA A 16/146, Sir Robert Peel to Queen Victoria, autumn 1844.

tury that Catholic bishops had been designated with their titles in an official announcement.

There was some annoyance among Catholics, however, that they were referred to as individuals rather than by their dioceses. Thus whereas the Protestant archbishop of Dublin was referred to as the "Most Rev. Richard, Lord Archbishop of Dublin," his Catholic counterpart was called the "Most Rev. Archbishop Daniel Murray." The *Freeman's Journal* lamented that the government that had been "so confided in by our too credulous archbishop, has thus meanly insulted him."[141]

Nonetheless, it was a clear setback for O'Connell. A delighted Prince Albert noted to Peel, "Every party seems sensible of the importance of the triumph and O'Connell's speech shows his anger, and at the same time his fear of making another false move in the present crisis. Persevere in your course, and I am sure the good cause, that of moderation and impartial justice, must in the end remain victorious."[142]

The maintenance of the Protestant Episcopalian Established Church in Ireland had come to be balanced by a grant to the Presbyterian Church and by government maintenance of Maynooth College, the principal seminary in Ireland for the training of Catholic priests. Peel proposed to increase the Maynooth grant substantially as a gesture toward Irish Catholics. In this he succeeded but not without intense opposition, though it came this time not from Ireland but from England.

He had the wholehearted support of the queen, however. She suffered from a less negative attitude toward Catholics than many of her contemporaries in England and saw that partial endowment of other churches would in fact increase the chances that the Established Church could be left in its position as state church. She told Peel in April 1845 that "[t]he measure is so great and good, that people must open their eyes, and will not oppose it."[143] She wrote to King Leopold that "I am sure poor Peel ought to be *blessed* by all Catholics for the manly and noble way in which he stands forth to protect and do good for poor Ireland." By contrast the bigotry and passions the measure had evoked in some quarters had caused her to "blush for Protestantism."[144]

141. *FJ*, 19 December 1844.

142. RA D 14/58, Prince Albert to Sir Robert Peel, 22 December 1844.

143. Queen Victoria to Sir Robert Peel, 9 April 1845, quoted in Parker, *Peel*, 3:173.

144. Queen Victoria to King Leopold of the Belgians, 15 April 1845, in Queen Victoria, *Letters of Queen Victoria*, first series, ed. A. C. Benson and Viscount Esher, vol. 2 (1844–1853) (London: John Murray, 1907), pp. 42–43.

The final measure was the provision of third-level education in Ireland, as until then the only significant third-level institution was Trinity College Dubin, which was under the auspices of the Established Church. This proved to be infinitely the most complex of the three reforms, beginning a controversy that was to last for sixty years centering on the extent to which the British state would endow denominational education at the third level in Ireland.

Peel proposed the setting up of several nondenominational colleges—Belfast, Cork, and Galway were eventually chosen as the sites—to provide education for Catholics, who were in a majority in most of the country, and for Presbyterians, of whom there were very large numbers in the northeast where Belfast was located. Initially, there was a good deal of support for the plan in Catholic Church circles, but over the years this hardened into outright opposition, bolstered by the condemnation of Rome, on account of the nondenominational issue.

O'Connell was an early and strenuous opponent. The issue helped to widen the growing gap between him and a group of radical young nationalists led by Thomas Davis, Charles Gavan Duffy, and John Blake Dillon, who had founded the *Nation* newspaper and who supported the colleges. Known eventually as "Young Ireland," they were advocates of a new cultural nationalism; their view of the nation was at once more romantic and more secular than O'Connell's.

Opponents of the scheme had a significant advantage when it came to the propaganda concerning the colleges. When the bill to establish the colleges was introduced in the Commons by Graham in May 1845 the project was immediately denounced by Sir Robert Inglis as "a gigantic scheme of godless education."[145] The term "godless colleges" stuck. The government had been slow to push its own name for the colleges and for several years they were called variously "academical institutions," "collegeiate institutions," "Irish colleges," "new colleges," "provincial colleges," or even "government colleges."

The title "queen's colleges" had been discussed as early as the autumn of 1844.[146] Clearly there were advantages in associating the name of the still popular queen with the scheme. Though Queen's College was officially

145. *FJ*, 12 May 1845.
146. RA D 14/11, "Memorandum on the Extension of Collegiate Education to Ireland drawn up for the Rt Hon. Sir James Graham by H. Maunsell M.D.," 10 October 1844. "I would propose that the new college, which for the sake of distinction, I will call Queen's College. . . ."

adopted as the name for the institutions, it took several years for the name to catch on—and it was too late to repair the damage done by the "god-less colleges" tag.

There were occasional protests against the ideological drift of the official name. In 1850, in an address to the "clergy and faithful," the Catholic bishops at the synod of Thurles condemned the colleges as "a system of education fraught with grievous and intrinsic errors. . . . It is presented to you, we deplore to say, in those collegiate institutions which have been established in this country and associated with the name of our august, most gracious and beloved Sovereign."[147]

The colleges survived, though the Cork and Galway ones hardly flourished. In 1850, under Lord John Russell's Whig government, they were federated into the Queen's University, with the support of Prince Albert. In September 1849 he wrote to his old mentor Baron Stockmar, "What principally occupies me just now is a plan for the establishment of a free University in Ireland in connection with the 'godless colleges,' in which I am supported by Peel and Lord Clarendon [the lord lieutenant]."[148]

Clarendon wanted Albert to be the first chancellor of the university. The latter refused, however, on the grounds that it would require personal attendance in Ireland and be politically controversial because the university had been founded against the wishes of "three disagreeing and fanatical churches and this of all countries in the world in Ireland, where it is most difficult to arrive at the truth in any matter."[149]

At the end of August 1844, while O'Connell was still in prison, the *Freeman's Journal* reprinted a tongue-in-cheek report that Prince de Joinville, son of Louis Philippe and then currently conducting a naval bombardment of Tangier, wished to visit Ireland:

147. *FJ,* 16 September 1850, quoted in Emmet Larkin, *The Making of the Roman Catholic Church in Ireland, 1850–1860* (Chapel Hill: University of North Carolina Press, 1980), 35.

148. Prince Albert to Baron von Stockmar, 10 September 1849, quoted in Kurt Jagow, *Letters of the Prince Consort 1831–1861* (London: John Murray, 1938), 153.

149. RA D 20/51, Prince Albert to Lord Clarendon, 15 October 1849. Other candidates considered were the astronomer Lord Rosse ("an odd indolent man, rather crotchety and Tory"; RA D 20/56, Lord Clarendon to Lord John Russell, 19 October 1849), Lord Landsdowne, and Sir Robert Peel. Eventually, Clarendon himself was appointed. In 1863 Lord Rosse was made chancellor of the University of Dublin.

Sir Robert Peel strongly urges the Queen to come over to prepare for his reception, further advising that O'Connell will be forthwith liberated and requested to act as master of ceremonies on the occasion. It is said that O'Connell has given by anticipation a peremptory refusal to being at all concerned in the matter and the Queen herself expresses strong objections to the arrangement, feeling that Ireland is not at present in the condition to afford the Prince the reception with which her Majesty as Queen of these realms would desire to salute him.[150]

The point was clear: O'Connell might have been checked in his repeal agenda but he still retained the power to check in turn. With the repeal movement still a strong force, no royal visit could safely take place to Ireland without his consent and a royal visit was not now in O'Connell's political interests. In the context of a Tory reform programme designed to wean the population from the idea of repeal it could only represent a danger, as far as the Liberator was concerned. If he caused trouble during the visit he would be accused of disloyalty. If the visit went peacefully, it would be used as evidence that repeal agitation was dead.

At the end of January 1845 the *Dublin Mercantile Advertiser* ran a story that the queen would visit Ireland that summer and that "great political changes are in contemplation for Ireland."[151] As the weeks moved on it came to be believed informally that a visit would be made and indeed that the queen would buy a residence on the coast near Dublin, between Killiney and Dalkey.[152]

On 7 April 1845 in the House of Lords Lord Stanley spoke of the queen's impending visit, which gave Lord Normanby an opportunity to raise the issue. As lord lieutenant he had had "the good fortune to witness the devotion of the Irish people, when their present Sovereign, upon her accession to the Throne, testified her sympathy with that people." She would "find more joyful enthusiasm in Ireland than she had met with anywhere else." But he warned the Tories against turning the visit into a "useless pageant" like the visit of George IV in order merely to advance their political agenda in Ireland. This would be "at variance with the expectations which it [the visit] would justly excite."[153]

The *Freeman's Journal* was initially equivocal about the visit. It hoped the

---

150. *FJ*, 29 August 1844.
151. Reported in *FJ*, 1 February 1845.
152. *Pilot*, reported in *FJ*, 8 April 1845.
153. 7 April 1845, *Parliamentary Debates*, 3d Series, vol. 79 (3 April–30 April 1845), col. 239.

Irish would not forget their loyalty to "a gracious and personally beloved sovereign." On the other hand, "nor will they forget the great obligations they owe to their country and their self-respect." O'Connell told the Dublin Corporation on 9 April that "there are no sides of the house on the question of loyalty to the Queen."[154] At his suggestion the question of how the Dublin Corporation should respond to the prospect of a visit was put off to a special meeting on 29 April. By then he had found a pretext for opposing it.

On 23 April the historian T. B. Macaulay accused Peel of having been humiliated in bringing forth the Maynooth grant measure, allegedly at O'Connell's behest. Both Peel and Graham rebutted the charge and once again spoke of their determination to bring about reform but also to resist repeal. Graham said that everyone in Britain and indeed most people in Ireland would "oppose . . . to the last extremity the Repeal of the Union, although by that resolve the foundations of this great Empire may in a convulsive struggle be shaken, and its stability endangered."[155] Though hyperbolic there was nothing new in Graham's rhetoric but it was enough for O'Connell.

The special meeting of the Dublin Corporation began with consideration of a joint Liberal and Conservative motion to ask the queen to visit Ireland. The Tories were in combative form. The Repeal Association was criticized for deciding to present the queen with a list of grievances, including a plea for repeal, if she visited Ireland. Two of the Tories, Hudson and Kinahan, even wanted the motion withdrawn and the queen discouraged from visiting, lest repealers make political capital from it.

It was at this point that O'Connell intervened. He had hoped to be "neutral on the question of Repeal during the Queen's visit." However, as he had told the Repeal Association the previous day, the recent debate in the Commons had changed all that:

It appears to me to have been a plan deliberately carried out to prevent us from combining to show our loyalty to our Sovereign in a spirit of complete harmony and in the absence of all discussion upon exciting topics. We had intended to do so but they have made it impossible by their declaration in parliament. It is possible I may be mistaken; but to me it seems that there was something of design in it.[156]

154. *FJ*, 10 April 1845.
155. 23 April 1845, *Parliamentary Debates*, 3d Series, vol. 79 (3 April–30 April 1845), cols. 1180–1207.
156. *FJ*, 30 April 1845.

He went on to claim that the design was to use any silence on the question of repeal as proof that it was losing support. As he had told the Repeal Association the previous day, when he had first revealed his new attitude to the visit, "We must not . . . give any pretence to our enemies for saying that there is any shrinking on the part of the Repealers."[157] He could not therefore take part in an address to the queen.

The lord lieutenant, Lord Heytesbury, told Graham that the debate in Parliament "has been seized upon by O'Connell and the more ardent of the Repealers as an excuse for and an incentive to further agitation."[158] Peel rather smugly told Prince Albert that they should expect extreme language from Irish separatists who "find their project thwarted by the conciliatory policy of the Government."[159]

There never had been a serious plan for a royal visit, but the government had not been unaware of the public speculation. In April Heytesbury told Peel that "[t]he inhabitants of Dublin, who for good reasons, anxiously desire the Queen's arrival, are constantly putting forth stories of decisions taken." But there were also practical reasons against it. George IV

> tho' he came as a Bachelor was much dissatisfied with the accommodation and I greatly fear that Her Majesty will be still more so. Both Castle and Lodge are in very bad repair, afford very indifferent and very little lodging room and the furniture is nearly worn out.[160]

He went on to suggest that an immediate visit would not be practical and that, in any event, the motive for some members of the Dublin Corporation who were urging it was the "visions of Baronetcies" floating before their eyes.

Whatever their reasons, the members of the Dublin Corporation defied O'Connell and pressed ahead with their petition to the queen. The lord mayor held a meeting attended by fifteen hundred in early May in support of the visit. Heytesbury reported that "[t]he tradesmen of Dublin [hopeful for increased commerce due to a visit] are exceedingly angry with O'Connell for they fear the violent line he has taken will prevent the Queen's visit."[161]

157. *FJ,* 29 April 1845.
158. RA D 14/134, Lord Heytesbury to Sir James Graham, 4 May 1845.
159. RA D 14/133, Sir Robert Peel to Prince Albert, 7 May 1845.
160. RA D 14/125, Lord Heytesbury to Sir Robert Peel, 23 April 1845.
161. RA D 14/136, Lord Heytesbury to Sir Thomas Freemantle, 1 May 1845.

O'Connell meanwhile was answering his critics at the Repeal Association on 5 May and meeting their criticism of his loyalty with defiance:

I cannot avoid remarking the contrast in the strength and purity of public feeling between 1821 and 1845. In 1821 the worst king, and the worst man that ever breathed, came here and received a monstrous tribute of servility by virtue of his office. In 1845 a queen is advised by her ministers to avoid our shores, lest she might hear the voice of a people demanding liberty (continued cheering).[162]

Conveniently forgetting his own role in the 1821 visit, he went on to try to sow division between the Whigs and the Tories by asserting that the debate in Parliament, on which he had based his objections to the visit, had been a Whig plot to frustrate it, "lest the Tories would have the *eclat* of a courtly visit, with all its kissings and forgivings."

A day or two before the *Observer* contained a report that the queen had changed her mind about a visit and would not now visit Ireland.[163] But Lord Mayor Arabin and the Dublin Corporation continued to hope for the best.[164] So they sought to exercise their right to present a petition to the queen's "person and throne." They arrived in London on 12 May with their address in favor of a royal visit.

The next day they met Graham, who rather unjustly, given the fact that they favored a visit, gave them the benefit of his icy sarcasm.[165] The queen was away and he did not know when she would be back to receive the address. She had never mentioned an Irish visit to him. He did not know why a speech in Parliament should alter the welcome the queen might get in Ireland:

[H]e asked how could it be expected that he would advise her Majesty to proceed to Ireland after it had been announced that the horses under the royal carriage were to be affrighted in the streets of Dublin with the shouts of Repeal—that the sound was to force like a shot into the Royal Councils—that certain gentlemen

162. *FJ,* 6 May 1845.

163. Reported in *FJ,* 6 May 1845.

164. *FJ,* 9 May 1845, reported the lord mayor's remark during a toast indicating that it might go ahead.

165. Graham's biographer claimed that O'Connell had once said "that Graham's statue should be place on a pedestal with the inscription 'Justice for Ireland.'" (Charles Stewart Parker, *Life and Letters of Sir James Graham, Second Baronet of Netherly, PC, GCB, 1792–1861,* 2 vols. [London: John Murray, 1907], 2:419). The *DNB* (vol. 8 [London: Smith Elder, 1908], p. 330) was less kind. Being home secretary was "a part scarcely well suited to one who was so little conciliatory in manner and so rash in utterance."

were to appear in their Repeal uniform of the Eighty-Two Club[166] at her Majesty's Levée?—Sir James Graham here paused, looking significantly at the Lord Mayor.[167]

Then remembering the purpose of the meeting, he told them that their address was "a document most gratifying to her Majesty."

Graham wrote to the queen that in any reply to the delegation she should not commit herself to "any fixed determination on this Point."[168] She met the delegation in Buckingham Palace on the afternoon of 21 May and gave them the most anodyne of answers. "Whenever I may be enabled to receive the Promised Welcome [in Ireland], I shall rely with confidence on the loyalty and affection of my faithful subjects."[169]

The *Nation* satirized the occasion:

There stood the velvet throne . . . there stood the aids-de-camp, gay as sparrows . . . there glowered Sir James Graham, dark as an inquisitor—and there sat the Queen, as grave as she would be—and there entered the Corporation, to—ask her to dinner.

But the Dublin Corporation could not offer her anything to compare with

the feudal cheer and forest game of Scotland, the galleries of Flanders or the policy of France. . . . [T]hey were answered with an imperious courtesy which thanked them for their loyalty, but forgot the invitation.[170]

The hoped-for visit had descended into farce and O'Connell was to add to that farce with one of the most outlandish burlesques of his career. He would provide his own royal visit to Dublin. On 30 May, the first "anniversary of the 'Martyrdom,'" of his imprisonment, as the *Times* sneeringly put it,[171] O'Connell held a national levee in Dublin with himself in the role of the monarch:

The representative of English domination holds a court to which creep the things that batten upon official patronage. The people take no heed of them. The

166. A repeal organization, with distinctive uniform, named after the year in which the Irish Parliament had gained a measure of legislative independence in 1782.

167. *Evening Post*, reported in *FJ*, 16 May 1845.

168. RA D 14/139, Sir James Graham to Queen Victoria, 16 May 1845.

169. *FJ*, 23 May 1845. RA QVJ, 21 May 1845: "Received on the Throne the Dublin address and read my answer."

170. *Nation*, 24 May 1845.

171. *Times*, 2 June 1845.

monarch of the Irish heart proclaims his levee, and from the confines of the south to the fortresses of the north pour in the chosen friends of Ireland.[172]

The meeting was held in the Rotundo in Dublin and was attended by the Dublin trades and town and city councilors from around the country. Wellington wrote to Graham that there were ten thousand people in the procession and a hundred thousand "idlers . . . lining the streets. . . . It was in short as impudent a demonstration of the popular force as ever was witnessed in Ireland."[173] In some ways it was the Clontarf meeting finally taking place. O'Connell's enemies in the press were livid. The *Evening Mail* was particularly savage about the "outrage on royalty":

Whilst we write this Mr O'Connell is sitting in aristocratic state in the throne room of the Rotundo, surrounded by his peers.[174]

A man, professing in words to be a subject—assuming in reality the prerogatives of a Sovereign, surrounded by a *regalia,* an etiquette resembling in all points that of a constitutional monarch.[175]

It ended by criticizing the lord lieutenant for allowing the levee to happen. "In short, if Lord Heytesbury were *de jure* the Lord Lieutenant of Ireland, Mr O'Connell was *de facto* Viceroy over him."

O'Connell repeated the exercise in Cork on 8 June. If he was now playing the monarch, it was not in the subdued middle-class manner that was to characterize most of Queen Victoria's reign. He was a monarch in the grand style of George IV who had processed through Dublin "in a full military uniform, decorated with the Order and Ribbon of St Patrick. His hat was ornamented with a rosette, composed of Shamocks of more than twice the size of a military cockade."[176] Everything about the presentation of O'Connell was oversized:

He sat on an elevated chair beneath a large canopy that towered twenty feet above the ground. Holding the canopy aloft were four female figures representing Justice, Truth, Fortitude, and Prudence. . . . An enormous repeal cap and a huge shamrock crowned the top of the vehicle.[177]

172. *FJ,* 31 May 1845.
173. RA D 14/147, The Duke of Wellington to Sir James Graham, 30 May 1845.
174. *Evening Mail,* quoted in *FJ,* 2 June 1845.
175. *Evening Mail,* quoted in *FJ,* 3 June 1845.
176. *FJ,* 18 August 1821.
177. *Cork Examiner,* 9 June 1845, quoted in Gary Owens, "Nationalism without Words: Symbolism and Ritual Behaviour in the Repeal 'Monster Meetings' of 1843–45," in James

The Dublin and Cork events in which O'Connell explicitly embraced his unofficial monarchical position were undoubtedly insults against the official monarchy of Queen Victoria. In a sense, though, O'Connell was admitting the defeat of his policy of winning the loyal center ground for Irish nationalism.

Nor did it distress Peel or the queen too much. Just over a fortnight after the Cork event Peel was writing to Queen Victoria about the debate in the Commons over the Irish colleges bill debate. He reported that "Mr O'Connell spoke at some length feebly and in a subdued manner."[178] Two months later he was telling her that "[t]ere are many symptoms of the decline of Repeal agitation in Ireland. The 'Repeal Rent' is fast declining in amount and the Roman Catholic Priests are in many instances actively cooperating with the Government in the detection of offenders and the maintenance of the public peace."[179]

The year 1846 witnessed the repeal of the corn laws, a measure that was helpful to Ireland during the famine. It caused a split in the Conservative Party between Protectionists and Peelites, who some years later were to join with the Whigs and the Radicals to form the Liberal Party. Immediately, it paved the way for the fall of Peel and the installation of a Whig government under Lord John Russell.

With the Young Ireland group appearing to grow in militancy, O'Connell seemed increasingly moderate to some in Britain, notably Prince Albert. "Young Ireland maintains that the employment of physical force is justifiable to carry the Repeal. O'Connell says that only *moral* force is justifiable and promises repeal within the year." He was thus pleased when O'Connell and his colleagues were restored to the magistracy. "On our suggestion the Orange Magistrates dismissed by the former Whig government were reinstated as well and the measure has been one of complete amnesty."[180]

In early 1847 a seriously ill Daniel O'Connell set out for Rome. The previous year he had delivered what Peel told the queen was a "temperate speech" on the Irish famine "which made a considerable impression."[181]

S. Donnelly Jr. and Kerby A. Miller, eds., *Irish Popular Culture, 1650–1850* (Dublin: Irish Academic Press, 1998), 250.

178. RA A 17/123, Sir Robert Peel to Queen Victoria, 24 June 1845.
179. RA A 17/167, Sir Robert Peel to Queen Victoria, 28 August 1845.
180. RA D 15/51, Prince Albert, memorandum, no date (c. August 1846).
181. RA C 23/78, Sir Robert Peel to Queen Victoria, 17 February 1846.

On 8 February 1847 he appealed to the Commons for famine relief for the last time. He died in Genoa on 15 May, having been received on his journey through the Continent as a statesman of legendary renown. His death was received in England with "little or no sensation."[182] But it did cause a sensation in Ireland when the news broke on 25 May. He was "[t]he Great Chieftan . . . [t]he foremost man of all the world . . . our staff, our safety, our pride, and our protection."[183]

The imagery that attended the discourse of his death was Gaelic or imperial or biblical, but it was not often kingly. It was as if the rivalry with the British monarch inherent in the uncrowned king appellation was now too petty for the occasion. For the *Freeman's Journal* he was an Alexander the Great whose "empire will endure until the Irish heart ceases to feel, or the Irish mind to think."[184] For Padre Ventura, who preached the funeral oration in Rome, where O'Connell's heart was interred, he was, perhaps surprisingly, a Napoleon.[185] For John Miley, who preached the sermon at his Dublin funeral, he was like Constantine the Great, as "both of them led forth the persecuted followers of Christ."[186]

The *Freeman's Journal* saw the return of O'Connell's body to Ireland in August and his burial as having sacral and messianic dimensions for the nation. "He comes to consecrate by mingling his bones with its earth this land so long desecrated by oppression."[187] And as for the funeral itself, "no monarch or statesman, or patriot of our own or any other country has had such a glorious tribute rendered to his memory as the people of Ireland afforded on yesterday to their departed chief."[188]

As far as Ireland's official monarchy was concerned, O'Connell was a paradox. He was Ireland's uncrowned king and yet no nationalist leader was ever again to offer such public loyalty to Queen Victoria as Daniel O'Connell.

182. Charles Greville, *The Greville Memoirs, Part 2: A Journal of the Reign of Queen Victoria from 1837 to 1852*, ed. Henry Reeve, 3 vols. (London: 1885), 3:85.

183. *FJ*, 26 May 1847.   184. *FJ*, 31 May 1847.
185. *FJ*, 28 July 1847.   186. *FJ*, 7 August 1847.
187. *FJ*, 2 August 1847.   188. *FJ*, 6 August 1847.

CHAPTER THREE

The Last Viceroy of Ireland (Perhaps)

Russell, Clarendon, and Completing
the Union, 1847–1852

The day after the death of O'Connell, the Irish Whig lord lieutenant Lord Bessborough, also died. Prince Albert believed that he had brought "great practical knowledge and influence" to his office.[1] According to the diarist Charles Greville, the prime minister initially wanted his brother, the duke of Bedford, to become lord lieutenant, while Lord Morpeth, later indeed to be lord lieutenant as Lord Carlisle, was "dying to go." Eventually, the president of the board of trade, George William Frederick Villiers, fourth earl of Clarendon, was appointed. Greville wrote that Clarendon, who was to become a favorite of Queen Victoria and serve three times as foreign secretary, was very keen on the position but "treated it as a sacrifice and a misfortune."[2] Greville was the clerk of the privy council; the posthumous publication of his diaries was to cause Queen Victoria great annoy-

---

1. RA D 15/63, Prince Albert, memorandum, 6 November 1846. "Lord Bessborough had great facilities for the Gov' of Ireland to which nobody else almost will have again, he is very popular with the people, from old association friend of O'Connell and the Priests, an excellent Irish Landlord and therefore much connected with his brother landlords, a capital man of business and himself thoroughly Irish" (RA D 16/69, Prince Albert, memorandum, 17 May 1847).

2. Reeve, *Greville, Part 2*, 3:85.

ance.[3] Clarendon's supporters were to dismiss Greville's views on him and to deride Greville himself as "a gouty and cynical old bachelor."[4]

Clarendon's own contemporary account of his appointment does indeed stress a sacrificial view of accepting the position:

J. R. [Lord John Russell] sent for me yesterday afternoon and proposed to me to go to Ireland; but it was done in his most cold, short, abrupt, indifferent manner—much as if he was disposing of a tide-waiter's place to an applicant. I made a string of objections and said I should take time to consider it; but I feel much embarrassed; for, if I consent, it would seem that I was accepting a small favour instead of making a great sacrifice.[5]

He would only go if opposition statesmen could be convinced of his altruism. Graham was to be told that it was "a patriotic, uncomplicated sacrifice." And Peel was to be told *"but in strict confidence, that the office will be abolished."* Clarendon was to be the last viceroy of Ireland, or so he thought. He left Ireland nearly five years later hated by Irish nationalists. He was vilified by the republican John Mitchel in *The Last Conquest of Ireland (Perhaps)*. The lord lieutenancy was to survive for over seventy more years. But of those who held the post under the union, none, apart from Earl Spencer, was to rival Clarendon in importance.

Clarendon's arrival coincided with the height of the great Irish famine caused by the failure of the potato crop. It had begun in the autumn of 1845 and was to rage over the next four years, though its consequences continued in various ways into the 1850s. One million people died of starvation or disease and one million more emigrated during those years. The country's population was immediately reduced by a quarter and the trauma initiated a population haemorrhage, caused by emigration and reduced domestic marriage rates, which resulted in Ireland's population in the mid-twentieth century, uniquely in Europe, being only half what it had been in the mid-nineteenth century.

Peel's Tory government had taken relatively effective remedial measures

3. The queen thought that the publication of the journals was "scurrilous." See Queen Victoria to Sir Theodore Martin, 26 October 1874, in Buckle, *Letters*, second series, vol. 2 (1870–1878) (London: John Murray, 1928), 354.

4. Herbert Maxwell, *Life and Letters of George William Frederick Fourth Earl of Clarendon*, 2 vols. (London: Edward Arnold, 1913),1:277.

5. Lord Clarendon to George Cornewall Lewis, May 1847, in Maxwell, *Clarendon*, 1:276.

and imported Indian corn. His decision to repeal the corn laws, which prohibited the importation of foreign grain ("corn" is the British term for all cereal grains) into the United Kingdom until domestic prices had reached a certain level, was spurred on by the famine. However, in the view of one recent historian of the famine, "[T]he tardy, frugal, short-sighted and ideologically-bound policies adopted by the Whig government made inevitable the slide from distress to the national calamity of the famine."[6]

The new government "viewed it as their moral responsibility to use the failure of the potato crop in 1846 to force economic change within Ireland."[7] Public works and soup kitchens were introduced, but the response was far from adequate. As the famine wore on into 1847 and 1848 British public opinion and opinion within the government became less sympathetic to Ireland. Though Russell himself was in favor of some further relief, most other members of the cabinet were not.

British opinion was fed by laissez faire economic theory and by a harsh *and racism* analysis of the Irish economic situation. The ordinary Irish people were seen as lazy and violent, while Irish landlords were viewed as indifferent to their responsibilities. It was judged that the size of the Irish population and its dependence on the potato for nutrition were unsustainable. So, too, was the Irish system of land tenure. In some quarters in Britain the famine was seen as an opportunity to reform the Irish economic system. Toward the end of the famine the government introduced a series of Encumbered Estates Acts to facilitate land reform and the removal of inefficient landlords. "The response of Russell's government to the Famine combined opportunism, arrogance and cynicism, deployed in such a way as to facilitate the long standing ambition to secure a reform of Ireland's economy."[8]

As early as the autumn of 1845 Queen Victoria had strongly supported Peel's moves to have the corn laws repealed. He had kept her informed of the worsening situation in Ireland and about cabinet divisions on how best to deal with it.[9] She had replied that such divisions "at a moment of im-

6. Christine Kinealy, *This Great Calamity: The Irish Famine, 1845–52* (Dublin: Gill and Macmillan, 1994), 71. For a variety of other judgments in the vigorous debate on the famine and the role of the British government in it, see Mary E. Daly, *The Famine in Ireland* (Dublin: Dun Dealgan, 1986), Cormac Ó Gráda, *The Great Irish Famine* (Dublin: Gill and Macmillan, 1989), and Peter Gray, *Famine, Land, and Politics: British Government and Irish Society, 1843–50* (Dublin: Irish Academic Press, 1999).

7. Kinealy, *Great Calamity*, 73.

8. Kinealy, *Great Calamity*, 355.

9. RA C 44/2 and 4, Sir Robert Peel to Queen Victoria, 5 and 27 November 1845.

pending calamity" were unfortunate. "The queen thinks the time is come when a removal of the restrictions on the importation of food cannot be successfully resisted. Should this be Sir Robert Peel's own opinion, the queen very much hopes that none of his colleagues will prevent him from doing what it is right to do."[10] Prince Albert was also concerned about the situation in Ireland where "half the potatoes were ruined by rot and no one could guarantee the remainder."[11] That autumn the queen received a number of memorials from Ireland asking for relief measures against the famine.[12]

As 1845 became 1846 the royal couple's sympathy and concern began to change to despair and then to exasperation at an unfolding tragedy that in some ways proved too great for them to imagine. It was easier to blame the Irish peasants and their leaders for what was happening and to seize on the outrages against landlords that had began to increase in frequency. Prince Albert composed two memoranda on Ireland toward the close of 1846. In early November he wrote, "The state of Ireland is most alarming and seems quite hopeless as every attempt on the part of the Government to relieve it, is turned by the Irish themselves to bad account." The landlords were to blame for not cooperating with the government and the people were to blame for exploiting the relief measures. "It is to be feared that the patience of England and Scotland will soon be at an end, seeing that all sacrifices are brought in vain and that they are only to be repaid in hatred and accusations."[13]

On 26 December Albert wrote:

10. RA C 44/6, Queen Victoria to Sir Robert Peel, 28 November 1845. See too Parker, *Peel Papers*, 3:237–38, quoted in *DNB*, vol. 22 (Supplement), pp. 1291–92.

11. Prince Albert, memorandum, 7 December 1845, in Benson and Esher, *Letters*, first series, 2:57.

12. RA D 14/182, Lord Heytesbury to Sir James Graham, 20 November 1845. He reports the resolutions of a meeting in the Dublin Mansion House under Lord Cloncurry. "They are of the most mischievous and inflammatory nature, and conclude by a Resolution to address Her Majesty upon the subject of the *famine* and *pestilence* with which Ireland is threatened." On 10 December 1845 the Dublin Corporation adopted a memorial to the queen on the famine; see *FJ*, 13 December 1845.

13. RA D 15/63, Prince Albert, memorandum, 6 November 1846. The view that England and Scotland had been charitable in helping Ireland, rather than being dutiful as members of a united kingdom, was a common one and is reflected by Albert's official biographer, Theodore Martin, in his *The Life of His Royal Highness The Prince Consort*, 5 vols. (London: Smith, Elder, 1875–1880), 1:403: "The immense votes of public money for Ireland were viewed by them [England and Scotland] without a grudge."

The state of Ireland seems to have arrived at its climax of confusion and misery. Every kind of iniquity is practised from the highest to the lowest. The magistrates who have to manage the distribution of relief in many instances give it to wealthy farmers, their own servants or relations, while people are actually starving around them.[14]

As for the people, he believed that they were content to accept government wages without working in return for them. Four days later Victoria had a discussion with Lord Broughton about "the wretched state of Ireland about which she had heard that morning from Lord John Russell. She said she saw no remedy for the distress."[15]

In January 1847 a petition was sponsored by Irish Tory peers to the queen to ask her to direct Parliament to help the starving people of Ireland.[16] Shortly thereafter a rival petition, proposed at a meeting attended by O'Connell, made similar demands.[17]

The government had more voluntary measures in mind for the immediate future. On 13 January 1847 a first Queen's Letter was issued, on the advice of Russell,[18] appealing for funds for famine relief in Ireland and Scotland. It was addressed to the archbishops of Canterbury and York and was read out at church services, at which collections for relief were taken.[19] Meanwhile, on 1 January 1847, Baron Lionel de Rothschild had founded the British Association for the Relief of Extreme Distress in Remote Parishes of Ireland and Scotland. The list of the principal public contributors was to be published.

The Irish nationalist myth about Queen Victoria and the famine has been, and still is, that she was utterly indifferent to it. Proof of this was the claim that she had merely donated £5 toward famine relief. In *The Great Hunger* Cecil Woodham Smith tried to alter this view by revealing that the queen had given £2,000 to the Rothshild appeal.[20] However, she misunder-

14. RA D 15/68, Prince Albert, memorandum, 26 December 1846.

15. John Hobhouse, Lord Broughton, *Recollections of a Long Life, with Additional Extracts from His Private Diaries*, 6 vols., ed. Lady Dorchester (London: John Murray, 1909–1911), 6:183.

16. *FJ*, 16 January 1847.

17. *FJ*, 15, 18 January 1847.

18. RA D 16/6 and 8, Lord John Russell to Queen Victoria, 6 January 1847, and Queen Victoria to Lord John Russell, 7 January 1847. The idea of a queen's letter had first been proposed a year earlier; see *FJ*, 7 January 1846.

19. *FJ*, 23 January 1847.

20. Cecil Woodham Smith, *The Great Hunger, Ireland 1845–49* (London: Penguin Books, 1962), 170.

stood the nature and purpose of the queen's donation. In the hierarchical society of early Victorian Britain there was a social etiquette concerning the size of donations. Queen Victoria's donation in fact came from government sources and its purpose was to set a marker by which others could estimate what they ought to give. Lord John Russell wrote to Prince Albert on 4 January:

In consequence of the number of Mercantile firms who have subscribed £1,000 each, I have ventured to intimate that Her Majesty will give £2,000. The Special Service Fund can bear this charge.

Should Your Royal Highness intend to subscribe in your own name, it will be desirable to do so now, as the subscription list will be in the newspaper list tomorrow.[21]

Prince Albert was duly recorded as having subscribed £500. The queen's uncle the duke of Cambridge gave £300 and her aunt the duchess of Gloucester £200.[22] The appeal raised £435,000.[23]

A second Queen's Letter in October 1847 raised little extra money, due to a hardening of attitudes in Britain.[24] In the summer of 1849 there was a private subscription among members of Parliament. Each MP gave £100 while the queen gave £500.

Two further donations merit note. The first was from the hated king of Hanover. His donation of £2,000 matched that initially made in his niece's name.[25] The second was from the sultan of Turkey. In the summer of 1849 he proposed to give £10,000 but, in view of the fact that this was five times greater than that officially given by the queen, the British government advised him to give £1,000. The *Freeman's Journal* put the disgust that many people felt at this eloquently, in a piece noticeably critical of the government rather than of the queen:

Those ministerial oppressors who have made this land a Haceldema for four whole years, limited the Queen's donation in the first instance. The paltry sum of

21. RA D 16/4, Lord John Russell to Prince Albert, 4 January 1847. See also Gray, *Famine, Land, and Politics*, 258.

22. RA D 16/5, newspaper cutting. In 1847 the duke of Cambridge's son, Prince George of Cambridge, was serving in the army in Ireland. On 15 March he attended the St. Patrick's Ball at Dublin Castle (*FJ*, 16 March 1847).

23. Peter Gray, *The Irish Famine* (London: Thames and Hudson, n.d.).

24. Gray, *Famine, Land, and Politics*, 289.

25. *FJ*, 20 November 1851.

two thousand pounds was as much as she could be *advised* to give consistently with Whig policy. To recommend to Queen Victoria to come to the aid of her perishing people with a contribution worthy of a wealthy Christian Sovereign, would be an admission on the part of her ministers that enough had not been done by them to save from ruin the support of the throne, her faithful subjects. They feared that *her* generosity would be *their* disgrace, and they sacrificed her fame to their own factious policy.... They committed a double treason—a treason against their Sovereign's glory and a treason against the lives of the people.[26]

Throughout 1847 the queen was by no means uninformed about the suffering of the people. Russell wrote to her, for example, on 8 January that "[t]he deaths in workhouses in one week have amounted to 662."[27] In some ways the queen's views were more progressive than those held by others in Britain about the famine. In March she reluctantly agreed to what she considered as the rather anachronistic expedient of a public "[f]ast day in connection with the distress in Ireland." She and Prince Albert went to Windsor, where they listened to a sermon, with which she strongly disagreed, by Samuel Wilberforce, bishop of Oxford, to go down in history as "Soapy Sam Wilberforce," one of Charles Darwin's fiercest opponents. Wilberforce's line reflected one of the least savory of contemporary attitudes to the famine, that it was a judgment of God. The queen recorded that he "stamped the famine as a punishment for our sins ... the heedless and improvident way in which the poor Irish [had] long lived" and because of "the wicked agitators ... and the deeds of violence there."[28] For Wilberforce, it seemed that O'Connell was to blame for the catastrophe.

The speech from the throne on 20 January 1847 was full of expressions of concern about Ireland. The *Freeman's Journal* greatly welcomed the speech's references to outrages which it saw as countering the impression of Ireland given in the British press:

We have ... no doubt her Majesty felt more than sovereigns on such occasions usually do when alluding to the melancholy condition of her brave, loyal but unfortunate Irish subjects. She also bears royal testimony to their signal endurance of ills, the most afflicting that ever befell an entire people. "It is satisfactory to me to observe that in many of *the most distressed* districts the patience and resignation of

26. *FJ*, 5 July 1849.
27. RA D 16/9, Lord John Russell to Queen Victoria, 8 January 1847.
28. RA QVJ, 9, 18, 24 March 1847, quoted in Walter L. Arnstein, "Queen Victoria's Speeches from the Throne: A New Look," in Alan O'Day, ed., *Government and Institutions in the Post-1832 United Kingdom* (Lewiston, N.Y.: Edward Mellen, 1995), 78.

the people have been *most exemplary.*" Such language, addressed to the British empire and the world, is calculated to remove most unfair and erroneous impressions of the conduct of the Irish peasantry under their unparalleled miseries. It is an imperial answer to the vicious slanders of caricaturists and malignant writers who gratified wicked passions and reflected national resentments by the most infamous representations.[29]

However, as the year wore on, the attention of both Victoria and Albert became fixed on the rising number of outrages in Ireland against landlords. In 1846 there were sixty-eight murders in Ireland. In 1847 there were ninety-eight. Clarendon pressed for coercion legislation and "became nearly hysterical" when the cabinet did not support him, even threatening to resign on 18 November.[30] Russell believed that the Irish problem was "a social one" and would not be solved by such legislation.[31]

Unable to comprehend the starvation of the faceless masses, Victoria and Albert were able to sympathize with the plight of individual landlords with whom they had often had personal contact. The most notorious incident was the murder of Major Denis Mahon in November. He was a close relative of Colonel Phipps, Prince Albert's private secretary. Queen Victoria wrote:

A shocking murder has again taken place in Ireland. An uncle by marriage of Mrs Phipps, Major Mahon, who had entirely devoted himself to being of use to the distressed Irish, was shot when driving home in his carriage. Really they are a terrible people, and there is no civilised country anywhere, which is in such a dreadful state and where such crimes are perpetuated! It is a constant source of anxiety and annoyance.[32]

Prince Albert sedulously kept press cuttings about the Mahon and other murders. "The state of Ireland is fearful at the moment, there does not pass a day that some atrocious murder does not take place."[33]

By December 1848 Clarendon despaired of the situation in Ireland and the willingness of the cabinet to support further relief measures.[34] He met

---

29. *FJ,* 21 January 1847.

30. J. Prest, *Lord John Russell* (London: Macmillan, 1972), 272–73.

31. Lord Russell to Lord Clarendon, 10 November 1847, in Spencer Walpole, *The Life of Lord John Russell,* 2 vols. (London: Longmans Green, 1889), 1:463.

32. RA QVJ, 5 November 1847.

33. RA D 16/112, Prince Albert, memorandum, 3 December 1847.

34. Woodham Smith, *Great Hunger,* 375.

Prince Albert, who recorded that "Lord Clarendon looks forward to the winter with perfect dismay. The poverty is dreadful and he is afraid that a great part of the population must die from absolute want." However, it was not all the fault of the government and other relief-providing bodies. The people "grow nothing but potatoes (in spite of every experience and caution) which have failed again entirely. Lord Clarendon knows an instance of a man having sown wheat which had come up beautifully and ploughing it up again for potatoes because he saw the potatoes of his neighbour look tolerably well."[35]

Queen Victoria's popularity remained high at least with many middle-class nationalists during the famine. In May 1849 there was a third apparent attempt on her life, this time by a lonely, unemployed Irishman, William Hamilton, from Adare, County Limerick, who fired at her with blanks on Constitution Hill in London. In Ireland there was a flurry of protestations of loyalty. "We believe there exists not a sovereign against whom there is less hostility felt by all classes of her subjects—for whom there is more of respect and towards whom there is more of general attachment than Queen Victoria," recorded the *Freeman's Journal*.[36]

Yet only nine days later she came in for a philippic from John MacHale, Catholic archbishop of Tuam. As early as 1847 Prince Albert had identified him as an agitator in the mold of O'Connell. "The people are full of 'impatience' and are excited by MacHale who was against relief works, and now that they are suspended, is against soup kitchens."[37] MacHale was accustomed to writing open letters to British politicians. In May 1849 he turned his sights against the queen but his real target was in fact the government.

He began by claiming, quite wrongly, that in the four years of the famine no "public document" or "deputation" had addressed the queen on the famine. Noting that the Irish people were delighted that their "beloved Queen" had survived the recent attempt on her life, he explained the lack of addresses to the queen in terms of the fact that "your Majesty's power is not at all commensurate with the well known benevolence of your feelings."

He went on to give a face to the faceless suffering of the people, telling the queen of a girl in Connemara who had carried her mother's corpse a

35. RA D 18/84, Prince Albert, memorandum, 30 October 1848.
36. *FJ*, 22 May 1849.
37. RA D 16/69, Prince Albert, memorandum, 17 May 1847.

mile for burial and had the next day been buried in the same grave herself so "that a parent and a child, whom such piety united in life, might not in death be desecrated."[38] "Your Majesty's ministers have neglected their duty, their indifference to the lives of the people must be an obvious conclusion. . . . It appears then that whilst your Majesty's sympathising breast could afford succour to your loving subjects, the ministers are unwilling to perform that paramount duty."

The queen was the caring mother of her people. He was pleading to her on behalf of "the doomed but innocent people" of Connaught. If the present government would not act, she should replace them with one willing "to provide for the safety of the lives of your Majesty's subjects."[39]

If there was one thing about which the government was assiduous it was the safety of the realm. The year 1848 was one of revolution in Europe. Prince Albert hoped that it might bring about the liberal federal Germany of which he had always dreamed, and lobbied several governments about the matter. "We never pressed on him *our* advice concerning the affairs of Ireland," commented the Austrian chancellor.[40]

In England the Chartist movement fizzled out without a revolution after the failure of the Kennington meeting. "We had our revolution yesterday, and it went up in smoke," wrote Albert to Baron Stockmar. "The law was victorious. . . . In Ireland things look still more serious."[41] This was true. There was indeed a greater prospect of revolution there.

Shortly after his arrival as lord lieutenant, Clarendon had reported to Russell that "Young Ireland has no money, some talent, very little influence and is losing ground."[42] All was changed early in 1848, when a revolution in France overthrew Louis Philippe and established the Second Republic. It electrified radical nationalists in Ireland. The *Freeman's Journal*

38. For a discussion on the use of female images in the depiction of the Irish famine, see Margaret Kelleher, *The Feminization of Famine: Expressions of the Inexpressible?* (Cork: Cork University Press, 1997).

39. John MacHale, archbishop of Tuam, to Queen Victoria, in *FJ*, 28 May 1849. He concluded the letter by promising that if no extra relief was forthcoming a delegation of Irish bishops would visit the queen.

40. Weintraub, *Albert*, 196.

41. Prince Albert to Baron von Stockmar, 11 April 1848, in Kurt Jagow, ed., *Letters of the Prince Consort, 1831–61* (London: John Murray, 1938), 135.

42. RA D 16/75, Lord Clarendon to Lord John Russell, 12 July 1847.

pointed to France as an example of what would happen in Ireland if its rights were denied.[43]

There were of course different strands of opinion within Young Ireland itself. John Mitchel and Thomas Francis Meagher represented the more radical wing. Mitchel founded the *United Irishman* as a breakaway from the more moderate *Nation* in February 1848. He wrote deliberately provocative open letters to Clarendon, addressed to "Her Majesty's Executioner-General and General Butcher of Ireland," inviting him to prosecute Mitchel— "yes, of course you will prosecute before long, in self-defence I hope you must"—and signing himself "I remain your enemy."[44] In March he sarcastically compared the programme of the new French government with the efforts in Britain to give refuge to the dispossessed royal families of Europe:

In fact England *will* not be out-done by France. While the Provisional Government is founding, as the *Times* says, a huge system of outdoor-relief for working people, London monarchy is busied in establishing an equally extensive system of outdoor-relief for destitute Royalties.[45]

The mainstream of Young Ireland had come under the influence of the not-so-young William Smith O'Brien, who was the leader of their political organization, the Irish Confederation. Educated at Harrow and Cambridge, Smith O'Brien had once been a Tory MP and then a supporter of O'Connell. His new radicalism alarmed his family, especially his mother. Prince Albert noted that "L[ad]y O'Brien has written to Sir R. Peel in the greatest alarm appealing to his generosity in case her son should get into danger by some *desperate* course which she fears he is likely to take."[46] But even at his most radical Smith O'Brien remained a royalist. In his last major speech in the Commons, in April 1848, he told the house that, unless it gave Ireland justice, Ireland would be a republic within three years. He went on to claim, however, that he himself was still loyal to the queen. It was with Parliament that he had the quarrel.[47]

43. *FJ*, 1 March 1848.

44. *United Irishman*, 25 March, 12 February, 11 March 1848.

45. *United Irishman*, 11 March 1848.

46. RA D 15/25, Prince Albert, memorandum, n.d. [1846].

47. Richard Davis, *Revolutionary Imperialist: William Smith O'Brien, 1803–64* (London: Lilliput, 1998), 246. At his trial on 15 May 1848 his counsel, Isaac Butt, vigorosly claimed that Smith O'Brien had disavowed republicanism and was a supported of a restored queen, lords, and commons of Ireland.

Enthusiastic for what was happening in France, Smith O'Brien tried to forge a united nationalist front by bringing about a reconciliation between the Confederation and the old, moderate Repeal Association, now under the leadership of O'Connell's son John, but nothing came of it.[48] Instead, things began to move in a more radical direction.

At a meeting of the Irish Confederation on 15 March, Meagher proposed that an Irish delegation be sent to Queen Victoria to ask for political change. If she refused to meet them they should "then and there make a solemn oath that when they next demand admission to the throne room of St James's, it shall be through the accredited ambassador of the Irish Republic." If, on the other hand, they got to meet the queen, they should call on her to use her royal prerogative, which Meagher must have known could only have been exercised on the advice of the government, to summon an Irish parliament:

If the call [to the queen] be obeyed . . . then, indeed, may we bless the constitution we have been taught to curse, and Irish loyalty, ceasing to be a mere ceremonious affectation, become with us a sincere devotion to the just ruler of an independent state (enthusiastic applause). If the claim be rejected—if the throne stand as a barrier between the Irish people and their supreme right—then loyalty will be a crime, and obedience to the executive will be treason to the country (more cheers).[49]

The meeting ended with Queen Victoria being toasted with cups of tea as queen of Ireland and "God Save the Queen" played on an Irish harp.[50]

A meeting of the Dublin trades was held at the behest of the Young Irelanders on 20 March and over ten thousand people attended. Clarendon fortified the city with troops, though the lord mayor claimed that "he knew the peace of the city was in no danger from the trades and working men of Dublin who were about to claim their political rights."[51] The meeting empowered a special delegation to bring an address to the people of France and it also adopted an address to the queen, which bluntly informed her:

48. Kevin B. Nowlan, *The Politics of Repeal: A Study in the Relations between Great Britain and Ireland, 1841–50* (London: Routledge and Kegan Paul, 1965), 183.

49. *FJ*, 18 March 1848.

50. Woodham Smith, *Great Hunger*, 385. She mistakenly gives the date as 15 April rather than 15 March.

51. *FJ*, 15 March 1848.

For the security of your throne, and for the salvation of this people, we ask you to restore to us that privilege which we have never forfeited—of which we have been so foully robbed. We seek no innovation. We desire to exist as our fathers existed—under native institutions; and to your Majesty, as the head of such institutions, we are willing to accord a free and generous allegiance. But our duty to your Majesty, and to ourselves, compels us to declare thus openly—that the freedom of our country and the welfare of its people are of more importance in our estimation than the security of the throne.[52]

The address portrayed Ireland before the union as a far more independent country than it ever was and offered only a very partial and provisional loyalty to the Crown. Even this was too much for the republican John Mitchel, however. Perhaps for the sake of harmony he offered only an implicit criticism of it in the course of his speech on the French address. He spoke of the "royal workmen of Paris. . . . I call those workmen royal, sir, because labour is the only king in France now and in his clemency, gentleness and wisdom as well as in his prowess, he is every inch a king (much cheering)."[53] Elsewhere in the city a rival meeting of the old and now declining Repeal Association was agreeing that in the case of an invasion Irishmen would "rally as one man for the defence of our Queen (cheers)."[54]

The next day Smith O'Brien, Mitchel, and Meagher were charged with sedition. Echoing the legal formula of a charge for treason, Clarendon told Russell that the charge had been sedition rather than treason because "these men have not actually levied war against the Queen and nobody can pretend that they have been compassing her death, with the channel between the two countries."[55] Yet the situation was far from secure from the government's point of view. The day after Clarendon wrote again to say that he was "becoming more convinced that we cannot weather the European storm in Ireland without pursuing a different course to that which six

52. *Nation*, 25 March 1848.

53. *Nation*, 25 March 1848.

54. *FJ*, 21 March 1848. John O'Connell had originally planned a great rally for 17 March. In view of Clarendon's increase in the number of troops in the city, however, he called it off. As a substitute, poorly attended ward meetings were held on 14 March. See RA D 17/36, Lord Clarendon to Sir George Gray, 27 March 1848. On 28 March in the wake of public sympathy with those charged with sedition, the Repeal Association agreed to send a petition to the queen—very similar to Meagher's—asking her to use her royal prerogative to summon a parliament in Dublin; see *FJ*, 29 March 1849.

55. RA D 17/34, Lord Clarendon to Lord John Russell, 22 March 1848.

weeks ago might have answered our purpose."[56] To this end he suggested paying the salaries of Catholic priests as a way of gaining their loyalty.

Though nothing came of this suggestion, the government did rush through a treason-felony act that widened the grounds of treason to include anyone involved in verbal "intimidation" of Parliament or the Crown and prescribed transportation for from fourteen years to life as the penalty.[57] Queen Victoria thought "[t]he state of Ireland is most alarming and most anxious."[58] Prince Albert urged the need for action in Ireland but innocently imagined that the government's position could be strengthened by conciliatory public statements:

The L[or]d Lieutenant ought not to postpone the issue of a Proclamation setting forth the evil intentions of the agitators, the certain misery which their success must bring upon Ireland and the readiness in the part of the Gov[t] to listen to any complaint and take any proposition for the amelioration of Ireland into their most serious consideration, that the way of petition is open to the Queen and to Parliament.[59]

The sedition charge only spurred Mitchel into further attacks. Released on bail like the others, he told a meeting of the Confederation on 23 March that he now opposed Meagher's plan to petition the queen. "I will never address the Queen of England (cheers). I have nothing to do with Kings or Queens and whatever may be the opinion of my brother Confederates there shall be no rest for me until I see Ireland a free Republic."[60] At Limerick on 30 April he told a crowd, "I am here not as a Jacobin (which I

56. RA D 17/35, Lord Clarendon to Lord John Russell, 23 March 1848.

57. The queen wrote in her journal, "A new law is going to be brought in against treason, to enable people holding treasonable language to be punished, making it [a] felony, and applicable to England as well as to Ireland." See RA QVJ, 4 April 1848.

58. Queen Victoria to Lord John Russell, 16 April 1848, in Benson and Esher, *Letters*, first series, 2:167.

59. RA D 17/53, Prince Albert to Lord John Russell [draft], 5 April 1848.

60. *United Irishman*, 25 March 1848. In fact he did address her frequently, albeit in the pages of his later published *Jail Journal*. Here Queen Victoria appears in the eerie guise of Queen Nice of Carthage: "You Sovereign Lady, Queen Nice, have charge of me now . . . but you may find, O Queen, that I am too dear at the price you have paid, and are like to pay. I will cost you most dread sovereign, rather more than my rations." See John Mitchel, *Jail Journal* (Dublin: Gill, 1913), 1 June 1848, p. 15. In some ways it was a prophetic promise as Mitchel was later to be responsible for propagating the view of the famine as a British genocide against the Irish which is still believed in America. The myth of Queen Victoria as the "famine queen" was later to be inserted into it.

am not)—nor as a Communist (which I am not)—nor even as a Republican (which I am) (loud cheers); but simply and merely because I am a bitter and irreconcilable enemy of the British government (here, hear). . . . [N]o Irishman ought to so much as speak to a man who has not provided himself with arms (loud cheering)."[61] A week before he had described the "'golden link of the Crown'" as "humbug."

In May the sedition charges against Smith O'Brien and Meagher collapsed, but Mitchel was rearrested, tried, convicted, and sentenced to transportation for fourteen years, under the new treason-felony act, specifically on account of articles in the *United Irishman* on 6 and 13 May 1848. One of the passages that the prosecution made most of was the following:

I tell you, frankly, that I, for one, am not "loyal." I am not wedded to the Queen of England, nor unalterably attached to the House of Brunswick. In fact I love my own barn better than I love that house. The time is long past when Jehovah *anointed* Kings . . . There is no divine right now but in the Sovereign People.[62]

Mitchel was here in part clearly satirizing the language of familial relationship that had been part of O'Connell's discourse on monarchy.[63] However, it was the collapse of the trials of Meagher and Smith O'Brien that had the greater consequences as far as the queen was concerned. In early April 1848 there had been reports that the queen would visit Ireland that summer.[64] The reaction in nationalist Ireland was not enthusiastic, but on political rather than personal grounds. The view of the *Freeman's Journal* was that "[i]f her Majesty came to Ireland to call together her faithful Irish Lords and Commons, we can promise her the warm welcome of loyal Irish hearts" but not if her visit is "to make a Royal pageant a substitute for justice." Criticism for the planned visit was reserved for the government which was betraying the Crown by seeking "to prostitute it to a foul purpose."[65]

61. *United Irishman*, 6 May 1848.

62. Reported in *FJ*, 26 May 1848.

63. In his *Jail Journal* (13 September 1848, 66), indeed, the queen is construed as an antifamilial figure: "Has not the Queen of England banished me from the land where my mother bore me, and where my father's bones are laid?"

64. Clarendon had been urging a royal visit on Russell since late 1847. "Whatever may be the political feelings or animosities of the Irish, their devotion to the Queen is unquestionable and whenever Her Majesty shall think proper to come to Ireland I am convinced she would be received with enthusiastic loyalty." See Lord Clarendon to Lord John Russell, in Woodham Smith, *Great Hunger*, 385.

65. *FJ*, 5 April 1848.

In John Martin's *Irish Felon*, the successor to the now defunct *United Irishman*, Meagher predicted that a royal visit would produce "Crowds—delirious with joy!" But he went on to ask:

[I]s it thus—with a bit of polished court plaster—that this wild and wounded nation will be cured and tamed? . . . I do not slander the Queen of England. . . . I have no aversion to royalty in the abstract. When it is encircled, and to a great extent controlled, by the will and interests of the commonwealth, I regard it as a safe and provident institution. . . . But I am neither an Englishman nor a hypocrite. . . . It is time we should have some reason for our loyalty, and until we have, we should withhold our loyalty, and all pretence of it.[66]

The collapse of the trials against Smith O'Brien and Meagher, however, apparently turned the government's mind away from advising the queen to visit Ireland, though the conviction of Mitchel caused them to reconsider briefly.[67]

Nothing had been absolutely settled as late as early July, however. On 3 July the queen wrote to Russell about speculation in the papers over the visit: "she regrets that it is still so doubtful. Indeed, the Queen has heard that many Irish Proprietors, including the Duke of Leinster, say that it would not at all be prudent for her to go to Ireland this summer."[68] He replied that "[i]t is understood that nothing is settled respecting Your Majesty's visit to Ireland. But it is impossible to prevent unauthorised paragraphs from appearing in the newspapers."[69]

On 10 July the *Times* of London announced that the visit was definitely off on the grounds that "the traitorous malice or the silly importunity of a very few persons might seriously mar the moral effect and the personal comfort of a progress otherwise entirely successful."[70] This was another unauthorized newspaper report but it effectively put paid to the matter. "It appears that at Your Majesty's Ball it was generally said that the visit would

66. *Irish Felon*, 1 July 1848.

67. Mitchel wrote (*Jail Journal*, 27 May 1846, 6) that he was glad that "Nice, Queen of Carthage, will not steer her yacht to Ireland this summer of 1848, as she graciously intended." He added in a note to the published text: "But the next year Her Gracious Majesty did carry her beneficent intention into effect, and the debased nation set its neck under her feet in a paroxysm of fictitious 'loyalty.' It is painful to relate but it is the disgraceful fact."

68. RA D 17/108, Queen Victoria to Lord John Russell, 3 July 1848.

69. RA D 17/109, Lord John Russell to Queen Victoria, 4 July 1848.

70. *Times*, 10 July 1848. "We should not believe that Ireland could furnish wretches capable of this crime, did they not declare themselves, and did not others give a tacit concurrence in the threatened outrage."

not take place and the report probably reached the *Times*," reported Russell to the queen.[71] Two days later he wrote that "Lord Clarendon complains much of the announcement made in the Times which he concludes to be official that Your Majesty's visit to Ireland will not take place this year."[72]

The *Freeman's Journal* denounced the motivations that it believed had been behind the abandoned visit. The government had wanted to lead "the Queen over here to help them to triumph over the utter prostration of national aspiration in Ireland. . . . No Queen or ministry will ever have the opportunity of coming over here to crow over the extinction of Irish national feeling, for it never will be extinct." It proceeded to attack Russell, who was of short stature, as "this miserable manikin, for whose moral dimensions no diminutive suffices—they are infinitely smaller than his physical, which are nature's imperfect expression of them."

"We had no Queen in Ireland in O'Connell's day." For the *Freeman's Journal* it was thus not Young Ireland as a movement "that veils against us the face of Majesty. . . . It is evident that Repeal must be either dead or triumphant before her English ministry will permit Victoria to grace Ireland with her presence."[73] It emphasized the point with a poem a few days later which ended with the verse:

> Then come at once—come like a Queen
> And fix your throne in College-green
> But first of all, afore you sail—
> Make up your mind to grant Repail [*sic*].[74]

Instead of visiting Ireland the royal couple spent their first extended period at Balmoral in Scotland in September 1848. By then it was just as well from their point of view that the Irish trip had been cancelled as during July and August the political and security situations had deteriorated. Habeas corpus was suspended and Young Ireland leaders were arrested. On 29 July Smith O'Brien led a brief and abortive uprising at Ballingarry, County Tipperary. As news of the uprising broke, the queen wrote confidently to her Uncle Leopold that "[t]here are ample means of crushing the Rebellion in Ireland and I think it now is very likely to go off without any contest."[75] The same day she wrote in her journal:

71. RA D 18/2, Lord John Russell to Queen Victoria, 11 July 1848.

72. RA A 19/206, Lord John Russell to Queen Victoria, 13 July 1848.

73. *FJ*, 12 July 1848.

74. *FJ*, 20 July 1848.

75. Queen Victoria to King Leopold of the Belgians, 1 August 1848, in Benson and Esher, *Letters*, first series, 2:223.

Good news of 4,000 of the Irish Rebels being dispersed by 50 of the Police, who got into a house, Smith O'Brien threatening them if they did not surrender which of course they refused to do. The Rebels then fired, the Police returning the fire, killing and wounding 12 or 14. They missed O'Brien who crawled away in a most cowardly manner.[76]

For the *Times* Smith O'Brien was "a spoilt child" whose efforts were "all in the vain expectation that he would step in to the seat of O'Connell, and pass thence, perhaps, to the presidency of a republic, if not the traditional throne of his ancestors."[77]

There was no great rejoicing in the government over the end of the rebellion. Prince Albert noted that "L[or]d C[larendon] does not believe that there is one loyal Roman Catholic in the country."[78] The possibility of paying Catholic priests as a way of buying their compliance was again seriously considered. On 25 August the queen recorded that at that day's privy council, Lord Gray "spoke of Ireland with keen interest and of the necessity of paying the Priests. The state of the country is still very bad, disaffection being so great that it is worse than open rebellion."[79]

Smith O'Brien was brought to trial in the autumn of 1848. Lord John Russell chose that moment to visit Ireland, one of the few prime ministers in office to do so, and found himself served with a subpoena to give evidence in the trial though it came to nothing.[80] Found guilty, Smith O'Brien was sentenced to death on 9 October for having "compassed the death of the Queen and levied war against the Sovereign with a view to her deposition." The *Freeman's Journal* hoped that "Queen Victoria, whose reign has been one of uninterrupted gentleness so far as she was concerned— would not execute vengeance."[81]

The government was anxious to draw a line under the late open rebellion. Not least of the reasons for this was British foreign policy in a turbulent Europe. In November the queen discussed Austria and its presence in Italy with Clarendon. "He agreed with me that it was most conflicting for us to urge other countries to give up part of their territory on account of

76. RA QVJ, 1 August 1848. In fact Smith O'Brien had only about a hundred followers with him.

77. *Times*, 25 October 1848. His O'Brien ancestors had once been Gaelic kings of Thomond.

78. RA D 18/84, Prince Albert, memorandum, 30 October 1848.

79. RA QVJ: 25 August 1848.

80. Walpole, *Russell*, 2:75.

81. *FJ*, 10 October 1848.

nationality, with Ireland protesting very urgently no doubt, but still protesting against our misrule."[82]

After Smith O'Brien's sentence Lord John Russell let it be known that he would advise the queen to grant a plea for clemency and commute the sentence to transportation. Smith O'Brien, however, preferred death to transportation. Special legislation had therefore to be introduced to enable clemency to be exercised in spite of Smith O'Brien's wishes.[83] It was passed with difficulty and the final order for transportation was only signed on 9 July 1849. Russell told Prince Albert that "[t]he exercise of mercy appears as difficult in Ireland as any other matter."[84]

The Crown, and Queen Victoria as wearer of that crown, had figured prominently in the rhetoric that had surrounded the political uncertainties of 1848 but largely in terms of a symbolic confrontation between Young Irelanders and the British government. No one really imagined that she had any personal power to summon an Irish parliament. Personal attacks were reserved for Russell and Clarendon. Indeed, in reading the speeches of people like Meagher and even Mitchel that refer to the queen it is possible to detect a tone of audacious novelty in their anti-monarchical attacks. After the O'Connellite era of professed loyalty this was something new in Irish public political discourse.

❖

A visit by the queen to Ireland had been a point of speculation for five years. It was thought that she might visit in the late summer of 1843 when the new royal yacht, *Victoria and Albert,* was ready.[85] In 1844 there were rumors about a visit in October.[86] The year 1845 was when it became clear that O'Connell's opposition could prevent a visit. In August 1846 the queen asked Russell's advice about the invitation she had received to visit Ireland from the lord lieutenant Lord Bessborough.[87] Russell discouraged it on account of the famine.[88] A week or so later Prince Albert wrote to Peel that "[t]he visit to Ireland is given up for this year."[89]

82. RA QVJ, 17 November 1848.

83. Charles Gavan Duffy, *Four Years of Irish History, 1845–1849* (London: Cassell, Petter, Galpin, 1883), 759.

84. RA D 19/52, Lord John Russell to Prince Albert, 19 June 1849.

85. *FJ,* 28 January, 15 May 1843.

86. *Globe,* 23 August 1844, reported in *FJ,* 26 August 1844.

87. RA D 15/52, Queen Victoria to Lord John Russell, 3 August 1846.

88. RA D 15/53, Lord John Russell to Queen Victoria, 4 August 1846.

89. Prince Albert to Sir Robert Peel, 16 August 1846, in Parker, *Peel Papers,* 3:463.

Russell suggested an impromptu visit in 1847 to avoid costly preparations. "The want of notice might in some respects be favourable, and would be an excuse to many Irish peers who might complete their ruin in preparations."[90] The visit did not take place, however, though that summer the *Spectator* reported that on her visit to Scotland the queen "passed in sight of the Irish shores 'with a sigh.'"[91] Comparisons were now common in Ireland between the time the queen was increasingly spending in Scotland and not spending in Ireland:

We admit a braccated Gael with a Lochaber axe is a more romantic object than a ragged and emaciated Irishman. . . . A people reduced by the misgovernment of England to the lowest condition of human existence would be a trying spectacle to the sovereign of the offending power.[92]

In 1848 there was some not very serious talk in government circles that the queen might go to Ireland and hold a parliament of the United Kingdom in Dublin.[93] A petition to this effect was even submitted to her.[94]

The year 1849 was the first in which, realistically, a royal visit became a possibility. O'Connell was dead, Young Ireland was crushed, and the famine showed signs of abating. It has often been suggested that Clarendon wanted a visit to help in the stabilization of the political system, to promote investment in Ireland, and to mark a symbolic end to the famine.[95] There was also a fourth reason that was in fact the most important. The royal visit was to be part of the rationalization of the Irish government, which was to involve the abolition of the lord lieutenancy, and the further integration of Ireland into the structures of the United Kingdom. It was to begin the process whereby the union would finally be completed. The *Freeman's Journal* called the visit "an insulting inauguration of the Clarendon era."[96]

Prince Albert wrote to Russell in early May 1849 on the question of the visit. The prince and queen had decided that "it should not be a *State* Visit, *but* one having more the character of a yachting excursion." A state visit

90. Lord John Russell to Queen Victoria, 21 August 1847, in Benson and Esher, *Letters*, first series, 2:149.

91. Reported in *FJ*, 23 August 1847.   92. *FJ*, 23 August 1847.

93. Prest, *Russell*, 300.   94. *FJ*, 1 September 1848.

95. Gray, *Famine, Land, and Politics*, 211: "it [the visit] would boost the morale of the country and give symbolic resonance to the Union."

96. *FJ*, 30 July 1849.

would involve "a very large expenditure, which Ireland is unable and unwilling to bear herself." If Parliament had to pay, there would be "a minute
investigation of the *details*" and this would lead to "discussions and obser-
vations, on the part of the meddling popularity hunters, which is much to
be deprecated in the present times."

The queen had long wished to visit Ireland and "[s]he accordingly sacrifices Her personal convenience by taking a long Sea Voyage for the purpose of Visiting Cork, Waterford, Wexford, Dublin and Belfast." In Dublin
there might be a levee and a drawing room; the royal party could stay
overnight on the yacht so as not to cause Clarendon to incur expense at the
Vice Regal Lodge. "We think politically this year particularly favourable
for a visit to Ireland."[97]

In reply Russell expressed general agreement but was worried that
"[a]ny expenditure might be open to the remark, 'If this money was to be
spent, why was it not spent on relieving the starving poor?'"[98] Privately
Russell was less enthusiastic and told Clarendon that he would not be responsible for the queen going to Ireland.[99] Clarendon, however, was delighted by the plan:

[T]here has been no period more publically propitious for Her coming here than
the present one—agitation is extinct, Repeal is forgotten—the Seditious associations are closed—the priests are frightened and the people are tranquil—Everything tends to secure for the Queen an enthusiastic reception and the one draw-
back, which is the general distress of all classes, has its advantages for it will
enable the Queen to do what is kind and considerate to those who are suffering,
and, at the same time what is convenient to herself, as it would be improper that
she should incur any great expense.[100]

It was obvious that great thought would have to be put into the details
of the visit. He advised that the queen should stay for four or five days lest
people "think she was in a hurry to leave a country so rarely visited by its
Sovereigns." He advised against sleeping on the yacht as it might give the
impression to people that the queen thought herself "unsafe among them."

97. RA D 19/46, Prince Albert to Lord John Russell, 6 June 1849.

98. RA D 19/47, Lord John Russell to Prince Albert, 6 June 1849.

99. Lord Clarendon to Sir George Grey, 15 August 1849, in Herbert Maxwell, *Life and
Letters of George William Frederick, Fourth Earl of Clarendon*, 2 vols. (London: Edward Arnold,
1913), 2:303. See also Stanley Weintraub, *Albert Uncrowned King* (London: John Murray,
1997), 121.

100. RA D 19/49, Lord Clarendon to Lord John Russell, 7 June 1849.

He recommended she add Killarney, the scenic destination in Kerry, to her itinerary and drop Waterford and Wexford, "an insignificant place" with "no harbour for large vessels."

Clarendon was also anxious that public funds not be used to finance the visit. In normal circumstances the salary of the lord lieutenant was far below the expenditure that the job required and lords lieutenant were required to finance much of their role from their own resources. The visit was going to place an extra strain on Clarendon's finances. However, though he insisted that "I have no Millionaire pretentions. . . . I would rather go to the Work house when I leave Ireland than have my name connected with any money Question in the House of Commons, or be accused by some of the vulgar gentlemen there of making a profit of the Queen's Visit."[101] The estimates he received from the Board of Works included £2,500 for decorating Dublin Castle and the Vice Regal Lodge, £500 for the reception marquee at Kingstown, and £400 for illuminations. He eventually submitted a bill to the exchequer for only £2,000.[102]

Drafts of the official announcement of the visit passed between Prince Albert and the government. The prince wanted it to state that the queen would "at some sacrifice of personal inconvenience take a long Sea Voyage" to enable her to make the visit.[103] Russell thought it best to remove the reference to "the sacrifice of convenience."[104]

Once the decision was taken reaction in government circles was positive. The foreign secretary, Lord Palmerston, himself an Irish peer, gave Russell his condescending prediction about the queen's reception in Ireland. "I shall be much mistaken in Paddy's character if the Queen is not satisfied with the demonstration of joy and loyalty with which her arrival in Ireland will be greeted."[105] In late July Russell wrote to the queen that "from all I hear . . . the Queen will find the Irish the most loyal of her subjects."[106]

Colonel Phipps wrote to the home secretary, Sir George Grey, who rather than Russell, to her disappointment,[107] was to accompany the queen as minister-in-attendance:

101. RA D 19/62, Lord Clarendon to Lord John Russell, 28 June 1849.

102. Woodham-Smith, *Great Hunger*, 391.

103. RA D 19/57, Redraft of announcement of queen's visit to Ireland.

104. RA D 19/58, Lord John Russell to Prince Albert, 25 June 1849.

105. Lord Palmeston to Lord John Russell, 5 August 1849, in G. P. Gooch, *The Later Correspondence of Lord John Russell 1840–1878*, 2 vols. (London: Longmans Green, 1925), 1:235.

106. RA D 19/97, Lord John Russell to Queen Victoria, 25 July 1849.

107. RA D 19/93, Queen Victoria to Lord John Russell, 19 July 1849: "We are sorry

I have seen the entry of several popular Vice Roys into Dublin (Normanby amongst them) and I quite agree with Lord Clarendon that no idea can be formed from anything that occurs in England of the scenes which will probably meet her Majesty in the towns.[108]

If it was the case that royal processions in Ireland were going to be met with enormous enthusiasm, then why not at least enhance them with an impressive equipage? Lord Fortescue told Phipps it was a pity that the queen would not have her own horses with her:

You who know the Irish must be aware how far more they attach to show than to substance and I really believe that nearly all of them from the highest to the lowest would be . . . gratified at seeing the Queen's equipage and red liveries in the streets of Dublin.[109]

Eventually, the carriages were taken to Ireland.

In Ireland the news of the visit was met with a mixed reception; even some members of the nobility were against it. Lord Monteagle decided to boycott the Dublin Castle levee and Lord Fitzwilliam wrote that "[a] great *lie* is going to be acted here. I would not have her go *now* unless she went to Killarney workhouse . . . Galway, Connemara and Castlebar. *That* would have been my tour for her."[110] The Tory *Dublin Evening Mail* painted a less-than-flattering picture of the Dublin through which the queen would process. Most of the houses on the main streets were "in a dirty and dilapidated condition, the windows broken, patched with brown paper . . . the shops closed and wooden shutters covered with auction bills, railway tables, quack advertisements and notices from the Poor Law Commissioners or the Insolvency Court."[111]

The visit was not welcomed by the *Freeman's Journal.* On the eve of the official announcement it adopted a similar objection to that of Fitzwilliam:

One visit to a hut in Connaught, one view of a "cleansed" estate in the south, a simple pencil etching by her Majesty of one unroofed cabin with its miserable

---

that Lord John does not intend going to Ireland but fully comprehend his wishes to remain quiet for 3 weeks."

108. RA D 19/71, Col. Charles Phipps to Sir George Grey, 7 July 1849.

109. RA D 19/72, Lord Fortescue to Col. Charles Phipps, 6 July 1849.

110. Lord Fitzwilliam to Lord Monteagle, 2 August 1849, quoted in Woodham-Smith, *Great Hunger*, 387, and Donal Kerr, *"A Nation of Beggars"? Priests, People, and Politics in Famine Ireland, 1846–1852* (Oxford: Oxford University Press, 1994), 204.

111. *Dublin Evening Mail*, 5 July 1849, quoted in Woodham Smith, *Great Hunger*, 386.

emaciated inmates cast out, and perishing on the dungheap beside it, would be a better result of this tour of the first magistrate of the empire, than a week's festivities in Dublin Castle, or the most enchanting sketch which her Majesty could treasure in her port folio of the picturesque beauties of Killarney.[112]

Once announced, the paper compared the impending arrival of the royal yacht with the recent departure of the ship bearing Smith O'Brien to Australia. It chose to misunderstand the government's efforts at frugality in the face of the famine. Dispensing with the use of formal court wear[113] was "lest Irish manufacturers flourish for a week." The lack of state formality was so that the queen would not receive addresses that might urge her "to dismiss her present advisers as men who had involved the country in irretrievable ruin—who had looked patiently on while hundreds of thousands of her subjects were passing to the grave."

As time went on certain formalities did begin to creep into the arrangements for the visit. It was announced that gentlemen accompanying the royal procession into Dublin on horseback should wear blue coats and scarfs and white waistcoats and trousers. The lord mayor thought that the provision of such attire "would give a good deal of employment."[114] But the *Freeman's Journal*'s view was that

the sables of black despair will better fit us than "the white vest and the blue coat" which, under the circumstances, would import *éclat* to the scene . . . We must not, by new attire or fresh paint, present to the eye appearances which facts and truth will not justify. . . . [A] repetition of the wild delirium with which the Irish received the profligate King in 1821 would be no compliment to the Queen of many virtues who is coming to see and judge for herself in 1849.[115]

As for members of the government, they should be met not with jeers but with "[a] calm stern silence."

Political opposition to the visit often took covert and always took symbolic form. The issues that galvinized it were those of the content of loyal addresses and of the illumination of the cities which the queen was to visit, especially Dublin. The Dublin Corporation learned officially of the visit at a meeting on 2 July. John Reynolds, MP, told the meeting that the queen

112. *FJ*, 29 June 1849.
113. Later it was announced by the lord chamberlain's office that the drawing room and levee would be in full dress (*FJ*, 26 July 1849).
114. *FJ*, 17 July 1849.
115. *FJ*, 23 July 1849.

ought not to be blamed for the actions of her ministers and should be welcomed to Ireland as "all believed that if it were in her power she would ameliorate the condition of her subjects."[116] He hoped that triennial meetings of Parliament might be held in Dublin and that the queen might establish a royal residence near the city. Indeed, toward the end of July the *Dublin Mercantile Advertiser* reported that the queen was considering building a "a marine villa" outside Dublin between Killiney and Bray for annual summer visits.[117]

The *Freeman's Journal* published an anonymous letter on 13 July from a member of the Dublin Corporation saying that the members of the Corporation, hoping for honors from the visit, were not going to mention repeal of the union or the "state" prisoners in their address to the queen.[118] Three days later at a meeting of the Corporation, the lord mayor, Timothy O'Brien, proposed the adoption of an uncontentious loyal address of welcome. The protests of councillor Loughman that the address should mention the famine and call for repeal were easily swept aside and the address was adopted.[119]

The *Dublin Evening Post*, whose views closely mirrored those of Clarendon, had called on the lord mayor to order an illumination of the city. Such an order would have required not only public institutions to be illuminated but also private houses, with householders having to place candles behind every pane of glass. At the 16 July meeting of the Corporation another councillor, Dr. Ryan, urged the lord mayor to issue a proclamation, asking the citizens not to illuminate but to give the money saved to the poor. O'Brien cut the debate short. It was clear that he did not want to get embroiled in the issue of the illuminations. Next day, however, a meeting of the ratepayers of the Post Office ward voted almost unanimously in favor of illuminations. One of the two dissenters at the meeting attacked the "base, bloody and brutal Whigs" and lamented that "men who had worked for so many years at the Repeal cause [were] now willing to compromise it." He would rather "allow his windows to be smashed" than to illuminate them.[120]

On 23 July the lord mayor had to fend off not only Loughman and Ryan but now Councillor Martin who wanted the queen to be petitioned

116. *FJ*, 3 July 1849.
118. *FJ*, 13 July 1849.
120. *FJ*, 18 July 1849.

117. Reported in *FJ*, 28 July 1849.
119. *FJ*, 17 July 1849.

for clemency for Young Ireland leaders such as Smith O'Brien, Mitchel, Meagher, and Terence Bellew MacManus. Fortunately for the lord mayor there was not a quorum at the meeting.[121] The *Freeman's Journal* argued that it was right for the Corporation to petition the queen concerning the prisoners on the increasingly anachronistically grounds that she was "an integral and independent power in the state."[122]

Several days later, and after a meeting at the Mansion House had backed illuminations, the *Dublin Evening Packet* reported that the lord mayor would issue a *ukase*—a tzarist edict—in favor of illuminations: "[B]y the use of a single word, a true idea [is given] of the edict that it appears our inhabitants will be ordered to obey. . . . We are called on to 'wake' with millions of candles the thousands slain by hunger." The *Freeman's Journal*, however, thought that the lord mayor was "too prudent to utterly defy public opinion so unequivocally expressed." Apparently a deputation in favor of illumination had told him that one thousand men would lose their jobs without a general illumination. "We did not believe the chandlers formed so numerous a body."[123]

By 30 July it seemed as if the vacillating O'Brien was not going to issue an order to illuminate.[124] Only a few days later, however, he did issue a proclamation but one merely "requesting a general illumination of all the houses of the city." "Dublin throws herself not upon her knees before Majesty—but on her face."[125] Meanwhile in Cork the mayor first decided to order an illumination and then, under public pressure, changed his mind.[126]

In Dublin, toward the end of the month, controversialists turned their attention to whether the carpets being bought for the viceregal apartments in which the royal family were to stay were English or Irish. It turned out that, though ordered from Irish shops, they were imported from England.[127]

121. *FJ*, 24 July 1849. The same issues were raised on 1 August (*FJ*, 2 August 1849), but again to no avail.

122. *FJ*, 3 August 1849. This was the basis for O'Connell's hope that she might act as a pro-Irish Whig partisan.

123. *FJ*, 26 July 1849.   124. *FJ*, 30 July 1849.

125. *FJ*, 2 August 1849.   126. *FJ*, 27 July, 2 August 1849.

127. *Dublin Evening Mail*, 27 July 1849, reported in *FJ*, 28 July 1849. In the summer of 1979 opponents of the impending visit to Ireland of Pope John Paul II claimed that expensive carpets had been ordered for his temporary altars.

At the same time as public political controversy over the visit was occupying the press, another important group in nationalist Ireland, the Catholic bishops, was considering what attitude to adopt toward the visit. The royal household, too, regarded the treatment of Catholic bishops during the visit as being a question of key political importance. The queen was keen that it be taken out of her hands, and so Phipps wrote to the home secretary, Sir George Grey:

The question with regard to the reception of the Roman Catholic Bishops, upon a par with those of the Established Church, is one entirely of state policy upon which the Queen would wish to be guided by the advice of Her Ministers.[128]

Two questions occupied the bishops. Should they attend the levee? What sort of an address should they make to her? With Crolly's death, there were only three active Catholic archbishops in Ireland at the time. Michael Slattery of Cashel wanted the bishops to present an address to the queen, detailing the suffering and grievances of the country. John MacHale of Tuam wanted the bishops to meet the queen in person with a similar agenda. If there was to be a formal address it should deal with "the terrible suffering of her subjects, as well as of the cruel neglect with which they have been treated by her ministers . . . [which] has probably been withheld from her."[129] The senior archbishop, the irenic Daniel Murray of Dublin, however, drafted an address of warm welcome.[130] MacHale rejected it and proposed an alternative which Murray said "would be extremely likely to do harm." Murray went on to offer a slightly modified version of the address with a mild reference to the sufferings of the poor.[131] This MacHale also rejected. Murray sent MacHale's letter on to Clarendon, telling him that "Your Excellency will perceive by the accompanying letter what I have to endure from some of my Bretheren."[132] In the end only twelve bishops signed the address.

As the time for the visit approached an even darker mood than normal

128. RA D 19/85, Col. Phipps to Sir George Grey, 13 July 1849.

129. John MacHale to Daniel Murray, 24 July 1849, in Thomas MacHale, *Correspondence between the Most Rev. Dr MacHale, Archbishop of Tuam and the Most Rev. Dr Murray, Archbishop of Dublin, Relative to an Address to Be Presented to Her Majesty Queen Victoria, on the Occasion of Her Visit to Ireland in 1849* (Dublin: M. H. Gill, 1885), 9.

130. Kerr, *"A Nation of Beggars?,"* 203.

131. Daniel Murray to John MacHale, 31 July 1849, in MacHale, *Correspondence,* 17.

132. Daniel Murray to Lord Clarendon, in Kerr, *"A Nation of Beggars?,"* 204.

descended on the *Freeman's Journal*. The London *Morning Post* had said that the Irish would receive the queen "in a frenzy of delight." The principal Irish daily paper took this as a sign that the English thought that the Irish "will insist upon exhibiting themselves in the character in which Paddy is best known to her Majesty—namely, as he appears upon the stage, mean, servile, extravagant and ludicrous. . . . There is no frenzy here." Instead, it advocated "a manly seriousness of deportment."[133] This was the first occasion on which opponents of royal occasions were to advocate that nationalists should adopt a reserved but respectful neutrality to the event in question. It was a policy that never worked. Over the years nationalist leaders were to discover that the only workable and politically effective alternative to cheering was jeering.

The previsit polemic between English and Irish papers touched off one of the periodic wars about Irish character: the Irish being either monsters or children in the English popular imagination, sometimes both. The short-lived Dublin *Press* published a poem on the visit and Irish national character:

> Our Queen, God bless her! Has been told
> That Irishmen are fools of old;
> Expects to find us one and all
> Vain, frivolous, theatrical;
> On ostentatious shows intent,
> Gay, fickle, and improvident;
> Fit stuff for soldiers, very good,
> For drawing water, hewing wood,
> And executing servile labours
> As menials of our English neighbours;
> Matchless as bulls, and merriest grigs,
> Alive at junketing and jigs;
> And better still than all I'm saying,
> The best in Europe at hurrahing
> And tossing up our hats and sticks
> At each new turn of politics.
> And now we think 'twould be unkind
> To disabuse the royal mind.[134]

133. *FJ*, 30 July 1849.
134. *FJ*, 30 July 1849.

The most insightful contribution to the debate came from the London *Morning Post* which was hostile to what it saw as the superficial nature of the visit and held that it would have been better had the trip been presented as "a visit of condolence" for the famine. It went on to draw attention to the English belief in the inherent enthusiasm of the Irish for the Crown and to suggest that this belief was reliant on the English stereotype of the Irish as emotional and childlike. Itself believing the stereotype, it warned its English readers not to rely on Irish enthusiasm for the royal visit on account both of the absence of any real government political agenda to conciliate the Irish and of another aspect of the same stereotype about the Irish: fickleness:

The susceptible nature of the Irish crowd, ever ready for extremes, may too easily give way to this brief excuse for making holiday even in the midst of ruin. . . . The Irish, no doubt, are a susceptible people, and now that contending parties are apparently broken down from combined misery and exhaustion, it may be a time to light the flame of loyalty throughout Ireland. But it will be a flame of straw—it will blaze up, and then expire from want of sustenance to feed upon, and then the darkness which must succeed will be all the more dismal from contrast with the delusive and momentary blaze which has passed away.[135]

"We left our dear Osborne almost immediately after luncheon, with the 4 eldest children," wrote the queen on 1 August.[136] Among the members of the royal household who accompanied the royal family was Fanny Jocelyn. There was potential for controversy in this as Lady Jocelyn was the daughter-in-law of the Orange leader, Lord Roden, on whose estate a massacre of Catholics by Orangemen, who had themselves been attacked by Ribbonmen, had recently taken place.[137]

The royal yacht *Victoria and Albert* sailed toward Cork with four other ships and arrived at Cove on the evening of 2 August, being joined by warships and many other vessels on its approach. Bonfires lit up the coastline.

Next morning, "[t]he day was grey and excessively muggy which is characteristic of the Irish climate."[138] The royal visitors had arrived earlier

135. *FJ,* 30 July 1849.
136. RA QVJ, 1 August 1849.
137. The Ribbonmen were members of a Catholic secret society.
138. RA QVJ, 3 August 1849.

than expected and the mayor of Cork asked Sir George Grey if the visit could be postponed for a day. The request was refused.[139] In spite of being the first destination on the queen's visit, Cork's capacity for feeling slighted did not let it down. The *Cork Examiner* reported that "many think that Cork has been treated with disrespect—assuming that disrespect *could* be shown by a monarch to a portion of that monarch's subjects." The reason for the request for the delay was because the "decorations were only half completed."[140]

The queen received visits on board the yacht from local military and naval officers and from Lords Bandon and Thomond. After lunch she boarded the steam tender *Fairy* and toured the harbor. She then landed at Cove, one of the Royal Navy's most important bases, received an address of welcome, and renamed the town "Queenstown," after the fashion of George IV's renaming of Dunleary in 1821. At 3:00 p.m. the queen and Prince Albert boarded the tender and journeyed up the River Lee toward Cork. Nearing the city they stopped "to receive a salmon and a very pretty Address from the poor Fishermen of Blackrock."[141] Arriving in Cork City at the Custom House the queen received city and county addresses—the former mentioning the distress of the country and hope for future good government[142]—and knighted the mayor, William Lyons, on board. Then the royal couple got into carriages, supplied by the county lord lieutenant, Lord Bandon, and, escorted by the 12th Lancers, drove round the principal streets of the city. The streets were decorated with flowers and triumphal arches. The queen noted that:

The heat and dust were great. We passed by the new [Queen's] College, in process of building. . . . Our reception was most enthusiastic. . . . Cork is not like an English town and has rather a foreign look about it. The crowds were very noisy and excitable but very good humoured.

This was another world to the queen. The men looked ragged and wore blue coats, short breeches, and blue stockings. The women wore long blue cloaks but no bonnets:

The beauty of the women is very remarkable and struck us very much, such beautiful dark eyes and hair, such fine teeth, nearly every 3rd woman was pretty, some

139. *FJ*, 6 August 1849.

140. Reported in *FJ*, 6 August 1849. In 1979 there was dismay in Cork when Pope John Paul II did not visit the city during the course of his trip to Ireland.

141. RA QVJ, 3 August 1849.   142. *FJ*, 6 August 1849.

remarkably so, also among the higher classes, there were pretty women to be seen.[143]

The *Freeman's Journal* claimed that though "[t]he crowds rushed through the city to-day with eagerness so as to obtain the best view of the processions," most of the real enthusiasm came from "the well-dressed occupiers of the windows, who certainly did cheer, waive hats and flutter handkerchiefs."[144]

On 4 August the royal yacht left Cove at 10:00 a.m., reaching Waterford harbor at 3:40 p.m. "We passed a little Fort called Duncannon from which no salute had been fired for 50 years and from which James IInd embarked, after the Battle of the Boyne."[145] They anchored for the night at Passage East. Prince Albert boarded the *Fairy* with his two sons and took it further up toward Waterford itself but returned at 7:00 p.m. without having landed. The queen remained on the *Victoria and Albert* sketching and receiving local dignitaries in the evening.

At 8:00 a.m. on Sunday, 5 August, the royal yacht set out once more, encountering rough seas until after Wexford. At 6:30 p.m. Dublin Bay came into sight and then Kingstown "covered with thousands and thousands of spectators, cheering most enthusiastically. . . . [T]he enthusiasm and excitement shown by the Irish people was extreme."[146] By the time that the royal yacht and the ten ships accompanying it had reached Kingstown, however, the lord mayor, who had been waiting there all day, had returned to Dublin by train. The royal family appeared on deck. To the correspondent of the *Freeman's Journal* who thought the crowd merely respectful, the queen "seemed . . . to be a comely, yet serious looking lady, somewhat full in person, and her features somewhat flushed and slightly embrowned by exposure to the sea air and summer's sun."

The next day the *Freeman's Journal* kept up its opposition to the visit:

In the emphatic language of the *Times* "Her heralds have been plague, pestilence and famine—the hunger which slays by hundreds and the disease which kills by

143. RA QVJ, 3 August 1849.

144. *FJ,* 6 August 1849.

145. RA QVJ, 4 August 1849.

146. RA QVJ, 5 August 1849. The next day she wrote to King Leopold about their arrival: "[W]e came in with ten steamers and the whole harbour, wharf and every place was *covered* with *thousands* and thousands of people who received us with great enthusiasm." Queen Victoria to King Leopold of the Belgians, 6 August 1849, in Benson and Esher, *Letters,* first series, 2:267.

tens of thousands" and though she comes not to stay the havoc made by "her heralds," not even, as we have been officially informed by her Viceroy, in his special
organ [the *Dublin Evening Post*], to inquire into the suffering, or *listen* to the complaints of her people, she will enter our city with royal pomp and pageantry, amid
the flattery of retainers, and the slavish adulation of expectants, and, we will add,
amid the respect of all.[147]

The opposition of the London *Times* and of Tories in general to the
visit gave nationalist opponents unexpected allies. The *Times* had said that a
lavish welcome for the queen in Dublin would be "an Insult to the sufferings of the living and the sepulchres of the dead."[148]

The morning of Monday, 6 August, began with the queen's thoughts
turning toward her son, Alfred, whose birthday it was. But this was the day
on which the success or otherwise of the visit was really to turn. *Punch* had
given its own prediction for the events of the day. "The Queen will . . .
proceed to the Lodge, where she will be met at the door by the Countess
of Clarendon with a dish of buttermilk and potatoes. Upon this the
Queen will lunch, and, afterward in a thimble, full of regal punch, drink [a
toast to the] Prosperity of Ireland."[149]

The day began with the queen being visited on the royal yacht by dignitaries who included Lord and Lady Clarendon and her cousin, Prince
George of Cambridge. At 10:00 a.m. the royal party went ashore. The
queen was impressed that "[a]n immense multitude was assembled who
cheered most enthusiastically."[150] The *Freeman's Journal* correspondent
thought the queen showed "impatient irritability."[151] The royal party took
the train to Sandymount Avenue, near Dublin. "Here we found our carriages, the postillions wearing their Ascot liveries."[152] The procession
through Dublin was for the queen "a never to be forgotten scene, particularly when one reflects on what state the country was in quite lately, in
open revolt and under martial law."[153]

The procession in open carriages moved from the south through Mer-
rion Square to College Green and then up Sackville (later O'Connell)
Street to the North Circular Road and thence to the Phoenix Park and the
Vice Regal Lodge. A special grand arch had been erected at the Baggot
Street Bridge, at which a ceremonial of entry into the city was enacted. An

147. *FJ*, 6 August 1849.
148. *FJ*, 6 August 1849.
149. Weintraub, *Albert*, 221.
150. RA QVJ, 6 August 1849.
151. *FJ*, 7 August 1849.
152. RA QVJ, 6 August 1849.
153. RA QVJ, 6 August 1849.

equerry demanded entry for the queen and the gates were duly opened by the city marshal. The lord mayor presented the queen with the keys of the city "with some appropriate words, spoken in an amazing brogue," noted the queen.[154] The scene was later caricatured in a hostile poem as follows:

> We saw a man 'neath the pond'rous frieze
> That toppled o'er the hatchway—
> We saw him fall on his bended knees
> As he handed up some rusty keys—
> She only took the latch-key.[155]

At the last triumphal arch on the route a dove, with an olive branch tied around its neck, was "let down into my lap."[156] The queen decided to keep the bird and had it put into a cage.

At midday the royal party reached the Vice Regal Lodge, "a nice comfortable house, reminding us of Claremont."[157] After lunch, with Prince Albert accompanying her on horseback, the queen drove in a carriage to see the Botanical Gardens in Glasnevin through streets "where there are wretched cottages, wretchedly ragged, dirty people and children, the latter very handsome." In the evening an inaugural dinner was held in the new dining room at the Lodge, which had been built by Lord Bessborough and never before used. The queen noted that the Irish lord lieutenant had a very large household which included twelve aides de camp, a chamberlain, an usher, a master of the horse, an under secretary, and a private secretary.

One aspect of the first day of the visit that the queen did not witness was the illumination of the city. This far surpassed expectations. It took the form not only of candles in windows but of colored transparencies lit from behind and of gas fittings shaped into royal motifs such as "V & A" and a crown. Some of the transparencies glorified an imperial theme. At the offices of W. Waterhouse on Dame Street the transparency showed a European officer, a Native American, an African, and a Chinese mandarin emptying cornucopias before the queen. Inscribed about was "The sun never sets on her dominions" and beneath "On the waters of the sea, in all parts of the earth, amongst every people and nation has she not posses-

154. RA QVJ, 6 August 1849.   155. *FJ*, 25 September 1849.
156. RA QVJ, 6 August 1849.

157. RA QVJ, 6 August 1849. Claremont was an English royal residence, once the home of King Leopold of the Belgians in his capacity as widower of Princess Charlotte. Louis Philippe and his family were currently living there.

sions."[158] On the other hand, the illuminated monogram "APW" for Albert Prince of Wales at the Bank of Ireland was popularly interpreted as supporting the repeal message, "A Parliament Wanted."[159]

The *Freeman's Journal* tried to minimize the strength of the enthusiasm for the queen's arrival. Only two hundred horsemen had accompanied the royal procession. Some of the stands along the royal route had been only one quarter full. In spite of all of this it was still the awkward fact that the welcome that the queen had received was much greater than the paper had hoped for and expected. The people were obviously confused and suffering from "mingled and conflicting feelings." In rather oblique language it admitted that the queen had been well received. This was due to "loyal feelings" toward the sovereign, "chivalrous feelings" toward Victoria as a woman, "personal affection" for Victoria who was both personally virtuous and a good constitutional monarch, and, finally, hopes that the queen would often come again. Nonetheless, it argued that the reception given by the people of Dublin was a humiliation for the Irish people and a victory for the backers of the royal visit.[160]

On Tuesday, 7 August, the queen drove into Dublin, where "I never saw more *real* enthusiasm."[161] She visited the Bank of Ireland, once the parliament house of the kingdom of Ireland. In the former chamber of the lords she met judges and in the former chamber of the commons she met members of the Irish nobility. At the Marlborough Street national schools she met the Established Church clergy and the Catholic archbishop of Dublin; the latter she found to be "a fine, remarkable-looking old man of 80."[162]

At Trinity College she and Prince Albert did not sign Ireland's premier ancient Celtic manuscript, the Book of Kells, as was later claimed. Instead they signed their names on a blank sheet of vellum that was then bound in with the manuscript.[163] On her arrival in the college there was a minor Orange demonstration from some of the students. It took the form of three rounds of Kentish fire, a form of applause associated with opposition to emancipation.

In the later afternoon the queen visited the Royal Hospital at Kilmainham, an institution for retired soldiers that predated the Chelsea Hospital

158. *FJ*, 7 August 1849.   159. *FJ*, 9 August 1849.
160. *FJ*, 7 August 1849.   161. RA QVJ, 7 August 1849.
162. RA QVJ, 7 August 1849.   163. Woodham-Smith, *Great Hunger*, 398.

in London. After that she drove round the principal streets of the city again. On her way back to the Phoenix Park a man called James Nugent, a poor law guardian from the North Union, approached her carriage and called out, "Mighty Monarch, Pardon Smith O'Brien." "Lord Clarendon rode up and put him aside."[164] That evening there was a dinner for twenty and a ball for three hundred at the Lodge. "I danced 3 Quadrilles and several Valses," wrote the queen.[165]

Much of the admiration for the queen was because she drove around in an open carriage unaccompanied by an escort. She left herself vulnerable to attack and it was taken as a sign that she was "confiding towards her people." It caused a *volte face* in the editorial attitude of the *Freeman's Journal.* "The more the citizens of Dublin see of Queen Victoria the more she wins their affection and the warmer becomes their feelings towards her." The paper went out in a rather embarrassed fashion to try to accuse the government of deceiving the queen into thinking she would not receive a warm welcome in Ireland.

None knew better than the Irish executive the fact that while Irishmen were most ardent in their pursuit of national rights they never harboured, much less entertained, an idea of placing themselves without the pale of her sceptre, or never devised to change the form of their constitution, but only to bring themselves more effectively within its operation.[166]

In fact there may well have been a plot against the queen during her visit. Many years later Charles Gavan Duffy wrote that during the visit he was told by a Dublin priest that there was a plan to kidnap the queen and hold her hostage in the Dublin mountains against the release of the "state prisoners." Accordingly, on one of the nights of the visit, two hundred members of the Confederate Clubs gathered at the Grand Canal, armed with pistols and daggers, but dispersed without undertaking any action.[167]

The next day, 8 August, was a day for formal ceremonial. Prince Albert, dressed in the uniform of a field marshal, one of the few honors the queen had been allowed by Parliament to confer on him, conducted a military review in the "fifteen acres" at the Phoenix Park. At 1:30 p.m. the queen left the Lodge and, escorted by two troops of the 7th Hussars, drove along the quays to Dublin Castle where she held a levee. Two thousand gentlemen were presented to her, among them eighty peers, three hundred officers,

164. *FJ*, 8 August 1849.
166. *FJ*, 8 August 1849.
165. RA QVJ, 7 August 1849.
167. Duffy, *Four Years*, 762.

and three hundred clergymen. This ceremony took three hours and was preceded by an hour of receiving loyal addresses from over forty civil, educational, and religious bodies.[168] The queen was well pleased with the occasion. She appeared in state with twenty-six pages carrying her train:

Everything was done in St James's style. The staircase and Throne Room are handsome and quite *like a Palace.* I sat myself on the throne, the seat of which was so high that I had great difficulty in sitting on it. . . . It [the levee] was hard work and the people were very awkward and some ridiculous, but what was more was the squeeze and the heat in the next room, which was such that the people were in a dreadful state of perspiration, not quite pleasant for my hand.[169]

But she found the whole event so exhilarating that by the time she arrived back at the Vice Regal Lodge at 7:00 p.m. "I really felt hardly at all tired."[170] An hour later she held a dinner for twenty that included prominent Catholics such as Chief Baron David Pigott and Lord Bellew. Several Catholic bishops attended. "Old Archbishop Murray has a fine head and he and his Bishops were in their full dress, the stockings and sash being violet and they wore gold crosses round their necks and a fine ring on their finger."[171] After dinner there was a concert of German music for another three hundred people. The queen was full of admiration for Clarendon. "He is an admirable Lord Lieutenant—quite 'un grand Seigneur' and all his young gentlemen are so active and have such good manners."[172]

On 9 August Prince Albert visited a variety of scholarly and educational establishments from the Royal Irish Academy to the Royal Agricultural Improvement Society of Ireland. The queen and prince attended a military review of over six thousand soldiers in the Phoenix Park, "the finest we have ever seen."[173] There was an infantry charge and then a cavalry charge. The soldiers "charged bayonets and rushed on at double quick time to the music of that terrible war cry, half British cheer and half Irish hurrah once so dreadful to the French legions, onward they rushed, and halted some twenty yards from the royal carriage."[174] The crowd cheered the queen and prince and their family—"most touching and beautiful"[175]—but, when

168. The *Times* mixed up the queen's reply to the Established and Catholic Churches and had her refer to the Catholic Church as "our church." RA D 20/10, Col. Phipps to Prince Albert, 11 August 1849.

169. RA QVJ, 8 August 1849.　　　　　170. RA QVJ, 8 August 1849.
171. RA QVJ, 8 August 1849.　　　　　172. RA QVJ, 8 August 1849.
173. RA QVJ, 9 August 1849.　　　　　174. *FJ,* 10 August 1849.
175. RA QVJ, 9 August 1849.

there was a call for a cheer for Lord Clarendon, the *Freeman's Journal* was not slow to record that "a shout of derisive laughter, the bitterest, the most scornful ever issuing from the outraged feelings of the people was the response."[176] It illustrated the paper's contention that "[t]he Irish people have ever drawn and now continue to draw a broad line between the Sovereign and the Minister."[177]

In the evening the queen returned to Dublin Castle for a drawing room at which sixteen hundred ladies were presented to her. Returning to the Lodge after midnight she saw the city's illuminations for herself and thought Dublin looked like Paris.[178] John Gray's *Freeman's Journal*, which, in the absence of any other significant political leadership, was acting as the voice of nationalist Ireland, was in agreement. "Dublin has been during the week like a city risen from the dead."[179]

The last day of the visit to the capital was 10 August. Accompanied by the 8th Hussars and 7th Lancers the queen drove down the Liffey Valley to the duke of Leinster's seat at Carton, near Maynooth. On the way she caught sight of some of the student priests of Maynooth "who I must say did not make a very attractive impression."[180] The Carton demesne had been thrown open for the day and many people traveled down from Dublin on special trains. She witnessed "a dance by some of the peasantry"[181] accompanied by two pipers. The Celtic note to the proceedings prompted the queen into private, unfavorable comparisons with her increasingly beloved Scotland. "There were 3 old ragged Pipers playing, but the Irish Pipers are inferior to the Scotch."[182]

The queen also visited the shell house that had been created in the previous century by Emily, duchess of Leinster, and traveled back to the main house for departure, not on the river by boat as planned, but on a Irish jaunting car, which the duke later had sent to England and presented to her. This incident gave rise to one of the more subtle of nationalist vengeances against the queen, a lyric in which Queen Victoria's speech is transposed into that of a stage Irishwoman:

"Be me sowl" says she, "I like the joultin' of yer Irish jauntin' car."[183]

---

176. *FJ*, 10 August 1849.   177. *FJ*, 9 August 1849.
178. RA QVJ, 9 August 1849.   179. *FJ*, 10 August 1849.
180. RA QVJ, 10 August 1849.   181. *FJ*, 11 August 1849.
182. RA QVJ, 10 August 1849.
183. Quoted in Woodham-Smith, *Great Hunger*, 403.

By 5:00 p.m. Queen Victoria was back at the Lodge. By 6:00 p.m. she was leaving for Kingstown. There the correspondent of the *Freeman's Journal* proved himself one of the few who had not been won over by the visit. He noted significantly that no member of the remaining political leadership of nationalist Ireland was present. "Not one could we observe of those whose names have been associated with the many moving appeals made to the justice of the British ministry on behalf of the suffering thousands in the west and south of Ireland." Had they been there, they "would at once see how little her Majesty knew of the barbarities committed in the name of the laws administered in her name."[184]

At Kingstown the queen heard people call, "Come every year."[185] As the royal yacht steamed out of the harbor she was seen to run "along the deck with the sprightliness of a young girl" to join Prince Albert high up on the paddle box. She then ordered the royal standard to be lowered three times and the paddle to be stopped so that the vessel glided out of Kingstown harbor under its own momentum, the queen continuing to wave at the people for a mile beyond the harbor:

We stood on the paddle box, as we slowly and majestically steamed out of Kingstown amidst the cheers of thousands and thousands and salutes, I waving my handkerchief as a parting acknowledgement of the loyalty shown me.[186]

The English radical MP John Bright, who saw what happened, was overcome with emotion. Clarendon told Sir George Grey that "there is not an individual in Dublin who does not take" the queen's behavior on her departure "as a personal compliment."[187]

The royal yacht steamed toward Belfast for a five-hour stay on 11 August which took in knighting the mayor and visits to the Linen Hall, Botanic Gardens, and new Queen's College. After Dublin it was a slight disappointment to the queen. Though she was attended by Lords Londonderry, Donegal, Enniskillen, Erne, and Fortescue, she thought the arrangements "were not so well managed as in Dublin":

The reception was hearty, though, I thought not quite as enthusiastic as in Dublin, I mean not quite so typically Irish. The people are a mixture of nations

---

184. *FJ*, 11 August 1849.   185. RA QVJ, 10 August 1849.
186. RA QVJ, 10 August 1849.
187. RA D 20/17, Lord Clarendon to Sir George Grey, 14 August 1849, in Benson and Esher, *Letters*, first series, 2:268–69.

and the Irish shriek was no longer to be heard and the female beauty had disappeared.[188]

The yacht stayed at anchor overnight and next day set sail for Scotland.
The visit to Ireland ended with a flourish. A baronetcy was conferred on
the lord mayor of Dublin and the title of earl of Dublin, once held by the
queen's father, the duke of Kent, was conferred on the Prince of Wales.[189]
This was at Clarendon's suggestion.[190]

Russell wrote to the queen to congratulate her "on the triumphant
manner in which your Majesty has been received in Ireland."[191] Charles
Greville soon had a firsthand report from Lord Lansdowne:

He said nothing could surpass the success of the Queen's visit in every respect . . .
much owing to the tact of Lord Clarendon and the care he had bestowed on all
the arrangements and details. . . . The Queen herself was delighted, and appears
to have played her part uncommonly well. Clarendon of course was overjoyed at
the complete success of what was his own plan. . . . In the beginning and while
the details were in preparation, he was considerably disgusted at the petty difficulties that were made, but he is satisfied now. Lord Lansdowne said the departure
was quite affecting; and he thinks beyond doubt that this visit will produce permanent effects in Ireland.[192]

Clarendon was indeed triumphant about the visit to Dublin. To Sir
George Grey he felt vindicated. "A vast many kind friends both here and in
England . . . [had been] denouncing the 'premature and hazardous experiment' and declaring that I alone was responsible for whatever mischief
happened. . . . I never doubted that the reception would be excellent; but I
did not expect the enthusiasm would have gone to the pitch it did, or that
the thermometer would have kept continually rising to the hour of her departure."[193] Privately to his brother-in-law, George Cornwall Lewis, he expressed relief: "When one considers how many things might have gone
wrong in bringing her and this excitable nation into contact for the first
time, it is a pleasure to reflect all went as if by clockwork as one could
most desire."[194]

188. RA QVJ, 11 August 1849.   189. RA QVJ, 12 August 1849.

190. RA D 19/93, Queen Victoria to Lord John Russell, 19 July 1849.

191. RA D 20/6, Lord John Russell to Queen Victoria, 11 August 1849.

192. Reeve, *Greville, Part 2*, 3:295.

193. Lord Clarendon to Sir George Grey, 15 August 1849, in Maxwell, *Clarendon*, 1:303.

194. Lord Clarendon to G. C. Lewis, 27 August 1849, in Maxwell, *Clarendon*, 1:304.

In the immediate aftermath of the visit Clarendon noted remarkable changes in public attitude. "Even the ex-[Confederate] Clubbists, who threatened broken heads and windows before the Queen came, are now among the most loyal of her subjects, and are ready, according to the police reports, to fight any one who dared say a disrespectful word of Her Majesty."[195] "The enthusiasm for her in Mayo was as great as here."[196]

"The presence of the Sovereign cannot of course produce social reformation . . . but it will produce more real good here than in any part of her Majesty's dominions."[197] "The Agitators and Ex-Clubbists will renew their Vocation and Mr [Charles Gavan] Duffy, the worst and most able of them all, will republish his paper,"[198] but they would not now be the force they were before. Furthermore, the good opinion of Ireland that the visit had created in England would, Clarendon hoped, act as a constraint against further Irish dissent. "The people are so delighted at finding they are loyal, and so proud of the good opinion of the Queen . . . that they feel they have a character to lose, and this may be a guarantee for future good behaviour."[199] Thus from round the country Clarendon had reports that ordinary people were saying with pride that "[s]he'd know now what sort of a lad Paddy was."[200]

In England the success of the visit was seen as a function of the role of the monarchy to help foster unity within the United Kingdom by overcoming divisions based on class or national identity. This was the theme of the public letter from Sir George Grey to Lord Clarendon which expressed the queen's views on the visit. She hoped that among all her subjects in Ireland there would be "that union of heart and affection which is essential to the prosperity of their common country."[201] For one English radical, on the contrary, what had happened was "the latest move . . . to pacify the naked Celt with a royal visit."[202]

For the London *Times* the bonding between the queen and her Irish sub-

195. RA D 20/17, Lord Clarendon to Sir George Grey, 14 August 1849, in Benson and Esher, *Letters*, first series, 2:268–69.

196. RA D 20/35, Lord Clarendon to Lord John Russell, 27 August 1849.

197. Lord Clarendon to Sir George Grey, 17 August 1849, in Maxwell, *Clarendon*, 1:303.

198. RA D 20/35, Lord Clarendon to Lord John Russell, 27 August 1849.

199. Lord Clarendon to C. G. Lewis, 27 August 1849, in Maxwell, *Clarendon*, 1:304.

200. RA D 20/20, Thomas Reddington to Lord Clarendon, 16 August 1849.

201. *FJ,* 17 August 1849.

202. Samuel Kydd, *Democratic Review*, September 1849, 137–39, quoted in Richard Williams, *The Contentious Crown: Public Discussion of the British Monarchy in the Reign of Queen Victoria* (Brookfield, Vt.: Ashgate, 1997), 56.

jects "will be the outward type of the unity which should in fact; as it does in theory, connect the two peoples on either side of the channel [the Irish Sea]."[203] And of course the welcome for the queen could also be used as a weapon to contradict the claimed mandate of Irish nationalist leaders. "But it is most strange, now we know what the real feeling of Irishness is, to reflect that for so many years they permitted a knot of professional demagogues to misrepresent their views and feelings without any kind of remonstrance or protest."[204]

The exiled John Mitchel addressed the same issue in his journal. "Plenty of blazing, vociferous excitement called 'loyalty' . . . [consisting] in a willingness to come out into the street and see a pageant pass . . . so her Gracious Majesty has come and enthroned herself in the hearts of her Irish subjects; and the newspapers are to say (at their peril) that a brighter day is just going to dawn for Ireland."[205]

Indeed, the *Freeman's Journal* itself briefly indulged in such sentiments. It looked to the queen's "personal influence" and hoped that she might be "the source from which many future enjoyments are destined to flow upon Ireland."[206] But it was only a brief reverie. By the beginning of November Prince Albert was complaining that the state of Ireland was "by no means satisfactory," with the Dolly's Brae controversy, on the one hand, and O'Connell's son reviving repeal agitation and Duffy restarting the *Nation*, on the other.[207]

As for John Gray's *Freeman's Journal*, it was soon defending Catholic bishops against the *Dublin Evening Mail*, which had called those bishops who had not attended the levee "rebels," and against the *Dublin University Magazine*, which took those bishops to task who had not signed the loyal address. For the *Freeman's Journal*, the bishops had been too busy in famine relief work, "saving the lives of her Majesty's subjects."[208] It then moved on to the attack. If the queen indeed wanted to promote union among her Irish subjects, she should abolish "every vestige of that ascendancy, laying prostrate every symbol of conquest and establishing as between all her Irish subjects *perfect equality*."[209] This was a call for the disestablishment of the

203. *Times*, 3 August 1849.
204. *Times*, 15 August 1849.
205. Mitchel, *Journal*, 26 October 1849, p. 202.
206. *FJ*, 17 August 1849.
207. RA D 20/59, Prince Albert, memorandum, 3 November 1849.
208. *FJ*, 18 August, 10 September 1849.
209. *FJ*, 10 September 1849.

Protestant Episcopal Church of Ireland. Within just over a year, however, the religious situation was to be even further soured by the "papal aggression" controversy.

❖

In 1850 the pope set up a system of Catholic territorial bishoprics in England. The move provoked one of the last great outbreaks of anti-Catholic paranoia in England. Russell's government passed the 1851 Ecclesiastical Titles Act which prohibited Catholic bishops from using territorial titles in the United Kingdom. It proved to be an ineffective piece of legislation, but the whole controversy worried the queen who thought it unnecessarily insulting to Catholics.[210]

There was great annoyance about the measure in Ireland. "1851 will be memorable in future history for the violence and wrong offered to a vast section of the Queen's subjects without any cause save that of giving full and free development to the theory of religious liberty, for which the constitution had provided and which had been grossly violated."[211]

In Ireland the Catholic hierarchy had continued in a mostly unbroken continuity of succession thorough the Reformation. Catholic and Established Church bishops used the same territorial designations, though even before the Ecclesiastical Titles Act the state did not legally recognize the use of them by Catholic bishops. The Irish Catholic bishops petitioned the queen to oppose the legislation and to think of "those principles of civil and religious liberty which your Majesty has vouchsafed to proclaim from the throne—principles which descended to your Majesty as a precious inheritance from your illustrious father."[212] The new act seemed about to force a matter of much more than protocol to a head that would openly involve the queen in her dealings with the religious leaders of the majority of Irish people.

"What is to be done with Dr [Paul] Cullen who has assumed the title of Archbishop of Armagh, Primate of all Ireland, which is punishable under the Emancipation Act?" enquired the queen of Russell at the end of 1850.[213] Russell consulted Clarendon. The latter had been warned, if he

210. Elizabeth Longford, *Victoria R.I.* (London: Pan, 1966), 254.

211. *FJ*, 2 January 1852.

212. *FJ*, 8 March 1851.

213. Queen Victoria to Lord John Russell, 14 December 1850, in Benson and Esher, *Letters*, first series, 2:336–37. The use of territorial titles by Catholic bishops was already illegal under the 1829 "Catholic Emancipation" Act.

needed warning, by the chief secretary, Sir William Sommerville, that prosecutions of Irish bishops for using territorial titles would prove politically disastrous.[214] So Clarendon replied to Russell that there was no need to stir up the issue in Ireland for, he claimed, Irish Catholic bishops rarely in practice used their territorial titles.

The issue eventually began to settle down, though Queen Victoria continued to be exasperated by the ambiguities that attended it. In April 1852 she wrote to Lord Derby, who was then prime minister of a short-lived, minority Protectionist Tory government, "Can no means by devised of laying down a permanent regulation after a full and fair investigation of the subject? The Queen could hardly call a Bishop 'Lord' one day and 'Rev. sir' the next according to the changes in her Gov[t]; and the L[or]d Lieutenant as her representative sh[d] not establish a usage which she could not follow."[215]

The major issue that dominated the later years of the Russell-Clarendon administration, however, was that of the abolition of the lord lieutenancy. Joseph Hume, the scourge of Orangeism, had been a longtime opponent of the office. He campaigned against it in 1830 and raised the issue again in the Commons in 1844. The lord lieutenancy was "a considerable cause of the existing agitation in Ireland" and its existence meant that "the Union had never in fact been completed." He was opposed by Peel, however, and withdrew his motion.[216] The *Freeman's Journal* was also adamantly opposed to abolition, as were most nationalists. The move toward abolition was a plot by those who held "that if the [viceregal] court be perpetuated the people of Ireland will thereby fancy that they are a nation!" The *Dublin Evening Mail* supported abolition on the grounds that the queen might herself visit Ireland occasionally instead. But for the *Freeman's Journal* "one viceregal residence in the hand is worth that of twenty monarchs in the bush."[217]

The plan for abolition of the lord lieutenancy began to take hold in government circles during Russell's government. As Lord Bessborough lay

214. RA D 21/52, Sir William Somerville to Lord Clarendon, 29 August 1851.

215. RA D 21/69, Queen Victoria to Lord Derby, 10 April 1852.

216. 9 May 1844, *Parliamentary Debates*, 3rd Series, vol. 74 (15 April–24 May 1844), cols. 834–61.

217. *FJ*, 22 May 1844.

dying in May 1847, Russell told Lansdowne that "[t]he office of Lord Lieutenant of Ireland has been one of separation, rather than union, between the two countries . . . [it] tends to separation, cabal, provincial jealousies, and diversity of administration . . . [and to] conceal from the Government the real aspect of Irish affairs." However, now was not a good time for its elimination, for a general election was looming.[218] Clarendon was therefore appointed to succeed Bessborough.

The idea continued to circulate among ministers and gained the support of Prince Albert. "The L[or]d Lieut[enant]'s Court is a mock court, he himself generally unacquainted with [the] country and in the hands of what are called the Castle advisers and dominated by one of the parties in the land." Clarendon was to be appointed as lord lieutenant because the current crises required "the presence of a determined Governor." In time Clarendon would become secretary of state for Ireland, with two under secretaries, one in London and one in Ireland.[219]

Several months later Albert wrote rather hopefully that abolition "should in the mind of the Irish not be considered as a degradation but as an elevation, not as a sinking to the level of a mere province but as an admission of equality with England and Scotland. Nothing will tend more to accomplish this end than a visit from the Sovereign in person after the departure of her representative and the providing of the means for the occasional Residence of the Sovereign in Ireland for the future." Dublin Castle and the Phoenix Park residence should be kept up and hereditary high offices created for the Irish aristocracy.[220] Given the growing famine and political crises in Ireland, however, the issue was put off indefinitely.[221]

It was the waning of the famine and of political agitation and the success of the queen's visit in 1849 that brought the issue back to the fore in

218. Lord Russell to Lord Lansdowne, 4 May 1847, in Walpole, *Russell,* 1:452.

219. RA D 16/69, Prince Albert, memorandum, 17 May 1847.

220. RA D 16/86, Prince Albert, memorandum, 26 September 1847. Clarendon thought that difficulties would arise over the maintenance of the Castle and Lodge and that the creation of Irish hereditary offices would cause jealousies (see RA D 16/90, Lord Clarendon to Lord John Russell, 10 October 1847).

221. RA D 16/88, Lord John Russell to Queen Victoria, 14 October 1847: "Lord John Russell thinks that in the present state of affairs the abolition of the Lord Lieutenancy must not be thought of." RA D 16/89, Queen Victoria to Lord John Russell, 14 October 1847: "The Queen must agree with L[or]d John Russell and L[or]d Clarendon that the present moment is not a favourable one for the experiment of abolishing the L[or]d Lieutenancy."

the government's mind as one among a number of measures that would tend to bring about a utilitarian reform in Ireland.[222] The matter was privately agreed in government very early in 1850, to the extent of determining the exact moment at which the office should be abolished. Lady Clarendon wrote in her journal that "George has remonstrated against the Viceroyalty ending in April 1851, as Lord John had proposed, on the ground of its being such an increase of expense to him to have all the Castle season. Lord John fully acquiesces in this and says he is quite as well pleased it should end on 1ˢᵗ January 1851, but he fancied George would like a leave-taking—rather an odd idea for George."[223]

Clarendon discussed the matter with Prince Albert in late February. Albert agreed that after the reform it would be "expedient that the Queen should then visit Ireland oftener and for a longer period at a time."[224] Clarendon warned him, however, that it would be an expensive new undertaking for the queen. In spite of his annual salary of £20,000 he expected to be £6,000 out of pocket by the time he left Ireland.

Public rumors about the move only began to circulate in early March.[225] Russell confirmed the plan on 16 March in a reply in the Commons to John Reynolds, who was then lord mayor of Dublin.[226] Opposition began to gather in Ireland. An early petition against the move offered four reasons against it. The first was that the lord lieutenancy was "a local governmental institution" that had existed for hundreds of years. The other reasons were that it would remove Dublin's metropolitan character, increase landlord absenteeism, and remove a vital source of income for the economy of Dublin.[227]

The *Freeman's Journal* cleverly pointed out that many of the Whigs' arguments against the lord lieutenancy—that it was a superfluous ceremonial office in a utilitarian age, a "sham seat of authority" when "all the power

222. Walpole, *Russell*, 2:86. RA D 21/14, Lord Clarendon to Lord John Russell, 4 May 1850: "Now, however, when tranquillity, such as has not been known for many years, prevails; when political agitation has ceased, and its evil consequences appear to be generally recognised, and the Queen for the first time in her reign has had the gratification of visiting this part of Her Dominions the period has arrived for doing away with the different system of govᵗ here."

223. Lady Clarendon's Journal, 13 January 1850, quoted in Maxwell, *Clarendon*, 1:305.

224. RA D 21/5, Prince Albert, memorandum, 21 February 1851.

225. *FJ*, 8, 12 March 1850.   226. *FJ*, 18 March 1850.

227. *FJ*, 25 March 1850.

[is] virtually exercised by the [prime] minister"—would equally apply to the monarchy itself. "We like the pageant; we have a natural affection for the royal office; it is a satisfaction to us to have a visible head of the executive before our eyes, and we can forget the individual in the institution."[228]

On 28 March the Dublin Corporation voted to oppose abolition and to petition Clarendon, the queen, and Irish MPs about the matter. "The Queen should be honestly told that the Irish people now regard her as a protectress" against the Whigs.[229] Abolition would open the way for the destruction of other Irish institutions and the ending of the entire Irish legal system. "I laugh to scorn Lord Clarendon's declaration that the work of spoilation is to stop with the abolition of the Viceroyalty," wrote John O'Connell.[230]

Abolition of the lord lieutenancy was becoming a nationalist issue, in a way that would appear surprising to subsequent generations of nationalists. The lord lieutenancy was being suddenly cherished as a native, even an independent, institution. The *Freeman's Journal* pushed the argument as far as it could possibly go:

The office is an Irish institution and . . . its demolition would be the destruction of a leading landmark of Irish nationhood. . . . [N]o people in Europe can claim their throne . . . with greater justice than the Irish can claim the Viceroyalty of Ireland as an Irish institution. It is older than the dynasty of Great Britain. It survived untouched the revolution which broke England's ancient throne and resulted in the establishment of a new one.[231]

The Union took from Ireland the power to make its laws. The abolition of the Viceroyalty takes from Ireland the power to execute its laws.[232]

The paper warned its readers not to let hatred of Clarendon deflect them from support for the office he occupied. If he wanted "to appear before her Majesty to beg for promotion" he ought not to be allowed to carry the lord lieutenancy with him as a trophy "to the foot of the throne." Rather, he ought to bring with him sketches of his true legacy in Ireland, "the unconsecrated graves into which, owing to his neglect, our famine-stricken people were thrown by the hundred like dogs without shroud or funeral."[233]

Initial Irish opposition culminated in a great public meeting at the Ro-

228. *FJ*, 27 March 1850.   229. *FJ*, 29 March 1850.
230. *FJ*, 2 April 1850.   231. *FJ*, 3 April 1850.
232. *FJ*, 4 April 1850.   233. *FJ*, 4 April 1850.

tundo in Dublin on 8 April.[234] Clarendon, however, remained passionately committed to the change as a measure likely to produce an improvement not only in Irish government but in Irish society. "I am sure that a Vice Roy—a man fixed at *the Castle,* who can be appealed to for every thing, asked for every thing and blamed for every thing, creates and encourages the habit of relying too much upon the Gov[t] and that when he is gone, People will be more ready to think and act for themselves."[235]

As the moment for introducing the abolition bill into Parliament was approaching, matters of detail began to cause difficulties in both royal and governmental circles. One such concerned the Buck hounds and their master, who were maintained at the expense of the civil list, the money designated by Parliament for the use of the monarch. Russell wanted them abolished and the money saved turned into a charity fund to be administered in Ireland after abolition by an officer to be called the lord high constable.[236] Prince Albert was against the move. The civil list had been fixed to provide for particular purposes even "useless" offices like the one under consideration. It would be dangerous in principle effectively to transfer civil list money to a public, political office. It would lead to other offices under the Crown coming under parliamentary scrutiny.[237]

On 17 May Russell introduced the bill to replace the lord lieutenant with a secretary of state for Ireland. Curiously, he first addressed possible objections from members of the aristocracy and gentry who attended formal functions at Dublin Castle. He saw no need "while the Queen herself is but twelve hours' distant, why there should be any need for any other court than that of her Majesty; and that those who wish to pay the homage of their loyalty may very well resort to her Majesty herself to pay the homage and respect that is due." He went on to say that the queen would visit Ireland "from time to time" and stay in the Phoenix Park residence.[238] For Russell, the trouble with the lord lieutenancy was its dangerously anachronistic constitutional position. The lord lieutenant "had the semblance of royalty without the power of defending himself."[239]

234. *FJ,* 8 April 1850.
235. RA D 21/14, Lord Clarendon to Lord John Russell, 4 May 1850.
236. RA D 21/11, Lord John Russell to Prince Albert, 11 March 1850.
237. RA D 21/12, Prince Albert to Lord John Russell, 18 March 1850.
238. 17 May 1850, *Parliamentary Debates,* 3d Series, vol. III (14 May–17 June 1850), cols. 178–80.
239. *FJ,* 20 May 1850.

Parliamentary reaction to the bill was surprising. Morgan John O'Connell, nephew of the late Liberator, broke with other nationalists and supported abolition. For him the lord lieutenancy combined "colonial government" and the functions of "a foreign ambassador."[240] But opposition to the bill came from the Peelites. Clarendon was particularly annoyed at the disapproval of Sir James Graham who, in Clarendon's view, had made many mistakes in Ireland as home secretary.[241] The most significant opposition came from a very influential quarter, the duke of Wellington.[242] Throughout June the government was occupied by the international crisis occasioned by the Don Pacifico incident and its will to pursue reform in Ireland ebbed away. In early July it effectively withdrew the measure for the time being at least.[243]

It was not quite the end of the matter. Preserving the lord lieutenancy was the principal issue in the Dublin municipal elections that autumn.[244] On 27 January 1851 another great meeting on the subject took place in the Rotundo,[245] and on 7 March the lord mayor and the Corporation of Dublin presented a petition to the queen against abolition.[246] Clarendon reported to Russell that opposition to abolition had greatly increased in Ireland.[247] Russell drew the obvious political conclusion and Clarendon wrote in depression to his sister, "I quite loathe the Irish as the cause of keeping us asunder for four years; and Heaven only knows how much longer they will do so, as I had a line from Lord John to say, 'We have determined not to proceed with the Abolition of the Lord Lieutenancy Bill this year.'"[248]

In December 1851 the foreign secretary, Lord Palmerston, left the government after a falling out over policy toward France. Clarendon was offered his post but turned it down—for fear of Palmerston, Greville

---

240. 17 May 1850, *Parliamentary Debates*, 3d Series, vol. III (14 May–17 June 1850), col. 229.

241. Lord Clarendon to G. C. Lewis, 7 June 1850, in Maxwell, *Clarendon*, 1:307–8.

242. *FJ*, 11 June 1850.

243. *FJ*, 5 July 1850.

244. *FJ*, 17 October; 4, 18, 22 November 1850.

245. *FJ*, 28 January 1851.

246. *FJ*, 10 March 1851.

247. Lady Clarendon's Journal, 7 February 1851, in Maxwell, *Clarendon*, 1:322.

248. Lord Clarendon to Lady Theresa Lewis, 8 March 1851, in Maxwell, *Clarendon*, 1:321. Clarendon had been told the year before by Russell's brother, the duke of Bedford, that when the lord lieutenancy was abolished Clarendon would not be appointed as secretary of state for Ireland but would be given "another very important place" (Duke of Bedford to Lord Clarendon, 12 March 1850, in Maxwell, *Clarendon*, 1:306).

thought.[249] In any event, the government itself fell in February 1852. Clarendon did not prove to be the last viceroy of Ireland as he had expected and he was replaced by Lord Eglinton. The issue of abolition continued to rumble on over the years.

In February 1853 Lord Cardigan delivered a satirical speech on the subject in the House of Lords. The lord lieutenant had

to undergo the task of saluting 300 or 400 ladies; an amusement very innocent in itself, but it appeared to him very extraordinary that any one of their Lordships should be placed in a position where he had to undergo such a ceremony as a point of duty.

The lord lieutenant was also obliged to "go to the theatre, on which occasion he proceeded through the quiet streets of Dublin attended by a cavalry escort." He appealed in the name of nineteenth-century progress for the government to do something about this anachronism. The then prime minister, Lord Aberdeen, replied, however, that the experience of the Russell government had been that abolition "would be received with so much aversion in that country [Ireland], that all the advantages which the noble Earl had described, even including the abolition of fêtes, dinners and processions, would not compensate for the ill-will and opposition which it would occasion." The government therefore had no plans to take any action on the matter.[250]

The next government, under Palmeston, also refused to adopt a policy of abolition.[251] Palmerston told the Commons in 1857 that he could not think of a suitable substitute for the lord lieutenant. He was supported from the opposition benches by Benjamin Disraeli who told the house that "[s]ome of the objections which have been made to the office of lord lieutenant of Ireland would apply to almost all the high offices of State, and . . . I am not sure that they would not apply to the monarchy itself."[252] A

249. 26 December 1851, in Charles Greville, *The Greville Memoirs, 1814–60*, 7 vols., ed. Lytton Strachey and Roger Fulford (London: Macmillan, 1938), vol. 6 (January 1848–December 1853), 317.

250. 17 February 1853, *Parliamentary Debates*, 3d Series, vol. 124 (10 February–10 March 1850), cols. 171–75.

251. 26 February 1855, *Parliamentary Debates*, 3d Series, vol. 136 (12 December 1854–1 March 1855), cols. 1869–71. Lord Granville told Lord Westmeath that the new government had no plans to abolish the lord lieutenancy.

252. 7 July 1857, *Parliamentary Debates*, 3d Series, vol. 146 (19 June–17 July 1857), cols. 1049–1097.

year later Palmerston, while in opposition during a second brief Derby government, told the house that "the decision of this question ought to be governed by the feelings of the people of Ireland" who were against abolition.[253]

So the issue that had been so central to Russell's plans for Ireland was allowed to lapse, though in private it was seriously considered by the Palmerston and Derby governments of the late 1850s and early 1860s.[254] From the point of view of the monarchy, the continuance of the lord lieutenancy, an office that mixed constitutional with political roles, was to be a very serious mistake, though it was to be a further thirty years before the effects of that mistake would be most clearly felt.

253. 25 March 1858, *Parliamentary Debates*, 3d Series, vol. 149 (23 February–3 May 1858), col. 775.

254. National Library of Ireland (hereafter cited as NLI), Larcom Papers, Ms 7504, memorandum from Lord Carlisle to Lord Palmeston on the abolition of the lord lieutenancy (copy), July 1857, pp. 1–8; General Sir Thomas Larcom to Lord Naas, 7 June 1858, pp. 35–38; "Query—Can anyone govern Ireland, out of Ireland?," memorandum from General Sir Thomas Larcom, 10 October 1860, pp. 77–108.

CHAPTER FOUR

Albertine Ireland

An Exhibition, an Excursion,
and a Statue, 1852–1864

The 1850s were the quietest of years in nineteenth-century Ireland. There were initiatives in constitutional nationalist politics but they tended to flounder. It was only toward the end of the 1850s that physical-force nationalism reemerged, first with the Cork-based Phoenix Clubs and from 1858 with the organization that came to be known as the Irish Republican Brotherhood (IRB) and its sibling organization in the United States, the Fenians.[1]

It was an ideal time for British attempts to refashion Ireland along lines more acceptable to Victorian sensibilities. The 1848 rebellion had failed. O'Connell was dead and repeal agitation was at an end. The famine had cleared the way for agricultural reform. An attempt had been made to reform the government of Ireland, albeit as yet unsuccessful. Britain, however, was preoccupied in the early 1850s with the Crimean War (1853–1855) and in the later 1850s with the anti-colonial uprising in India that the British called the Indian Mutiny (1857) and with fears of a French invasion of Britain. In spite of these preoccupations, at least for some in Britain the decade was a time of minor experiment that boded well for the emergence of a progressive Ireland, freed from sectarianism and nationalism.

1. In this work the term "Fenian" will be used in a general sense to refer to both the American Fenians and the Irish IRB.

Queen Victoria and especially Prince Albert longed for an Ireland that they and their fellow Victorians could understand, an Ireland that in their estimation was progressive and scenic rather than backward and brutal. Their visits to Ireland in 1853 and 1861 can be seen in the light of the role they had forged for themselves and the monarchy so successfully in early Victorian Britain, as patrons of education, industry, and the arts, on the one hand, and as promoters of a new sort of engagement with the countryside as a resort from urban life, on the other.

Ireland could be shaped, they thought, and it could be shaped along the lines of progressive Albertine ideals and examples. The visit of Victoria and Albert to William Dargan's 1853 Dublin exhibition of industry and arts, which was inspired by Prince Albert's Crystal Palace Exhibition in London in 1851, was their way of promoting an Ireland whose interests were commercial and industrial rather than atavistic. Their visit to Killarney in 1861 was on a par with their periods of residence in the Highlands of Scotland and their purchase of the Balmoral estate which had done so much to reduce the "otherness" of the Celtic fringe to the safety of a tourist destination in the public imagination.

Conventional constitutional politics might have appeared lackluster in nationalist Ireland in the 1850s and 1860s. In fact, political energies were often devoted to struggles over symbols, struggles that took explicit cultural form. Throughout most of the nineteenth century Irish nationalist politicians were without political power. They were forced faute de mieux to make themselves visible through symbol.

The view of nineteenth-century Ireland that sees a brief literary renaissance in the 1830s and 1840s followed by a period of cultural desuetude until the Anglo-Irish literary revival of the 1890s needs to be modified at least to the extent of recognizing the explicitly cultural texture, albeit of a nonliterary variety, of Irish political life. The promotion of science and the arts through exhibitions was a novel form of cultural activity; these became occasions for struggles of political ideology. Processions, funerals, great public meetings, and the drawing up of petitions and addresses were forms of political public theater.

Another even more explicitly cultural locus for the politics of symbol was public statuary. In the early 1860s, in particular, Irish "party" politics became the politics of statutes, with the streets of Dublin as the ideological battleground. This is the context for understanding the controversy that descended on proposals to erect a statue there to Prince Albert, who had died in 1861.

The twelve-month period from December 1851 to December 1852 was a time of interesting proposals for the filling of the Irish lord lieutenancy, none of which came to fruition. In December 1851 the Russell government was weakened by the departure of the foreign secretary, Lord Palmerston, over a disagreement concerning France. Russell offered Palmerston the Irish lord lieutenancy "either with or without a British peerage," assuring him "that Lord Clarendon, without looking for any other office, will be happy to relinquish."[2] Palmeston took the offer as an insult and turned it down.

A year later Lord Aberdeen became prime minister at the head of a coalition of Whigs and Peelites which was to last just over two years. Again Palmerston was offered the lord lieutenancy but turned it down on the grounds that it might have involved him in reforming the Church of Ireland, which he was unwilling to do.[3] He joined the government as home secretary but his sights continued to be set on foreign affairs. Palmerston would go on to serve as prime minister for two terms of three and six years, respectively. Ironically, though, for a man whose personal and property links with Ireland were so strong, his political interaction with Ireland was negligible.

In 1852, between the fall of Russell and the appointment of Aberdeen, Lord Derby served as a minority Tory, protectionist prime minister. His entry into office was the occasion for the second move to install a member of the royal family as an apolitical lord lieutenant. In this case the candidate was the queen's cousin, George, who had succeeded his father as duke of Cambridge in July 1850. He was in the army and had been serving in Dublin for five years. The queen was pleased with the proposal but it did not work out.[4]

A Scottish sportsman, Lord Eglinton, was appointed instead. Initially popular, he and the Derby government quickly sank in the estimation of Irish nationalists on account of their alleged anti-Catholicism.[5] There was annoyance in July when Derby was reported as having ordered the channel

2. Lord John Russell to Lord Palmerston, 17 December 1851, in Walpole, *Russell*, 2:139. Palmerston was a member of the House of Commons because, as an Irish peer, he did not have a seat in the House of Lords—hence Russell's offer of a British peerage.

3. *FJ*, 23 December 1852.

4. *FJ*, 23, 24 February 1852.

5. *FJ*, 18 June 1852.

fleet away from Queenstown. This was interpreted as a slight to Cork on account of Tory party political setbacks there. The fleet's visit had coincided with the hosting by the city of an exhibition of arts and industry, modeled on the great Crystal Palace exhibition of 1851, and anticipating the Dublin exhibition of 1853. There had been hopes that the queen herself might visit the Cork exhibition, but it was not to be.[6]

※

Prince Albert was anxious to help Ireland but along lines consonant with his own analysis of the country. He believed that Catholicism was a superstitious religion and that education might help to liberate Irish Catholics from their superstitious ways. In October 1852 he wrote to Lord Derby in connection with Lord Eglinton's views on "national education" in Ireland, a system of primary education that had been established on multidenominational lines in 1831 by Lord Derby himself, when he was serving as Irish chief secretary, but which had eventually slipped into denominational control. Albert noted Eglinton's view that national education had failed *"as a system of united education"* but he believed it had succeeded in giving *"a liberal and secular* education to the Roman Catholic population, which is beginning to tell upon their moral and religious state." In a postscript he advised Derby to read a newspaper report of a miracle in France and to ponder as to "whether to educate the mind, irrespective of doctrinal differences, is not the *first* importance."[7]

In fact, the 1850s saw Catholicism in Ireland growing in vigor and self-confidence. The significance of the letter, however, lies in the prince's view that Ireland was not only in need of improvement, but also ripe for it. It soon became clear to Prince Albert that the man who could lead Ireland to that improvement was William Dargan, sponsor of the 1853 Dublin exhibition. He seemed to conform to all the Victorian tenets of self-improvement for "not long ago [he was] a *common* labourer himself, who has raised himself solely by his own industry and energy . . . [making him] an example of national hope":

What he has done has been done on the field of Industry and not of politics or Religion, without the Priest or factious conspiracy; without the promise of distant extraordinary advantages, but with immediate apparent benefit.[8]

6. *FJ,* 30 July 1852.

7. Prince Albert to Lord Derby, 26 October 1852, in Martin, *Prince Consort,* 5 vols. (London: Smith, Elder, 1875–1880), 2:476–77.

8. RA D/21 86, Prince Albert, memorandum, 28 September 1853.

Dargan had made his fortune building roads, canals, and railways. He had come from humble origins and had learned his trade through working with Thomas Telford in England. By 1853 he had built six hundred miles of railway and had contracts for two thousand more. He lent as much as £100,000 to the Dublin exhibition committee and though he recouped much of it the project eventually left him £20,000 out of pocket.[9] It was to be an exhibition of the arts but principally of the work of Irish manufacturers. The latter, unable to be as competitive as their English rivals, specialized in "ornamentation more than utility."[10]

The exhibition was a cause of pride in nationalist quarters. It was not going to be as magnificent as the Crystal Palace exhibition,

yet we feel confident that, comparing all things . . . remembering that one was the work of one of the greatest Sovereigns of Europe, supported by the commercial wealth of a great commercial nation; and that the other will be the work of one man, supported by the purse of one man—a Celtic man—we believe history will pronounce the Irish Exhibition of 1853 to be the more remarkable of the two—a more direct emanation from the genius of industry, and a more marked demonstration of the industrial progress of the age.[11]

On 12 May 1853 the Dublin exhibition was opened by the lord lieutenant, Lord St. Germans, who had won popularity in Ireland by indicating his personal opposition to the abolition of the lord lieutenancy.[12] Shortly thereafter St. Germans offered a baronetcy to Dargan. The latter refused and was praised for doing so by the nationalist press, though on grounds that it made his contribution seem the more selfless and thus more valued in public esteem.[13] The refusal, however, did not diminish the interest in him that was becoming evident in royal circles. The *Morning Chronicle* reported that Queen Victoria would visit the exhibition in the company of Prince William of Prussia, later to be the first German emper-

9. *DNB*, 5:504.

10. T. D. Jones, quoted in Alun C. Davies, "Ireland's Crystal Palace, 1853," in *Irish Population, Economy, and Society: Essays in Honour of the Late K. H. Connell*, ed. J. M. Goldstrom and L. A. Clarkson (Oxford: Clarendon Press, 1981), 258.

11. *FJ*, 21 October 1852.

12. *FJ*, 8, 18 February 1853. For further discussion of the Dublin exhibition of 1853, see Leon Litvack, "Exhibiting Ireland, 1851–3: Colonial Mimicry in London, Cork and Dublin," and Jamie A. Saris, "Imagining Ireland in the Great Exhibition of 1853," in *Ireland in the Nineteenth Century*, ed. Leon Litvack and Glenn Hooper (Dublin: Four Courts, 2000), 15–57, 66–86.

13. *FJ*, 21 May 1853.

or, and the king of the Belgians.[14] On this occasion the *Freeman's Journal* was warm in its welcome of a visit, whether or not it was a state visit:

No matter how brief the visit, we accept it as a token of her kindness and her reception will be just as cordial in her plain bonnet as if she came with a diamond crown and the aristocracy of England in her train.[15]

A minor controversy rumbled on for a while over whether the visit should be a grand, state occasion and how long it should last, with nationalists arguing that if it was not a state occasion and only lasted a few days it would be seen as a "supercilious looking in on the 'poor relation.'"[16] In early July it was announced that the visit would last between 12 and 16 July.[17] On 7 July Dr. John Gray, who was gaining increasing stature in his own right as a Liberal politician of moderate nationalist views, urged the Dublin Corporation in its loyal address of welcome to ask the queen to return for a proper state visit on a future occasion. He also argued that the address ought not to overstress Ireland's prosperity or to speak of the cessation of repeal agitation as a gain.[18]

The visit had to be postponed, however, due to illness in the royal family. First Prince Albert and then Queen Victoria herself contracted measles.[19] It was not therefore until at 8:00 a.m. on 29 August that the royal yacht *Victoria and Albert* steamed into Kingstown Harbor from Holyhead, the royal party having traveled there by train. The queen was accompanied by Lord Granville, who in spite of the grandeur of his ministerial title, lord president of the council, was considered to be a rather junior minister to accompany the monarch on such an occasion.[20] As the yacht entered the harbor the royal family stood on the bridge between the paddle boxes with Granville and Rear Admiral Lord Adolphus Fitzclarence, a son of William IV.

The *Nation* was not warm in its welcome of the queen:

Dublin Flunkeydom is in tears this moment because this English Queen will not appear in our streets in the fully glory of imperial state. . . . All of you who feel

14. *FJ*, 21 May 1853. 15. *FJ*, 25 May 1853.
16. *FJ*, 2 July 1853. 17. *FJ*, 6 July 1853.
18. *FJ*, 8 July 1853.
19. *FJ*, 9 July 1853; RA QVJ, 3 July 1853. Prince Albert to Lord Aberdeen, July 1853, in J. B. Conacher, *The Aberdeen Coalition* (Cambridge: Cambridge University Press, 1968), 126.
20. 28 August 1853: "This is new, because hitherto she has always had with her either the Premier or a Secretary of State," in Strachey and Fulford, *Greville Memoirs*, 6:441.

that this Queen's reign has done much to consummate the conquest of your country by a system of silent, and crafty, and assassin statesmanship; whose houses have given martyrs to Irish freedom in the past; who can recognise in the wasted form of the captive nation the true queen of your hearts and allegiance; who have struggled with our banished patriots;—shun this ovation, and progress, and procession.[21]

In an apparent retort to this call, the *Freeman's Journal* welcomed the queen's arrival for what it construed as being a nonparty political visit:

It is not a political move—a part of state policy—a triumph over fallen men or in mockery of an afflicted people. It is the reverse of all these. It is a visit of congratulations from a Queen to her subjects on the achievement of a great work—a visit of sympathy to the sons of toil—a visit in honour of the progress of industry—an act of royal homage to the mind, the labours, and the recognised greatness of a Celtic man, who, born to no patrimony, made for himself a patrimony which nobles might envy, and earned for himself and his country a world-wide fame by deeds which monarchs might proudly emulate.[22]

Accounts of the visit tend to repeat a claim that one million people turned out at Kingstown to see the queen's arrival.[23] Though the *Freeman's Journal* recorded that the queen was very warmly received and the London *Times* that the welcome was "in every way worthy of a loyal and warmhearted people," there is no contemporary record of such a number.[24] Nonetheless, the welcoming crowd was very large.

On this occasion the train journey took the queen into the city center at Westland Row. She processed through the streets, once again in her own carriages[25] and thence to the Vice Regal Lodge. Bad weather prevented a visit to Dargan at Mount Anville, south of the city, that day. Instead the queen took a carriage drive through the adjacent Strawberry Beds area. In the evening twenty-four guests had dinner at the Lodge. "It put me in mind of 4 years ago," she wrote.[26] That evening the city was lit with gas illuminations.

The queen had come to see the exhibition and visited it on the follow-

21. *Nation*, 27 August 1853, reported in the *Times*, 29 August 1853.

22. *FJ*, 29 August 1853.

23. Lee, *Victoria*, 235: "A million Irishmen and women are said to have met her on her landing at Kingstown."

24. *FJ*, 30 August 1853; *Times*, 31 August 1853.

25. *FJ*, 27 August 1853.

26. RA QVJ, 29 August 1853.

ing four successive days. This had the effect of boosting considerably the numbers attending the exhibition. These reached 15,207, for example, on 30 August alone.[27] On her first visit Victoria, Albert, and their two elder sons, the Prince of Wales and Prince Alfred, received addresses from the exhibition committee and the Dublin Corporation and saw the fine arts court and Irish antiquities section. "The exhibition buildings [on Leinster Lawn] are ugly on the outside but very fine in the interior," wrote the queen.[28] The queen wore a white silk dress, the ribbon of the order of St. Patrick, an Irish lace shawl, and a pink bonnet. She thought the best pictures were those loaned by "Uncle Leopold."[29]

This first visit occasioned a rather public display of sibling rivalry among the queen's two sons. The exhibition committee had presented bound catalogues to the royal party but did not give one to Prince Alfred. He approached one of the organizers with this plea: "Mr Roe, my brother, the Prince of Wales, has been presented with a catalogue, and I can't see why I should not get one."[30] One was duly ordered.

On her second visit the Queen saw ceramic work; on her third, machinery, linen, antiquities, and Hogan's statue of Hibernia supporting a bust of Lord Cloncurry—who was to die on the day the exhibition closed; and on her fourth and final visit fabrics and whiskey.[31] There was a variety of other engagements too during the visit. Prince Albert inspected public baths, workhouses, and a lodging house.[32] On 31 August the two young princes visited Dublin Zoo and the queen attended a military review in the Phoenix Park at the fifteen acres, though during it one cavalryman broke his leg.[33] Bad weather prevented a royal visit to Powerscourt House the next day, however.

On 2 September Prince Albert inspected the cavalry at the fifteen acres, the Prince of Wales presented new colors to the boys of the Royal Hibernian Military Academy, and the queen visited Howth Castle via Clontarf, "famous," she recalled, "for O'Connell's monster meeting, which was dispersed."[34] On 3 September, the last day of the visit, the queen let it be known that "[w]e have spent a delightful week and are quite sorry to leave so soon."[35]

27. *FJ*, 31 August 1853.
28. RA QVJ, 30 August 1853.
29. RA QVJ, 30 August 1853.
30. *FJ*, 5 September 1853.
31. *FJ*, 1, 2, 3 September 1853.
32. *FJ*, 31 August 1853.
33. *FJ*, 1 September 1853.
34. RA QVJ, 2 September 1853.
35. *FJ*, 5 September 1853.

The visit had gone almost without a hitch. Controversy centered on only two issues. The first was an incident in which a "respectably dressed" man had thrown a paper into the queen's carriage. It turned out to be a petition to help him recover £50 that he had lent to an officer. The man, who was a church organist, later claimed that he had not intended to alarm or insult the queen.[36]

The second issue concerned the virtual boycotting of the visit by the Catholic bishops. They were attacked for it by the English *Morning Post* but defended by the *Freeman's Journal* on the grounds that they had saved the queen embarrassment for, under the Ecclesiastical Titles Act, she would have had to have refused to meet them had they used their territorial titles.[37] In fact, Paul Cullen, newly translated to the see of Dublin, had wanted the bishops to deliver a loyal address to the queen. "But the Lion [John MacHale] does not want to. We will do what we can. It is better not to leave the field all to the Protestants."[38]

On the last day there were final royal visits to the Marlborough Street National Schools, the Glasnevin Model Farm, the Botanical Gardens, and Dublin Castle before the queen and her family left for Kingstown and the sea journey home. "The Queen gazed with evident admiration at the scene, and, as cheer after cheer burst from the people, seemed to be deeply moved at this unmistakable manifestation of the affection of her Irish subjects."[39] She stood on the deck of the royal yacht for half an hour as it prepared to leave. "It was a gay fine evening," she wrote. Prince Albert, in a comparison that he intended to be flattering, had thought the people looked like "Italian beggars." Now the queen herself thought that the "constant singing, cheering etc. and the noise the people made, made me quite imagine one was in a foreign port, in the south."[40]

But it was not just the Irish people who had shown themselves to be "in a state of feverish excitement."[41] The queen had evinced a startling enthusiasm for Dargan both in private and in public, to an extent almost unseemly

36. *FJ,* 5 September 1853.

37. *FJ,* 9 September 1853.

38. Paul Cullen to Tobias Kirby, 18 August 1853, in Emmet Larkin, *The Making of the Roman Catholic Church in Ireland, 1850–1860* (Chapel Hill: University of North Carolina Press, 1980), 207.

39. *FJ,* 5 September 1853.

40. RA QVJ, 30 August, 3 September 1853.

41. *Times,* 1 September 1853.

by the standards of royal etiquette. The *Freeman's Journal* noted on her first visit to the exhibition the "almost affectionate reception which the greatest Monarch gave to her greatest subject when he was yesterday presented by her minister." Because the queen had "the impulse of a woman possessed of intellect to understand and of heart to appreciate" what Dargan had done, she "pressed the arm of William Dargan."

The queen cut short her visit to the exhibition that day to enable her to undertake the visit to Dargan's home that bad weather had prevented the previous day, "the first ever visit paid by the Queen to an untitled subject."[42] The queen found Dargan "touchingly modest and simple, I would have made him a baronet but he was anxious it should not be done."[43] She was almost as enthusiastic and as forgetful of her royal dignity in connection with those associated with Dargan. She sat in Mrs. Dargan's chair at the exhibition at the latter's request and on her return to Kingstown she sought out Sir John Benson, architect of the exhibition building, in the crowd to thank him for his work.[44]

For Victoria and Albert William Dargan was the template for a new sort of Irishman and Irish leader. "Mr Dargan is the man of the people. He is a simple unobtrusive, retiring man, a thorough Irishman." Both of them recorded a story that they had been told at dinner on 1 September by the duke of Leinster. His cabman had told him that Dargan "has put plenty of money into our pockets and never took any out of them." This was taken as a reference to Daniel O'Connell and the "repeal rent" that his supporters had been asked to pay.

Prince Albert was delighted by the news that O'Connell was now so forgotten that when his library and furniture had been recently sold "hardly a bidder could be found, who would have taken an interest in possessing some relique of the *great Liberator*, his name is never heard mentioned, as if he had never existed." The Catholic clergy was also discredited. The fact of "the potatoe [*sic*] disease and famine having occurred without his [the priest's] having been able to stop it, has broken the spell of superstition by which he had been considered entrusted with the power of God."[45]

Queen Victoria thought Ireland "wonderfully improved" since her first visit:

42. *FJ*, 31 August 1853.
43. RA QVJ, 30 August 1853.
44. *FJ*, 5 September 1853.
45. RA D 21/86, Prince Albert, memorandum, 28 September 1853.

There is a great inclination amongst the people to apply themselves to industry and to foster this, the Exhibition will be of great use. It has raised the feeling of enterprise amongst the people, showing them that if they try, they *can* succeed. Mr Dargan's own life story they are inclined to study and reflect upon.[46]

The *Times* thought that the queen's visit to the exhibition was "destined to inaugurate the new era of prosperity at length opening upon the country."[47] The *Morning Post* judged that the visit was a closing of the door on one sort of Irish past:

The jargon with which the few remaining traders in sedition seek to keep up a blind animosity against all things English has long lost its influence, and the trash and humbug of the agitator will vanish rapidly as the successful enterprise of such men as Dargan increases the intercourse and identifies the interests of Ireland with those of the rest of her Majesty's dominions.

However, it went on to be savagely scathing about the people of rural Ireland:

To the great mass of the people, the very elements of civilisation and progress are still wanting. They have not made the first steps of an advancing race even in the manufacture of food. The lazy root is their bone. When that fails them their resource is flight. The loss of the potato should have taught them to grow wheat and to bake bread. It has only driven them to emigration.[48]

The *Freeman's Journal*, while not sharing any of the above criticisms, warned that a future of economic progress for Ireland was not the easy course that it seemed to be in the light of the success of the exhibition:

[W]e hope that those who have adopted the cry [for industrial progress] will not use it as a mere parrot cry ... but will set themselves to work in good sober earnest—ascertain what are the impediments to industrial progress and remove them with all convenient despatch, in order that industry may flourish and bring happiness and comfort to the poor man's home while giving fame and wealth to the nation.[49]

And, indeed, industrial progress turned out to be as false a future for most of the Irish economy as life without nationalism was for Irish politics. The failure of one version of an Albertine Ireland, an Ireland of eco-

46. RA QVJ, 1 September 1853.
47. *Times*, 5 September 1853.
48. *Morning Post*, 2 September 1853; RA D 21/91.
49. *FJ*, 5 September 1853.

nomic and industrial prosperity, was poignantly encapsulated in the fate of its icon, William Dargan. After the exhibition he went on to invest his money in a flax-growing project that failed. Then he established mills around Dublin that did not prosper. Finally he returned to building railways but was seriously injured in a fall from his horse in 1866, dying the next year. His impoverished widow was forced to rely on a civil list pension of £100 that she was awarded in 1870.[50]

After the visit to Ireland the royal couple returned to a Britain troubled by the outbreak of war between Turkey and Russia. Britain was eventually to become involved on the side of Turkey in what became known as the Crimean War. Nothing was yet certain in the autumn of 1853, however, except that there was a tense political atmosphere that was exacerbated by the resignation of the popular and pro-Turkish Palmerston from the cabinet in mid-December. Prince Albert by contrast was labeled pro-Russian and his public popularity diminished.

On 30 December 1853 the *Freeman's Journal* published an open letter to Prince Albert from the "distinguished and eminently popular pulpit orator"[51] Dr. D. W. Cahill. It ranged over a large number of topics. "Why should any one dare to compare the drunken profligacy of Oxford and Cambridge with the spotless character of our [Irish] Catholic colleges?" he asked at one point. At another he offered the view that "I could love England, if she would only do justice to the administration of law in Ireland."

The main reason for the letter, however, was political. Cahill thought that the Aberdeen government was good for Ireland and that Palmerston should be kept out of government, especially the foreign office, because he hated Catholicism. Though Albert was addressed as "a spectator, not an actor, in British policy," it was clear that Cahill thought that Albert sympathized with his views on Palmerston and foreign policy.

On 3 January 1854 the London *Morning Herald* printed an anonymous attack on Albert's influence on government. "Is it too much that one man, and not an Englishman by birth, should be at once Foreign Secretary, Commander-in-Chief and Prime Minister, under all administrations?" A week later the *Freeman's Journal* published a defense of the prince and of his

50. *DNB*, 5:505.
51. *FJ*, 22 April 1853.

advice to his wife by Thomas Mulock of Killiney, County Dublin. This letter caused a sensation in the British press and led to a heightened controversy over the prince's influence. There were rumors that he and the queen had been sent to the Tower of London. Lord Palmerston had to have the *Morning Post*[52] deny that Albert had caused his resignation and on 31 January Lord Aberdeen made a speech in Parliament defending the prince.[53] The crisis passed but it was noteworthy for the part that the Irish press had played in a United Kingdom issue rather than simply an Irish issue. This was not to happen often.

❖

In February 1855 Palmeston himself, whom Queen Victoria disliked but came to tolerate, became prime minister. "To the Irish tenantry the premiership of Lord Palmerston bodes no good," claimed the *Freeman's Journal*.[54] One welcome result for nationalists was the removal as lord lieutenant of Lord St. Germans, who "did much to restore the bitter spirit of the old ascendancy party,"[55] and his replacement by Lord Carlisle, who as Lord Morpeth had been such a popular chief secretary in the 1830s and who was to win a reputation as lord lieutenant for "vigorous common sense."[56] He was also popular as a stout defender of the office of the lord lieutenancy against moves to abolish it.[57] On his departure in February 1858 he was described as "the most popular Viceroy who ever administered affairs in this country."[58] Replaced by Lord Eglinton during the brief Derby government of 1858–1859, Carlisle was reappointed with the return of Palmerston in June 1859.

The middle years of the 1850s were the period when Ireland loomed least in British minds throughout the nineteenth century. In August 1855 the *Freeman's Journal* complained that the queen's speech on the ending of the parliamentary session had praised the colonies' contribution to the Crimean War but omitted any reference to Ireland:

But no man would discover from this royal effusion, so full of thanks for the past and of hopes for the future that there was such a kingdom as Ireland, that her

52. Weintraub, *Albert*, 296.
53. 31 January 1854, *Parliamentary Debates*, 3d Series, vol. 130 (31 January–27 February 1854), cols. 96–97.

54. *FJ*, 27 February 1855.   55. *FJ*, 13 March 1855.
56. *FJ*, 19 August 1856.   57. *FJ*, 5, 16 February 1858.
58. *FJ*, 10 March 1858.

Majesty had any sympathy, interest, or connexion with the people of this king-dom or that one gallant Irish heart had ever throbbed its last in defence of her crown.[59]

A year and a half later it was purporting to be pleased at the omission of any reference to Ireland from the speech at the opening of Parliament:

Ireland is omitted from the speech. Of late years it has dropped out of the stand-ing roll of topics which ministers had always ready for the consideration of par-liament, and we do not regret the omission, for cold disregard is almost preferable to the grating prominence which Ireland usually occupied in royal speeches.[60]

During the spring of 1858, just after his confirmation, the young Prince of Wales paid a visit to Ireland accompanied by his tutor. It was the first royal visit not to center on Dublin. From 12–14 April he visited the West Cork towns of Bandon, Clonakilty, and Skibbereen and journeyed thence by the royal yacht *Osborne* to Killarney in County Kerry.[61] At Skibbereen, which he judged to be "a rising place," he stayed at Doyle's Commercial Hotel, which was promptly renamed the Prince of Wales Hotel. A month later James Stephens visited the town and swore in Jeremiah O'Donovan Rossa and others as early members of the IRB.[62]

The prince went on to spend a fortnight in Kerry, under the care of Colonel Henry Herbert of Muckross Park, Killarney, who had briefly been chief secretary toward the end of Palmerston's first administration. The Cork *Southern Reporter* described him as follows: "Although a large landed proprietor, he warmly supported the corn law movement and has shown himself the friend of progressive and enlightened reform."[63] The prince climbed mountains and viewed lakes, during which, in a gesture of royal domestication of the native environment, "[t]he 'Gun Rock' near Brickeen-Bridge was 'baptised' in a bottle of Mr Finn's best wine 'the Prince of Wales Island.'"[64]

59. *FJ*, 15 August 1855; *FJ*, 31 October 1857, reported that there were 43,000 Irish soldiers and only 47,000 English and Scots soldiers in the British army.

60. *FJ*, 4 February 1857.

61. *FJ*, 16, 17 April 1858.

62. R. V. Comerford, *The Fenians in Context: Irish Politics and Society, 1848–82* (Dublin: Wolfhound, 1885), 49.

63. *FJ*, 28 May 1857.

64. *FJ*, 3 May 1858.

On his next visit to Ireland the prince referred to his 1858 visit, saying that "he conceived a strong attachment to the peasantry" during it. This, according to the *Freeman's Journal*, which could not resist an opportunity to enter into the wars about Ireland's "national character," was because he was a "rollicking lad who talked so pleasantly, and dispensed his gold and silver so liberally" and because of the difference between the behaviour of "well-dressed mobs in England" and that of "the ill clad but gentle mannered Irish peasant [who] observed all the proprieties and stood respectfully apart until good-humouredly challenged by the Prince to answer a question."[65]

Two months later Prince Alfred also visited Killarney, albeit for a shorter duration. On a boat trip round the lakes of Killarney his guide, Jeremiah O'Connor, played "Rule Britannia" and later "God Save the Queen" on a bugle.[66] Both visits were dry runs for a visit from the queen but both were overshadowed by the triumphal progress throughout the country that autumn by the English Cardinal Wiseman, the first prince of the Catholic Church to visit Ireland since the Reformation. To the chagrin of the British press, there was a toast to the pope but not to the queen at a special banquet for him held in the Mansion House in Dublin, an event that was boycotted by Lord Eglinton.[67] What was clear from the incident, though, was that Catholic nationalist Ireland, after a decade of quietude, was regaining the capacity for self-assertion.

Lord Eglinton departed from office in 1859 with a relatively popular reputation in nationalist Ireland for a Tory lord lieutenant.[68] Indeed, Tory administrations during this period went out of their way to woo Irish Catholic opinion.[69] The returning Lord Carlisle caused some initial consternation by asking that the formal ceremony of entry into the city of Dublin be dispensed with and that the Dublin Corporation should not make a formal address of welcome to him or express any view to him con-

65. *FJ*, 2 July 1861.
66. *FJ*, 6 July 1858.
67. *FJ*, 2, 3 September 1858.
68. *FJ*, 6 July 1859: "Lord Eglinton fared better than any Conservative Viceroy within our recollection, and came nearer to a popular Viceroy than any other Lord Deputy of the old breed since the Duke of Rutland."
69. I am grateful to Professor R. V. Comerford for this point.

cerning the future of the lord lieutenancy.[70] The alarm that this caused was so great that he had to relent somewhat. He duly received an address from the Corporation and in reply reassured it that he had "no apprehensions" of any attempt to abolish the lord lieutenancy.[71] Irish susceptibilities were further disturbed several months later when the government allowed the formation in Britain of volunteer defense corps against a French invasion but disallowed them in Ireland. Irish loyalties could not be relied on was the inference that was drawn.[72]

Royal relations with Ireland had their ups and downs in 1860. In March the letters of the German polymath Alexander von Humboldt, to the diplomat Karl Varnhagen von Ense, were published. Both men were by then dead. One of the letters was dated 27 February 1847 and recounted a conversation between von Humboldt and Prince Albert when they met at Stolzenfels in 1845. "'I know,' he [Albert] said to me [von Humboldt] 'that you sympathise greatly with the misfortunes of the Russian Poles. Unfortunately, the Poles are as little deserving of our sympathy as the Irish.' This is what he said to me, one who is the glorious husband of the Queen of Great Britain."[73] The *Times* reported that the publication of the letters had been the cause of "exciting a painful interest" in the views of the prince.[74]

In private, for it would not have been constitutionally proper for him to have done so in public, the prince consort protested his innocence:

[M]ost assuredly I never said that the Poles and Irish deserved to be thrown overboard together, although it is quite possible we had some conversation about the similarities and faults in character of both nations. The matter is of no importance, for what does a man not write or say to his intimate friends under the impulse of the moment? But the publication is a great indiscretion. How many deadly enemies may be made if publicity be given to what one man has said of another, or perhaps even in cases has not said?[75]

70. *FJ,* 29 June 1859.

71. *FJ,* 15 July 1859. On her 1861 visit Queen Victoria was to note that Lord Carlisle was "exceedingly popular" (RA QVJ, 23 August 1861).

72. *FJ,* 7 December 1859.

73. Kurt Jagow, *Letters of the Prince Consort 1831–1861,* trans. E. T. S. Dugdale (London: John Murray, 1938), 346.

74. *Times,* 22 March 1860.

75. Prince Albert to the princess royal, 21 March 1860, quoted in Jagow, *Prince Consort,* 346.

The incident did indeed cause damage to Prince Albert's standing and to that of the royal family in general in Ireland and was not soon forgotten. In the short term, though, the damage done by Prince Albert was eclipsed by an incident involving his eldest son, about whose abilities both the queen and prince consort were coming to have such doubts. In July 1860 the Prince of Wales, accompanied by the duke of Newcastle, was sent to tour Canada and to represent the queen there. In late August he received a rapturous reception in Montreal and other areas of Quebec, the Catholic, French-speaking region of Lower Canada.[76] The bishop of Montreal had his episcopal residence illuminated in welcome.[77]

Sectarian tensions were high in Canada, and the Orange Order was strong in the Protestant, English-speaking region of Upper Canada. The prince's advisers were anxious to prevent him from doing anything that might exacerbate such tensions. Newcastle advised the mayor of Toronto that the prince ought not to be put in the position of having to pass under Orange arches on his route through that city.[78] A problem arose, however, at the town of Kingston, "this dirty, stagnant little town [which created] a most unfavourable impression of both place and people," according to the *Times* correspondent.[79]

The prince's party reached the town by steamer. Newcastle, however, ordered the steamer not to land because the local Orangemen had erected a triumphal arch with a picture of William of Orange on one side and of the Prince of Wales and the Italian revolutionary Garibaldi, who had repeatedly attacked the Papal States, on the other.[80] The Canadian prime minister, J. A. Macdonald, who was on the steamer and who was the MP for Kingston, was furious.[81] Newcastle was adamant and issued a public appeal to the Orangemen

to abstain from displaying in the presence of a young Prince of 19 years of age, the heir to a sceptre which rules over millions of every form of Christianity, symbols of religious and political organisation which are notoriously offensive to the members of another creed, and which in one portion of the Empire have repeatedly produced not only discord and heart burning, but riot and bloodshed.[82]

76. *Times*, 4, 10 September 1860.
77. *FJ*, 14 September 1860.
78. *Times*, 20 September 1860.
79. *Times*, 20 September 1860.
80. *FJ*, 20 September 1860.
81. Sidney Lee, *King Edward VII: A Biography*, 2 vols. (London: Macmillan, 1927), 1:94.
82. *Times*, 20 September 1860.

There was an angry public meeting in Kingston and Orangemen harried the prince's steamer along its route. When the news reached Ireland, though, there was great satisfaction in nationalist quarters at the royal rebuff to the Orangemen.[83]

❊

On 5 February 1861 the queen went to see an Irish play, Dion Boucicault's *The Colleen Bawn*, an adaptation of Gerald Griffin's *The Collegians*, at the Adelphi theater in London. "People are wild about it—and the scene when the poor Colleen is thrown into the water and all but drowned is wonderfully done," she wrote to her daughter Vicky.[84] But the year was to be one of grief for the queen, with the death of her mother in March—"I know that no one . . . ever loved me as she did!"[85]—and of Prince Albert in December. After the death of her mother Queen Victoria entered into a period of depression and withdrew from public activities.

She could not therefore have welcomed the constitutionally inappropriate attempts in May 1861 of the Irish nationalist leader, the O'Donoghue of the Glens, to present her directly with a petition on Irish self-government, rather than to present it through the home secretary.[86] Eventually, there were rumors about the state of her emotional health and it was thought that these might be quashed by a summer visit to Ireland, to see the Prince of Wales who was then undergoing military training at the Curragh in County Kildare.[87]

The prince arrived in Dublin at the end of June and spent a few days at the Vice Regal Lodge engaged in official duties before joining the Second Battalion of the Grenadier Guards, under Colonel Percy, at the Curragh Camp for ten weeks of military training, where he had the use of the headquarters hut of the Irish commander-in-chief, General Sir George Brown. It was anticipated that the prince would be promoted a rank every fortnight so that by the end of the period he would be in a position to command a full battalion before his parents.[88]

83. *FJ*, 26 September 1860.

84. Queen Victoria to the princess royal, 6 February 1861, in Roger Fulford, *Dearest Child, Private Correspondence of Queen Victoria and the Princess Royal, 1858–61* (London: Evans, 1977), 305.

85. Queen Victoria to the princess royal, 23 August 1861, in Fulford, *Dearest Child*, 345.

86. Comerford, *Fenians*, 64.

87. Weintraub, *Albert*, 403.

88. Weintraub, *Albert*, 403.

In early August, however, the duke of Cambridge inspected the Curragh Camp and thought the prince "lacking in energy."[89] Queen Victoria was later to thank Colonel Percy for treating her son like any other officer and pointing out to him the deficiencies in his abilities as an officer.[90] Months after the end of the prince's training at the Curragh it was felt necessary to issue a statement about his behavior there in the *Court Circular.* It recorded that on one occasion he had marched twenty miles on foot in a day with his men rather than go by horse and that "all his demeanour while in the camp was modest and retiring, and in all his conduct he acted up to the noble example of his father,"[91] who had died a short time before the statement was issued.

There were thus doubts not only about the prince's military prowess but also about his personal conduct. The posting was of course notoriously the occasion for the prince's sexual initiation through his relationship with the actress Nellie Cliften. It led to rows later in 1861 between the prince and his father, Prince Albert, shortly before the latter's death. The queen came to blame her husband's demise in part on the incident.[92]

But all of that was yet in the future. The queen, Prince Albert, and three of their children, Princesses Alice and Helena (known as Lenchen) and Prince Alfred, arrived in Kingstown late on the evening of 21 August on what was billed as being a private visit to Dublin. As they drove through the city the next day on their way to the Phoenix Park the queen found the people "most friendly and enthusiastic."[93] Prince Albert visited public institutions in the afternoon while the Prince of Wales called on his family at the Vice Regal Lodge before returning to the Curragh with his brother Affie.

On 23 August Prince Albert went to the Curragh while the queen received an address from the Dublin Corporation. In the late afternoon the royal family drove round the principal streets of Dublin again. One member of the Corporation had wanted to include a reference in its address to the decline in Ireland's population since 1851 of one million people, as recorded in a recent census, a figure that did not include the decline immediately caused by the famine. However, there had been little support for

89. Lee, *Edward VII*, 1:118.

90. Philip Magnus, *King Edward the Seventh* (London: John Murray, 1964), 47.

91. Reported in *FJ,* 22 January 1862.

92. Weintraub, *Victoria*, 292–93, 313.

93. RA QVJ, 22 August 1861.

the inclusion of such a pointed statistic in the address.[94] But the reduction in Ireland's population was not lost on the queen herself. As she traveled south by train a few days later she noted:

[I]t is astonishing how utterly denuded of population the whole of the country is; large plains, a good deal cultivated, with here and there a small house, and awful cabins, but no villages and hardly any towns.[95]

Saturday, 24 August, was the day for the queen's day trip by train to the Curragh to see the Prince of Wales command his troops. "As we approached the Cavalry they began to play one of dearest Mama's marches which entirely upset me," she wrote. "Bertie came by, looking very nice and I recognised many Aldershot acquaintances."[96] After the review the queen and Prince Albert met some of the officers at their son's hut, before returning to Dublin. While at the Curragh Prince Albert complained to Lord Carlisle that the prince was not earnest enough about his soldiership.[97] But to the king of Prussia he loyally reported that Bertie "did his part at the Curragh Camp very well, holds himself better, and has learned everything methodically from the bottom up to command of a company. He has been drilling three times a day and appears to have enjoyed it."[98]

On Sunday Prince Albert and his sons visited Mountjoy and Smithfield prisons while Queen Victoria and her daughters called on the commander-in-chief at Kilmainham. The queen again felt depressed: "I have felt weak and very nervous, and so low at times; I think so much of dearest *mamma* and miss her love and interest and solicitude *dreadfully*. I feel as if I were no longer cared for."[99] The next day was Prince Albert's birthday. The queen arranged a birthday table for him at the Vice Regal Lodge with wreaths of flowers and presents. She gave him a half-length portrait of a Sicilian woman by the Belgian painter Portaels:

God bless and ever preserve my precious Albert, my adored Husband! Alas! so much is so different this year, nothing festive—we on a journey and separated

94. *FJ*, 14 August 1861.   95. RA QVJ, 26 August 1861.

96. RA QVJ, 24 August 1861.   97. Lee, *Edward VII*, 1:119.

98. Prince Albert to King William I of Prussia, 1 September 1861, in Jagow, *Prince Consort*, 367.

99. Queen Victoria to King Leopold of the Belgians, 26 August 1861, in Queen Victoria, *Letters of Queen Victoria*, first series, ed. A. C. Benson and Viscount Esher (London: John Murray, 1907), vol. 3 (1854–1861), pp. 577–58.

from many of our children. I am still in such low spirits, but already quite early I wished him warmly and tenderly joy and he was as ever so loving and affectionate. May God mercifully grant that we may long, very long, be spared to live together and that I may *never* survive him![100]

❋

The 1861 visit had a second part to it, a visit to Ireland's then only really developed tourist area, Killarney in County Kerry. Walter Scott had made Scotland attractive to the English: "The fashion for the trimmings of an imaginary Highland culture was part of the dominant romantic ideology of the first half of the nineteenth century."[101] George IV had been enthusiastic for the Scottish fashion and Victoria and Albert had gone further and bought a home in Scotland, where they interacted directly and even affectionately with the peasantry on their Balmoral estate.

The *London Review* saw their residences there as helping in the process of bringing about a change in the relationship between England and Scotland, with the former no longer fearing the latter as a place of rebellion but viewing it as a tranquil holiday resort:

It is a singular and cheering sight in these modern days to see Queen Victoria treading the heather and wandering among the mountains and streams where the people once rose *en masse* to resist the dynasty of which she is so illustrious an ornament.[102]

Could not the same be done with Ireland? Could not Ireland be reenvisioned through a renewing royal perspective as a peaceful rural retreat rather than as an arena of agrarian conflict? The visit to Killarney was an Albertine experiment in that direction.

On 26 August the royal family traveled south by train. They stopped at various points on the route. At Thurles, County Tipperary, the queen noted that "the crowd was tremendous, very noisy and the people very wild and dark looking—all giving that peculiar shriek, which one hears here instead of cheers. The girls are handsome with long dishevelled hair."[103]

At 6:30 p.m. they arrived in Killarney, where they were to be the guests of the county's Liberal political establishment. They stayed at the old Kil-

100. RA QVJ, 26 August 1861.
101. Dorothy Thompson, *Queen Victoria, Gender and Power* (London: Virago, 1990), 38–39.
102. Reported in *FJ,* 10 September 1861.
103. RA QVJ, 26 August 1861.

larney or Kenmare House which the queen thought looked like a French chateau[104] but which was to be demolished in 1872 and replaced by the Victorian mansion in which the Prince and Princess of Wales were to stay during their fateful visit in 1885. The queen and her family were the guests there of Lord Castlerosse who was then a Liberal MP for Kerry. He was to have a career of service in the royal household and, as Lord Kenmare, eventually to rise to the position of lord chamberlain.

The evening was warm and Queen Victoria was to have an unusual complaint for a tourist in Ireland: "All the windows open and yet not a breath of air." On the other hand, there was "[a]n excellent dinner served *à la Russe* with merely dessert and fruit on the table." Among the dinner guests on that first evening were the local Catholic bishop, "a tall, stout, very intelligent clever man," and James O'Connell, "brother of *the* O'Connell, the last of that generation, a very good man, with quite different views to his brother."[105] James O'Connell was in fact a keen supporter of the Liberal party; in 1869, on Gladstone's recommendation, the queen would confer a baronetcy on him.[106]

The next day the royal family boarded Castlerosse's great, eight-oar barge at Ross Castle for a journey on the lakes to the cheers of thousands of local onlookers.[107] By lunch time they had reached Lady Castlerosse's cottage at the foot of the Hill of Glena. The queen noted that all the hills were wooded "which gives them a different character to those in the Highlands."[108] Jeremiah O'Connor was on hand once again to play "God Save the Queen" as the party got back into the barge.[109] They then traveled into the upper lake where further refreshments were to be had in a marquee that had been set up in "a lonely spot but terribly infested with midges."[110]

That evening the royal family moved as arranged to Muckross Park, the home of another local Liberal magnate, Colonel Herbert, lord lieutenant of County Kerry and the Prince of Wales's host in 1858. "The Herberts are very agreeable, clever people. We retired early. It was again dreadfully hot."[111]

On the second full day of the visit the queen saw the Muckross demesne. "We were enchanted with the extreme beauty of the scenery. . . .

104. RA QVJ, 26 August 1861.　　　105. RA QVJ, 26 August 1861.
106. *FJ*, 15 September 1869.　　　107. *FJ*, 28 August 1861.
108. RA QVJ, 27 August 1861.　　　109. *FJ*, 29 August 1861.
110. RA QVJ, 27 August 1861.　　　111. RA QVJ, 27 August 1861.

It is one of the finest drives I have every taken."[112] Princess Alice wrote of Killarney to the duchess of Manchester, "This is the place I admire most almost of any I have ever seen."[113]

In the afternoon, during the course of a boat trip, the queen took part in a symbolic re-creation of part of the landscape:

By the Herberts' request I christened one of the points which runs into the lake, with a bottle of wine, Albert holding my arm when we came close, so that the bottle was successfully smashed.[114]

The only unsuccessful part of the choreography of the day was the failure of the pack of hounds belonging to Maurice James O'Connell, son of James O'Connell, to drive a stag along the shore as the royal boats passed by.[115]

There was something highly stylized in the countryside that was presented for the queen to observe and that seemed somehow to have been called into existence by her very act of observation. At the dinner that evening she noted that "[e]veryone [was] so pleased at Killarney having been duly admired." And yet the next sentence in her journal entry acknowledges, apparently with a certain alarm, the existence of yet other Irelands besides the one that had been created for her: "Mr Herbert told me that about them all the inhabitants were Roman Catholics, the same at Killarney, where there are 3 Nunneries and several Brotherhoods, including Franciscan Monks."[116]

There was obviously something disconcerting in this realization for the queen. Tourism always reduces the complexity of a culture to simple and acceptable images. The next day, shortly before her departure for Dublin, the queen actually visited a Franciscan foundation, but it was the ruins of Muckross Abbey, a late medieval friary that had finally been suppressed by order of Cromwell in 1652. For the queen, though, it betokened not the bewildering complexity of Ireland's alien political and religious identity but the safety of Gothic romanticism. "The Cloisters are perfect and very ghost like," she wrote, "No one high or low, will pass it alone at night."[117]

112. RA QVJ, 28 August 1861.

113. Princess Alice to the Duchess of Manchester, 4 September 1861, in *"My Dear Duchess": Social and Political Letters to the Duchess of Manchester, 1858–1869*, ed. A. L. Kennedy (London: John Murray, 1956), 174.

114. RA QVJ, 28 August 1861.   115. *FJ*, 29 August 1861.

116. RA QVJ, 28 August 1861.   117. RA QVJ, 29 August 1861.

An Ireland that was a safe tourist destination for the English was one in which the images of counterrealities to those pleasing images necessary for tourism were being held at bay. For this reason, tourism was often recommended by English commentators as a cure for Ireland and tended to be regarded by radical nationalists with hostility.

Thus, on the one hand, the London *Times* was a consistent advocate of Ireland being seen as as welcoming a part of the Celtic fringe as Scotland had become. In 1849 it thought that the queen's visit could only help in the process. "She will draw in her train an imitative host of tourists and travellers."[118] On the other hand, however, John Mitchel had sarcastically confided to his diary that once famine had cleared the West of Ireland of its population, "The Prince Albert will then take a hunting lodge in Connemara."[119]

In their newspaper, the *Irish People*, the Fenians too evinced great hostility to what they derided as the "picturesque" Ireland that would attract tourism and that was advocated by the *Times*. "The time will come when the annual stream of tourists will lead the way, and when wealthy Englishmen, one after another, in rapid succession, will seize the fairest spots, and fix here their summer quarters."[120] They need not have worried. The Albertine image of a peaceful and scenic Irish countryside did not prevail against the negative images of Ireland in British newspapers that were occasioned over the following decades by the Fenians and the land war.

Just before their departure from Dublin on 29 August the royal family drove round the principal streets of the city for the last time to cheering crowds though, according to the queen, with "many dirty ragged people running along near the carriage decidedly the worse for whisky."[121] Two and a half months later, on 10 November, the streets of Dublin were to become the scene for another public spectacle, the massively attended funeral of the exiled, though quite minor, Young Ireland activist, Terence Bellew MacManus. This event has often been characterized as at least a symbolic turning point in nineteenth-century Irish politics, marking the reemergence of a confident, radical, and uncompromising nationalism. It was arranged by a group called the National Brotherhood of St. Patrick, an organization

118. *Times*, 3 August 1849.
119. 26 October 1849, Mitchel, *Jail Journal*, 203.
120. *Irish People*, 12 March 1864.   121. RA QVJ, 29 August 1861.

that had been infiltrated by the Fenians, and the Fenians were certainly the principal beneficiaries of the propaganda value generated by it.

The funeral gained the opprobrium of Archbishop Cullen and the Catholic Church. The elaborate demonstration that he organized nine months later on 20 July 1862 to lay the foundation stone of the Catholic university was certainly intended as a counter to the MacManus funeral. The MacManus funeral had been months in the planning. However, at least in some partial way, it is also surely legitimate to see the energy that went into it as a counter to the royal visit that had preceded it only weeks before.

When the MacManus funeral took place the queen's recent triumphal journey through some of the same streets was still fresh in the minds of the people of Dublin. And a week before the funeral copies of a letter from Patrick Lavelle, the priest who defied Cullen to conduct a funeral service for MacManus, were distributed throughout the city. It made no direct mention of the queen but it is strong in its denunciations of those who were cooperating socially and politically with the British administration in Ireland:

[H]e [MacManus] abandoned all for Ireland, wealth, friendship, peace and human happiness . . . he is denied the honours accorded to every Castle-slave, time serving hypocrite and Whigling sycophant . . . the crawling place-hunter who worships only the one God of Dublin Castle.[122]

It has to be admitted that whatever link there was between the royal visit of 1861 and the MacManus funeral was of a minor nature. In the years to follow, however, the correlation between royal events and some nationalist demonstrations in Ireland was to become more obvious and deliberate. Over the next few years, however, nationalist interaction with royalty would take place through the surrogate of the proposed statue of Prince Albert.

In the nineteenth century London was the largest city in the world and the capital of the world's most important industrial economy and of a great empire which, by the end of the century, embraced one quarter of the earth's surface. Its public statuary came to reflect this preeminence. Whereas in Washington, the capital of the United States, ten public statues were erected between 1851 and 1880, in London during the same period

122. *FJ,* 6 November 1861.

thirty public statues were erected.[123] In contrast to England, Ireland was a poor country, and in contrast to London, Dublin was a small and impoverished city. And yet during the same period twenty-five public statues were erected in Ireland, most of them of individuals who fitted into the canon of Irish nationalism. More remarkably still, fourteen of these statues were erected in Dublin alone.[124]

There were at least five reasons for the extraordinary investment in public statuary by sculptors of international renown such as J. H. Foley. First, it was a cultural expression of nationalism—one of the legacies of the Young Ireland movement was a consciousness that nationalism had to be a cultural as well as a political force. Second, and this was especially true of Dublin itself, it was a way of marking out civic space for Irish nationalism. The only area of government in which nationalists could exercise any control was that of chartered towns and cities, under the Municipal Corporations Act. The countryside was still controlled by ascendancy-dominated grand juries.

Third, in a country in which the nationalist majority held very little political power, it became a way of conducting politics through symbolism, not only against Britain but, perhaps even more importantly, between internecine groups within Irish nationalism itself. Fourth, and relatedly, most of the statues were erected during the period from the death of O'Connell to the rise of Parnell in which nationalist leadership was itself relatively weak. The construction of statues of the great nationalist leaders of the past was a means by which the minor nationalist leaders of the present might claim their mantles. This was part of the reason for John Gray's advocacy of the statue of O'Connell and for A. M. Sullivan's support of that of Henry Grattan. Finally, during the same period, statues of great nationalist leaders of the past could be used to at least disconcert British visitors, especially royal visitors, who imagined that Ireland might be becoming more amenable.

In June 1858 Prince Alfred arrived in Limerick and was conducted on a

123. David Cannadine, "The Context, Performance, and Meaning of Ritual: The British Monarchy and the 'Invention of Tradition' c 1820–1977," in *The Invention of Tradition*, ed. Eric Hobsbaum and Terence Ranger (Cambridge: Cambridge University Press, 1983), 64.

124. Judith Hill, "Ideology and Cultural Production: Nationalism and the Public Monument in Mid Nineteenth-Century Ireland," in *Ideology and Ireland in the Nineteenth Century*, ed. Tadhg Foley and Seán Ryder (Dublin: Four Courts, 1998), 56.

tour of the city by the mayor. The *Munster News* reported that "[h]e proceeded on foot through George-street *until he came to the O'Connell Statute*
[emphasis added], which the Mayor pointed out to him, and of which he
took particular notice."[125] Something rather similar happened to his elder
brother the next year. On St. Patrick's Day 1859 the Prince of Wales found
himself in Rome on the grand tour and decided to visit the Irish College,
which was a Catholic seminary. He was greeted by the rector, Tobias Kirby,
and by the archbishop of Dublin, Paul Cullen, who was on one of his frequent visits to the city. Instead of asking the prince into the college, however, they first suggested he visit the nearby church of St. Agatha, where
the prince "examined minutely the monument raised by Mr Bianconi to
O'Connell in which the Liberator is represented at the bar of the House
of Commons refusing to take the Protestant oath."[126]

Even Victoria and Albert had had a brush with Irish statuary, albeit of a
miniature variety. On their fourth visit to the Dublin exhibition in September 1853 they examined some parian statuettes:

[T]he largest of the group represented the late Mr O'Connell, surrounded by a
number of peasants, male and female—the figures being about five or six inches in
height and moulded with great spirit and expression. Her Majesty attracted by the
figures, stopped to examine them, and instantly exclaimed—"Ah, that is O'Connell." "Yes," said Prince Albert, "and an excellent likeness it is of him, too." . . . Mr
Leland has designed and modelled another group, in which Mr Dargan is represented surrounded by Irish artisans and labourers, whose condition he has done so
much to elevate and improve, but unfortunately it was not quite ready for exhibition, otherwise it is not improbable that it would have found a purchaser in the
Queen.

In fact, the queen, showing no doubt where her interests really lay, went on
to buy a parian statuary group entitled "Burns and Highland Mary."[127]

❖

Prince Albert died on 14 December 1861, apparently of typhoid but perhaps really of stomach cancer,[128] and a grief-stricken Queen Victoria began
her retirement from public duties. After initial sympathy for the queen,
public opinion became restive with her effective disappearance and within
a couple of years her popularity was at a low ebb.

125. Reported in *FJ,* 28 June 1858.   126. *FJ,* 29 March 1859.
127. *FJ,* 3 September 1853.   128. Weintraub, *Victoria,* 299–300.

The *Freeman's Journal* announced the death of the prince as "[a] Great Calamity" for England. Next day it apologized that for technical printing reasons it had not been able to use black borders for the columns in which the announcement had been made.[129]

Within months of the prince's death there were moves to memorialize him throughout the United Kingdom. The lord mayor of Dublin, Denis Moylan, wrote to the queen's private secretary, General Grey, on 28 February 1862 to propose erection of a bronze statue of the prince in Dublin as Ireland's national memorial "to commemorate the exalted private virtues and the eminent public services of the late Prince Consort as well as to make their high appreciation of his devotion to the Sovereign who so well deserves and so highly enjoys the affectionate attachment of all her subjects." The general replied on 3 March, indicating the queen's approval.[130]

On 15 March 1862 Moylan held the first of a series of meetings in the Mansion House to drum up support for the statue.[131] Those who attended included William Dargan and the well-known physician Dr. Dominic Corrigan. Lord Derby contributed £50 toward the enterprise.[132]

In the *Freeman's Journal* Dr. John Gray—who was to be knighted in July 1863 for his work as a member of the Dublin Corporation on the Vartry water scheme—began to speculate on the need for more statues in Dublin. One had already been erected to the poet Tom Moore. A fund for a statue of the playwright Oliver Goldsmith was already in existence and a proposal had been made for a statue of Edmund Burke. The *Freeman's Journal* thought that Dublin needed statues of Henry Grattan and Daniel O'Connell.

There was already an indoors municipal statue of O'Connell by John Hogan in Dublin and a public statue also by Hogan in Limerick. The people of Ennis, County Clare, were also in the process of erecting a statue to him but were running out of money. Another £100 was needed and Gray appealed for it in his newspaper.[133] The Tory *Dublin Evening Mail* did not miss the opportunity to claim that the people of County Clare had been reluctant to pay for the statue and that it was a sign that O'Connell was being forgotten.[134]

On 23 September Gray announced that £105 17s had been received and

129. *FJ*, 16, 17 December 1861.

131. *FJ*, 17 March 1862.

133. *FJ*, 11 September 1862.

130. *FJ*, 5 March 1862.

132. *FJ*, 28 June 1862.

134. Reported in *FJ*, 13 September 1862.

that he was going to put the excess amount toward the erection of a national monument to O'Connell in Dublin. Within days Gray had seen to the formation of a committee and had applied to the Dublin town clerk for a site at the intersection of Sackville Street and Carlisle Bridge for "the statue of O'Connell, about to be erected by the Irish nation and the Catholics of the world."[135] There was at this stage a considerable overlap in the membership of the O'Connell and Albert committees, with Moylan and Corrigan attending the O'Connell committee meetings, for example.[136] "At the Albert committee he [Moylan] was a constant attendant. From the O'Connell Statute Committee he was rarely absent."[137]

On the other hand, the by now middle-aged Young Irelander John Blake Dillon was a member of the O'Connell committee but was presumably not an enthusiast for the Albert statue; equally, some of the Tory members of the Albert committee would not have been enthusiasts for the O'Connell statue. Nonetheless, Gray was delighted to receive donations from unexpected quarters: £10 from Judge Fitzgerald, the main force behind the Albert committee, and £10 from Viscount Southwell.[138] By mid-November 1862 two and a half thousand pounds had been collected for the O'Connell monument.[139] A month and a half later it had reached nearly four and a half thousand pounds. Thereafter the rate of giving fell off somewhat.[140] Ten thousand pounds was the target sum.

Meanwhile the Albert committee was itself looking for a site and hit upon St. Stephen's Green, then a private park for residents of the area, which they thought might be renamed Albert Park.[141] Their proposal provoked the setting up of another committee, with the separate but related agenda of opening up St. Stephen's Green as a public park for Dublin working men. This was a cause and a controversy that was to entail the presentation of petitions to Parliament and that would not be settled until 1880; it even outlasted the controversy surrounding the statues themselves.[142]

In November the first murmurings against the O'Connell statue from

135. *FJ*, 23, 24, 27 September 1862. This is the site at the intersection of what are now known as O'Connell Street and O'Connell Bridge where the great statue was eventually unveiled on 15 August 1882.

136. *FJ*, 14 September 1862. 137. *FJ*, 2 January 1863.

138. *FJ*, 25 October 1862. 139. *FJ*, 10 November 1862.

140. *FJ*, 1, 22 January 1863. 141. *FJ*, 29 September 1862.

142. *FJ*, 23 October 1862.

the other end of the political spectrum began to be heard. It was reported that the militant "National Brotherhood of St Patrick" was against the O'Connell statue and in favor of the money raised being used in the struggle against landlordism.[143] The Brotherhood went on sponsor a lecture on O'Connell, given by John Martin, who in spite of being a brother-in-law of John Mitchel, was by then becoming decidedly moderate in his political views.[144]

Almost immediately disputes also began to break out among the moderate nationalists and Liberals who were supporting the O'Connell statue. Peter Paul McSwiney was a prosperous Dublin businessman with aspirations to public life.[145] He owned the *Morning News*, whose editor A. M. Sullivan had his own political ambitions. McSwiney and Sullivan fell out with the O'Connell committee and with John Blake Dillon, in particular, over the committee's refusal to allow the press access to all its proceedings.[146] The committee tried to make amends by adopting Sullivan's suggestion that the O'Connell monument celebrate not just Catholic emancipation but all of O'Connell's achievements.[147]

On 24 January the Albert committee heard the results of a poll among the householders of St. Stephen's Green about the proposal to turn it into an Albert park. Forty-seven were in favor and only fourteen against, but a great majority of households, eighty in fact, had refused to take part in the vote. There seemed to be no prospect therefore of the scheme going ahead,[148] though late the next month a private bill was presented to the Commons, asking that St. Stephen's Green be converted into the Albert Park.[149] At the same time the public mood in Ireland, as it had done in Britain, was turning against the withdrawn royal family. This was evidenced in the reaction in Ireland to the marriage of the Prince of Wales to Princess Alexandra of Denmark on 10 March 1863.

Opposition to a loyal address for the occasion was led in the Dublin Corporation by Alderman Plunkett. "There are many other matters on the paper—such as outdoor relief—of more importance than the marriage of the Prince of Wales."[150] At the end of February a committee of the Corporation under the Liberal Protestant lord mayor, John Prendergast Verek-

---

143. *FJ*, 11 November 1862.
144. *FJ*, 31 December 1862.
145. He was also a cousin of James Joyce's father.
146. *FJ*, 13, 17, 23 December 1862.
147. *FJ*, 1 January 1863.
148. *FJ*, 26 January 1863.
149. *FJ*, 2 March 1863.
150. *FJ*, 20 February 1863.

er, tried to come up with compromise proposals on how the royal marriage ought to be celebrated in Dublin. City buildings would be illuminated but not other buildings. There should be fireworks and it should be a general holiday "as much as possible" and people should be urged to mark the wedding by giving to charity. This compromise did not please Plunkett, who used a procedural motion to prevent the Corporation from adopting the proposals. Plunkett's plea that the Corporation move on to consider more urgent matters such as relief was itself frustrated by a motion to adjourn the house that was supported by a large majority, including Gray and McSwiney.[151]

The Corporation met again a few days later and agreed to a loyal address, Plunkett having been persuaded to raise no further objection. In Britain the beautiful Princess Alexandra had caused a sensation with her arrival in the country. In Ireland the public mood began to warm toward the marriage. The *Freeman's Journal* sarcastically congratulated "our contemporary" the *Morning News* on McSwiney's decision to illuminate his newspaper offices for the wedding.[152] The *Freeman's Journal* praised the princess for appearing in London in an Irish-made gown. "A few ill-conditioned malignants may advise 'black flags' and 'death's head and crossbones' as a greeting for the wedding day of the Princess who thus uses her position to benefit the working men of Dublin."[153] One very elderly man had indeed paraded around Dublin two days before the wedding with a flagpole and black flag surmounted with a death's head and cross bones: a calf's skull and ox bones had been used. He was arrested and fined 5 s., though his alleged mysterious employer was never found.[154]

On the wedding day itself things went smoothly enough in Dublin, though some windows were broken, students sabotaged the machine that was to have illuminated the Catholic university, and a handbill was distributed that attacked Princess Alexandra, on the xenophobic grounds that she was a Dane and thus part of the race that King Brian Boru had fought at the Battle of Clontarf in 1014.[155] There were also disturbances in Cork and in Ballina, County Mayo.[156]

151. *FJ*, 28 February 1863.   152. *FJ*, 3 March 1863.
153. *FJ*, 10 March 1863.   154. *FJ*, 10 March 1863.
155. *FJ*, 11, 21 March 1863.
156. NLI, Larcom Papers, Ms 7487, *Daily Express*, 14 March 1863.

Further feuding afflicted the O'Connell committee in October 1863, though this time from a new source. William Smith O'Brien, long released and returned to Ireland, wrote publicly that the O'Connell statue should be located on a new street to be cut through the old Liberties area of Dublin. For Gray, this was tantamount to relegating the statue to the Dublin slums.[157]

In January 1864 the O'Connell committee ran into a dispute with the lord lieutenant, Lord Carlisle, who managed to suggest that the planned erection of so many statues was a sign of Irish civic immaturity rather than of the converse. The planned statues were "undertaken in obedience to a rage and passion for erecting testimonials" to people who did not deserve them. In response, John O'Hanlon, secretary of the O'Connell committee, resiling from a maladroit comparison between the relative merits of Burke and O'Connell for a statue, asked the lord lieutenant if Prince Albert was included in his list of those who did not deserve a statue.[158] Ironically, Carlisle was himself memorialized in 1870, the same year as William Smith O'Brien.

In 1864 McSwiney became lord mayor of Dublin. On 13 January 1864 A. M. Sullivan began to flex his own independent political muscles in the Dublin Corporation when he opposed an address of congratulations on the birth of a son to the Prince and Princess of Wales. "He wished the child more happiness than would befall it if born of poor parents in this country."[159] Tempers frayed in the Corporation over a proposal to move the existing statue of O'Connell into a position of greater prominence in the City Hall, with some members seeing in it a plan by Sullivan to reduce Gray's influence.[160]

By this time the Albert committee had commissioned J. H. Foley, who was ironically also to be given the O'Connell commission in 1867, to create the statue of the prince consort. It had also abandoned all hopes for St. Stephen's Green, especially as the Corporation had received a report from one of its own committees urging it not to sacrifice the rents that the changing of St. Stephen's Green would entail.[161] Instead, the Albert committee set its sights on College Green, the area between Trinity College and the Bank of Ireland, formerly the parliament house.

157. *FJ*, 27, 29 October 1863.
159. *FJ*, 14 January 1864.
161. *FJ*, 2 February 1864.

158. *FJ*, 8 January 1864.
160. *FJ*, 18 January 1864.

When this plan was proposed to the Corporation on 9 February, it was vehemently rejected by Plunkett who said that only statues of O'Connell and Grattan, father of the independent parliament, were worthy of that site. It certainly should not go "to the memorial to a foreign prince."[162] In passing, it is worth noting that Albert was being considered foreign because he was German rather than British! Sullivan temporized about the issue at the meeting but afterward decided to use Plunkett's objections to his own political advantage. The *Nation,* of which Sullivan was then editor, called the Albert statue for College Green proposal "an outrage."[163]

At the next and highly dramatic meeting of the Corporation a week later a letter was read out from Sullivan proposing a statue of Grattan for the College Green site:

No other man, unless it be Daniel O'Connell, could advance a claim as powerful as that of Henry Grattan to the place in College-green. . . . [A]ny other site in the city would suit equally well for the statue of Prince Albert, but no other site in Dublin is no imperatively marked out as the right one for that of Henry Grattan.

The report of a committee of the Corporation on the matter, however, was also read. It recommended that the Albert statue be placed in College Green. There was a heated debate and then the matter was voted on. An amendment denying College Green to the Albert statue was lost by fourteen votes to thirty-two. Plunkett and Sullivan were among those who voted in favor, while a coalition of Tories, Liberals, and moderate Liberal nationalists, which included Gray, voted against. The original motion allowing the Albert statue to be placed on College Green was passed by the same margin. Sullivan, who had earlier said he intended no disrespect to the memory of Prince Albert, was bitter about the decision:

The names of those who had voted for the resolution would be branded with infamy for all posterity. The statue of a foreign prince would be hateful in the eyes of the Irish people and would provoke the hissing and execration of every true-hearted Irishman who went by it.

Albert was "the slanderer of Poland," a reference to the von Humboldt letter,[164] and should not be "revered in Ireland." Sullivan's supporters in the

162. *FJ,* 9 February 1864.   163. *Nation,* 13 February 1864.

164. NLI, Larcom Papers, Ms 7587, Supplement to the *Nation,* 21 March 1863. This includes a cartoon of Erin turning away in disgust as the the lord lieutenant unveils the Albert memorial, inscribed with the offending comment about Ireland and Poland.

gallery booed anyone who tried to speak against him. Gray, trying to draw a parallel between the dispute between O'Connell and Young Ireland and that between himself and Sullivan, accused Sullivan's supporters of being "the successors and followers of the men who dealt thus with the Emancipator of Catholic Ireland."[165]

But the evening was a triumph for Sullivan. In Grattan he now had the political podium of a statue to rival that of Gray and, as quickly became apparent, he also had public opinion on his side, to such an extent that his activities and increasing prominence peaked the hostile interest of the Fenians. They had long regarded Sullivan as an enemy and had accused him of being a "fellon-setter" for having printed the names of those who had attended the MacManus funeral.[166]

On 22 February Sullivan helped arrange a mass meeting in the Rotundo, under the notional nationalist leader, the O'Donoghue of the Glens, to protest against the Corporation's decision. However, it was broken up by a group of Fenians calling out "Goulah" at Sullivan. The Fenian leader, James Stephens, "himself took charge of the preparations for the break up of the meeting and the hunting of A. M. Sullivan and his friends from the room."[167] This was political calculation on the part of the Fenians and was certainly not, as the *Weekly Register* reported, "a scandalous tumult in which Irishmen professing to be of the same political tint assaulted each other without an assigned or intelligible cause."[168]

What the Fenians were afraid of was that Sullivan and the O'Donoghue were on the point of founding a new parliamentary movement that might deflect support from their own physical-force movement. In the *Irish People* they called the controversy over the College Green site "the Albert Dodge." They thought it was merely an excuse for a parliamentary initiative.[169]

Thirty years later Sullivan's brother was scathing about the actions of the Fenians at the Rotundo meeting. Recalling that one of them had, after the meeting, shaken Stephens "warmly by the hand" and told him "'You are great; I'll never doubt you again,'" T. D. Sullivan scoffed that their actions had been

---

165. *FJ*, 16 February 1864.
166. *Irish People*, 27 February 1864.
167. T. D. Sullivan, *A. M. Sullivan: A Memoir* (Dublin: T. D. Sullivan, 1885), 75.
168. Reported in *FJ*, 29 February 1864.
169. *Irish People*, 20 February 1864.

an astonishing display of military genius. After this who could doubt that Ireland would soon by free? Had there not been a great smashing of chairs and tables in the Rotundo? Had not the green flag, consisting of the baize from a reporters' table, been hoisted and waved triumphantly? Did not countenances that had been red with the rage of the "engagement" become radiant with the joys of "victory"?[170]

For the Fenian John O'Leary, though, the incident "showed the strength of the Fenian element in Dublin."[171]

The meeting was rearranged by A. M. Sullivan for the following week and Sullivan ensured that the Fenians were for the most part excluded by making it a ticket-only event. Even this strategy did not stop a certain amount of heckling. The O'Donoghue said that he intended no personal disrespect to the memory of Prince Albert. "When he heard of his death he felt as he always felt when——. A voice—Glad. The O'Donoghue—No. He did not feel glad."[172] Nonetheless, the meeting was a success from Sullivan's point of view, though the *Irish People* accused him of having committed "political suicide" by relying on "the protection of the police of Prince Albert's royal widow" at a meeting to protest against the Albert statue.[173]

But this was far from the case, as the tide was beginning to run in Sullivan's favor. A report from the Rotundo meeting was sent to the Corporation.[174] It was referred to a committee, though this continued to favor the College Green site for the Albert statue.[175] By now, however, feeling on the Corporation itself was turning against the plan. A compromise suggested on 2 May that no statues be allowed on College Green and that even the existing statue of William III be removed was not passed, however.[176]

There was a dramatic new development two weeks later when it was revealed by the lord chancellor, Sir Maziere Brady, on behalf of the Albert

170. Sullivan, *Sullivan*, 75.

171. John O'Leary, *Recollections of Fenians and Fenianism*, 2 vols. (London: Downey, 1898), 2:10.

172. *FJ*, 1 March 1864.

173. *Irish People*, 5 March 1864.

174. *FJ*, 5 April 1864.

175. *FJ*, 19 April 1864.

176. *FJ*, 3 May 1864. NLI, Larcom Papers, Ms 7587, Supplement to the *Nation*, 21 May 1864. A cartoon in this edition proposed a novel solution to the problem by depicting the equestrian statue of William III with Prince Albert sitting behind William III.

committee, that the queen had officially given her sanction for the use of the College Green site as long ago as the end of February, though as he confessed to the under secretary, Sir Thomas Larcom, "I have no apprehension whatever of any change in the resolution of the Corporation."[177] And, indeed, the Corporation voted by twenty-nine to twenty-four not to allow the Albert statue to proceed on the College Green site.[178] "I expect this will wound the Queen mentally," confided Lord Carlisle to Larcom.[179]

The matter of the site was referred to private negotiations. It was a year and a half, however, before a diplomatic formula could be found that allowed the Albert committee to opt for Leinster Lawn, the site of the 1853 Exhibition, rather than College Green, for the Albert statue. Eventually the lord mayor received a letter from the duke of Leinster saying that "[t]he committee of the memorial to the Prince Consort are anxious to place it on the lawn. They have her Majesty's approval, provided the Corporation of Dublin, who kindly granted a site in College-green, would consent to the change."[180]

In the *Nation* Sullivan—who was later to donate the £400 from a national testimonial to him to the Grattan statue[181]—was far from magnanimous about the people he referred to as "Albertites" who had promoted "the German invasion of College-green":

When first it was proposed to desecrate by an Alien's statue a spot so solemnly consecrated to National memories, all Ireland felt the stroke like a barbarous wound; a wanton and heartless insult to a prostrate nation.

The man who in one heartless sentence smote the cause of Poland and of Ireland, who hated our name and creed and race, to have his Statue placed in the spot most sacred to Irish Nationality![182]

---

177. NLI, Larcom Papers, Ms7587, Sir Maziere Brady to General Sir Thomas Larcom, 8 May 1864.

178. *FJ*, 18 May 1864. Brady did not hold the lord mayor or Sir John Gray responsible for the débâcle as they were away on business when the move was made against the Albert statue at the Corporation and "advantage was taken of their absence to carry the new proposition."

179. NLI, Larcom Papers, Ms 7587, Lord Carlisle to General Sir Thomas Larcom [n.d.].

180. *FJ*, 20 December 1865.

181. *FJ*, 28 December 1868.

182. *Nation*, 23 December 1865.

In the early months of 1864, as the controversy raged in Dublin, Queen Victoria was much preoccupied with the building of the Frogmore mausoleum for her husband.[183] On 11 May she visited the studios of a leading sculptor to see "the colossal statue of dearest Albert (without the horse) for Glasgow. It is most beautiful, so like and the figure and expression excellent."[184] Many years later, Frederick Ponsonby, who got some of the details wrong,[185] wrote that the queen had been deeply hurt by the Dublin controversy over the statue to her husband:

The Irish people always resented the coldness of the Royal Family towards Ireland and complained that the Sovereign did not set food in Ireland since 1861. They quite overlooked the fact that there had been occurrences which were calculated to implant in Her Majesty's mind a distrust and even a dislike of Ireland. The first was that when the Prince Consort died the Queen presented a statue of him to the city of Dublin, but the Mayor and Corporation refused to accept it and sent it back to her. This occurred when she was in such deep grief that it completely overshadowed her whole life, and she is reported to have said that she would never forgive Ireland.[186]

In fact the relationship between Irish nationalists and the Crown was never especially the issue in the College Green controversy. The real issue was between at least three very different factions within nationalism. One of them, the Fenian movement, was to come to dominate the queen's perceptions of Ireland for decades to come.

183. RA QVJ, January to February 1846.

184. RA QVJ, 11 May 1864.

185. This shows that the court was as capable of creating myths about Ireland as the Irish were at creating myths about the Crown.

186. Frederick Ponsonby, *Recollections of Three Reigns* (London: Eyre and Spottiswood, 1951), 62.

CHAPTER FIVE

"God Save the Green"

Royal Residents and Fenian Prisoners, 1865–1878

With Lord Carlisle falling ill and dying in the autumn of 1864 there was a need to find a replacement. Palmerston and Russell both agreed that "the best arrangement, and the most conducive to the completion of the Union, would be the abolition of the office of Vice Roy in Ireland, and either the transfer of Irish affairs to the Home Office, or the appointment of an additional Secretary of State for Ireland," but they also agreed that the time was not right because an election was looming. The initial choice for successor was the fifth earl of Bessborough, an Irish peer whose father had been lord lieutenant in the 1840s.[1] Bessborough was a first cousin of Sir Henry Ponsonby, who spent most of his career as equerry to Prince Albert and then as equerry and later private secretary and keeper of the privy purse to Queen Victoria. Ponsonby, who backed up the queen's views of Ireland during the crucial years of the 1880s, had been an aide de camp to the fourth Lord Bessborough and to Lord Clarendon and private secretary to Lords Clarendon, St. Germans, and Eglinton during their lord lieutenancies.[2]

Bessborough refused the position of lord lieutenant. The next nominee was Lord Wodehouse, who was later to be known as Lord Kimberley. The queen objected to him on the grounds that "[h]e is *not* popular and is a

1. RA D 22/7, Lord Palmerston to Queen Victoria, 10 September 1864.
2. *DNB*, 16:81.

great Talker."[3] Palmerston disagreed. Lord and Lady Wodehouse were "agreeable persons" and he had been a good British ambassador to Russia. Besides, there were problems with the alternatives whom the queen had suggested. Lord Ailesbury, for example, was no doubt "an excellent man" but "shy."[4] Russell and Sir George Grey added their weight to the nomination of Wodehouse, who was eventually appointed and proved relatively popular with moderate nationalists, though the Fenians derided him as Lord Woodlouse.[5]

※

The Fenians reached their optimum strength in terms of numbers and preparedness for an uprising in 1865. However, in September of that year the government moved to arrest the movement's leaders and suppress its newspaper, the *Irish People.* "The conspiracy will now probably break out into insurrection or collapse," the queen was told by Russell—who was soon to be prime minister again on the death of Palmerston.[6] In February 1866 an act suspending habeas corpus was hastily passed and the news telegraphed to Osborne House on the Isle of Wight so that the queen could sign the act into law and send it back to London by special messenger. Lord Wodehouse was very grateful for the queen's "confidence" and support in the matter.[7]

The moment had indeed passed for the Fenians to be a significant military force; this was borne out by the ease with which its various military ventures in 1867 were suppressed, though fear of the Fenian threat continued unabated in government circles. But as one door closed a new, and potentially more significant, door opened, especially for those Fenians who faced execution or long terms of imprisonment for their activities. It was

3. RA D 22/8, Queen Victoria to Lord Palmerston, 12 September 1864.

4. RA D 22/11, Lord Palmerston to Queen Victoria, 16 September 1864.

5. RA D 22/12, Lord Russell to Queen Victoria, 18 September 1864. RA D 22/14, Sir George Grey to Lord Palmerston, 16 September 1864. *FJ*, 6 August 1866. Wodehouse nearly made the mistake of dispensing with the ceremonial entry into the city of Dublin at the beginning of his terms of office. However, when the under secretary General Sir Thomas Larcom warned him that this "would not be acceptable to the Dublin public," Wodehouse relented. See NLI, Larcom Papers, Ms 7586, Lord Wodehouse to General Sir Thomas Larcom, 13 October 1864; General Sir Thomas Larcom to Lord Wodehouse, 14 October 1864; Lord Wodehouse to General Sir Thomas Larcom, 15 October 1864.

6. RA D 22/16, Lord Russell to Queen Victoria, 19 September 1865.

7. RA D 22/40, Lord Wodehouse to Sir George Grey, 17 February 1866.

the role of Irish nationalist martyrs. They garnered sympathy and calls for amnesty and their cause contributed to a new political mobilization that helped the home rule movement to flourish in the 1870s.

In the canon of Irish republican mythology, the Fenians are the strongest link in the chain of continuity between the United Irishmen of 1798 and the revolutionaries of 1916 and their heirs, the Irish Republican Army (IRA) of the subsequent Irish "Troubles" or "War of Independence." The Fenian membership oath certainly mentioned "the Irish Republic, now virtually established"[8] and the Fenian proclamation of 1867 included the following passage:

We therefore declare that, unable longer to endure the curse of Monarchical government, we aim at founding a Republic based on universal suffrage, which shall secure to all the intrinsic value of their labour.[9]

It is ironic therefore that, in spite of such evidence, the Fenian leadership was in practice not especially concerned with the role of monarchy or particularly caught up with anti-monarchical sentiment. In the early days of the IRB there was some doubt indeed as to what the initials stood for. Thomas Clarke Luby, a founder of the movement, claimed that they originally stood for "Irish Revolutionary Brotherhood" and that it was only at the insistence of James Stephens that the name became "Irish Republican Brotherhood."[10] And the 1867 proclamation, quoted above, owed more to English republican sentiment than to Irish imperatives.[11] For John O'Leary, indeed, the issue of a republic was not the central one. He wrote late in life:

Let England cease to govern Ireland, and then I shall swear to be true to Ireland and the Queen or King of Ireland, even though that Queen or King should also happen to be Queen or King of England. It has not, nor has it ever been with me, any question of forms of government, but simply of freedom from foreign control.[12]

The agenda of the *Irish People* in the early 1860s was also less concerned with the constitutional superstructure of Ireland, monarchy or republic, than with the reality of political independence. "We have insisted, over

8. O'Leary, *Fenians*, 1:101.

9. Alan O'Day, *Irish Home Rule, 1867–192* (Manchester: Manchester University Press, 1998), 8.

10. O'Leary, *Fenians*, 1:123.   11. Comerford, *Fenians*, 136.

12. O'Leary, *Fenians*, 1:27.

and over again, that there is but one way in which Irishmen can benefit themselves fundamentally, and that is by regaining their lost independence, and at the same time reconquering the land for the people."[13]

The anxieties of the paper had to do with the threat to Fenianism from rival, new, nationalist constitutional political movements, which it derided as "agitation," and the opposition to the movement by the Catholic Church. "We are not 'going against the Priests' at all. It is the priests who are going against us. We should be glad to see the Priests of Ireland, like the Priests of Poland, encouraging and aiding the people in the struggle for independence."[14] Its references to the queen were rather mild.[15] The closest it came to attacking the Crown was an assault on the influence within Irish nationalism of Irish Catholic peers, whom it attacked as an enemy within:

It is a remarkable fact that nearly every man who received from an English sovereign an Irish title perpetrated some horrible crime, some treachery of the most heinous nature against the lives and interest of the Irish people, inasmuch that the peerage of Ireland may be considered as a calendar of national criminals. It would be very dangerous to admit into the councils of a patriotic movement a liar so unblushing as Fingal, or a knave so dishonest as Trimlestone, or political swindlers like the Bellews.[16]

Nor did Fenian anti-monarchism have the visceral quality of that evinced by the Irish parliamentarians of the early 1880s, a comparison that serves as evidence for the fact that there was never a necessary correlation between a person's or a group's views on the issue of home rule under the Crown or a republic without it, on the one hand, and the degree of that same person or group's feelings of enthusiasm, indifference, or hostility toward the monarchy, on the other. The Irish parliamentarians of the 1880s had, in theory, a much more accepting attitude toward the continuing role of the monarchy in a home rule Ireland than did the Fenians of the 1860s. In practice, their emotional antipathy toward the monarchy was much greater.

Reports of Fenian assassination plots against the royal family proved ei-

13. *Irish People,* 6 February 1864.   14. *Irish People,* 17 December 1864.

15. *Irish People,* 8 July 1865. "Her Majesty the Queen of England has just had her say— by deputy of course—to her Parliament before dismissing it. Her Majesty seems to be immensely well satisfied with the world in general, and her North American subjects in particular. Perhaps it is enough for us to say that it is very easy to satisfy Her Majesty."

16. *Irish People,* 24 September 1864.

ther to be false or, if true, the work of rogue elements, though under-
standably they were, nonetheless, to loom large in the minds of the members of the royal family and their advisers. Fenian antipathy to monarchy
was undoubtedly more visceral in the United States, a country whose own
foundational mythology was bound up with antipathy to a British
monarch and where such antipathy was therefore welcome. Thus a man
called Willy Tully was nearly lynched by the crowd at an American Fenian
meeting at Jones's Wood on 28 October 1866 for calling out to James
Stephens that "Queen Victoria had plenty of rope in Canada with which
to hang the Fenians,"[17] who were to organize several military raids on
Canada from the United States.

For the most part the Irish Fenians contented themselves with a certain
degree of monarchical parody rather than with lynchings. In January 1866 a
youth called Denis Boland was caught by the police with a Fenian proclamation that ended with the words "God Save the Green."[18] As a parody of

the British national anthem, this phrase was soon overtaken by "God Save
Ireland." These words were famously used by Edward O'Meagher Condon
when he was sentenced to death for his part in the killing of Sergeant
Charles Brett in Manchester in September 1867. T. D. Sullivan used it in his
ballad about the three "Manchester martyrs" who were executed for the
crime, though ironically Condon himself was reprieved.

During the 1860s, when Queen Victoria was decidedly unpopular in
Britain, the public attitude to her among the Fenians and in Ireland generally was remarkable for the fact that it did not amount to much more than
apathy. John O'Leary claimed that "my feeling towards England's Queen
was then, as it is now, one of complete indifference":[19]

I looked upon her as a highly respectable foreign lady, apparently with the merits
and demerits of the English *bourgeoise*. . . . [S]he symbolized that British rule which
was so hateful to my soul. As a woman she was indifferent, as the ruler disliked,
but scarcely actively, seeing that she reigned rather than ruled, and that she could
not well help being English and a Queen, or, rather the English Queen of
Ireland.[20]

Indifference, however, was no great position for the monarchy to be occupying. The final edition of the *Irish People* contained the view that "we

17. *New York Herald*, 31 October 1866, reported in *FJ*, 12 November 1866.
18. *FJ*, 5 January 1866.   19. O'Leary, *Fenians*, 2:62.
20. O'Leary, *Fenians*, 2:131.

cannot help feeling more than sceptical about Irish loyalty, as we believe the masses of our countrymen as little ultra-loyal as we are ourselves."[21] An anonymous writer to the *Star* addressed the same subject:

[T]he people of Ireland are about the easiest in the world to govern through loyalty if only the loyal appetite gets something to feed on. Sir, I am almost ashamed to think how prone to the most exuberant abject loyalty the Irish people naturally are.... They tried to idolise even George the Fourth.... The late Prince Consort, a placid and excellent personage, did not like the Irish.... In Ireland at all events the people say the Queen does not care about the Irish people—does not like them.

He went on to assert that, due to royal neglect, "we in Ireland are not loyal at present" and that the Irish "have no warmer sentiment towards the Queen of Great Britain than they have towards the Queen of Sheba."[22] As the decade wore on it became clear to supporters of the monarchy and particularly to those in government that something needed to be done. For the sake of the monarchy in Britain as well as in Ireland, there ought to be more frequent royal visits to Ireland, perhaps even a royal residence in Ireland. In Ireland, however, adherence to the monarchy was the index of adherence to the United Kingdom in a way in which it was not in England. If the Irish were discontented, it must mean that the Crown was not doing its job properly, ran one line of thought in Britain. It was easier to think this than to take the demands of Irish nationalism seriously. The decade thus also saw the beginnings of a British scapegoating of the monarchy for Irish discontent.

The early months of 1865 were an anxious time for Lord Palmerston. Rumors had been circulating that the queen would resume her public duties and open Parliament in person, and so there was discontent when she did not do so. The Fenian issue was pressing in Ireland, but it was not until later in the year that the government moved to suppress the movement.

A suggestion made in the Commons that the Irish situation would be helped if the Prince of Wales was to visit there was greeted with laughter.[23] But for Palmerston it was a serious suggestion. There was to be another exhibition in 1865 and this would provide the occasion. He wrote to the queen about alarming reports on the imminence of a Fenian uprising that

21. *Irish People*, 16 September 1865.   22. Reported in *FJ*, 21 September 1865.
23. *Irish People*, 11 February 1865.

"these accounts seem to him [Palmeston] to afford additional reasons for the Prince of Wales's visit to Dublin at the opening of the Exhibition. . . . It is not a matter of small importance to your Majesty's interests and to those of the Country, whether the Irish people should be attached to or alienated from the Royal Family."[24]

The queen was sensitive on the subject on two counts: the criticism of her own retirement from public duties and the promotion of the Prince of Wales, whose abilities she doubted and of whose personal conduct she disapproved. She could not agree with Wodehouse that "the Irish are naturally disaffected because they are differently treated in these matters from England and Scotland; the fact being that neither in England nor Scotland have the Prince and Princess of Wales attended such a ceremony as that for which their presence is now solicited."[25]

It was in fact a fair point. Nonetheless, the queen consented to a visit from the Prince of Wales, but not from the princess who would have been eight months pregnant with the future King George V during the week of the visit. Irritated by Palmerston having called the visit "a journey for a political purpose in place of Her Majesty, the queen prevented the prince from holding a levee at Dublin Castle during the visit on the grounds that her representative was the lord lieutenant and that he should not be superseded. A final problem was caused by the chancellor of the exchequer, W. E. Gladstone, who refused to pay for the visit from additional public funds.[26]

The prince himself was very much in favor of the visit and seems to have agreed with the analysis that saw the popularity of the Crown as a sedative for Irish discontent. "I think it is of great importance that some one should go over, as a great deal depends on the popularity of the Crown there, if they are humoured a little and taken notice of."[27] He was disappointed, though, at the decision about his wife. "I fear the visit will be considered rather flat if the Princess does not accompany me."[28]

The prince's intimation proved to be correct. There was great disap-

24. Lord Palmerston to Queen Victoria, 17 February 1865, in Queen Victoria, *Letters of Queen Victoria*, second series, ed. George Earle Buckle(London: John Murray, 1926), vol. 1 (1862–1869), pp. 250–51.

25. Sir Charles Phipps to Lord Palmerston (draft), 18 February 1865, in Buckle, *Letters*, second series, 1:251–52.

26. Lee, *Edward VII*, 1:226.   27. Lee, *Edward VII*, 1:225–26.

28. Lee, *Edward VII*, 1:225.

pointment that the princess did not come. The *Freeman's Journal* hoped she would visit one day:

Denmark has many friends in Ireland. Danish is largely interfused with Irish blood. Many Danish names, slightly altered, abound in Ireland. The Princess Alexandra then would find relatives amongst us, though very distant ones.[29]

The visit took place between 8 and 12 May. The exhibition was opened by the prince on 9 May. It was a very different sort of exhibition of manufacturing and the arts to that of 1853. The exhibition and the restoration of St. Patrick's Cathedral, which the prince also visited, were being sponsored by the Guinness family, whose members were keen to effect their translation from trade to the aristocracy. Those invited to the opening were for the most part members of the aristocracy or "the gentry without limit" and the knights of St. Patrick paraded in their regalia.[30] It was thus more a pageant to the nobility than to industrial progress.

Crowds lined the streets for the prince's trip to the exhibition, but many in the crowd were disappointed because the prince traveled in a closed carriage. Sullivan's *Nation* charitably allowed that this was due to the bad weather.[31] Later it was to be portrayed as being due to security fears. The *Irish People* was delighted at the annoyance that the closed carriage had caused to supporters of the monarchy. It went on to claim that the heir to the throne had "got the coldest of all possible receptions. . . . The poor Prince made the most of the next to no cheering he got. Bows and smiles were lavishly bestowed on the few small boys who were the representatives of Irish loyalty."[32] The reception was warm enough, though, for the *Times* to call it "most acceptable":

Ireland has suffered long and deeply from absenteeism; but of all absenteeism that which is most keenly felt is the inveterate absence of Royalty. . . . Loyal sentiments are inherent in the Irish character but they require to be kindled.[33]

⁂

In mid-1866 there were a number of Fenian raids on Canada from the two principal factions within American Fenianism. James Stephens promised that there would be an uprising in Ireland before the end of the year,

29. *FJ*, 10 May 1865.

30. *FJ*, 10 May 1865.

31. *Nation*, 13 May 1865.

32. *Irish People*, 13 May 1865.

33. *Times*, 13 May 1865.

but he was deposed by more determined elements when there were no signs of it. In February 1867 there was an abortive raid on Chester Castle in England and a mustering of one hundred Fenians on the Iveragh peninsula beyond Killarney in a wood that the queen had visited. "Your Majesty will remember the point we moved up to the day of the Stag Hunt, and the large wood close to the side of the mountain."[34] The Kerry Fenians dispersed after several days.

In early March there were skirmishes in the Dublin mountains and also in Munster. "This in addition to the well founded alarm at Chester shows how widely spread and unquenched the spirit of Fenianism still is. Under these new circumstances, the Queen concludes that the suspension of the Habeas Corpus Act will have to be renewed,"[35] wrote the queen to Lord Derby, who after the fall of Russell over parliamentary reform was now Tory prime minister. One hundred and seventy suspects were tried by special commission, habeas corpus was duly suspended, and in September 1867 the queen allowed the Irish constabulary to be called the Royal Irish Constabulary in recognition of its contribution to the crushing of revolt.

On 1 May two Fenians, Thomas Burke and Patrick Doran, were sentenced to death for treason. Doran's sentence was commuted and there was public sympathy in Ireland for Burke, an American, as his actions had not resulted in any deaths. On 14 May a meeting at the Mansion House in Dublin drew up a memorial for clemency to the lord lieutenant, Lord Abercorn, and this was supported by a letter from Cardinal Cullen, as he had recently become.[36] The memorial was formally presented to Abercorn on 24 May by a delegation headed by prominent members of the clergy, Dr. Spratt and Canon Pope. Spratt presented the memorial and Abercorn made his formal reply that Doran was to be reprieved but that Burke would not be. Pope repeatedly asked the subdued Abercorn to reconsider but to no avail.

The lord lieutenant received the memorial as representative of the sovereign whose birthday it was. The *Freeman's Journal* referred to "the affection

34. RA D 22/48, General Grey to Queen Victoria, 15 February 1867.

35. RA D 22/45, Queen Victoria to Lord Derby, 14 February 1867.

36. *FJ*, 15 May 1867. Unusually, Cullen had attended the lord mayor's banquet that year and been given precedence after the lord lieutenant and Lady Abercorn. Disraeli had defended this in the Commons because of Cullen's "rightful rank of a Roman Prince" (25 January 1867, *Parliamentary Debates*, 3d Series, vol. 185 [5 February–15 March 1867], cols. 933–36).

of the Irish people for their humane and tender-hearted Sovereign" from whom they hoped for a reprieve. Meanwhile, at Westminster over one hundred MPs had signed a petition for clemency. Many of them were English or Scots MPs, among them John Stuart Mill. A delegation of Irish MPs that included The O'Donoghue and Sir John Gray waited on Lord Derby and announced that if that failed they would travel to Balmoral to appeal to the queen directly.[37]

Burke was reprieved on 27 May. The queen thought the decision "unfortunate, as it will look as if such people were always to be pardoned which is a bad example. But the execution had been too long delayed for it to have had any deterrent effect."[38] Ironically, the reprieve was accompanied by an outburst of gratitude toward the queen in Ireland, which took the rather dangerous view for her constitutionally that she had been personally responsible for the decision:

Then the Queen, who is as much beloved in America as in England has shrunk from the two-fold responsibility of taking away life for a political offence and the life of an American. Of course if her Ministers persisted she must yield. They wisely yielded and saved England from the indelible disgrace and Ireland from the mischief which the martyrdom of Burke was almost certain to produce, and of which we would feel the deplorable consequences for many generations.[39]

James Haughton, a member of the delegation to the lord lieutenant, wrote to Abercorn with an even more explicit view of the importance of the queen's role. He told Abercorn that he had felt hopeful after the meeting:

Partly because of the well known kindly feelings of our beloved Queen on the subject of death-punishment; partly because we all believed your Excellency sympathised fully with her Majesty in regard to the awful nature of the punishment; partly because we felt that it would prove a political error to make martyrs of these criminal and misguided men, and partly because your Excellency named to meet us, the birthday of our loved and honoured Sovereign.[40]

The government, too, or at least one government minister, had rather dangerously implicated the queen personally in the decision. A petition from people in Birmingham in favor of clemency to the queen was sent to Balmoral and, contrary to established constitutional practice, under which a petition to the queen ought to have been sent to the home secretary, re-

37. *FJ*, 25, 27 May 1867.   38. RA QVJ, 27 May 1867.
39. *FJ*, 28 May 1867.   40. *FJ*, 28 May 1867.

ceived a speedy reply from Spencer Walpole, minister in attendance there, to say that he had shown it to the queen.[41] The danger for the standing of the queen lay in what would happen if and when a less popular decision was taken in a similar case.

And this is exactly what happened within six months. On 11 September two prominent Fenians, Colonel Thomas Kelly and Captain Timothy Deasy, were arrested in Manchester. A week later an attempt to free them from a police van by a group of thirty armed Fenians resulted in the death of an unarmed policeman, Sergeant Charles Brett. On 1 November five men, none of whom were actually thought to have fired the fatal shot, were sentenced to death for the crime, though two, Maguire and Condon, were quickly reprieved, one because he was an American and the other because of doubts about his guilt.

In Ireland it was believed that the death of the policeman was not intended. It was "an unfortunate accident in the course of what was otherwise a splendid exercise in Irish gallantry."[42] The *Freeman's Journal* hoped "the Government will complete the work of mercy, and advise the Queen, who, though she dislikes Fenianism, dislikes to shed the blood of her subjects still more, to commute the sentence." It reminded its readers of the reprieve of Burke: "[T]he government divided with the Queen the popularity of that most politic act."[43]

The queen herself was very exercised about the issue. She had her private secretary, General Grey, write to Lord Derby:

The Queen is very anxious and nervous about these Fenian Convicts, lest by any change H[er] M[ajesty] should be placed in the most painful position of having to decide—or even to express an opinion which might influence the decision—on the fate of these unfortunate men.

It is impossible for H.M. not to feel that the future tranquillity of the country may depend on the course now adopted. It may prove a very mistaken mercy should the extreme penalty of the law which they—the Leaders at all events—have so fully incurred, be remitted. Yet the Queen can only wish that that shall be done which the safety of the country requires.[44]

The queen obviously wanted the executions to go ahead without herself becoming directly involved with the decision. Grey reported to the queen

41. *FJ*, 1 June 1867. 42. Comerford, *Fenians*, 148.
43. *FJ*, 18 November 1867.
44. RA D 22/65, General Grey to Lord Derby, 2 November 1867.

that he had "endeavoured to avoid giving a direct opinion in the name of Your Majesty that any of the men should be left for execution further than is implied in calling L[or]d Derby's particular attention to the fact that it might be mistaken mercy not to do so—as the general opinion is that the continuance of the movement is owing to the mercy shown the Canadians."[45] The queen had come to the conclusion that mercy for the Fenians was a mistaken policy several months before.[46] So she continued to keep up the pressure on the government.

On 11 November she spoke with Disraeli, who was soon to take over as prime minister from the ailing Derby, about "the Fenian prisoners and the necessity (dreadful as it sounded and is, to press for such a thing) of an example being made and of no irresolution being shown for the safety of others and the country at large."[47] Grey wrote to Derby on 14 November and used stories of threats against the queen's life to urge strong action. "She must deprecate in the strongest manner any appearance of irresolution or weakness in dealing with the outrageous crime of which these men have been convicted."

The queen met Derby and other ministers herself on 18 November and discussed "these wretched Fenians," in a conversation that revealed something of the shades of opinion within the cabinet. The duke of Marlborough, lord president of the council, thought their "wicked machinations" would be checked by "an example" being made. A less certain Lord Mayo, the Irish chief secretary, said "it would be very difficult to grapple with the Fenians, though in Ireland there was far less trouble than here, but he feared it would take long to put things right. Still no man of good character or property belonged to the Fenians nor any Protestant Irish."[48]

On 20 November the home secretary, Gathorne Hardy, wrote with the news the queen had been waiting for. "It has been decided finally and irrevocably that the law shall take its course in the case of Allen, Larkin and Gould [O'Brien]."[49] General Grey replied expressing a dispassionate royal

45. RA D 22/66, General Grey to Queen Victoria, 4 November 1867.

46. 22 September 1867, *The Diary of Gathorne Hardy, Later Lord Cranbrook: Political Selections, 1866–92*, ed. Nancy E. Johnson (Oxford: Clarendon Press, 1981), 50; RA QVJ, 22 September 1867.

47. RA QVJ, 11 November 1867.

48. RA QVJ, 18 November 1867.

49. RA D 22/70, Gathorne Hardy to Queen Victoria, 20 November 1867, in Buckle, *Letters*, second series, 1:469.

approval, "Sad as it is to Her Majesty to give an opinion in favour of what may appear to be a severe decision."[50] Grey himself thought the executions would prove "that the laws are not to be broken with impunity, a death blow will have been given to this wicked conspiracy."[51]

It was at this point that the queen became publicly involved with the issue. A torch-lit public meeting at Clerkenwell decided to send a delegation to petition the queen for clemency at Windsor Castle. The delegation of three arrived at Windsor on 22 November, the day before the executions, accompanied to the castle by a hostile local crowd of "100 dirty looking workpeople . . . cheering for Your Majesty"[52] who wished "to duck them in the river and hooted them."[53] Consonant with constitutional practice but contrary to Walpole's actions earlier in the year at Balmoral, they were rebuffed by Grey and told that the petition would have to come through the home secretary. By then the crowd had grown so hostile to the delegation that its members had to be escorted out of the town.[54]

The next day the three "Manchester martyrs," as they became known in Ireland, were executed. "I prayed for these poor men last night," wrote the queen.[55] The executions caused outrage to public opinion in Ireland which had come to anticipate a milder response to Fenianism from the government: "the Queen would be unwilling to shed the blood of her English subjects."[56] There were protests and A. M. Sullivan was imprisoned for seditious libel for having printed a cartoon about the executions in the *Weekly News*, an offshoot of the *Nation*, showing a fiendish woman with a dagger in her hand, said to represent "the government of England."[57]

Then on 13 December there was an explosion at Clerkenwell prison where Fenians were being held. Twelve people died in the explosion and, in the short term anyway, this eclipsed the publicity surrounding the Manchester executions. The queen's "heart bleeds to think of the misery which was wantonly inflicted on so many innocent victims of this atrocious wickedness."[58] William Jenner, the royal physician, visited some of the in-

50. General Grey to Gathorne Hardy, 20 November 1867, in Buckle, *Letters*, second series, 1:469.

51. RA D 22/74, General Grey to Queen Victoria, 22 November 1867.

52. RA D 22/75, General Grey to Queen Victoria, 22 November 1867.

53. RA QVJ, 22 November 1867.   54. *FJ*, 23 November 1867.

55. RA QVJ, 23 November 1867.   56. *FJ*, 25 November 1867.

57. *FJ*, 17 February, 30 March 1868; *Weekly News*, 7 December 1867.

58. RA D 22/80, General Grey to Gathorne Hardy, 14 December 1867.

jured at St. Bart's and at the Royal Free Hospital on her behalf.[59] The Prince of Wales also visited them and told his mother how sad it was "that so many people should in one moment be reduced to the fearful misery they are now in."[60] The queen urged the suspension of habeas corpus in England but Derby did not think it would be desirable as "the great mass of the people are eminently loyal and actively hostile to the conspirators."[61]

❈

Throughout the latter months of 1867 the Fenian issue came also to have a very personal aspect for Queen Victoria, though one that was unknown to the general public. It was to make her feel almost as much a "state prisoner" as the imprisoned Fenians themselves. In mid-October the home secretary telegramed Grey at Balmoral with information from the mayor of Manchester of reports that the Fenians intended to seize the queen at Balmoral "and were starting to-day or to-morrow." "Too foolish!" was the queen's robust dismissal of the story, setting the tone for her future attitude to such rumors.[62] Nonetheless, locals were asked to keep a lookout for strangers, extra police were drafted in,[63] and it was agreed that the queen's return journey south would take place in daylight so as to minimize the risk of Fenian attack.[64]

Extra precautions were forced on a reluctant monarch and resulted in her being pursued by her protectors. Lord Stanley, foreign secretary and son of the prime minister, wrote on 4 December:

I heard at Windsor that the Queen refusing to allow an equerry to be in attendance when she is driven about by John Brown [her Highland servant] and the possibility of a Fenian attack on her thought to make precautions desirable, she is followed in these drives by two of the suite, who keep a distance, and are armed with revolvers.[65]

59. RA D 22/84, William Jenner to Queen Victoria, 16 December 1867.

60. The Prince of Wales to Queen Victoria, 10 January 1868, in Lee, *Edward VII*, 1:227.

61. RA D 22/90, 92, Queen Victoria to Gathorne Hardy, 19 December 1867; Lord Derby to Queen Victoria, 19 December 1867; in Buckle, *Letters*, second series, 1:479–83.

62. RA QVJ, 14 October 1867, in Buckle, *Letters*, second series, 1:466.

63. RA D 22/56, General Grey to Queen Victoria, 15 October 1867.

64. Johnson, *Hardy*, 52.

65. John Vincent, *Disraeli, Derby, and the Conservative Party: Journals and Memoirs of Edward Henry, Lord Stanley, 1849–1869* (Hassocks: Harvester, 1978), Journal 4 December 1867, p. 324.

Alarm really began to grow on 16 and 18 December with telegrams from the governor-general of Canada, Lord Monck, to the effect that first one and then two Danish ships had recently left New York carrying dozens of Fenians who planned to land in Bristol Channel and were "sworn to assassinate the Queen" and members of the government.[66] On 19 December the queen, who had moved to the more vulnerable Osborne on the Isle of Wight for the Christmas season, confided to her journal that she had been "[m]uch upset by a long letter from Gen. Grey, written in the most dreadful alarm, saying he heard people had sailed from America with the intention of assassinating me."[67]

Grey had spoken to the queen of the danger on 18 December. His letter on 19 December was because he felt he had not persuaded her of the danger. "Your Majesty should be under no delusion as to the designs which are harboured against Your Majesty ... real danger exists ... he [Grey] would on his knees beseech Your Majesty to consider whether it would not be better for Your Majesty to be at Windsor."[68] The queen hid her own upset and replied that "[s]he is sorry to see him *so very much* alarmed tho' she knows well from what kind and devoted motives his anxiety springs." Nonetheless, "she thinks any *panic* or show of fear would be most injurious as well as unnecessary."[69] That same day the queen wrote to the home secretary to communicate with her directly in future as "General Grey has become *so dreadfully* nervous that he thinks the Queen is in *constant danger.*"[70]

The next day the duke of Marlborough visited the queen on behalf of the cabinet. As he told her the full story of the information from Monck, the queen noted how "nervous" he seemed.[71] That day she also wrote robustly to Derby that she would not return to Windsor, as he had wanted. She also had words for him on his cautioning her about "unattended late drives [which] afford an opportunity for desperate adventurers against which no vigilance can effectively provide":[72]

Also to explain to him how groundless his apprehensions are as to her *late and distant drives after dark*—which *never at any time* hardly, take place *here*, and scarcely *ever* at

66. RA D 22/99, 100. Lord Monck telegrams, 16, 18 December 1867.

67. RA QVJ, 19 December 1867.

68. RA D 22/86, General Grey to Queen Victoria, 18 December 1867.

69. RA D 22/87, Queen Victoria to General Grey, 19 December 1867.

70. RA D 22/90, Queen Victoria to Gathorne Hardy, 19 December 1867.

71. RA QVJ, 20 December 1867.

72. Lord Derby to Queen Victoria, 19 December 1867, in Buckle, *Letters*, second series, 1:479–83.

Windsor, and then *never without* an Equerry riding in attendance. The Queen does not consider Windsor *at all safe.* And to London *nothing* will make her go, *till* the present state of affairs is *altered.*

Such precautions are taken here that the Queen will be little better than a *State* prisoner. She may consent to this for a *short time,* but she *could not* for long.[73]

She wrote to Hardy in the same vein about Windsor, "there are many nasty people always about there, and indeed she would not for her health remain there. The air is so foggy, damp and unwholesome and the vicinity to the town makes it so unruly and so noisy that her health and nerves would not admit of her remaining there." Nonetheless, she asked him to make sure to inform her of any "suspicious persons" leaving from London for South-ampton, across the Solent from the Isle of Wight and Osborne.[74] In pri-vate that night she "[p]rayed earnestly for help and protection in these anxious painful times."[75]

On 22 December Hardy wrote to the queen with an even more alarming story, this time about a takeover of London beginning with "the destruc-tion of gasometers," telegraphs, and railways "and the use of some deadly explosive or chemical implements by which ships or buildings may be de-stroyed and their defenders half suffocated." Those behind it were "not Fe-nians but Republicans engaged not against England only but Monarchy everywhere." Hardy confessed that he himself did not believe the story and was beginning to have his doubts about Monck's report.[76]

The latter story began to crumble when a further report from Monck indicated that the three Fenian potential assassins of the queen were code-named Robert Emmet, Daniel O'Connell, and Edward Fitzgerald, and that one of them was claiming to be a relative of the man who shot President Lincoln.[77] Panic continued, nonetheless, within the royal household and the queen found herself personally having to reprimand junior officers for sending alarming security reports directly to the government. In future they should "tell [John] Brown instead."[78]

In early January 1868 it was revealed that there was no truth at all in the

73. RA D 22/93, Queen Victoria to Lord Derby, 20 December 1867, in Buckle, *Letters,* second series, 1:484.

74. RA D 22/96, Queen Victoria to Gathorne Hardy, 20 December 1867.

75. RA QVJ, 20 December 1867.

76. RA D 22/101, Gathorne Hardy to Queen Victoria, 22 December 1867.

77. RA D 22/111, G. K. to Sir J. Macdonald, sent by Lord Monck to the colonial sec-retary, the duke of Buckingham, and by him to Queen Victoria.

78. RA D 22/108, Queen Victoria to Lieutenant Charles Fitzroy, 30 December 1867.

story from Canada. Queen Victoria's abashed courtiers acknowledged that the queen had acted with great courage during the crisis and all were "proud of your Majesty's honest confidence and fearless trust in your people."[79] Solid government intelligence had always indicated that Queen Victoria was in no danger and that the Fenians saw the queen as sympathetic to Ireland and that "as far as Your Majesty yourself was concerned, Your Majesty could go *anywhere* in perfect safety."[80]

The queen herself considered it was "*a great triumph*" for the position she had taken. She was forty-eight years old, had been shot at three times and knocked on the head and received threatening letters "and yet *we never* changed our mode of living or going on." She wrote to Hardy about

this *absurd* and *mad* story from Canada, which she must say Lord Monck ought to be ashamed at having credited—and (Mr Hardy must forgive her for saying so) the *Government also*—tho' *she* thinks *he* was never inclined himself to share in the extravagant alarm which took possession of everyone about.[81]

The urbane and skeptical Hardy thought her letter "amusing. She is charmed at the explosion of the Canada canard."[82] The trusting queen, however, told her daughter Vicky that she thought that "Mr Hardy is the right man in the right place, besides being a most delightful person, he is so calm and quite. . . . But the country was never more loyal or sound. I would throw myself amongst my English or dear Scotch subjects alone (London excepted as it is so enormous and full of Irish) and I should be as safe as in my room."[83]

The year 1868 saw the second, and most successfully, episode of what might be termed the Prince of Wales's Irish reign manqué. Lord Abercorn, whose son was a friend of the prince, had been keen for some time for another visit from the prince to Ireland but the visit had been postponed due

79. RA D 23/5, Lieutenant Charles Fitzroy to Queen Victoria, 5 January 1868.

80. RA D 22/63, General Grey to Queen Victoria, 20 October 1867, reporting on the views of a detective who had attended Fenian meetings.

81. RA D 23/10, Queen Victoria to Gathorne Hardy, 8 January 1868.

82. 10 January 1868, Johnson, *Hardy*, 61.

83. Queen Victoria to the Crown Princess of Prussia, 11 January 1868, in Roger Fulford, *Your Dear Letter: Private Correspondence of Queen Victoria and the Crown Princess of Prussia, 1865–71* (London: Evans, 1971), 169.

to the Fenians.[84] Abercorn wrote to Disraeli, now prime minister, of the need to steer "the Irish National feeling into direct sentiments of loyalty to the Royal Family."[85]

In March Disraeli raised the issue with the queen. Perhaps, he casually suggested, the prince might make a formal visit and also return later in the year for hunting in Kildare or Meath and thus "combine the fulfilment of public duty with pastime, a combination which befits a princely life."[86] The queen replied that she would allow only a short visit as otherwise "every other part of the Queen's dominions" would soon want similar attention. In the case of the Prince of Wales, "any encouragement of his constant love of running about, and not keeping at home, or near the Queen, is most earnestly and seriously to be deprecated."

If the Irish "behave properly" during the visit she promised to consider sending other members of the royal family over, especially Prince Arthur "(who is called Patrick)." But she went on to make it clear that the government would have to pay for such visits and they ought to be considered as work not pleasure trips: "For health and relaxation, no one would go to Ireland and people only go who have their estates to attend to. But for health and relaxation thousands go to Scotland."[87] Her days at Killarney were obviously now a fading memory.

Disraeli thought that Ireland was at a "turning point" and that the visit could be important. In retrospect 1868 was not a turning point in the obvious way that 1849 had been. However, the success of the 1868 visit from the point of view of monarchy and the government was due to the feeling in Ireland at the time that, especially with Irish Church disestablishment on the horizon, Ireland was indeed at such a turning point.

Disraeli also warmed to the suggestion that the centerpiece for the visit ought to be the ceremonial installation of the prince as a Knight of St. Patrick at St. Patrick's Cathedral. This would provide a more acceptable pretext to the queen than the alternative, a visit to the races. The queen wrote to her son that the latter plan "strengthens the belief, already far too

84. Lee, *Edward VII*, 1:277.

85. RA D 23/31, Lord Abercorn to Benjamin Disraeli, 5 March 1868.

86. RA D 23/30, Benjamin Disraeli to Queen Victoria, 6 March 1868, in Buckle, *Letters*, second series, 1:513.

87. RA D 23/32, Queen Victoria to Bejamin Disraeli, 7 March 1868, in Buckle, *Letters*, second series, 1:513–14.

prevalent, that your chief object is amusement."[88] The wounded prince replied that he was going to Ireland for duty, not amusement. The chief secretary, Lord Mayo, and Abercorn's son, Lord Hamilton, had suggested that he visit Punchestown Races because so many people went there and it was "a kind of annual national festival." It was a better place than Dublin for people "to display their loyalty to you and your family if (as it is to be hoped) such a feeling exists."[89]

Disraeli wrote to the queen stressing "that the peace and contentment of Ireland may be favoured, perhaps even secured, by members of the Royal Family, from time to time, paying visits to that country" and pressed that the Princess of Wales be allowed to accompany her husband on the trip.[90] A month later the queen was writing to the prime minister that there were stories that she was forcing the prince to go to Ireland. She wanted him to issue a statement that it was the government's idea and responsibility but Disraeli politely declined.[91]

In Ireland the prospect of the visit became the focus of hopes from the nascent amnesty movement for Fenian prisoners.[92] The visit lasted from 15–24 April and some Fenian prisoners were indeed released before it,[93] though not enough for the *Nation*, which reflected that "[o]ur felons will remain felons still."[94] Just before the visit the Commons had voted in favor of Gladstone's resolutions favoring the disestablishment of the Church of Ireland. This made the Prince and Princess of Wales all the more welcome in Catholic nationalist Ireland.

> Our future King and Queen come to us, however, at a time when the Imperial Commons, by an overwhelming majority, have declared that the past must be redeemed . . . that justice, equality and conciliation must henceforth be the distinctive features of English rule in Ireland. [The Irish are] instinctively monarchical, hereditarily loyal, lovers of order and good government.[95]

88. RA D 23/37, Queen Victoria to the Prince of Wales, 9 March 1868, in Buckle, *Letters*, second series, 1:514–15.

89. RA D 23/42, Prince of Wales to Queen Victoria, 11 March 1868, in Buckle, *Letters*, second series, 1:515.

90. RA D 23/46, Benjamin Disraeli to Queen Victoria, 14 March 1868.

91. RA D 24/15, 16, Queen Victoria to Benjamin Disraeli, 10 April 1868, Benjamin Disraeli to Queen Victoria, 11 April 1868.

92. *FJ*, 17 March, 1 April 1868.

93. Lee, *Edward VII*, 1:228.

94. Reported in the *Belfast Newsletter*, 16 April 1868.

95. *FJ*, 15 April 1868.

They understand no other form of Government. Republics are the dreams of enthusiasts. . . . All thinking men are of opinion that Ireland should be governed as much as possible with Royal state.[96]

The prince and princess, together with the duke of Cambridge and Prince Teck, all of them wearing shamrock, arrived at Kingstown at 9:00 a.m. and traveled in a carriage procession into Dublin. The public reception was very enthusiastic and the decoration of the city of Dublin at times remarkable. In Merrion Square, Sir William Wilde, father of the playwright, displayed an emblem in which "Faith, Loyalty and Patriotism were happily combined in a large blue and red flag, having in the centre a green crown, containing a Prince of Wales feather, and surmounted by an ancient Irish cross in gold. Below the banner hung an ancient Irish harp surmounted by an ancient spear." In Dame Street there was a banner that read "Welcome Prince and Princess of Wales" on one side and "The Earl and Countess of Dublin forever, God save the Queen" on the other.

The Dublin Corporation address, delivered in Dublin Castle, was a diplomatic balancing of differing political views. Because it contained no complaint and was looking to the future, it did not mean that the Irish were lacking in "self-respect." The Corporation hoped the visit would open "a new era for Ireland."[97]

The Waleses visited Punchestown Races on 16 April and the prince went again the next day while the princess visited Alexandra College, an educational institution for women, named after her. That evening they called in on a ball at the Mansion House, arriving at 11:00 p.m. and departing at 2:00 a.m.[98] Saturday, 18 April, was the day of the installation, the first such ceremony in its elaborate form since George IV's visit in 1821.

Lord Abercorn fulfilled his role as grand master while Lord Mayo carried the sword of state and Lord Waterford, as hereditary great seneschal of Ireland, greeted the Princess of Wales at the door of St. Patrick's Cathedral. The knights first met in the chapter room to hear the queen's message that the prince should be installed as a knight. They then processed into their stalls in the cathedral, where the prince was clothed in the robes of the order, his banner was unfurled, and the Ulster king at arms read out his royal titles to a flourish of trumpets.[99] That night there was a banquet at the Castle and next day a military review, attended by

96. *FJ*, 16 April 1868.

97. *FJ*, 16 April 1868.

98. *FJ*, 17, 18 April 1868.

99. *FJ*, 8 April 1868.

150,000 people, in the Phoenix Park.[100] The entire spectacle was all a prolepsis of the late Victorian ceremonial monarchy.

Over the remaining days of the visit the prince and princess visited numerous public institutions but showed a special diplomatic care to balance visits to Protestant institutions with visits to Catholic ones. On 21 April the prince inaugurated the statue of Edmund Burke and received a honorary degree at the Protestant Trinity College. He went on immediately to visit the state-unrecognized Catholic University, where Cardinal Cullen introduced him to an array of Catholic peers and judges. Cullen had pointedly arranged the iconography, with pictures of Queen Victoria and Pope Pius IX hanging side by side.[101] On the last day of the visit the Waleses visited the Mater Hospital and were once more met by Cullen "attired in his robes as a Prince of the Church." In the reception room a picture of the Madonna was flanked by pictures of two princes, the Prince of Wales and Cardinal Cullen.

The prince wrote to his mother:

I only wish, dear Mama, that you could have been here instead of us; as I feel sure that you would have been astounded by the expressions of loyalty you would have received, and the people, though excited, were so good-humoured and orderly.[102]

The queen was already receiving other positive reports of the visit. Mayo wrote that "[n]othing could have been more successful than the Installation has been. The day was very fine and the Streets were literally crammed with People."[103] Abercorn wrote that a hundred thousand people had seen the Waleses at Punchestown on the first day and that on the second the prince had gone about informally and been very well received.[104]

But the unfortunate prince could do little right in his mother's eyes and the queen deprecated his second visit to the races. Abercorn found himself having to defend the prince[105] and the visit. Even Fenian sympathizers had "cheered with real cordiality":

[A] foundation has been laid by which the loyalty of the Irish people, and their strong natural attachment to Your Majesty's person, and to the Royal Family, has

100. *FJ,* 21 April 1868.
101. *FJ,* 22 April 1868.
102. Lee, *Edward VII,* 1:229.
103. RA D 24/22, Lord Mayo to General Grey, 18 April 1868.
104. RA D 24/23, Lord Abercorn to General Grey, 19 April 1868.
105. RA D 24/30, Lord Abercorn to General Grey, 22 April 1868.

been aroused to a point that may easily be kept up and even augmented by any further similar occurrences.[106]

Abercorn's attitude reflected the growing belief among British politicians of most political persuasions in the potential power of the monarchy to act as a unifying force and as a means of transcending divisions based not only on nationalism, as in the case of Ireland, but also on class, as in the case of newly enfranchised industrial Britain.

George Cambridge told his cousin how much good the visit had done to a childlike people whose discontents could be dismissed as the work of manipulative political leaders:

I never doubted the joy they [the Irish people] would feel and express on having the leading members of the Family, after Yourself, amongst them. . . . The fact is that the Irish people are very impressionable people. They are very easily guided to mischief by bad and designing persons, but they are as easily guided to good if only the occasion offer such as the present and of which they have availed themselves to the fullest extent.[107]

However, aware that such attitudes would be put about in Britain after the visit, the *Freeman's Journal*, while looking forward to further visits from the Waleses, warned against the view "that discontent has vanished in the light of the Royal countenance."[108]

The royal family was about to receive an unpleasant postscript to what everyone, except perhaps Queen Victoria herself, agreed was a highly successful visit. On 7 January 1868, though this did not become known until some time later, a Fenian assassin called Lennon waited to strike at Lord Mayo outside Dublin Castle. Luckily for him the chief secretary did not turn up at the Castle that day.[109] On 7 April Thomas D'Arcy McGee, a former Young Irelander and now a prominent Canadian politician and opponent of the Fenians, was assassinated in Ottawa. Then on 25 April came the news that on 12 March there had been an attempt on the life of Queen Victoria's second son, Prince Alfred, duke of Edinburgh since May 1866, in Australia. The queen's journal entry for the day read:

106. RA D 24/34, Lord Abercorn to Queen Victoria, 25 April 1868, in Lee, *Edward VII*, 1:229.

107. RA D 24/26, Duke of Cambridge to Queen Victoria, 21 April 1868.

108. *FJ*, 24 April 1868.

109. In 1872 Lord Mayo was assassinated while serving as viceroy of India.

Much started by a telegram from the Duke of Buckingham, saying that dear Affie had been shot at, at Sydney, but was going on well, thereby showing however that he had been wounded! All, greatly shocked.—On coming in from a drive with Lenchen heard that the Duke of Buckingham had arrived, which alarmed me and I dreaded the worst! However, thank God! It was not.[110]

Prince Alfred had been on the royal navy ship *Galatea*, which was visiting Australia. He was attending a public charity picnic for a sailors' home at a place ironically called Clontarf. As he was in the process of formally presenting a check he was shot in the back. As he collapsed he cried out, "My God, my God! My back is broken." As the attempted assassin, Henry James O'Farrell, was wrestled to the ground by bystanders two further shots went off, one of them wounding the mayor of Sydney in the foot. The wound to the prince was not serious. He was operated on by two naval officers and made a complete recovery.

When captured, O'Farrell shouted, "I'm a Fenian. God save Ireland." Later he confessed, "I've made a mess of it, and all for no good." The assassination was the idea of a small group of Australian Fenians and was to have been a retaliation for the Manchester executions. O'Farrell had been born in Australia but had visited Ireland. He claimed to have once been ordained as a deacon and to also have worked in property dealing and mining.[111]

"It is so shamefully wicked for poor dear Affie is so entirely unconnected with anything political or Irish," wrote his mother.[112] The *Freeman's Journal* agreed, hoping "that the perpetration of this horrible outrage will turn out to be a maniac. Fenians in every part of the world will disavow such a dastardly attempt on the life of a young man who never did them harm."[113] Anxious to distance moderate nationalism from an event that was, significantly, obviously seen to be well beyond the pale of what could be tolerated from extreme nationalism, the *Freeman's Journal* refused to allow O'Farrell the usual dignity of political martyrdom when he was eventually executed. He was dismissed as "a miserable lunatic."

Meanwhile £40,000 was subscribed for a Prince Alfred Hospital and some consideration was given to renaming New South Wales, the Australian colony in which the incident had taken place, Alfredia or Prince Alfred Land.[114] For the *Times*, though "coupled with the recent assassination

---

110. RA QVJ, 25 April 1868.
112. RA QVJ, 24 April 1868.
114. *FJ*, 27 May 1868.

111. *FJ*, 19 May 1868.
113. *FJ*, 27 April 1868.

of Mr McGee, this deed will bring home to the most doubting minds the true character of the Fenian conspiracy."[115] The Fenian threat continued to hang over the royal family, though a sensational newspaper report in the *Gazette de France* of a planned Fenian attack on the queen while she was visiting Lucerne in Switzerland on 19 August 1868 turned out to be a hoax.[116]

❖

W. E. Gladstone was now leader of the Liberal Party in opposition. Shocked as most other British politicians were by the activities of the Fenians, he became convinced that he ought to pursue a "justice for Ireland" policy as a way of winning round moderate Irish nationalists. Not the least of the reasons for this was that it would remove the international embarrassment that British policy in Ireland had long proved to be, especially to a Liberal statesman such as Gladstone who had been such a champion abroad of what today would be called "human rights":

> Ireland has been strong in her controversy with Great Britain, because she has had justice on her side, and at her back the deliberate judgment of the civilised and Christian world. . . . We are resolved, so to speak, to deprive her of them by doing justice.[117]

Land reform and university education were among the issues he was eventually to tackle, but first came the issue of the Established Church. Though it only had a small number of adherents, this reformed, episcopal church, often also known as the Irish Church, which was united with the Church of England under the Act of Union, was, to the *chagrin* of Irish Catholics, still the state-recognized church in Ireland.[118]

Some Tories, such as Lord Mayo, favored a "leveling up" of the position of the Catholic and other churches rather than the disestablishment of the Irish Church. Gladstone took the opposite view. In March and early April 1868, with the Tories still in power, he convinced the House of Commons to support his position by 336 votes to 270.[119] Lord Downshire told a meeting in Ulster, where opposition to disestablishment was strongest, that "[o]ur religion is assailed, our endowments threatened, the Union be-

115. *Times*, 27 April 1868.
116. NLI, Larcom Papers, Ms 7696; *Daily Express*, 22 August 1868; *FJ*, 24 August 1868.
117. RA D 27/29, W. E. Gladstone to Paul Cardinal Cullen, 6 March 1870.
118. After disestablishment it became known as the Church of Ireland.
119. *FJ*, 23 March, 4 April 1868.

tween Great Britain and Ireland endangered and the Queen's Coronation oath set at nought."[120]

On the day of the vote Queen Victoria went to visit Lord Derby on his sickbed. This was taken as having "political significance" and as indicating the queen's disapproval of the measure.[121] It was true that the queen disapproved of what Disraeli had told her was Gladstone's "revolution."[122] She told Gladstone's colleague Lord Granville that she had "never concealed her disapproval of the course pursued by Mr Gladstone" because it would stir up "religious animosities which have so long been the bane of Ireland."[123]

On 1 May Gladstone's formal resolution in favor of disestablishment was passed by the Commons by a majority of sixty-five. The *Belfast Newsletter* thought the Irish Church was a sacrifice to appease Irish terrorism. "There is no Irish Church to oppress the population of England."[124] The defeat of the government was obviously a resigning issue for the Tories, so Disraeli repaired to Osborne House to see the queen, as constitutional etiquette demanded. However, he had already arranged with her not to resign at once but to remain in office several months longer so that any general election might take place with new constituencies under the terms of the 1867 Reform Act.[125]

The Commons accepted the arrangement on 4 May but at the price of asking the queen three days later "to place at the disposal of Parliament her interest in Irish Church temporalities."[126] This meant that the queen could not use the royal prerogative, which was in any event exercised in her name by the government, to make appointments in the Irish Church until the question of disestablishment had been settled. The request raised constitutional issues to do with the royal prerogative and practical political issues inasmuch as the Suspensory Bill, which would accompany such a move, was likely to be passed by the Commons but not by the Lords.

General Grey advised the queen that withholding the requested permission would mire her in the political debate.[127] So it was announced on 12

120. *Belfast Newsletter,* 21 April 1868.   121. *FJ,* 6 April 1868.
122. RA D 23/47, Benjamin Disraeli to Queen Victoria, 17 March 1868.
123. RA D 24/19, Queen Victoria to Lord Granville, 16 April 1868.
124. *Belfast Newsletter,* 1 May 1868.
125. RA D 24/29, Benjamin Disraeli to Queen Victoria, 22 April 1868.
126. *FJ,* 5, 8 May 1868.
127. RA D 24/43, General Grey to Queen Victoria, 5 May 1868.

May that, on the advice of the cabinet, the queen would not interfere with moves to introduce a Suspensory Bill.[128] The bill failed to get through the Lords but the queen won respect in Catholic Ireland for her action. She did not "place herself in opposition to her people and set up the Throne in hostility to the will of the Empire."[129]

Queen Victoria soon became the object of lobbying from both sides. On 14 May 1868 the archbishops of Dublin, Armagh, Canterbury, and York presented her with an address against disestablishment. Four days later the home secretary forwarded a petition from four thousand Irish Protestants also against.[130] On 15 March 1869 a delegation from the Dublin Corporation presented the queen with a "humble address" at Windsor Castle in favor of the measure.[131] Two months later it was the turn of the Grand Orange Lodge to send her a petition against.[132]

The general election in November 1868 gave the Liberals a majority. Gladstone became prime minister in December, declaring that his "mission is to pacify Ireland." Throughout her reign the queen got on best with urbane ministers who were often ironic about her behind her back. The tragedy of the relationship between Gladstone and Queen Victoria was that both were alike in their passion over political issues, but whereas Gladstone relied on argument the queen relied on instinct. Over the years he earnestly bombarded the monarch with memoranda on a huge variety of subjects whose details she had not the patience or the intellectual curiosity to follow. Surprisingly, disestablishment was one issue on which, despite their differing views, they managed to establish a working partnership.

Mr. and Mrs. Gladstone visited the queen at Osborne on 22 January 1869. The next day he outlined his plans for disestablishment to her, telling her that he had discussed them in part with only two others.[133] He gave her his papers on the subject, but the queen had to ask her late husband's biographer, Sir Theodore Martin, to write a summary of them for her.[134]

At an early stage the queen decided that as Gladstone had won an election on the issue, it was up to her to help to smooth the way for disestablishment in a fashion that was most advantageous to an Irish Church facing disendowment as well as disestablishment. She also strove to avoid the

128. *FJ*, 13 May 1868.   129. *FJ*, 27 March 1869.

130. *Belfast Newsletter*, 15 May 1868; *FJ*, 16, 19 May 1868.

131. *FJ*, 16 March 1869.   132. *FJ*, 21 May 1869.

133. RA QVJ, 23 January 1869.

134. Roy Jenkins, *Gladstone* (London: Macmillan, 1995), 295.

constitutional crisis that would arise if the unelected House of Lords rejected the measure.[135]

There were no lines of communication between Gladstone and the Irish Church, so the queen set about establishing them through senior clerics in the Church of England, such as Dean Stanley of Westminster, who was married to Lady Augusta Bruce, a former lady in waiting to the queen, and Dr. W. C. Magee, the bishop of Peterborough.[136] She refused to open Parliament in person lest it be thought that she supported disestablishment,[137] but told the prime minister that, though she did not approve of it, "if she could be of any assistance to Mr Gladstone . . . he may entirely depend on her affording it."[138] Gladstone was delighted by the queen's efforts and urged her to continue.[139] So she persuaded the new archbishop of Canterbury, Archibald Campbell Tait, to enter into discussions with Gladstone, telling him that Gladstone "shows the most conciliatory disposition" and was "really moderate in his views."[140]

The bill was introduced in the Commons on 1 March and was passed by the end of the month. By the beginning of June the queen was alarmed by the prospect that it would be thrown out by the Lords, with its Tory majority, thus causing a clash with the Commons and preventing the bill being amended to soften what she saw as its more severe provisions.[141] She

135. Queen Victoria to Lord Derby, 7 June 1869, in Buckle, *Letters*, second series, 1:603–4.

136. RA D 25/12, 13, 33, Lady August Stanley to Queen Victoria; memorandum of the Dean of Westminster; the Bishop of Peterborough to Queen Victoria, 12 February 1869.

137. Queen Victoria to the Crown Princess of Prussia, 6 February 1869, in Fulford, *Your Dear Letter*, 222–23. "You ask me if I am going to open Parliament. No I am not going to do so—purposely and on sound grounds. I had intended not doing so when I still thought and hoped the late Government would have been in, and told Mr Disraeli that I wished not to appear personally to take a part in this Irish Church question—which was the cry with which everyone went to the elections, and which resulted in a large majority against the very principle which I cannot conscientiously but consider to be the right one, though I am quite ready to give way to what may be inevitable. But I will not give it the sanction of my presence. And this I have told to Mr Gladstone (who however had never asked or expected me to go) who is quite satisfied."

138. RA D 25/9, Queen Victoria to W. E. Gladstone, 31 January 1869, in Buckle, *Letters*, second series, 1:578–89.

139. RA D 25/40, W. E. Gladstone to Queen Victoria, 14 February 1869.

140. RA D 25/44, Queen Victoria to the archbishop of Canterbury, 15 February 1869, in Randall Thomas Davidson and William Benham, *The Life of Archibald Campbell Tait Archbishop of Canterbury*, 2 vols. (London: Macmillan, 1891), 2:8–9.

141. RA D 26/16, General Grey to the archbishop of Canterbury, 4 June 1869.

was especially concerned with the terms of the church's disendowment, which she called "the really bad, dangerous and unjust part."[142] At the same time she received warnings about the constitutional dangers of her interfering in the deliberations of the House of Lords.[143]

Nonetheless, she persisted and came to form part of a line of communication that led from Tory peers, opposed to the bill, to Archbishop Tait, to the queen, and thence to the Liberal leader in the Lords, Lord Granville, and back again.[144] The pressure was not all from the Tories on the Liberals to make concessions. Granville told the queen with apparent sincerity about how he had tried to discourage public meetings against the obduracy of the Tory-dominated second chamber. The real question at issue was "the dignity, efficiency and *permanence* [emphasis added] of that Assembly [the Lords]."[145] Intended to alarm the Tories, it actually frightened the queen, who told him she hoped he "will do *all* he *can* to enable the moderate Conservatives to *prevail*."[146] On 19 June the second reading of the bill was carried in the Lords by a majority of thirty-three, with the archbishops of Canterbury and York abstaining.

But the Lords had amended the bill and Gladstone had to tell the queen in early July that the government could not accept the changes that had reduced the disendowment to "a mere shadow."[147] She tried to turn the democratic card against him, saying that though the election had been won on the issue of disestablishment, the removal of state backing for the church, there had been little said during the campaign on disendowment, the removal of the church's investments. He should therefore be prepared to make concessions on the latter issue.[148] This was calculated to infuriate the "people's William." When Tait had made a similar point, Gladstone had replied that "[h]is means of information must be inferior to the means of information of those, who were every where in contact with the people."[149] It was a rebuke also to the queen.

142. Queen Victoria to the Crown Princess of Prussia, 24 March 1869, in Fulford, *Your Dear Letter*, 230.

143. RA D 26/25, Lord Grey to General Grey, 6 June 1869.

144. RA D 26/26, 28, Archbishop of Canterbury to Queen Victoria, 7 June 1869 (in Davidson and Benham, *Tait*, 2:26–27), Queen Victoria to Lord Granville, 8 June 1869.

145. RA D 26/29, Lord Granville to Queen Victoria, 8 June 1869.

146. RA D 26/31, Queen Victoria to Lord Granville, 9 June 1869.

147. RA D 26/60, W. E. Gladstone to Queen Victoria, 10 July 1869.

148. RA D 26/65, Queen Victoria to W. E. Gladstone, 11 July 1869.

149. RA D 26/67, W. E. Gladstone to Queen Victoria, 12 July 1869.

An impasse had developed between Commons and Lords. Once again Queen Victoria arranged a meeting between the prime minister and Tait.[150] Several tense days followed, but eventually the outstanding points were settled, the bill passed the Lords on 22 July, became law four days later, and "a formidable constitutional conflict" was avoided.[151] The Church of Ireland was allowed to keep half its endowment, amounting to eight million pounds. One million went to Maynooth and the Presbyterian Church, both of which lost their existing state subsidies, and seven million was set aside for charity.[152]

Her daughter Vicky told the queen that disestablishment had been a very popular issue on the Continent and "indeed it has wonderfully increased your popularity."[153] The queen thought that "the Irish don't care the least" for disestablishment and that their interest was in land reform.[154] Yet many Irish Protestants did care and there was great disappointment that the monarch, whom they had toasted as "Defender of the Faith" at some of their meetings, had not taken a stand in defense of establishment.[155] There was talk of the queen's treachery. Indeed, some Protestants, as a symbolic gesture of protest against the measure, were said to have threatened to "kick the Queen's Crown into the Boyne" if it was passed.[156]

Obstacles overcome are soon forgotten. Had the Lords thrown out the bill and had the second chamber survived to continue to block disestablishment, the issue would have eventually become as enormous a source of grievance in Ireland as home rule and the land issue were to become. Gladstone's action had forestalled all of that, but he had only been able to achieve it with the active help of the queen.

Why had she been so helpful to Gladstone on this issue when in years to come she would oppose his efforts to bring about home rule

---

150. RA D 26/89, W. E. Gladstone to Queen Victoria, 19 July 1869.

151. RA D 26/103, W. E. Gladstone to Queen Victoria, 22 July 1869.

152. Comerford, *Fenians*, 163.

153. The Crown Princess of Prussia to Queen Victoria, 4 May 1869, in Fulford, *Your Dear Letter*, 234.

154. Queen Victoria to the Crown Princess of Prussia, 13 March 1869, in Fulford, *Your Dear Letter*, 228.

155. *FJ*, 11 June 1869.

156. *FJ*, 4 February 1888. See too *FJ*, 12 January 1892, which reports a meeting of the Dublin Corporation in which it was said that the remark had been attributed to a William Johnston who had denied ever making it.

tooth and nail? Even more than home rule, disestablishment seemed to involve an issue of principle, for the monarch's coronation oath had pledged the queen to uphold the Protestant religion. Nor can her actions be explained in terms of any great sympathy for Ireland at the time or for Catholicism.

Personally, Queen Victoria was beginning to move toward a pronounced Protestantism in her own religious stance. In November 1873 she famously took communion in the Presbyterian, Established Church of Scotland at Crathie Church on her Balmoral Estate.[157] A year later she told Vicky with reference to the situation on the continent that Catholicism was "so aggressive, so full of every sort of falseness and uncharitableness and bigotry (unlike any other) that it must be resisted and opposed."[158] Six months later she was telling her daughter "how very anti-Catholic I am."[159]

The answer may lie in the political formation that Queen Victoria had received from the prime ministers of her youth. In 1838 Melbourne had told her "that the Established Church was *generally* kept up for the Poor, as the rich could afford that themselves; whereas in Ireland . . . the Established Church is *only* kept up for the Protestant feeling of the United Kingdom and not for the Poor who are almost all Roman Catholics."[160]

More important was the formative influence that Sir Robert Peel had exerted over twenty years before. On 30 March 1846 Prince Albert had a discussion on the subject of the church establishment with him. Peel had had his share of having to deal with monarchs who stood out against ecclesiastical reform on the grounds of principle and therefore "advised the greatest secrecy upon that subject, that neither the Queen nor myself should say a word upon the subject to any body as it was most dangerous ground." The issue had split up five governments that Peel could name and caused other enormous difficulties.

"The Coronation oath was a ground which he had always avoided in debate as a most dangerous one, being a most difficult and obtuse question

157. *FJ,* 4 November 1873.

158. Queen Victoria to the Crown Princess of Prussia, 20 October 1874, in Roger Fulford, *Darling Child: Private Correspondence of Queen Victoria and the Crown Princess of Prussia, 1871–78* (London: Evans, 1976), 158.

159. Queen Victoria to the Crown Princess of Prussia, 16 April 1875, in Fulford, *Darling Child,* 178.

160. RA QVJ, 16 May 1838, quoted in Esher, *Girlhood,* 1:327.

which exposed the Sovereign personally to bear the whole brunt of furious party contest lead [*sic*] by religious fanaticism."[161] The combined influence of Peel and an impressed Prince Albert may have been the reason why Queen Victoria did everything in her power to prevent Irish Church disestablishment from becoming a divisive constitutional issue or an issue of principle for the monarchy.

❖

It was decided early in 1869 that Prince Arthur should be the next member of the royal family to visit Ireland. Queen Victoria had concerns about the popular agitation for the release of Fenian prisoners and about growing agrarian agitation. The new lord lieutenant, Lord Spencer, the "red earl," was reassuring.[162] Indeed, the queen would have done well to have been more concerned about possible trouble from the opponents of disestablishment.

The visit was a long one, lasting from the 3 April to 4 May. Prince Arthur was hailed by Dr. Russell of Maynooth as "a Prince whom our beloved Queen in a manner dedicated to Ireland" by giving him Patrick as one of his names.[163] The prince carried out what was by now becoming the usual round of royal visits in Dublin and followed his elder brother's example with a visit to Punchestown. He stayed with the Count de Jarnac, a French diplomat under Louis Philippe with Irish family connections who was later to be ambassador of the Third Republic to London,[164] at Thomastown Castle, County Tipperary, before traveling to Killarney.[165] At Kenmare Convent school the children sang him a special song that began with an allusion to his godfather:

> Like Wellington, whose name he bears,
> Brave to repeal his country's foes;

---

161. RA D 15/15, Prince Albert, memorandum, 30 March 1846. Peel proceeded to recommend reading on the subject to Prince Albert (RA D 15/11, 12, Sir Robert Peel to Prince Albert, 30, 31 March 1846). Two days later Peel was uncomfortable with the fact that the prince had written a memo about their conversation. Prince Albert accordingly threw the memo on the fire (RA D 15/13, Prince Albert, memorandum, 1 April 1846), but then wrote another memo about that meeting and seems to have kept a copy of the original.

162. RA D 25/57, 59, General Grey to W. E. Gladstone, 26 March 1869; Lord Spencer to W. E. Gladstone, 30 March 1869.

163. *FJ*, 9 April 1869.   164. *FJ*, 23 March 1875.

165. *FJ*, 6–10, 12–14, 17, 21–22 April 1869.

> Like Patrick, helping all their needs,
> And thoughtful for his country's woes.[166]

Several days later he was in Derry where the Protestant Apprentice Boys organization tried to politicize his visit by shouting "No Surrender" at an anti-Liberal demonstration. Later in the day there was a riot in another part of the city and three people died.[167] This was the first occasion on which there had been any trouble during a royal visit and it was significant that it was caused not by nationalists but by the supporters of Protestant ascendancy. "When the daily and hourly talk is about the Queen's treachery, if she disregarded the Coronation oath, and the appeal of power and bayonets, one is not surprised at the ring of revolvers on the walls of Derry."[168]

The prince went on to spend several successful days in Belfast before his departure,[169] though he was too early to see the completed statue to his father there.[170] Later in the year Arthur traveled to Canada to serve with the rifle brigade. He visited Buffalo in New York State, which was notorious for its Fenian connections. The visit gave rise to a false story that he had been kidnapped by the Fenians. In May 1870 he was in command of troops at St. John's during a Fenian skirmish.[171]

"Arthur has had a perfect triumph in Ireland—even in the worst and most dangerous part," the queen wrote to Vicky.[172] She dismissed the "unfortunate riots, which had nothing to do with his visit, being purely political and religious. Arthur was in bed at the time."[173]

In Ireland in 1869 mainstream nationalist politicians might express sympathy for the plight of Fenians prisoners but not directly for the cause of Fenianism. That was beyond the bounds of the politically acceptable. Daniel O'Sullivan thought himself an exception. On 1 January he was installed as mayor of Cork, accepting a green flag with "God Save Ireland" on it.[174] Early in 1868 he had been dismissed from the magistracy by Lord

---

166. *FJ*, 23 April 1869.   167. *FJ*, 29 April 1869.

168. *FJ*, 30 April 1869.   169. *FJ*, 1, 3, 4 May 1869.

170. *Belfast Newsletter*, 1, 11 May 1869.

171. Noble Frankland, *Witness of a Century: The Life and Times of Prince Arthur, Duke of Connaught, 1850–1942* (London: Shepheard, Walwyn, 1993), 36–37, 40.

172. Queen Victoria to the Crown Princess of Prussia, in Fulford, *Your Dear Letter*, 232.

173. RA QVJ, 30 April 1869.

174. *FJ*, 2 January 1869.

Mayo for subscribing to relieve the families of Fenian prisoners.[175] During Prince Arthur's visit he had blocked an invitation to have him open a new racecourse.[176] The same evening, 27 April, O'Sullivan presided at a banquet for two released Fenians prisoners, John Warren and Augustine E. Costello, who were about to set out for America. O'Sullivan made a speech:

There was at this moment in the country a young Prince of the English nation.
A Voice—He be d[amne]d.
Another Voice—No, he's welcome.
The Mayor continued to say that, when that noble Irishman O'Farrell fired at the Prince in Australia he was imbued with as noble and patriotic feelings as Larkin, Allen and O'Brien (great cheering, and cries of "he was").[177]

Queen Victoria was horrified at such "atrocious language, almost with reference to Arthur's visit to Ireland, praising O'Farrell who shot at Affie, and the criminals at Manchester and Clekenwell!!" What was worse, she had received O'Sullivan at a levee less than two months before as part of a Fenian amnesty deputation.[178] She demanded action against O'Sullivan, and Gladstone promised to oblige. However, when it was discovered that O'Sullivan had not contravened any law Gladstone found himself having to resort to the arcane and judicially dubious expedient of introducing a bill of pains and penalities into Parliament to disbar the mayor from office.[179] This was a parliamentary declaration of guilt and imposition of punishment, without recourse to trial before the courts or impeachment before the Lords, and differed from the similar procedure of attainder only inasmuch as death was the penalty for the latter.[180] O'Sullivan himself had made a speech at a committee of the Cork Corporation that began as a retraction but turned into a reiteration, illustrative of the ambivalence toward political violence among some nationalists:

He would be the last man in Ireland to countenance the taking of the life of either prince or peasant; and if he saw a pistol aimed at a royal prince or at anyone tomorrow, he would be the first to turn it aside, though he turned it on himself.

---

175. Oliver MacDonagh, "The Last Bill of Pains and Penalties: The Case of Daniel O'Sullivan, 1869," *Irish Historical Studies* 19 (1974–1975): 138.
176. *FJ*, 28 April 1869.
177. *FJ*, 29 April 1869.
178. RA QVJ, 29 April 1869.
179. RA D 26/2, 5, W. E. Gladstone to Queen Victoria, 1, 4 May 1869.
180. MacDonagh, "O'Sullivan," 136.

He did not approve of O'Farrell's act, but, at the same time, he would not deny him credit for pure and honourable motives (oh!). He would not and could not deny such motives to Allen, Larkin and O'Brien, or even the unhappy man Barrett who blew up Clerkenwell.[181]

Gladstone's bill was introduced into the Commons on 5 May. It accused O'Sullivan of misconduct not only on account of the speech but also because of his mayoral performance as an ex officio magistrate. N. D. Murphy, the MP for Cork, said he felt "shame and humiliation" over the affair.[182] Things began to get more complicated, however, when it was agreed that a copy of the bill be sent to O'Sullivan, that the Irish attorney general be ordered to produce evidence against O'Sullivan, and that witnesses and counsel be produced before the House.[183] It was turning into a trial after all. Next there was news of public meetings in Cork in support of the mayor and three Irish Liberals spoke up for him.[184]

The whole procedure was becoming deeply embarrassing to a Liberal government and was garnering international notoriety:[185]

A Bill of Pains and Penalties brings to remembrance the worst times of our history, and, mingled with the feeling that such a process was an engine which had been abused and ever must be capable of great abuse, there was a sense that it was almost ludicrous to bring the whole force of Parliament to bear against such a person as Mr. O'Sullivan.[186]

Fortunately for Gladstone, O'Sullivan himself came to Parliament's rescue. On 11 May J. F. Maguire, another MP from Cork, read to the Commons O'Sullivan's letter of resignation as mayor.[187] A relieved government announced that it would not proceed with the bill. Gladstone told the queen that "on this occasion, perhaps, for the first time, public sentiment in Ireland has refused the invitation to array itself against the authority of the Crown and the Law."[188]

If by "the Crown" Gladstone meant the monarchy, he was right that the incident certainly illustrated the existence of a deference toward it in Irish public discourse. But, whereas public defiance of the Crown as government

---

181. *FJ*, 1 May 1869.
182. 5 May 1869, *Parliamentary Debates*, 3d Series, vol. 196 (1 May–16 June 1869), col. 229.
183. *FJ*, 7 May 1869.   184. MacDonagh, "O'Sullivan," 147–48.
185. *FJ*, 7 May 1869.   186. *Times*, 12 May 1869.
187. *FJ*, 12 May 1869.
188. RA D 26/9, W. E. Gladstone to Queen Victoria, 11 May 1869.

was commonplace in nationalist Ireland, public defiance of the Crown as monarchy in public had always been a rarity. Gladstone was wrong to see anything new in the deference shown but also wrong to suggest, as he seemed to do, that it might be a growing trend. During the next decade deference to the Crown as monarchy would in fact begin to crumble in Ireland.

⁂

Gladstone continued to pursue his policy of conciliation toward Ireland through two measures, the release of Fenian prisoners and the 1870 land act that increased the rights of tenant farmers. The queen disapproved of the first and was skeptical of the second. If security of tenure was a tenant aspiration that was being entertained, then "the lawless determination neither to pay rent, nor to suffer evictions, should have been denounced . . . as a violation of the rights of property which could not be allowed for a moment."[189]

On 22 February 1869 half of the remaining Fenian prisoners in custody were released. Eight months later Gladstone was telling the queen that as a result "the feeling of the people of Ireland towards the Throne and the Legislature has perceptibly improved."[190] The queen disagreed.[191] Releasing the Fenians was a sign of weakness.[192]

The momentum for amnesty continued in Ireland and paved the way for the first really serious movement to press for domestic government since O'Connell. Its leader was Isaac Butt, president of the Amnesty Association, who was to go on to found the Home Government Association in 1870 and the Home Rule League in 1873. On 28 June 1869 Butt recalled being part of the group that had presented an amnesty petition to the queen at a levee in March. "I believe that those who waited on her at the levee formed the opinion that if her personal feelings of humanity were consulted these men would not now be in prison."[193]

In October 1871, while the queen was ill, the home secretary, H. A. Bruce, replied negatively on her behalf to an amnesty petition that had been sent to her. In the reply he denied that amnesty should be extended

189. RA D 27/10, Queen Victoria to W. E. Gladstone, 19 January 1870.
190. RA D 26/118, W. E. Gladstone to Queen Victoria, 2 October 1869.
191. RA D 26/116, Sir Thomas Biddulph to W. E. Gladstone, 29 September 1869.
192. RA D 26/121, Queen Victoria to W. E. Gladstone, 5 October 1869.
193. *FJ,* 29 June 1869.

to Fenians in the army or those who had killed Sergeant Brett. It was a policy statement in a message supposedly from the queen. Butt was quick to capitalize on the home secretary's blunder. He expressed himself to be outraged, refusing to believe that the views in the letter could have been authorized by the queen:

> The Queen, we are told, is too ill to attend to government business. What impression would be produced upon the minds of the Irish people if they believed that the only time and the first time she took an active part in public business was to command an angry letter, refusing the request of her Irish subjects. I believe that nothing could be more calculated to prevent her Majesty from receiving the attachment or regard of the Irish people. The minister who dictated that letter committed a crime against the Queen.[194]

In 1875 the Irish MP Mitchel Henry appealed to the House of Commons for the release of Fenians who had been in the army. He blamed their continuing detention on "the military authorities," hinting that the commander-in-chief the Duke of Cambridge was to blame. He then appealed rhetorically "to that tender spot in the heart of the Sovereign" for their amnesty.[195]

Some moderate nationalist opinion—and Butt was a moderate—believed at the time and for some time afterward that the queen was well disposed to Ireland, meaning Irish nationalists, while in private she was actually working to frustrate Gladstone's plans for Irish reform. In some ways it was necessary to the political strategy for moderate nationalists to believe this, even if the evidence to the contrary had been available, as it enabled them to invoke the hope of a constitutional authority greater than that of the government with which they were often at loggerheads. It added weight to their advocacy of the constitutional rather than the physical-force path in politics.

The amnesty movement was politically broad and included Fenians and others who were less deferential than Butt. This was evidenced at the end of yet another visit from the Prince of Wales to Dublin, this time from 31 July to 7 August 1871. The monarchy was at a low ebb in England and the

---

194. *FJ*, 24 October 1871.
195. 7 August 1875, *Parliamentary Debates*, 3d Series, vol. 226 (26 July–13 August 1875), cols. 683–86.

English republican movement was enjoying its brief flowering at the time. In July 1871 there was great criticism in the press of the fact that no members of the royal family had been on duty to receive the emperor and empress of Brazil on their visit to London.[196]

The Prince of Wales himself was becoming an increasingly discredited figure in the eyes of Victorian moralists. His involvement in the 1870 Mordaunt divorce case had not been a help. However, his popularity in Ireland had been enhanced by the publication of an apparently purloined letter from him to his brother, Alfred, officially denounced as a hoax, on the topic of visiting Ireland in the summer of 1870:

Alix does not like it as she says we are not called upon to run in the way of being shot. . . . It is a pity they [the Irish] are so discontented and the shooting at landlords from behind hedges is really too bad. For all that I would willingly spend the summer or autumn in Ireland, and knock about a bit, and take my chance, if it would do any good. I can't see if there are any Irishmen who would like to shoot me, why they would not do so in London instead of waiting until I took the trouble of visiting their own country. I don't mean to say I'd like to be shot; far from it, as I am a great believer in unbroken bones; but one can't be over nice now-a-days. Besides I am getting a bit tired of my life here, and would like to assist in making friends with the Irish who are excellent fellows at heart and the best soldiers in the world.[197]

In the early part of 1871 most public attention on royal circles was focused on the queen's fourth daughter, Louise, who contracted what was to turn out to be her unhappy marriage to the marquis of Lorne, heir to the duke of Argyll, in March. A week before the wedding she was presented with a memorial from "the ladies of Ireland" in support of Fenian amnesty.[198] The Lornes were to accompany the Prince of Wales on his visit, as was Prince Arthur. The queen chose the moment of the beginning of the visit to request that Arthur be given the usual annuity for her unmarried sons who had come of age of £15,000. It was agreed by Parliament, though in the Commons fifty-one MPs, twenty-eight of them Irish, voted to reduce the sum to £10,000.[199]

The *Freeman's Journal*, while admitting that "the seclusion of his [the

196. *FJ*, 24 July 1871.   197. *FJ*, 19 May 1870.
198. *FJ*, 14 March 1871.
199. 31 July 1871, *Parliamentary Debates*, 3d Series, vol. 208 (20 July–21 August 1871), cols. 570–90.

Prince of Wales's] Royal mother may have tended to diminish her personal popularity," nonetheless welcomed the visit:

> The warmest Nationalists, either of past times or of the present, have acknowledged, and acknowledge now, that it is for the common good of Great Britain and Ireland that the same monarch should preside over both islands. The "golden link of the Crown" has never been felt as a grievance, even by those who have chafed the most at the hands of the legislative connexion.

The programme of events for the visit was unremarkable, centering on a visit to the Royal Agricultural Society show. The only controversial event was the visit of the Prince of Wales to the Masonic Hall in Molesworth Street; Catholic Ireland was deeply suspicious of the Freemasons.[200] The prince was very pleased with the welcome in Dublin. He wrote to his mother that Arthur "is always hailed as 'Prince Patrick' or 'Pathrick' tout court and they quite look upon him as their special Prince."[201]

Lord Lorne, straying from the principle of noblesse oblige, wrote rather patronizingly of the lord mayor of Dublin, John Campbell, to his new mother-in-law. The "ball at the Mansion House was a dreadful infliction for there were over 2,000 people crowed into a round room with very little ventilation but he [the lord mayor] was in great spirits and said the most wonderful things." At a dinner Lorne was amused by the lord mayor's interest in the aristocracy and his accent, which Lorne thought it would be acceptable to mock. "'Well, Markiss, will ye tell me who's that young man?'" he asked of several persons there, all of whom happened to hold the title of marquess. When Lorne told him who each one was the lord mayor acknowledged receipt of the information with "'Eigh, that's the Markiss!'"[202]

But there was trouble in store for the royal visitors. An amnesty meeting was called for Sunday, 6 August, by P. J. Smyth, MP for Meath, and by A. M. and T. D. Sullivan. The venue was the Phoenix Park not too far away from the Vice Regal Lodge where the royal visitors were staying. It was banned by an official of the Board of Works but was held nonetheless. There was a baton charge by the police and several people were injured, in-

---

200. *FJ*, 2, 5 August 1871.

201. RA D 27/89, Prince of Wales to Queen Victoria, 3 August 1871, in Lee, *Edward VII*, 1:230.

202. RA D 27/91, Lord Lorne to Queen Victoria, 5 August 1871, in Buckle, *Letters*, second series, 2:155–56.

cluding A. M. Sullivan. The riot caused outrage in England as well as in Ireland at the brutality of the police action and it soured attitudes to what had been turning into a highly successful royal visit. The *Pall Mall Gazette* was caustic about the visit and about British expectations concerning the monarchy's role in Ireland:

The assumption that Irish grievances are so fanciful that a couple of Princes and Princesses have only to pay a hurried visit to the capital, and eat, drink and dance with gay activity for two or three days, within sight of the select circles of the Castle to set them right has been universally resisted.[203]

Lord Mayor Campbell, days before the subject of Lorne's mockery, became a nationalist hero when he refused a knighthood from the departing Prince of Wales in protest of the police action. A. M. Sullivan exacted his own revenge within the month by acting as host to a high-level delegation of French republicans, headed by Count de Flavigny, who had come on a fact-finding tour of Ireland and were treated to a banquet at the Mansion House and given a tellingly royal reception.[204] "The reception of the French delegation seemed to me to be scandalous & their language as reported little better," wrote Gladstone. "But I hope the reception at least is in some degree to be referred to temporary irritation."[205]

The royal party were still considering the visit a success. Lorne told the queen that "there never was more loyalty shown than during the last days" and that in spite of the amnesty meeting incident "there was a very hearty reception given us this m[ornin]g on leaving Dublin."[206] The lord lieutenant, Lord Spencer, wrote to Queen Victoria that he was "more convinced than ever that the influence of a visit from the Royal family is great for Ireland. The mass of the Irish people are loyal but require to realize and see the object of their loyalty." As for the amnesty meeting, it had been the work of "the Fenian element in the city [who] dreaded the effect of the successful Royal visit upon their funds and organization."[207]

203. Reported in *FJ*, 8 August 1871.

204. *FJ*, 17, 28 August 1871.

205. W. E. Gladstone to Lord Spencer, 25 August 1871, in H. C. G. Matthew, *The Gladstone Diaries*, 14 vols. (Oxford: Clarendon Press, 1968–1994), vol. 8 (July 1871–December 1874), p. 27.

206. RA D 27/92, Lord Lorne to Queen Victoria, 7 August 1871.

207. RA D 27/93, Lord Spencer to Queen Victoria, 8 August 1871, in Peter Gordon, *The Red Earl. Papers of the Fifth Earl Spencer, Vol. 1: 1835–1885* (Northampton: Northampton Records Society, 1981), no. 84, pp. 95–96.

Gladstone was furious that the meeting had been banned and that the riot had been precipitated by a police action. This was "the first occasion on which your proceedings have been the subject of serious criticism," he warned Spencer.[208] In the Commons the government was blamed for having "played the game of their opponents" and having undone all the good of the royal visit. Their sternest critic was Colonel White, the MP for Tipperary:

No doubt the promoters [of the demonstration] thought the close proximity of Members of the Royal Family would add to the effect of their agitation; and if this were so, although the design constituted a breach of hospitality, no one would say it was an occasion for battering and bludgeoning the people almost to the extremity of murder.

Had the Prince of Wales been "hooted out of the city the next day, who would have been responsible for that?" The fact that the royal party continued to be well received after the riot was a tribute to "the good feeling and the hospitality of those Dublin people whom they [the government] had taken upon themselves to batter and maim and send to hospital for nothing at all."[209]

In early September Smyth and the Sullivans held another amnesty meeting in the Phoenix Park. The royal visitors were high on the agenda of topics for the speakers:

The royal party visited this country with great dread of being shot sitting in their carriages (laughter). To guard against that they attached to the hind portion of their carriages two ten inch barrel revolvers in case an attempt to injure them was made.

Did the Prince of Wales love the Irish? On a recent occasion he said in an outburst of passion that he wished he was on the throne. And for what? Was it to allay the sufferings or better the condition of Ireland? It was not, but to rule Ireland with an iron hand, and with the intention that all he could not coerce to be loyal subjects he would exterminate from the land (loud cheers and hisses).

Someone else claimed that Lord Lorne had written that the Irish were "lower than the Hottentots." The speeches having reached this point of extravagance, Smyth intervened to point out that there was no evidence to

208. W. E. Gladstone to Lord Spencer, 25 August 1871, in H. C. G. Matthew, *The Gladstone Diaries*, 8:26.

209. 17 August 1871, *Parliamentary Debates*, 3d Series, vol. 208 (20 July–21 August 1871), cols. 1774–75.

suggest that the royal visitors had had anything directly to do with the suppression of the original meeting.[210]

"Royal visits to Ireland have always been successful," claimed the *Times* before the Phoenix Park riot.[211] The 1871 visit was an important one for the relationship between monarchy and nationalism in Ireland. The original Phoenix Park meeting had been called as a counter to the royal visit. One nationalist newspaper had put it to its readers that it was "the duty of the people to demonstrate that patriots are dearer to their hearts than princes."[212] Apart from the O'Sullivan incident, whose public dimension was inadvertent, this was the first occasion on which a royal visit was directly marked by a nationalist counterevent. It had not yet taken the form of an explicit challenge to royalty. However, the inept way in which the meeting was first banned and then suppressed was an added lesson to more radical nationalists regarding the publicity value of anti-royal confrontation.

❖

The Prince of Wales returned to England only to fall ill later in the year. Following the queen's own recovery from serious illness, his recovery was accompanied by public rejoicing and marked the beginning of the rehabilitation of the monarchy in English popular opinion. Lord Spencer noted a change of mood in Ireland too.[213] The queen's own popularity rose further after an apparent assassination attempt on her on 29 February 1872 by a madman called Arthur O'Connor, a nephew of the Chartist leader Feargus O'Connor, with an unloaded pistol. He had wanted to get her to sign a Fenian amnesty petition, though he had no connection with the Fenians himself.

O'Connor was only given twelve months hard labor and twenty strokes of the birch in punishment, to the annoyance of his potential victim.[214] Meanwhile, the queen presented John Brown with a medal for saving her life.[215] Her assassin's Irish background "certainly is not tended to increase the Queen's wish to visit Ireland."[216] Nor could have a later incident. In

---

210. *FJ*, 4 September 1871.

211. *Times*, 2 August 1871.

212. Lee, *Edward VII*, 1:231.

213. RA D 27/95, 96, Lord Spencer to Queen Victoria, 27 December 1871, 11 February 1872.

214. Weintraub, *Victoria*, 402.   215. *FJ*, 1 March, 8, 12 April 1872.

216. Lady Mary Biddulph to Lord Spencer, 16 March 1872, Spencer Papers, in Gordon, *The Red Earl*, vol. 1, no. 90, p. 100.

December 1878 a man called Edward Byrne Madden, subsequently judged to be of unsound mind, wrote to the government threatening to shoot the queen. He later claimed that he had been acting under the instructions of the late Prince Albert.[217]

The 1871 Irish visit was important for the Prince of Wales. It dented his ambition to make the cause of the monarchy in Ireland his special project. It would be fourteen years before he would visit Ireland again. Only a day or two before the Phoenix Park débâcle he had written to his mother from Dublin that an Irish royal residence "would do more than any political measure which might be brought forward in parliament and Lord Spencer is very strong in that opinion."[218]

A related issue to royal visits was a royal residence. O'Connell had suggested an Irish royal residence during George IV's visit in 1821 and had subscribed £20 annually thereafter toward it.[219] William Dargan had told the queen that the greatest honor she could give him would be to order him to build her a palace in Ireland.[220] The issues of a royal residence in Ireland and of a role for the Prince of Wales in Ireland were the cause of a running battle between Queen Victoria and Gladstone during most of the five years of his first term as prime minister. But the idea of the prince living in Ireland for a part of each year predated even Gladstone. The *Daily Telegraph* suggested it in 1864.[221] There was laughter in the Commons the next year when it was suggested that the lord lieutenant be replaced by the Prince of Wales residing in Ireland for three months each year.[222] In May 1867 the *Court Circular*, however, intimated that such an arrangement was indeed likely.[223]

In December 1868 the departing Abercorn, now a duke, had urged more frequent royal visits to Ireland. General Grey summed up his view as being based on the position that "the grievances of Ireland are rather sentimental than such as can be removed by Acts of Parliament . . . [the Irish people feel] that they are considered and treated as an inferior People who had no *right* to ask from their Sovereign and the Royal Family, those attentions which are paid to other parts of Your Majesty's dominions."[224]

The queen apparently toyed with the idea of a trip to Ireland "for a few

217. *FJ*, 13, 20 December 1878.
218. RA D 27/89, Prince of Wales to Queen Victoria, 3 August 1871.
219. *FJ*, 21 December 1878.   220. *JF*, 20 February 1867.
221. *FJ*, 16 August 1864.
222. *FJ*, 9 February 1865.223. *FJ*, 5 February 1867.
224. RA D 24/63, General Grey to Queen Victoria, 23 December 1868.

weeks to see the country" but not for long.[225] Grey, however, had over-reached his mandate in the matter by discussing with the new lord lieu-tenant, Lord Spencer, the queen's wish "to become better acquainted with the fine scenery of the country and with the peasantry if it could be done privately and quietly as Your Majesty visits Scotland."[226]

Spencer had responded with alacrity to the possibility of a visit from the queen. He told Grey that the Dublin banker, John La Touche, was offering to give the queen his residence in the Wicklow mountains if there were occasional royal visits.[227] But the queen was too ambivalent about vis-iting Ireland to accept the offer.[228]

In May 1868 the matter of a royal residence had been raised in the Commons by the veteran Irish lawyer Sir Colman O'Loghlen. The royal family were Ireland's "greatest absentees." A royal residence would "aid in the work of pacification." Borrowing a phrase from the Young Irelanders, he claimed it "would reconcile the dynasty to them [the people] and make it, so to speak, racy of the soil." He was particularly keen that the queen would "visit the cottages of the poor as she did in Scotland."[229] During Gladstone's first ministry the matter became a campaigning issue for anoth-er MP called Stacpoole. He raised the matter in July 1870, February and July 1871, and February, April, and July 1872. At one point Gladstone told him that "if there were any risk of the Government forgetting its duty [on the matter], I am sensible that by his agitation we should be reminded of it."[230]

Much had in fact been going on behind the scenes, in a complex debate that involved several rather separate issues. The first was that of a royal res-idence in Ireland. The second was that of a role in Ireland for the Prince of Wales, either as lord lieutenant or as an intermittent royal resident. The third was the that of the role of lord lieutenant himself. As Henry Ponsonby shrewdly put it to the queen after a year and a half of debate,

225. RA D 24/64, General Grey to Queen Victoria, 23 December 1868.

226. RA D 24/65, General Grey to Queen Victoria, 29 December 1868.

227. RA D 24/65, General Grey to Queen Victoria, 29 December 1868.

228. RA D 25/3, General Grey to W. E. Gladstone, 8 January 1869, in Buckle, *Letters,* second series, 1:575–77.

229. 15 May 1868, *Parliamentary Debates,* 3d Series, vol. 192 (11 May–25 June 1868), cols. 346–50.

230. 23 April 1872, *Parliamentary Debates,* 3d Series, vol. 210 (15 March–30 April 1872), col. 1678.

Gladstone was really interested in securing a role for the Prince of Wales and Spencer was really interested in securing a royal residence.[231]

Gladstone broached the subject with the queen in June 1871. She was against a residence being bought because it would oblige the royal family to visit Ireland very regularly "when Scotland and England deserved it much more." If a member of the royal family had to be stationed regularly in Ireland for a third or even half of the year she thought it would be better if it was Prince Arthur, though she agreed with Gladstone that if it was the Prince of Wales the venture would at least keep him away from London.[232] Gladstone concluded that the queen was opposed to a royal residence but at least persuadable on the question of a royal lord lieutenant or of a prince as a substitute for the lord lieutenant.[233]

Sir Thomas Biddulph set the topic in the context of the growing republican movement in Britain itself. If a resident prince helped to "reclaim Ireland," it "would tend to popularize the Royal Family" generally.[234] This was a position with which the prime minister also agreed.[235] Gladstone tried to bring matters to a head by asking the queen what he should reply to Stacpoole's latest resolution. But it did not work and the queen told the prime minister to be vague about any commitment to a royal residence.[236]

Spencer, at Gladstone's request, had also been setting forth his views on the pros and cons of the issue. If a prince were appointed as lord lieutenant, there would be a danger that flatterers would gather around him and that he would be drawn into party politics. If the lord lieutenancy were replaced by a secretaryship of state with the promise of a royal residence in Ireland, there might be a problem of getting members of the royal family to visit frequently enough. Spencer therefore recommended the retention of the lord lieutenancy together with the setting up of a royal

231. RA D 27/120, Henry Ponsonby to Queen Victoria, 13 December 1872.

232. RA D 27/74, Queen Victoria, memorandum, 25 June 1871, in Buckle, *Letters* (London: John Murray, 1926), second series, vol. 2 (1870–1878), pp. 136–38.

233. H. G. C. Matthew, *The Gladstone Diaries* (Oxford: Clarendon Press, 1982), vol. 7 (1869–1871), pp. 514–15.

234. RA D 27/75, Sir Thomas Biddulph to Queen Victoria, 27 June 1871.

235. William M. Kuhn, "Ceremony and Politics: The British Monarchy 1871–72," *Journal of British Studies* 26, no. 2 (April 1987): 157.

236. RA D 27/80, 81, W. E. Gladstone to Queen Victoria, 5 July 1871; Queen Victoria to W. E. Gladstone, 6 July 1871.

residence.[237] In short, he did not think that it would be suitable for the Prince of Wales to take on the role of lord lieutenant or to substitute for that role. Gladstone did not agree. He thought that sending the prince to Ireland would both help him and the monarchy generally.[238]

Spencer continued to favor a royal residence as a way of mending Ireland's "sentimental grievance" about the royal family and toward the end of the next year was suggesting that Lord Portarlington's house, Emo Court in Queen's County, would be a suitable location for it.[239] Lord Bessborough, government chief whip in the Lords, had come up with the idea of abolishing the lord lieutenancy and having the Prince of Wales spend several months a year in Ireland in the first place.[240] Now he was saying that the Irish liked novelty and that if members of the royal family stayed in Ireland for long the novelty would wear off.[241]

By the end of 1872 Gladstone had also run out of steam on the matter.[242] So too had Queen Victoria's eldest son. In October 1872 he acknowledged that there was little likelihood that his mother would allow him any significant role in Ireland.[243] He contented himself with making recommendations concerning the appointment of lords lieutenant, Lord Hardwicke in 1876 and Lord Lorne in 1880, neither of whom was appointed. He refused requests from the duke of Marlborough, with whose family he had a personal grievance, to visit Ireland during his own tenure as lord lieutenant.[244]

In 1877 home rulers looked back with surprised amusement at their own

---

237. Lord Spencer, memorandum, 4 July 1871, in Gordon, *The Red Earl*, vol. 1, no. 83, pp. 93–95.

238. Lord Spencer, memorandum, 14 October 1871, in Gordon, *The Red Earl*, vol. 1, no. 89, pp. 98–99. Spencer also sought the advice of the retired Irish under secretary General Sir Thomas Larcom, but the latter warned him against change and taking "a false step" over the issue. See NLI, Larcom Papers, Ms 7504, Lord Spencer to General Sir Thomas Larcom, 24 October 1871, pp. 193–200; General Sir Thomas Larcom to Lord Spencer, 30 October 1871, pp. 203–11.

239. RA D 27/117, Lord Spencer, memorandum, November 1872.

240. Gordon, *The Red Earl*, vol. 1, p. 12.

241. RA D 27/116, Henry Ponsonby to Queen Victoria, 11 December 1872.

242. RA D 27/119, W. E. Gladstone to Queen Victoria, 12 December 1872.

243. Lee, *Edward VII*, 1:220.

244. Lee, *Edward VII*, vol. 1, p. 233. The duke's son Lord Randolph Churchill had tried to blackmail the prince over a case of marital discord. The prince had written innocent letters to Lady Aylesford. Lord Aylesford wanted to divorce her on account of her affair with

interest in a royal residence in 1870.[245] About the only person who persisted with the issue of the royal residence into Disraeli's second ministry was Captain Stacpoole. He raised it once more in July 1875 only to be ridiculed by A. M. Sullivan with the news that noblemen in Dublin tried to boost the prices for their houses by planting stories in the newspapers that the Prince of Wales was about to buy their premises.[246] Prime Minister Benjamin Disraeli was insouciant on the subject: "I am very much in favour of royal residences, particularly when they are inhabited."[247]

One prince who had not been much mentioned in the debate was Prince Alfred, duke of Edinburgh. He visited Dublin from 4–8 June 1872, to open an exhibition and inaugurate the statue of his father the prince consort on Leinster Lawn.[248] The exhibition, backed again by the Guinnesses, was to have the usual dimensions of industry and manufacture, on the one hand, and the arts, on the other, except that the artistic side centered on a national portrait exhibition that seemed to emphasize the canon of nationalist leaders from Sarsfield and Grattan to the "genius-stamped features of O'Connell."[249]

The unveiling of the Albert statue could not take place during the visit because only the supporting figures of science, labor, agriculture, and art were in place. Foley's maquette had to be hoisted into position for the prince to view. Three days after the prince had seen the statue there was an attempt to blow up both it and the statue of Lord Carlisle in the Phoenix

---

Lord Randolph's brother Lord Blandford, and in early 1876 Lord Randolph had threatened the Princess of Wales that the prince's letters would come out in court if he did not put pressure on Lord Aylesford to stop the divorce proceedings. See Richard Hough, *Edward and Alexandra: Their Private and Public Lives* (London: Hodder and Stoughton, 1992), 165–68.

245. *FJ*, 2 February 1877. "A great many speeches were made [at the founding of the Home Government Association in 1870]—some of a very foolish character—some stating that a Royal residence was needed and that if the Duke of Connaught were made a sort of perpetual Viceroy or resident all the evils of which they complained in Ireland would be removed (hear, hear and laughter)."

246. 25 June 1875, *Parliamentary Debates*, 3d Series, vol. 225 (16 June–23 July 1875), col. 564.

247. 24 July 1874, *Parliamentary Debates*, 3d Series, vol. 221 (15 July–7 August 1871), col. 625. Disraeli was replying to a question from Sir Eardley Wilmot.

248. *FJ*, 7 June 1872.

249. *FJ*, 1 May 1872.

Park. Lord Spencer wrote to the queen that "as last year the Fenian element of the population disliked the success of the Royal visit and showed their feelings in the meeting of the Phoenix Park, so this year the same party took the despicable course of attempting to damage the Memorial which the Duke had visited."[250]

Neither statue was really damaged.[251] But the attempt contributed to Queen Victoria's growing dislike of Ireland.[252] Nor was it to be the last attack on the statue. On 29 June 1875 two men, Joseph Barry and Martin Hopkins, were in the process of placing on the statue "a large piece of zinc in the shape of a helmet with the words 'No Royal Residence for Prince' painted on it in red letters" when they were arrested. They had covered the statue in canvas and paper saturated in coal tar. Had it been ignited it would have had a corrosive oxidixing effect on the bronze of the statue and disfigured it. A revolver was also found at the scene. The two men were fined £10 each and given a year in prison.[253] Ironically, the Albert statue has survived in an unobtrusive position on Leinster Lawn to the present day.

Gladstone's Irish university measure was defeated in March 1873 but it was not until after the general election of February 1874, at which sixty Irish home rulers were returned, that Disraeli resumed office. Spencer was offered a "step" in the peerage to marquess but refused it. He had been quite popular in Ireland and his departure was lamented. His successor turned out eventually to be his predecessor, the duke of Abercorn.[254] The chief secretary was to be Sir Michael Hicks-Beach whom Disraeli told the queen was "a rising man."[255]

During the following years there were a number of minor royal interactions with Ireland. There were reports that the Prince of Wales would visit in 1873[256] and that the duke of Edinbugh would attend the Dublin horse

250. RA D27/104, Lord Spencer to Queen Victoria, 10 June 1872.

251. *FJ*, 11 June 1872.

252. Frank Hardie, *The Political Influence of Queen Victoria, 1861–1901* (Oxford: Oxford University Press, 1935), 178.

253. *FJ*, 12 August 1875, p. 7.

254. *FJ*, 24, 26 February 1874.

255. Queen Victoria, memorandum, 20 February 1874, in Buckle, *Letters*, second series, 2:321.

256. *Daily News*, 30 August 1873, quoted in *FJ*, 1 September 1873.

show in 1874[257] with his new wife, but nothing came of them. In May 1874 Prince Arthur was confirmed in his Irish identity with the title of duke of Connaught.[258] He himself was stationed in Ireland for nearly two years from October 1876 to May 1878 in command of the first battalion of the Rifle Brigade, first in Dublin, then at the Curragh, and finally in Fermoy, County Cork. In 1879 Queen Victoria's youngest, Prince Leopold, who suffered from haemophilia and was to be created duke of Albany two years later and to die prematurely in 1884, made his only visit to Ireland. He cruised around the north coast, visiting Derry, Coleraine, Portrush, and the Giant's Causeway.[259]

Meanwhile nationalist Ireland was developing a confidence of its own when it came to welcoming international figures. In September 1872 there was a flurry of interest at reports that the exiled former emperor Napoleon III was going to buy a house at Bray, County Dublin.[260] That same month the Burmese ambassador visited Dublin.[261] The Chinese ambassador also visited in August 1877.[262] In August 1875 delegations from France, Gemany, Poland, and Switzerland attended the celebrations in Dublin to mark the centenary of O'Connell's birth.[263]

Then in July 1877 there was a visit from "the first crowned sovereign who (not being a King or Queen of England) has visited Ireland since King Robert the Bruce" in the person of the emperor of Brazil, though he was hissed by one "very excited bystander" who mistook him for the French general "what guv up Metz" to the Prussians in the Franco-Prussian War.[264] Finally, much was made of Gladstone, the once and future leader of the Liberal Party, who visited Dublin in a bid to woo home rulers from 17 October to 12 November 1877. The Dublin Corporation used its new powers under the 1876 Municipal Privileges (Ireland) Act to make him only the city's second honorary freeman, the first being Isaac Butt.[265]

The new sense of confidence and independence extended to formal etiquette. It was remarkable how long even at public banquets in the national-

257. *FJ*, 9 May 1874.
258. *London Gazette*, 26 May 1874, quoted in *FJ*, 27 May 1874.
259. *Times*, 9 September 1879.   260. *FJ*, 25 September 1872.
261. *FJ*, 28 September 1872.   262. *FJ*, 29 August 1877.
263. *FJ*, 9 August 1875.   264. *FJ*, 7, 9 July 1877.
265. *FJ*, 8 November 1877.

ist cause the use of the traditional three toasts to the queen, the other members of the royal family, and "The Lord Lieutenant and Prosperity to Ireland" persisted. "God Save the Queen" was sung and a toast to Queen Victoria was made at the Mansion House banquet in connection with the O'Connell centenary, for example.[266] It was not until August 1876 at a Dublin banquet of the Home Rule Confederation of Great Britain that Butt, "an experienced and not unskilled barrister," according to Disraeli,[267] changed the toasts to "The Queen, Lords, and Commons of Ireland" and "Prosperity to Ireland" with no mention of the lord lieutenant.[268]

The year 1876 saw the passing through Parliament by the government of Disraeli, soon to be earl of Beaconsfield, of the act to confer the title empress of India on Queen Victoria. There was extreme unease in England about the introduction of a title associated with the populist despots of Europe.[269] It was also unpopular in Ireland. For Sir John Gray's son Edmund Dwyer Gray it was a title "held by African potentates and Continental upstarts."[270] Several dozen Irish MPs voted against the measure. Butt, however, abstained in the hope of winning concessions on Fenian amnesty, as did two rising members of the Irish Home Rule Party, Joseph Biggar and Charles Stewart Parnell.[271]

These two were soon to pursue a policy of obstructing parliamentary business by means of long speeches and the use of procedural devices. Biggar once used such a device to have the Prince of Wales removed from the visitors' gallery of the House of Commons.[272] Before long Parnell had taken over the leadership of the Irish Parliamentary Party and was negotiating to secure the support of the Fenian movement for parliamentary agitation. Theodore Martin told the queen that Parnell and his followers "use the organs of a very desperate party in Ireland who are quite ready to seize the first favourable opportunity for a seditious outbreak."[273]

266. *FJ,* 6 August 1875.

267. RA D 28/5, Benjamin Disraeli to Queen Victoria, 1 July 1874.

268. *FJ,* 23 August 1876.

269. Richard Williams, *The Contentious Crown: Public Discussion of the British Monarchy in the Reign of Queen Victoria* (Brookfield, Vt: Ashgate, 1997), 115.

270. *FJ,* 25 April 1876.

271. Comerford, *Fenians,* 219.

272. Anna Parnell, "How They Do in the House of Commons: Notes from the Ladies' Cage," *Celtic Monthly,* May 1880, p. 469.

273. RA D 28/19c, Sir Theodore Martin to Queen Victoria, 30 July 1877.

In 1875 Joseph Biggar had been vociferous in his opposition to a visit by the Prince of Wales to India during a debate on the costs of the visit. Biggar saw the royal family being used for the same purpose in India as it was in Ireland, to excite popular enthusiasm for the Crown as proof against the need to acknowledge the reality of the discontent of the people:

In Ireland they had had two or three Royal visits, and great things had been expected from them by some people; but the agitation for the Repeal of the Union, for Catholic Emancipation, against tithes, still continued as strong after George IV's visit as it was before. Her present Majesty, when she visited Ireland, was right well received; but the people were still dissatisfied because they were misgoverned and they still agitated for Repeal, for Home Rule, for the improvement of the Land Laws, and the Fenian agitation had supervened.

Royal visits to Ireland or to India enabled the British governing classes to live in "a fool's paradise" about the lands they governed.[274]

The Prince of Wales's visit to India was accounted a great success and the Corporations of Dublin and London presented an address of congratulations to the queen at Osborne House on 24 July 1876.[275] There had been some opposition to the address in Dublin on the grounds that the prince on his way home had refused to lay the foundation stone for a Catholic orphanage in Malta.[276] He made up for it, however, by visiting the Irish Dominican nuns at Lisbon.[277]

In May 1878 Prince Arthur became engaged to Princess Louise of Prussia. In July the Commons approved a marriage grant for the couple but not without the opposition of Sir Charles Dilke, a leading scourge of the monarchy. Several Irish members spoke in favor, though there was laughter in the chamber when the prince's connections with Ireland were raised in his favor.[278]

In view of those links the lord mayor of Dublin, Hugh Tarpey, suggested an Irish national wedding gift for the couple.[279] When the mayor of Cork, W. V. Gregg, tried to hold a meeting about the gift, however, it

---

274. 15 July 1875, *Parliamentary Debates*, 3d Series, vol. 225 (16 June–23 July 1875), col. 1525.
275. *FJ*, 25 July 1876.
276. *FJ*, 26 April 1876.
277. *FJ*, 11 May 1876.
278. 25 July 1878, *Parliamentary Debates*, 3d Series, vol. 243 (23 July–16 August 1878), cols. 231–61.
279. *FJ*, 20 November 1878.

turned into a shambles.[280] The issue of the gift continued to cause controversy in 1879. There were objections that it was to be a silver dinner service bought in London and was not to be of Irish manufacture.[281] The marriage was in early March and the full gift was not presented until October.[282] As a token before the wedding a single silver candlestick was presented to the prince by the lord mayor of Dublin. However, there was a feeling in Ireland that Arthur had been rather peremptory in his gratitude and ought at least to have invited the lord mayor to the wedding.[283]

❖

The year 1879 was to see Ireland plunged into its worst agricultural depression since the famine. This led to the Land War and home rule crisis of the 1880s, which were accompanied by tenant evictions, outrages against landlords, and terrorist attacks in Britain. For this reason the killing of the unpopular landlord, Lord Leitrim, in 1878 seemed in retrospect to be a foretaste of what was to come.

There may, though, be a more specific reason for its importance to the story of monarchy and nationalism in Ireland. After his death Leitrim's remains were brought for burial to the family vault at St. Michan's Church in Dublin, which is located not far from the River Liffey. On its approach to the church the hearse was attacked by a crowd, some of whose members seemed intent on getting hold of the body, perhaps with a view to throwing it in the Liffey.[284] Queen Victoria received a much more benign account of the proceedings: "A good many rogues had collected, and there was the usual pushing and shouting common in such assemblages. The conduct was certainly unseemly but the crowd appeared to me to be good humoured." The rush toward the coffin was apparently only to get a better view.[285]

Whatever the truth, the darker version of events became canonized in nationalist mythology. Over twenty years later it may have provided the template for the symbolic funeral in Dublin of the British Empire, and by extension of the aged Queen Victoria, which climaxed with Maud Gonne and James Connolly pushing a coffin into the Liffey.

❖

280. *FJ,* 21 December 1878.
281. *FJ,* 15 February 1879.   282. *FJ,* 27 October 1879.
283. *FJ,* 13 March 1879.   284. *FJ,* 11 April 1878.
285. RA D 28/77, Lt. Col. J. A. Caulfield to Henry Ponsonby, 12 April 1878.

The mid- and late 1870s were not years of as special significance for the monarchy in Ireland as the late 1860s and early 1870s had been. By the conclusion of the Fenian and post-Fenian eras, though, the monarchy had been left in a very dangerous position in Ireland. At the end of the 1870s with the Home Rule Party gaining ground, the Irish Liberal Party was virtually dead and Irish Tories were all but confined to Ulster.

Thus as democracy grew and the capacity of English politicians directly to control events in Ireland, by means of internal party politics or of forceful imposition, diminished, so the same politicians began to have greater expectations and to make greater demands on the monarchy's role in Ireland. English political ideology needed to believe that Ireland could be won over and that Irish grievances were merely sentimental.

The monarchy could address such grievances through royal visits that would produce cheering crowds and thus the proof that the British political establishment needed to reassure itself. If British belief in the shallowness of Irish grievances crumbled, so too might the will and ability to remain in control of Ireland. The real importance of royal visits thus lay not in any actual acquiescence to British rule they might create in Ireland so much as in the illusion of such acquiescence they might be used to create for England.

The more politically discerning of Irish nationalists knew all this. If the price of their attrition against the ruling mind-set of the English was the undoubted continuing popularity of the royal family, then so be it. The monarchy was thus soon to find itself in the unenviable position of being the punching bag between English political ideology, on the one hand, and Irish political aspirations, on the other.

Beginning of outright rejection

CHAPTER SIX

"Avoid Foxy Jack"

Spencer, Parnell, and the End of Deference, 1879–1885

The years 1879 and 1880 marked a great transition in Ireland. By the end of 1880 C. S. Parnell, with Isaac Butt dead, was chairman of the Irish Parliamentary Party, though it would be some time yet before he would achieve complete dominance within it.[1] He was also president of the recently formed Irish National Land League, whose principal organizer was Michael Davitt and which had been formed to aid tenant farmers who were fearful of eviction because they were unable to pay their rents, due to the worsening agricultural depression. This move was to lead to the first stage of the "Land War" over the next three years which was characterized by evictions, withholding rents, boycotting, mass meetings, agrarian outrages, and land reform. Parnell had the advantage of a loose understanding, known as the "new departure," with some significant elements of the Fenians, by which they gave him their qualified blessing for his activities.

Parnell wished to gain as much political independence for Ireland from Britain as was attainable. He was most careful to accept the idea that the two countries would be linked by the monarchy: "The Queen would be our Queen; she would be the link that would attach Ireland to Great Britain."[2] To Queen Victoria, however, Sir Henry Ponsonby reported that

1. The Irish Parliamentary Party was also informally known as the Irish Party, the Irish Home Rule Party, and the Irish Nationalist Party.

2. *United Ireland*, 31 March 1883.

Parnell had said that "[n]one of us . . . will be satisfied until we have destroyed the last link which keeps Ireland bound to England."[3] Parnell was indeed reported as having said as much at Cincinnati, Ohio, in February 1880 but adamantly denied it.

Parnell's speeches in Ireland often came closer to a rejection of monarchy than was prudent for someone who knew he needed British political cooperation to achieve his goals. He urged a meeting in Cork to "convince our rulers that . . . if they wish to maintain the link of the Crown, that the link of the Crown shall be the only link between the two countries (loud cheering!)."[4] At the end of his career in 1891, while fighting desperate by-elections in Ireland after the split in his party, Parnell dropped the public pretense of an acceptance of monarchy. Addressing a crowd at Navan he began, "Men of Royal Meath, perhaps some day or other in the long, waiting future, some one may arise who may have the privilege of addressing you as men of Republican Meath (loud cheers)."[5] This was to lead to a falling out with Cecil Rhodes, one of his few remaining friends, who thought that Parnell agreed with him on the value of imperial federation for the British Empire.

It was perhaps inevitable, given Parnell's absolute ascendancy in Irish nationalist politics throughout the 1880s, that he should have emerged in iconic terms as the first Irish nationalist countermonarch since O'Connell. It was in Montreal, during the course of a tour of North America in early 1880, that Parnell was first hailed as the "uncrowned king of Ireland."[6] Tim Healy, watching Parnell wave from the ship that bore him back to Ireland from New York at the end of his tour, thought Parnell was "looking like a king."[7] In *A Portrait of the Artist as a Young Man*, James Joyce was to capture the grief of Parnell's supporters at his defeat and death over ten years later in the character of Mr. Casey: "—Poor Parnell! He cried loudly. My dead king!"[8]

3. RA D 29/227, Sir Henry Ponsonby to Queen Victoria, 21 December 1880.

4. *United Ireland*, 8 October 1881.

5. *Times*, 2 March 1891.

6. Herbert Tingsten, *Victoria and the Victorians* (London: George Allen and Unwin, 1972), 326.

7. Frank Callanan, *T. M. Healy* (Cork: University Press, 1996), 35, quoting R. B. O'Brien, *The Life of Charles Stewart Parnell, 1846–1891*, 2 vols. (London: Smith, Elder, 1898), 1:85.

8. James Joyce, *A Portrait of the Artist as a Young Man* (1916; London: Penguin Books, 1992), 39.

O'Connell had generally wanted to claim loyalty to the Crown for Irish nationalism. As a result he had been ambivalent about the implications of the sobriquet of "uncrowned king." It was not so in the 1880s. Queen Victoria was increasingly known to have Conservative political tendencies. But this did not matter as her power was now quite limited. What did matter was that, encouraged both by the Liberals, who wanted a focus for domestic unity to transcend class divisions, and by the Conservatives, who wanted a unifying national ideology to support imperial expansion abroad, the monarchy had become the symbolic focus of British national cohesion.

In 1889 John Morley, one of the most popular Liberal politicians ever to hold office in Ireland, told the Commons that "the Monarchy has entered into the very web of English national life, and is the outward and visible symbol of the historic character of the nation."[9] The *Dictionary of National Biography* put the matter succinctly:

The crown after 1880 became the living symbol of imperial unity, and every year events deepened the impression that the queen in her own person typified the common interest and the common sympathy which spread a feeling of brotherhood through the continents that formed the British empire.[10]

This judgment was generally true, except in the case of nationalist Ireland, where Queen Victoria's embodiment of imperial Britain was to the detriment of her popular standing. "Another war is imminent," reported the *Freeman's Journal* in 1879, "and at any moment we may hear that Queen Victoria has commenced hostilities against Theehow, King of Burmah [*sic*]."[11] Nor were nationalist activists slow to draw comparisons between Parnell and Queen Victoria, unflattering to the latter, as in the following piece which contrasts the Irish taxation money going to support the queen with Parnell's service gratis to Ireland. This was written in 1880, in an American journal, three years before Parnell received a testimonial of £37,000 from the Irish people:

The contrast presented by the character of Queen Victoria and Mr. Parnell is not only striking—it is even startling. Nothing can be more noble and generous than the one; nothing more selfish, mean, and vixenish that the other. Mr Parnell donates his talents, his fortune, his life to the Irish. He loves them with all his heart. Victoria deprives them of £8,000, and hates them with all the mean spite and petty malice of her waspish nature. He is the "uncrowned king of Ireland." She is re-

9. *FJ*, 30 July 1889.   10. *DNB*, 22:1366.

11. *FJ*, 8 October 1879.

garded as a sceptred impostor. He would exalt the Irish into free men; she would degrade them into slaves and beggars. She gives them "an alms out of her own bag" and sinks them into involuntary mendicancy, which galls and humiliates their national pride.[12]

In America Irish and Irish-American public anti-monarchism was always more pronounced than it was in Ireland. But in this respect things were changing even at home. The early 1880s saw a significant cultural change in Ireland and the emergence of a more assertive and much less deferential form of nationalism. Anti-monarchism now became publicly acceptable in the mainstream of political life in a way in which it had never been before.

There were various causes for this. One was the radicalizing nature of the urgent political and agrarian issues of the times. Another was the disappearance of any restraining influence on the Nationalist Party, when it came to the building of an Irish consensus on important issues, from Irish Tories and non–home rule Liberals. Such Liberals were in steep decline and in 1881 the last Tory was in office as lord mayor of Dublin. Nationalists dominated Irish politics except in Ulster, the first signs of partitionist practice becoming apparent as early as the December 1881 controversy over the national exhibition.

A third reason was the rise of members of the Catholic lower middle class to positions of political influence. In Dublin, for example, the relative numbers of professionals and richer merchants, epitomized by the likes of Sir John Gray and Peter Paul McSwiney, on the Corporation declined as the numbers of publicans and grocers increased.[13] This new political establishment was much less likely to be impressed by the allure of tradition, precedent, and decorum than its upper-middle-class predecessor had been.

A fourth reason was the advent of a new generation of young, firebrand, nationalist leaders at a national level under Parnell, such as William O'Brien, John Dillon, Tim Healy (a relative of A. M. Sullivan), and John and William Redmond. Within twenty years they had followed the usual trajectory from youthful radicalism to middle-aged moderation associated with the waves of new leadership that had arisen in the 1840s, and which included the O'Connellite John Gray and the Young Irelander Charles Gavan Duffy, and in the 1860s, and which had included the Fenians and A. M.

---

12. C. M. O'Keeffe, "Queen Victoria and Mr Parnell," *Celtic Monthly,* June 1880, p. 521.

13. Mary E. Daly, *Dublin the Deposed Capital: A Social and Economic History, 1860–1914* (Cork: Cork University Press, 1984), 204, 209. Also see *FJ,* 20 April 1885.

Sullivan. In the 1880s, however, these Irish parliamentary leaders were at the height of their youthful certainties.

Finally, the Irish lack of deference of the 1880s may have been learned from an English lack of deference in the 1870s. Just as some of the virulent Irish anti-monarchism of the late 1890s was due to people of English background such as Maud Gonne, so the anti-monarchism of Irish politicians in the early 1880s may have been learned from the anti-monarchism of English radicals and republicans from the 1870s onward.[14]

In November 1882 a controversy arose over a proposal to offer the freedom of the city of Dublin to the distinguished Anglo-Irish soldier Lord Wolseley. The *Freeman's Journal* dismissed it as a ruse by the Tory and Liberal rump on the Corporation to embarrass the nationalist majority. Wolseley "is a distinguished English soldier and it is right for England to do him honour." The paper took the opportunity to reflect on the cultural change that had happened in recent years:

> The wave of National sentiment, which within the past two years has passed over Ireland, did not, however, leave Dublin untouched. Recently, the Corporation of the Capital has . . . cast aside their tone of subserviency which up to that time had more or less characterised it.[15]

This casting aside of subservience took both serious and not-so-serious forms. Among the latter were a prank by students at Trinity College inviting people to a nonexistent viceregal function[16] and the loud official complaints of the Royal College of Surgeons in Ireland that prominent Irish doctors were not getting the same level of honors as their English counterparts.[17] Finally, in February 1885 the novelist George Moore wrote to Dublin Castle asking for an invitation to a state dinner so that he might conduct research for a novel he was writing.[18] The Vice Regal Court had

---

14. I am grateful to Professor R. V. Comerford for drawing my attention to the similar dependence of the anti-landlordism of the Ireland of the 1880s on opposition to the principle of landlordism in British and American radical thinking in the 1870s.

15. *FJ*, 9 November 1882. Wolseley was eventually conferred with the freedom of Drogheda and professed himself glad to be thought an Irish soldier (*FJ*, 31 March 1883). On 30 June 1882 Dublin Tories held a banquet for Wolseley in the Rotundo while the lord mayor hosted a banquet for a U.S. senator in the Mansion House (*FJ*, 2 July 1883).

16. *FJ*, 27 June 1884.

17. *FJ*, 14, 16, 17, 21 July 1883.

18. *FJ*, 9 February 1885. The novel, published the next year, was *A Drama in Muslin*, which contains scenes set at official functions in Dublin Castle.

been reduced to being the object of a novelist's mocking anthropological investigations.

❖

Queen Victoria was greatly distressed by the rising tide of Irish agrarian outrages and terrorist attacks in Britain during the 1880s. Early on in the period a delicate diplomatic issue arose over the desire of Elizabeth of Bavaria, the semi-estranged wife of Emperor Franz-Josef of Austria-Hungary, to visit Ireland for the purposes of hunting. Empress Elizabeth loved hunting both for itself and because of her English instructor in the sport, Captain "Bay" Middleton of the 12th Lancers, who was also her current lover.

In the autumn of 1878 Sisi, as she was generally known, arranged to rent Summerhill House, in County Kildare, home of Lord Langford.[19] It was a sensible choice as it placed her geographically in a position to participate in fox and stag hunting with the Ward Union, Meath, and Kildare hunts, three of the top hunts in the country.

Queen Victoria was worried about the situation, however, and sent the prince of Teck to Vienna to ask the empress not to go. The *Freeman's Journal's* version of his message, unlikely because of its directness, was one implicitly humiliating to Queen Victoria. "It was represented that Ireland was a Catholic country, and that its people would be likely to make demonstration in favour of a Catholic Empress on their soil which might contrast strongly when compared with a welcome given a Protestant sovereign."[20] In fact, though the queen's real fears may have been along such lines, the warning was in the form of advice that Ireland was not a safe country. Acting on the counsel of Lord Spencer, a friend of the empress who was to accompany her on the trip, the emperor chose to ignore the queen's advice and Sisi duly departed for Ireland, promising to travel incognito.[21] Meanwhile at Summerhill a private chapel was constructed, the stables extended, five Irish hunters bought, and an independent telegraphic link established to the Continent, to prevent British interception of her messages home.[22]

The empress arrived in Dublin on 22 February 1879 as the Countess

19. *FJ*, 26 August 1878.

20. *FJ*, 9 January 1879.

21. Andrew Sinclair, *Death by Fame: A Life of Elizabeth Empress of Austria* (London: Constable, 1998), 96.

22. Sinclair, *Death by Fame*, 96.

Hohenembs, an alias that was announced in the Irish press days before.[23] Her attempts to maintain her incognito only caused offense in Dublin, where civic officials were intent on giving her an official welcome. The lord mayor of Dublin made himself seem ludicrous when he scrambled uninvited aboard the empress's special train and traveled down to County Kildare in the baggage compartment.[24] One of her attendants was wont "to snarl down the very slightest exhibition of interest in her movements . . . [and] roamed, magnificently about, showing his teeth and his contempt to all about whom it might concern."[25] The empress stayed until 23 March, hunting almost every day, even on Ash Wednesday—to the dismay of the members of the hunts that she joined.[26]

On 24 February, while pursuing a deer, Elizabeth, accompanied by Middleton and Spencer, strayed into the grounds of Maynooth College.[27] She was introduced by Spencer to the vice president, William Walsh, the future fervently nationalist archbishop of Dublin. He ushered her into the college refectory and "when she asked for a shawl gave her his College gown which Her Majesty put on and most becoming it was."[28] The next Sunday she returned for mass and later in the year sent the college a silver statuette of Ireland's patron whom she apparently thought was Saint George. The following year she again attended mass in the college and this time sent a present of cloth-of-gold vestments decorated with shamrocks.[29]

Sticking overrigidly to her official incognito as a form of revenge against Queen Victoria, Sisi refused to meet the Irish lord lieutenant, the duke of Marlborough, during her visit.[30] The latter was determined to find a way around this. On 7 March his son, Lord Randolph Churchill, joined the Meaths to hunt with the empress.[31] She finally conceded and lunched with Marlborough on the day of her departure.[32]

Sisi's second and last trip to Ireland lasted between 4 February and 7

23. *FJ*, 20 February 1879.   24. *FJ*, 17 March 1879.

25. *FJ*, 24 February 1879.

26. *FJ*, 27 February 1879. Sinclair, *Death by Fame*, 98.

27. *FJ*, 26 February 1879.

28. Lord Spencer to Lady Spencer, 25 February 1879, Spencer Papers, in Gordon, *The Red Earl*, vol. 1, no. 141, p. 134.

29. Patrick J. Corish, *Maynooth College, 1795–1995* (Dublin: Gill and Macmillan, 1995), 237.

30. *FJ*, 13 March 1879.   31. *FJ*, 8 March 1879.

32. *FJ*, 24 March 1879.

March 1880. A party from the Vice Regal Lodge joined her and the "killing" Kildares on 14 February.[33] On her way home through England she stopped to call on Queen Victoria and the coolness which her visits had caused between them was overcome.[34] Late in 1880 the empress's mind turned toward visiting Ireland once more for hunting early in 1881. But enough was enough for the queen. "I have written confidentially to the Empress of Austria," Queen Victoria told her daughter Vicky, "that she would be exposed to very great danger if she came over to hunt in Ireland, where the hounds are even in danger of being shot or poisoned and several popular landlords have been stopped from hunting."[35]

Queen Victoria's fears that the empress might have been hailed as an alternative sovereign had proved groundless, not least because the Empress Elizabeth had had no purpose beyond enjoying herself. But the visit did occasion one reminder of the de facto influence of Ireland's informal countermonarch. In January 1881 Lord Granville told the queen that "Parnell & Co. have asked Count Karolyi [the Austrian ambassador in London] to present a memorial to the Empress of Austria telling her Majesty how quiet Ireland is, that there is no reason why she should not come to hunt here, and promising her Majesty a hearty welcome."[36] For Parnell to act in such a matter, addressing a foreign monarch about her travel plans in the United Kingdom, was too much for Queen Victoria for whom he was now "Pretender Parnell."[37]

With agricultural distress increasing in the autumn of 1879, the duchess of Marlborough, wife of the lord lieutenant, set up a relief committee, which appealed for public funds.[38] But charity was no longer as controlled and stratified as it was in the 1840s. Queen Victoria donated £500 to it.[39]

---

33. *FJ*, 5, 16, February, 8 March 1880.   34. Sinclair, *Death by Fame*, 104.

35. Queen Victoria to the Crown Princess of Prussia, 8 December 1880, in Roger Fulford, ed., *Beloved Mamma: Private Correspondence of Queen Victoria and the German Crown Princess, 1878–85* (London: Evans, 1981), 92.

36. RA D 30/68, Lord Granville to Queen Victoria, 26 January 1881, in Buckle, *Letters* (London: John Murray, 1928), second series, vol. 3 (1879–85), p. 185.

37. RA D 30/85, Queen Victoria to Lord Granville, 29 January 1881, in Buckle, *Letters*, second series, 3:186.

38. *FJ*, 19 December 1879.

39. *FJ*, 26 December 1879. RA D 28/43, 43a, Sir Henry Ponsonby to Queen Victoria, 21 December 1879, Queen Victoria to Sir Henry Ponsonby.

Six weeks later the banking heiress, Lady Angela Burdett-Coutts, gave a vastly greater sum.[40] Charity was now also more directly politicized. Thus a rival nationalist organization to that of the duchess, known as the Mansion House Committee, was set up 2 January 1880.

Then on 20 January the lord mayor of Dublin, Edmund Dwyer Gray, who was also MP for Tipperary, presided at a meeting of Irish nationalist MPs that was critical of government relief efforts. In retaliation Marlborough refused to attend that year's annual banquet given for the lord lieutenant by the lord mayor at the Mansion House. Gray attacked him on the grounds that he had "voluntarily descended from his position as representative of the Queen and constituted himself the representative of a political party." He then went on to make a great show of attending the lord lieutenant's levee out of respect "for the Sovereign whom he represents and indicated my opinion that the respect should be paid to the office irrespective of the holder." Gray donated the £500 saved from the banquet to the poor of Dublin.[41]

Marlborough's action was not only constitutionally suspect, it was also a grave political mistake. In gradually assuming positions of political power, nationalists had entered political structures and a political culture of deference to the monarchy and other institutions of the United Kingdom. The lord mayor's banquet for the lord lieutenant was a most important occasion for viceregal political circles to intersect not only with Dublin but also with Irish political circles generally with a view to the sustaining of a common political culture. The lord lieutenant needed the banquet more than the lord mayor did. Marlborough's actions had undermined the custom. In 1881 the traditional banquet was held, but held for the last time, under Dublin's final Tory lord mayor, George Moyers.[42] By 1883 Charles Dawson, the charismatic and highly accomplished two-term nationalist lord mayor, had devised an alternative. In 1882 he had refused to hold the banquet for the lord lieutenant, to the chagrin of Dublin Tories and the delight of nationalists.[43] On 7 December 1882 he was feted in Thurles for "dispensing with the annual banquet to the representative in Ireland of her Majesty the Queen at a time when some of the best and bravest of our citizens were imprisoned for devotion to their native land and when thousands of our fellow countrymen were on the verge of starvation."[44] On 1

40. *FJ*, 11 February 1880.　　　　41. *FJ*, 2 February 1880.
42. *FJ*, 16 February 1881.　　　　43. *FJ*, 2 December 1882.
44. *FJ*, 9 December 1882.

January 1883 Dawson held a "civic banquet" for four hundred guests, and the lord lieutenant was not invited. The queen was toasted and "God Save the Queen" sung, but to the accompaniment of a trade rather than a British military band. The other toasts were to "The Irish Members" and "The Progress of Irish Industry."[45]

In March 1880 Disraeli, now Lord Beaconsfield, called an election. He decided to make home rule an issue in Britain by writing a public letter to Marlborough, attacking home rulers as "false to their Queen and country." William Shaw, then briefly leader of the Irish parliamentarians, accused the prime minister of anti-Irishness. The Nationalist Party in turn issued a manifesto attacking Beaconsfield.[46] The latter's real object of attack was the Liberal Party, which was thought to be sympathetic to the home rulers. As the *Morning Post* put it,

He who votes for a Liberal candidate furthers the views of men who scarcely profess to be loyal to the Crown and the British connection. He who votes for a supporter of the Ministry takes a course by which he can manifest true loyalty alike to Irish, to English and to Imperial interest and to the Queen and to the country.[47]

In the event, the Liberals won the election with 349 seats to the Conservatives' 243. The Irish Parliamentary Party picked up sixty-one seats, though only twenty-four of them were initially firmly pledged to support Parnell. After some prompting from Lord Granville and Lord Hartington, who took over as Liberal leader from Gladstone in 1875 and who was her own choice for prime minister, Queen Victoria reluctantly called on Gladstone to form a new government. However, "though her antipathies were well concealed, in practical terms she was not unlike the House of Lords—politically quiescent when a Conservative Administration was in office, and a vigilant defender of the national interest when the Liberals were in power."[48]

Meanwhile in Ireland, the duke of Edinburgh, who held the rank of rear admiral in the royal navy, was assisting with relief efforts, at the end of a fishing holiday in the west of Galway.[49] When an American ship, *The Constellation*, with supplies for Ireland landed in Cork, the duke arranged

45. *FJ*, 2 January 1883.

46. *FJ*, 9, 18 March 1880.

47. *Morning Post*, 31 March 1880, reported in *FJ*, 1 April 1880.

48. Robert Rhodes James, *The British Revolution: British Politics 1880–1939, Vol. 1: From Gladstone to Asquith, 1880–1914* (London: Hamish Hamilton, 1976), 137.

49. *FJ*, 9, 12 April 1880.

for a small fleet of gunboats to ferry supplies "for the use of the perishing poor in the islands and nooks and crannies of the western coast."[50] However, it was Commander Potter of the *Constellation* on whom the freedom of the city of Dublin was conferred and not the duke.[51]

Agrarian outrages were a constant preoccupation of the government during the Land War of the early 1880s. In 1878 there had been 301. The figures for 1880, 1881, and 1882 were 2,585, 4,439, and 3,433, respectively. In 1883 the figure fell back to 870.[52] Gladstone's policy, on entering into office, was to try reform rather than coercion. In June he introduced a bill to compensate evicted tenants. The queen told Lord Granville that she thought the bill "a great misfortune" and that she was alarmed "at the Radical tendency of the Government."[53] Her strategy was to influence the government through the Whig aristocrats, such as Granville and Hartington, whom she trusted.[54] However, when the bill was thrown out by the House of Lords in August it led to increased violence in Ireland. A significant number of Irish landlords were murdered in August and September, most notably Viscount Mountmorres in late September, to whose wife the queen sent condolences.[55] Queen Victoria had feared that things could only get worse in Ireland.[56]

On 19 September Parnell had called for the ostracism of farmers who had taken over the farms of evicted tenants. This process was soon to be known as "boycotting" after its most famous victim, Captain Boycott, in whose fate the queen took a sympathetic interest.[57] Parnell's strategy paid off but at the price of increased violence. Of 1,893 families evicted in 1880, only 152 were evicted in the last quarter. However, of the 2,590 outrages,

50. *FJ*, 22, 24 April 1880.

51. *FJ*, 5 May 1880.

52. T. W. Moody, *Davitt and the Irish Revolution, 1846–82* (1982; Oxford: Clarendon Press, 1984), Appendix E1, p. 565.

53. RA D 29/26, Queen Victoria to Lord Granville, 10 July 1880.

54. RA D 29/42, Queen Victoria to Lord Granville, 20 July 1880, in Buckle, *Letters*, second series, 3:121.

55. RA D 29/100, Lady Mountmorres to Lady Ely, 6 October 1880.

56. RA D 29/42, Queen Victoria to Lord Granville, 20 July 1880, in Buckle, *Letters*, second series, 3:121.

57. RA D 29/125, 143, Sir Henry Ponsonby to Queen Victoria, 2 November 1880; Lord Cowper to Queen Victoria, 13 November 1880. Ponsonby reported that Boycott was receiving help. "This is a good sign—but it verges on civil war." Cowper wrote that Boycott "has kept up his spirits in a wonderful manner."

1,696 were committed during the same period.[58] On 2 November Parnell and thirteen others were charged with conspiracy to prevent the payment of rent, a move that the government had been contemplating since September. In early October the queen had written to Gladstone that she was glad to learn that the government was going to take action against the Land League, "which is doing such terrible mischief and producing by Mr Parnell's language, encouraging as it does murder, a state of affairs unequalled in any civilised nation."[59] On 23 January 1881, however, the trial of Parnell on the charge collapsed when the jury could not reach a verdict. Three months before Granville had warned the queen that he was "not sanguine with regard to the outcome of the Irish prosecutions."[60]

Beaconsfield told the queen that the Liberal administration in Ireland "has taken the form of anarchy."[61] The queen herself was becoming restive with the Liberal government over Ireland, not least because she felt she it was not keeping her up to date with events. "Her Majesty received so little information that she was compelled to rely chiefly on newspaper reports," Ponsonby acidly wrote to the lord lieutenant, Lord Cowper.[62] She also felt that the government was not keeping itself properly informed about the outrages. She took to forwarding correspondence from Ireland to Gladstone so as to be sure he "hears from all sides what passes there."[63] Gladstone told her that it would be foolish to embark on "hurried legislation" for Ireland, but the queen argued that it was necessary as "the Irish are rapidly becoming the slaves of the Land League organisation, whose law is obeyed while that of the realm is defied."[64]

In December there were newspaper reports that effectively she had urged the cabinet to adopt coercion in Ireland.[65] She had indeed written a letter to Gladstone to be read to the cabinet hoping that "the law may first be vindicated in Ireland" and that "careful consideration may then be giv-

---

58. Moody, *Davitt*, Appendix F, p. 567. Appendix E1 puts the number of agrarian outrages in 1880 at 2,585. Appendix F puts it at 2,590.

59. RA D 29/96, Queen Victoria to W. E. Gladstone, 2 October 1880.

60. RA D 29/97, Lord Granville to Queen Victoria, 15 October 1880.

61. Lord Beaconsfield to Queen Victoria, 28 October 1880, in Buckle, *Letters*, second series, 3:151.

62. RA D 28/46, Sir Henry Ponsonby to Lord Cowper, 7 November 1880.

63. RA D 29/108, Queen Victoria to W. E. Gladstone, 14 October 1880.

64. RA D 29/161, Queen Victoria to W. E. Gladstone, 22 November 1880.

65. *FJ*, 16 December 1880.

en without haste to a Land bill for ameliorating the evils complained of."[66] She had written, too, to Cowper, about whose abilities she had some doubts,[67] that the situation in Ireland was "very dreadful and very disheartening and the more one does for the Irish the more unruly and ungrateful they seem to be." She told him she hoped that W. E. Forster, the chief secretary, who was a member of the cabinet, would convince Gladstone of the need for "strong measures to make the law respected."[68] She urged on Forster, for whom she had "always had a sincere regard,"[69] and wrote in a similar vein to Hartington, hoping that the cabinet would not be deterred by threats from radical members such as Joseph Chamberlain and John Bright to resign. "The law is *openly defied, disobeyed,* and such an example *may* spread to England, if it prove successful in Ireland. . . . *Don't* yield to *threats* of resignation from the two before-named people. *Let them go. All* right minded and loyal people will support you, if you do what is right."[70]

In the event, she was pleased when the cabinet, against Gladstone's better judgment, agreed to coercion without immediate land reform.[71] Even Bright and Chamberlain agreed.[72] Forster introduced a Protection of Property and Person Bill into the Commons. The queen was annoyed at the attempts of "these dreadful Irish people," meaning home rule MPs, to obstruct its passage.[73] She also hoped "it may be possible to shut up Davitt" who was indeed arrested when his parole as a ticket-of-leave Fenian prisoner was withdrawn on 3 February.[74] Around the same time O'Donovan Rossa's Fenian organization set off a number of explosions in Britain. Extra police were dispatched to guard the queen at Osborne even though no spe-

66. RA D 29/203, Queen Victoria to W. E. Gladstone, 13 December 1880.

67. RA QVJ, 15 December 1880, in Buckle, *Letters,* second series, 3:164.

68. RA D 29/179, Queen Victoria to Lord Cowper, 5 December 1880, in Buckle, *Letters,* second series, 3:162.

69. RA D 29/233, Queen Victoria to W. E. Forster, 25 December 1880, in Buckle, *Letters,* second series, 3:165–66. She ended her letter with the statement that "[s]he *cannot* and will not be the Queen of a *democratic monarchy.*"

70. RA D 29/200, Queen Victoria to Lord Hartington, 12 December 1880, in Buckle, *Letters,* second series, 3:163.

71. RA D 29/209, Lord Hartington to Queen Victoria, 14 December 1880.

72. RA D 30/1, Queen Victoria to W. E. Gladstone, 2 January 1881.

73. RA D 30/35, Queen Victoria to Lord Hartington, 16 January 1881, in Buckle, *Letters,* second series, 3:183.

74. Queen Victoria to W. E. Gladstone, 25 January 1881, in Buckle, *Letters,* second series, 3:185.

cific threat had been made against her.[75] The Irish coercion measure became law on 2 March. Habeas corpus was suspended and dozens of suspects were arrested.

In early May 1881 John Dillon, one of the rising Irish parliamentarians and "a violent and dangerous fanatic," in the view of Forster,[76] was arrested and detained under the coercion powers. He was the first parliamentarian to be arrested under the legislation and among the reactions which it provoked was a series of reported threats in the United States to the lives of the queen and the Prince of Wales. "If Dillon dies in prison, the Queen will not live a year, the Prince of Wales will have to be ironclad like the Czar"[77] (Tzar Alexander had been assassinated in March of that year). Queen Victoria was very surprised, even at the very suggestion of a threat against her in the United States. "In *America generally* she is a *great favourite* she knows."[78] Nothing came of the threat and Dillon was released in August, but the queen warned the prince to be careful about his security.[79]

In April 1881 Gladstone made an attempt at another land act. It gave further rights to tenants and allowed for legal redress over the question of the fairness of rents. The queen was initially persuaded that it was a moderate measure.[80] However, she began to change her mind when Lorne's father, the duke of Argyll, resigned from the government in protest.[81] Victoria urged Gladstone to accept Lords' amendments favorable to the landlords.[82] For Gladstone, however, the bill was to be the means whereby the government would "beat the Land League."[83] But the queen was not reassured and believed that "no moderate people like the Bill tho' they have not the courage to support amendments to improve it."[84] The meas-

75. RA D 28/55, Sir E. Y. W. Henderson to Sir Henry Ponsonby, 20 January 1881.

76. RA D 30/48, W. E. Forster to Queen Victoria, [19 January 1881].

77. RA D 28/74, J. A. Godley to Sir Henry Ponsonby, 16 June 1881, quoting American newspaper reports.

78. RA D 31/102, Queen Victoria to W. E. Gladstone, 15 June 1881.

79. RA D 28/74a, Sir Henry Ponsonby to F. Knollys, 17 June 1881.

80. RA D 28/69, Sir Henry Ponsonby to Queen Victoria, 1 May 1881.

81. RA D 31/44, Queen Victoria to the duke of Argyll, 7 April 1881, in Buckle, *Letters,* second series, 3:222.

82. RA D 31/183, Queen Victoria to W. E. Gladstone, 7 August 1881, in Buckle, *Letters,* second series, 3:229.

83. RA D 31/186, W. E. Gladstone to Queen Victoria, 8 August 1881, in Buckle, *Letters,* second series, 3:230.

84. Queen Victoria to Sir Henry Ponsonby, 13 August 1881, in Arthur Ponsonby, *Henry Ponsonby, Queen Victoria's Private Secretary* (London: Macmillan, 1942), 190.

ure became law in August, the queen complaining of Gladstone's "high handed dictatorial style" when it came to the Lords.[85]

The new legislation disconcerted the members of the Irish Home Rule Party. Should they oppose it or support it? The party duly decided to abstain on the second reading of the bill. In September the Land League Conference agreed with the policy of partial engagement that Parnell had come up with in order to "test the act."[86] At the same time Parnell's rhetoric for domestic audiences became more extreme. It was on 2 October at Cork that Parnell made his remark about the link with the Crown. Gladstone responded at a speech in Leeds on 7 October, comparing Parnell with O'Connell:

O'Connell professed his unconditional and unswerving fidelity to the Crown of England. Mr Parnell says if the Crown of England is to be the link between the two countries it must be the only link, and whether it is to be the link at all (I am not now quoting his words) is a matter which he has not yet I believe given an opinion (laughter).[87]

Parnell replied to Gladstone on 9 October in a speech in Wexford. The next night at a banquet for Parnell in the same town, Tim Healy mocked the allure of assimilation to the culture of Westminster politics which gave a person "the ability to wear a cocked hat, a court suit and a sword by your side at a Queen's levee."[88]

On 12 October the cabinet decided the time had come to arrest the Irish Parliamentary Party leadership.[89] Parnell and several others were detained over the following days and in retaliation the Irish Party issued its "no rent manifesto"—though it had little appreciable effect on the payment of rent. On 20 October the Land League was outlawed and the new government land court opened. The queen told Gladstone that she was "much pleased that you are acting with vigour in Ireland."[90]

"The Queen desires reports from Ireland," Gladstone told Forster in early October.[91] But the reports were not promising. Cowper was afraid to leave the Vice Regal Lodge:

85. RA D 31/217, Queen Victoria to Lord Granville, 17 August 1881.

86. *FJ*, 19 September 1881.   87. *FJ*, 8 October 1881.

88. *FJ*, 10, 11 October 1881.

89. RA D 31/228, W. E. Gladstone to Queen Victoria, 12 October 1881.

90. RA D 31/237a, Queen Victoria to W. E. Gladstone, 13 October 1881.

91. W. E. Gladstone to W. E. Forster, 3 October 1881, in H. C. G. Matthew, *The Gladstone Diaries* (Oxford: Clarendon Press, 1990), vol. 10 (January 1881–June 1883), p. 137.

We had intended to visit different parts of the Country this winter but, now that we have done Belfast, there is no other place to which we could go with the smallest prospect of being well received—and to go anywhere with the result of being hissed and insulted would only do harm. We shall remain quietly here for the present.[92]

The *Freeman's Journal* concurred. "The Viceroyalty has long been only a show, but in the hands of the present lord lieutenant it has been almost forgotten."[93] The queen wrote to Gladstone in December about the deteriorating situation generally:

The Queen continues to read in the newspapers and to hear from various sources the most distressing accounts of the disaster and anarchy that seem to prevail and has today seen the copy of a manifesto signed "Patrick Egan" stating that the tenants are at war with the Government and ordering them to pay no rent. . . . [L]et no effort be spared for putting an end to a state of affairs which is a *disgrace* to *any civilized* country.[94]

Late in 1881 the queen became directly involved in affairs in Ireland in connection with plans for the 1882 National Exhibition of Irish Manufactures. The exhibition was under the auspices of a general committee on which there were representatives of committees from around the country. In early December a dispute arose at the general committee over a proposal to have Queen Victoria as the patron of the exhibition and nominal president of the general committee. The Irish Party's new newspaper, *United Ireland*, sneered at the invitation to the queen to open the exhibition "with her own sainted touch."[95] The Belfast committee was strongly in favor of the queen's involvement but it was opposed by southern nationalists.[96] They knew that, given the state of the country, the move would be widely unpopular. The issue had been raised in September when a decision was taken not to have a patron. In early October, at a Cork banquet for Parnell, T. P. O'Connor alluded to it during his speech in which he proposed that the Irish people themselves should be patrons of the exhibition. When he had referred, however, to the possibility of the queen being patron there were

---

92. Lord Cowper to Sir Henry Ponsonby, 3 December 1881, in Ponsonby, *Henry Ponsonby*, 336.

93. *FJ*, 23 November 1881.

94. Queen Victoria to W. E. Gladstone, 31 December 1881, in Buckle, *Letters*, second series, 3:249.

95. *United Ireland*, 10 December 1881.

96. *FJ*, 10 December 1881.

hisses, and then there were groans at the mention of the Prince of Wales.[97]

A further meeting of the general committee was held on 22 December. Motions both in favor and against the queen's patronage were defeated, but a motion abandoning the exhibition was passed. For the Belfast delegation, working within a United Kingdom perspective, the inclusion of the queen would have shown that the exhibition "was not political in a party sense." For the southern nationalists, her inclusion would have shown precisely the opposite; as a delegate from Waterford put it, "[U]nder a constitution like theirs her Majesty's name had been used in such a way that if it were put at the head of this Exhibition he was afraid it would lead to the failure of the project." The meeting ended in rancor over whether Queen Victoria should be described as queen or England or of Ireland.[98]

It was a sign that the dominant political interests both north and the south no longer had that shared set of symbolic attachments that would have enabled them to work together as one nation. As such there was an implicitly partitionist flavor to the moment. For the northerners, the queen stood above party conflict in her position within the constitution. For nationalists, there was something wrong with the constitution and the visceral expression of their sense of grievance about it took the form of the exclusion of the queen.

In January of 1882 Lord Mayor Dawson revived the idea of an exhibition but now as an explicitly nationalist enterprise. No attempt was made this time to forge common ground with the north. Its opening would coincide with the unveiling of the long-awaited O'Connell statue in Dublin.[99] The 1853 exhibition had been about Victorian, utilitarian progress; the 1865 exhibition was a celebration of aristocracy; and the 1872 exhibition had seen the mood change toward nationalism; now the 1882 exhibition was a full-bodied celebration of nationalist Ireland. Belfast was unrepresented and the Guinnesses refused permission for their Coburg Gardens exhibition palace to be used.[100] Indeed, it was subsequently demolished. Members of the aristocracy generally refused invitations to loan art works to the exhibition and the South Kensington institution would not lend its traveling collection.[101]

On 15 August 1882 the O'Connell statue was inaugurated and the na-

97. *FJ,* 3 October 1881.   98. *FJ,* 23 December 1881.
99. *FJ,* 26 January 1882.   100. *FJ,* 23 November 1882.
101. *FJ,* 8 January 1883.

tional exhibition opened in the Rotundo Gardens. Edmund Dwyer Gray formally handed over the statue to the lord mayor, in the presence of Parnell and his lieutenants.[102] The next day Gray was arrested for publicizing a letter from William O'Brien criticizing recent judicial decisions. That evening at a Mansion House banquet to mark the opening, for the first time there was some hissing when the band played "God Save the Queen." Dawson tried to defuse the incident by remarking in his speech that "if the other estates of the realm should do their duty to this country, the Queen would not be wanting in giving to the measure the final stroke of her pen (cheers)." However, when Mayor Galvin of Cork said that the co-ercion measures could not be blamed on the queen, there was more hissing at the mention of her name.[103]

Queen Victoria had been kept informed of the controversy surrounding the exhibition. There was something disconcerting for Lord Spencer, now returned as lord lieutenant, in the vigor and confidence of a nationalist political culture from which the institutions designed to promote the common political culture of the United Kingdom were now excluded. He told the queen, more in hope than in realism, at the end of July 1882 that "[t]he exhibition is expected to be a failure and neither the Statue or [*sic*] the Exhibition will be ready for the ceremonies, but that unfrequently occurs in Irish ceremonials."[104] After the ceremonies he had to report that fifty thousand people had attended and that there had been no disturbances, though he could not help adding that there had always been the fear "of a sudden drunken row developing into a riot."[105]

The next year there was an exhibition in Cork whose organization rested on an uneasy alliance of nationalists and Tories, in the form of Lord Bandon. Parnell attended the banquet connected with the opening.[106] However, the procession through the streets of Cork to the opening ceremony of the exhibition the day before had been greeted with great public apathy. The public boycott was thought to have had something to do with the decision of the organizing committee to have "God Save the Queen" sung during the opening ceremony.[107] There was some unease in official nationalist circles about this development. The *Freeman's Journal* insisted that

102. *FJ*, 16 August 1882.   103. *FJ*, 17 August 1882.
104. RA D 34/72, Lord Spencer to Queen Victoria, 31 July 1882.
105. RA D 34/104, Lord Spencer to Queen Victoria, 17 August 1882.
106. *FJ*, 5 July 1883.
107. *FJ*, 4 July 1883.

nationalists were not Revolutionaries" and did not aim at "the disintegration of the Empire or the dethronement of her Majesty."

On the contrary, their contention is that if Ireland were conceded the right of Local Government or Home Rule, it would consolidate and strengthen her Majesty's Empire, and render all classes of Irishmen loyal and contented as well as prosperous.[108]

Spencer visited the exhibition a few weeks after the opening. He reported receiving "loyal cheers" and that "a hostile demonstration had been arranged" but that its "failure was very satisfactory."[109]

❈

The early months of 1881 were full of minor matters for the queen in her relationship with Ireland before the events of early May gave the year its definitive, tragic focus. The year began with the drawing up of a petition to Queen Victoria, of "utmost loyalty to the Queen and constitution," at a meeting of Irish landlords.[110] In early February the queen made one of her few public interventions in the Land War with a letter to Lord Aberdare, reported in the *Daily Telegraph,* on whether the Society for the Prevention of Cruelty to Animals might look into the mutilation of cattle in Ireland, which was a feature of some agrarian outrages.[111] It was an issue that had been upsetting the queen for some time.[112]

In Ireland the duke of Edinburgh conducted a tour of Irish lifeguard stations.[113] Then in early March at Windsor came the seventh and last attempt on the queen's life. It was the work of a Roderick Maclean. "Even in this country there is general condemnation of the atrocious crime which has been attempted," wrote Lord Cowper to her.[114] The Dublin Corporation passed a resolution of sympathy with the queen and a delegation went to communicate it to her at Windsor Castle.[115]

108. *FJ,* 27 June 1883.

109. RA D 36/78, Lord Spencer to Queen Victoria, 1 September 1883.

110. RA D 28/95, 147, Duchess of Abercorn to Lady Ely, 4 January 1882; Sir Henry Ponsonby to Queen Victoria, 9 March 1882.

111. *FJ,* 4 February 1882.

112. RA D 31/261, 262, W. E. Forster to Queen Victoria, 5 December 1881; Sir Henry Ponsonby to Queen Victoria, 6 December 1881. Ponsonby wrote, "There is apparently no feeling for man or beast among the agitators in Ireland and the degradation is worse than that of savages."

113. *FJ,* 6 February 1882.

114. RA D 28/137a, Lord Cowper to Queen Victoria, 3 March 1882.

115. *FJ,* 7 March, 21 April 1882.

At the beginning of February 1882 a home rule motion was brought forward in the Commons.[116] It had no chance of passing, but allowed Gladstone to say that he was in favor of local government in Ireland. This alarmed Queen Victoria and she sought to extract from him an undertaking that he would never support home rule. The best he would do was to say that it was "most improbable" that he would do so.[117]

Toward the end of March Gladstone requested that Parliament increase the annuity to Prince Leopold, duke of Albany, from £15,000 to £25,000 on account of his impending marriage. It was in line with previous requests and was overwhelmingly approved, though forty-two MPs, most of them Irish, opposed it. Tim Healy's speech caused the queen special offense:

For his own part, he did not care whether he was regarded as loyal or disloyal; but he intended to vote against the Motion on the ground that he was opposed to these people having anything whatever. [Order!] The right hon. Gentleman the Prime Minister had stated that Her Majesty had been truly happy in the matrimonial alliances which had been formed by Her children; but he thought that happiness might consist, to a very great extent, of the £25,000 a year which those children got. [Cries of "Oh!" and "Divide!"] ... Then he thought the best thing that this illustrious Prince could do with his excellent understanding was to employ it in earning his living. ["Cries of Order!"] ... If the Duke of Albany was a Prince, he should set a good example, and work for his living.[118]

The queen was at Mentone with the ailing Prince Leopold when she heard the news. She thought Healy's language was "shocking, but was strongly condemned." However, her greatest anger was reserved for Sir Charles Dilke, the erstwhile republican and now a member of the government, who had abstained in the vote. "This is very wrong and shows that such people ought not to be in the Gov^t and can never be in the Cabinet."[119]

In early April the *Daily Telegraph* reported that the queen had enquired after the health of Lady Henrietta Monck. She was in a carriage in County Westmeath with W. B. Smythe and his sister-in-law, Mrs. Henry Smythe, when it came under attack and Mrs. Smythe was shot dead.[120] A week later

116. RA D 28/105, W. E. Gladstone to Queen Victoria, 9 February 1882.

117. Queen Victoria to W. E. Gladstone, 11 February 1882; W. E. Gladstone to Queen Victoria, 13 February 1882, in Buckle, *Letters*, second series, 3:260.

118. 23 March 1882, *Parliamentary Debates*, 3d Series, vol. 267 (3 March–24 March 1882), col. 1690.

119. RA QVJ, 26 March 1882.

120. RA D 32/10a; *Daily Telegraph*, 8 April 1882.

Gladstone had to explain to the queen why it was that Parnell had been released from prison to attend his nephew's funeral in Paris.[121] A few days after that Queen Victoria was writing to her daughter Vicky about Lord Kenmare, her lord chamberlain, who had entertained her at Killarney, "once a rich man, a Liberal and Roman Catholic and a most popular, kind-hearted man." Now the effects of the Land War had impoverished him.[122] Around the same time, Sir Henry Ponsonby received a letter from Albert Young, a Doncaster telegraph clerk. He claimed to be a Catholic priest with five evicted men in his parish who blamed the queen for their condition and were threatening to kill her unless they each got £40 with which to emigrate. Ponsonby was advised that the money could be paid to his correspondent's "dupe" in Doncaster. He reported the matter to the police and Young was apprehended.[123]

❖

The Kilmainham Treaty of early May was a grandiose name for the agreement between Parnell and Gladstone's government, named after the prison in which Parnell was being held, whereby in return for the release of Parnell and his associates, the easing of coercion, and the bringing of tenants in arrears and leaseholders within the terms of the 1881 land act, Parnell agreed to help end the Land War and cooperate with Liberal policy in Ireland.

In late April Gladstone had replaced Cowper as lord lieutenant with Lord Spencer, though the latter was to retain his existing position of lord president of the council.[124] On 1 May 1882 the prime minister wrote to the queen with the news that Parnell and the other Irish MPs were to be released.[125] Sir Henry Ponsonby's initial reaction was that it was a risk worth trying.[126]

Forster, however, did not think so and resigned from the cabinet. The queen hastily telegraphed him the necessary permission to make a statement in the Commons on the reasons for his resignation. She told him

121. RA D 32/15, W. E. Gladstone to Queen Victoria, 14 April 1882.

122. Queen Victoria to the Crown Princess of Prussia, 19 April 1882, in Fulford, *Beloved Mamma*, 118. Lord Kenmare had written to Ponsonby of his plight on 10 April 1882 (RA D 32/10).

123. *FJ*, 1 May 1882.

124. RA D 32/27, W. E. Gladstone to Queen Victoria, 27 April 1882.

125. RA D 32/39, W. E. Gladstone to Queen Victoria, 1 May 1882.

126. RA D 32/40, Sir Henry Ponsonby to Queen Victoria, 1 May 1882.

that she had always had great "faith and confidence" in his work for "un-happy Ireland." "The Queen owns she considers the experiment about to be tried a very hazardous one."[127] That night the queen confided her misgivings at agreeing to the releases to her journal. "Alas! I cannot cease regretting this consent [to the releases] which I ought never to have been asked to give in such a hurry."[128]

Next day at the privy council meeting, at which Spencer officially took office, the new lord lieutenant told the queen he hoped that the releases would not be taken as a triumph for Parnell. "I said I feared it would."[129] At the same meeting Lord Frederick Cavendish, brother of Hartington and a relative by marriage to Gladstone, was appointed to succeed Forster, though as very much a secondary figure to Spencer, who was to be a lord lieutenant with executive authority.

On 4 May Forster attacked the treaty and Parnell in his resignation speech. If Parnell "had not been placed in Kilmainham when he was placed there, he would soon have become in reality what he was called by many of his friends, the uncrowned King of Ireland."[130] The same day the queen heard that Michael Davitt had also been released. Gladstone had not mentioned this to her and she sent him an angry telegram. "Is it possible that Michael Davitt known as one of the worst of the treasonable agitators is also to be released?"[131] The next day Forster called to see the queen, who congratulated him on his speech, "entirely agreeing with him."[132]

On Saturday 6 May Spencer arrived in Dublin. He had just reached the Vice Regal Lodge when news arrived that Lord Frederick Cavendish and T. H. Burke, the under secretary, had been stabbed while walking within sight of the lodge by men, later identified as members of a group calling itself the Irish National Invincibles. They had used surgical knives. In London the same evening the walls of Spencer House in St. James's Place were posted with placards bearing the word "Death."[133]

That Saturday Queen Victoria had been out visiting Epping Forrest. After dinner a telegram arrived from Spencer to say that Burke was dead

127. RA D 32/44, Queen Victoria to W. E. Forster, 2 May 1882, in Buckle, *Letters*, second series, 3:277.

128. RA QVJ, 2 May 1882.   129. RA QVJ, 3 May 1882.

130. *FJ*, 5 May 1882.

131. RA D 32/56, in Buckle, *Letters*, second series, 3:281.

132. RA QVJ, 5 May 1882.

133. [Lady Lytton], *The Notebooks of a Spinster Lady, 1878–1903* (London: Cassel, 1919), 64.

and Cavendish "most dangerously wounded." The queen's first thought, after sending a telegram to Cavendish's wife, Lucy, was that the warnings of
Forster, who had actually been the Invincibles' initial, intended target,
about the treaty had been "almost prophetic." Then came a further
telegram with the news that Cavendish was dead. "How could Mr Gladstone and his violent radical advisers proceed with such a policy, which inevitably has led to all this? Surely his eyes must be opened now."[134] The funeral was held at Chatsworth on 8 May. The Prince of Wales attended.[135]
The same day G. O. Trevelyan was appointed chief secretary, Sir Charles
Dilke having refused the position.[136]

The queen was not slow to apportion blame. The day after the murders
she wrote to Granville: "Her heart bleeds for poor dear Lucy Cavendish.
. . . [The queen] considers this horrible event the direct result of what she
has always considered and has stated to Mr Gladstone and to Lord
Spencer as a most fated and hazardous step."[137] Granville told Ponsonby
that "[i]t is quite natural that the Queen should feel strongly on this ghast-
ly tragedy, but some sentences in her letter are such as would almost require our resignation if I were to show the letter to my colleagues."[138]

Gladstone took a completely opposite view of things to the queen.
"Some think that the immediate stimulus to the Fenian crime was rage at
being abandoned by the chiefs of the Land League movement and at their
apparent desertion to the cause of order."[139] By her own standards the
queen's reply to Gladstone, who was grieving the loss of a relative as well
as a colleague, was mild. She lamented "the fatal policy which was intended as a message of conciliation to Ireland and has been responded to in so
startling a manner."[140] The murders shocked Victorian Britain; many of
Gladstone's supporters would have agreed with the queen rather than with
him. Lady Monkswell wrote that the murders "forced upon me the convic-

134. RA QVJ, 6 May 1882.

135. Lee, *Edward VII*, 1:235.

136. W. E. Gladstone to Lord Hartington, 8 May 1882, in *The Gladstone Diaries*, 10:256.

137. RA D 32/82, 7 May 1882, Queen Victoria to Lord Granville, in Buckle, *Letters*, second series, 3:285.

138. Ponsonby, *Henry Ponsonby*, 191.

139. W. E. Gladstone to Queen Victoria, 7 May 1882, in Buckle, *Letters*, second series, .
3:287.

140. RA D 32/116, Queen Victoria to W. E. Gladstone, 9 May 1882, in Buckle, *Letters*,
second series, 3:293.

tion that our dear beloved Gladstone has been wrong in releasing the 800 or so suspects, and the Irish Members, Parnell & Dillon & Davitt, in the course of last week."[141]

Queen Victoria herself was not satisfied with the prime minister's views in the aftermath of the murders. "Mr Gladstone's eyes are not yet opened. It is too dreadful."[142] She was, however, rather taken aback by the obvious effects on him personally of the tragedy when she met him on 13 May, though this did not prevent her from driving home her views on the issue:

I saw Mr Gladstone yesterday; greatly shaken—and seemingly despondent and as if his energy was gone; very pale. I of course spoke of the necessity of strengthening measures—but also how fatal I thought the step of letting the suspects out was, before a stringent measure had been passed. He defended himself but when I said I knew Mr Burke (one of the victims) had been of the same opinion and greatly deprecated it, it seemed to shake him and he said the catastrophe had certainly followed very rapidly. People however begin to feel that the many other poor people who were murdered were comparatively unavenged till a Lord and a relation were killed. There is much truth in this alas!—at the same time the alarm of course is caused by the daringness of the act—killing a member of the Government and as it were under the windows of the Lord Lieutenant.[143]

The government's response to the murders was the introduction of the Prevention of Crime Bill and the Arrears Bill promised to the Irish Party. Despairing of her influence over events,[144] the queen found herself in the unusual position of enlisting the help of the Prince of Wales to influence Hartington. She wrote that "the utter disregard of all my opinions after 45 years of experience ought to be considered, . . . [makes] me very miserable and disgust[s] me. . . . The mischief Mr Gladstone does is *incalculable*."[145] Nor was she to be appeased by Spencer's reports of cheering at her birthday review in Dublin. "The Queen cannot but fear that the feeling of the lower classes in Dublin sympathises more cordially with criminals than

141. E. C. F. Collier, *A Victorian Diarist: Extracts from the Journals of Mary Lady Monkswell, 1873–1985* (London: John Murray, 1944), 101.

142. Queen Victoria to the Crown Princess of Prussia, 10 May 1882, in Fulford, *Beloved Mamma,* 119.

143. Queen Victoria to the Crown Princess of Prussia, 10 May 1882, in Fulford, *Beloved Mamma,* 119–20.

144. Queen Victoria to Sir Henry Ponsonby, 27 May 1882, in Ponsonby, *Henry Ponsonby,* 191.

145. RA D 33/60, Queen Victoria to the Prince of Wales, 27 May 1882.

with the supporters of law and order."[146] In early July Queen Victoria went on to reject Spencer's view that things were improving in Ireland. He replied that things had improved and that this was making the extremists all the more desperate.[147]

Gladstone tried to convince her that Parnell, who had condemned the murders, was now committed to legality: "He spoke decisively against outrages."[148] Ponsonby thought that if Parnell wanted "to restore legality" he ought to "check the utterance of his sister [Anna Parnell] who denounced Spencer as a murderer."[149] But to the queen it was simply the case that "Mr Gladstone is determined to trust in these rebels. . . . His retirement & that of his evil genius Mr Chamberlain w[oul]d make a g[rea]t difference & be a g[rea]t blessing to the country."[150]

In the Commons the members of the Irish Party tried to prevent the passage of the Prevention of Crime Bill. The queen described them as being "Irish rebels"[151] and was particularly enraged by one speech from Tim Healy. John Bright had taken him to task for supporting a conference in Chicago in which "wild words" had been spoken. Healy said he was no more responsible for them than the queen was for everything that happened in Parliament:

The right hon. Gentleman taunted Irish Members with being traitors to the Crown. What was the Crown? Was it the Mace on the Table? Was it the Sovereign of these Realms? He remembered, and, no doubt, the Chairman, as a Caledonian, remembered the words of the old Jacobite song

> Wha' the De'il ha' ye gotten for a King,
> But a wee wee German lairdie?

That was the view Predecessors of the same hon. Gentlemen in that House took of the Crown. But when he heard the Crown referred to in vague and shadowy terms, he was bound to confess that he did not know what it meant. But he

146. RA D 33/84, Sir Henry Ponsonby to Lord Spencer, 7 June 1882.

147. RA D 34/47, 48, Queen Victoria to Lord Spencer, 13 July 1882; Lord Spencer to Queen Victoria, 14 July 1882.

148. RA D 28/154, W. E. Gladstone to Queen Victoria, 25 May 1882.

149. RA D 33/90, Sir Henry Ponsonby to Queen Victoria, 8 June 1882.

150. Queen Victoria to Sir Henry Ponsonby, 21 May 1882, in Ponsonby, *Henry Ponsonby*, 191.

151. RA D 34/9, Queen Victoria to Lord Spencer, 1 July 1882, in Buckle, *Letters*, second series, 3:303.

did know to whom his allegiance was due; his allegiance was due to his country-men and any allegiance that stood in the way of the betterance, improvement and advancement of his country he should despise.[152]

This infuriated the queen. Gladstone agreed that the remarks were "both insolent and disloyal," but had to tell her that because the chair had not adverted to the matter at the time nothing now could be done about it. He promised that the government would be vigilant to prevent such occur-rences in future.[153]

Lord Spencer believed that ceremonial displays impressed Irish people and could help to win them away from nationalism. This was to lead him to urge a royal visit for 1885. In 1882 he tested out his theory with a vicere-gal visit to the west of Ireland in September. His carriage was preceded by eight hussars and eight mounted constables in front and two armed con-stables and two detectives behind.[154] "The Irish are impressed by what they see and the display of escorts of Police attending the Lord Lieu-tenant is likely to make an impression upon them and make them realize that there is a strong Government who notice what they do and are ready to punish crime as well as redress grievance."[155]

By the end of 1882 Ponsonby was reporting to the queen that the situa-tion in Ireland was improving. Parnell was hard up; the National League, the successor of the Land League, was not a success; and Michael Davitt had fallen out with the other Irish leaders.[156] Meanwhile, early in 1883, the trials of the Invincibles began. The evidence at the trials seemed to confirm all the queen's views about Irish politics:

The disclosures are *fearful*, and the connection between the Land League, Fenians, and Assassination Society is *appalling* but most important and will surely open the eyes of many Home Rulers and miserable sympathisers.[157]

Queen Victoria continued to take a minute interest in the trials. "The Queen has been most painfully interested by the examinations at Kilmain-ham [court] which are quite *thrilling*. Will the not finding of the knives

152. 23 June 1882, *Parliamentary Debates*, 3d Series, vol. 271 (22 June–10 July 1882), col. 295.

153. RA D 33/154, W. E. Gladstone to Queen Victoria, 25 June 1882.

154. Gordon, *The Red Earl*, 1:23.

155. RA D 34/145, Lord Spencer to Queen Victoria, 18 September 1882.

156. RA D 34/185, Sir Henry Ponsonby to Queen Victoria, 25 December 1882.

157. Queen Victoria to Sir William Harcourt, 18 February 1882, in Buckle, *Letters*, second series, 3:411.

(which she fears is likely) cause any difficulty in condemning these monsters? She *trusts not.*[158] In May and early June those convicted were executed. There was little or no public opposition to the executions in Ireland, so horrific had the crime been perceived to be.[159] In a sequel to the executions, James Carey, who had provided information against his fellow Invincibles, was shot dead in South Africa in June; the man who shot him was executed in turn in December, leading to rumors of an Invincible revenge assassination plot against Gladstone himself.

By the end of June Spencer was satisfied that things were definitely quietening down in Ireland. "Lord Spencer trusts that with a steady continuation of firm administration that in time the feeling towards England may be turned into one of friendship, but much patience will yet be needed."[160]

A new source of worry for the Liberals, anxious to create a center ground in Ireland by appeasing nationalists, was the policy of Conservatives such as Sir Stafford Northcote and, later, Lord Randolph Churchill of stirring up the fears of Ulster Protestants against home rule. Liberals tended to be suspicious of the helpfulness of the loyalty of Ulster. Spencer wrote to the queen of Northcote's intervention in Ulster that "[a]s far as a display of loyalty such gatherings will do good but the danger is with the excitable Orangemen, that they will stir up religious differences and drive into the ranks of Nationalists moderate Roman Catholics and others who dislike intensely the usual violent tactics of the Orange party."[161]

It was in Britain itself that the security situation was now deteriorating. In January 1883 there were explosions in Glasgow, in then in March more explosions in London at Whitehall and at the offices of the *Times.* The queen thought the bombing of Whitehall "a grievous and alarming occurrence following as it did close upon the threats of reprisals, which the queen long expected but Mr Gladstone did not." She noted that O'Donovan Rossa "speaks in triumph and says *more* and *worse* will follow."[162] There were discoveries of dynamite in London, Liverpool, Glasgow, and Birmingham.

158. RA D 35/19, Queen Victoria to Lord Spencer, 15 February 1883.

159. RA D 35/57, Lord Spencer to Queen Victoria, 4 June 1883, in Buckle, *Letters,* second series, 3:423. "There has been but little pressure to obtain commutation of the death sentences."

160. RA D 36/65, Lord Spencer to Queen Victoria, 28 June 1883.

161. RA D 36/98, Lord Spencer to Queen Victoria, 17 October 1883.

162. RA D 35/72, Queen Victoria to W. E. Gladstone, 17 March 1883.

On 9 April a new Explosives Act was passed through Parliament in one day. The spate of Ireland-related terrorism continued, however. In September there was an explosion at the Woolich Royal Arsenal and the next month one on the London Underground near Charing Cross Station. Three days later the duke and duchess of Connaught set out from the same station on a trip that was to take them to India. Arthur's three brothers and their wives turned up to see him off. There was a very large security operation to assure their safety.[163]

Explosions and dynamite finds continued throughout 1884, from successful and not-so-successful attempts to cause explosions at London train stations in February, to explosions in St. James's Square and Scotland Yard in May, to an attempt to destroy London Bridge in December. When the Prince of Wales attended the races at Aintree in March great security measures were taken for his safety.[164]

In Ireland Spencer's efforts to maintain a distance from the Orange Order had led him to dismiss Lord Rossmore from the magistracy. This move was denounced by Colonel E. R. King-Harman at a meeting in Dublin attended by the leading Conservative W. H. Smith. King-Harman was not from Ulster but from Boyle, County Roscommon, and had once been a moderate home ruler. His speech on this occasion was an attempt to reclaim all of Ireland, and not simply the northern province, for loyalty to the Crown:

A very large proportion of Irishmen of all classes and creeds were loyal to the British connection, loyal to the Queen, loyal to the Constitution, and the integrity of the Empire and loyal to truth, honour and honesty. . . . [It was not] only a sect of the Irish nation that were loyal to the connection with the Empire.[164]

Some Irish Tories boycotted Spencer's levee in retaliation for his action, concerning Rossmore and generally, and Tim Healy stirred the pot by issuing a pamphlet on Orangeism entitled *Loyalty, plus Murder.*[165] In June Spencer visited Ulster but the Orange grand master, Lord Enniskillen, ordered that there be no protests against him lest "it would be put down by our enemies, especially in this country, as an insult to her Majesty."[166]

In March 1884 John Redmond returned to Ireland and controversy after a visit to Australia. The controversy is illustrative of the hostility to monarchy then current in nationalist political circles. Archibald Forbes of the

163. *FJ*, 3 November 1883.
165. *FJ*, 30 January, 5 February 1884.
164. *FJ*, 25 January 1884.
166. *FJ*, 18 June 1884.

Nineteenth Century had charged that while in Australia Redmond had been speaking in his "usual seditious manner" but, encountering resistance to his nationalist views, had to change tack and "ask meetings of Irishmen to cheer for the Queen." For Redmond, this latter allegation was a serious slander that he vigorously refuted.[167]

That same month Prince Leopold, duke of Albany, died. The *Freeman's Journal*, setting aside its "political feelings" toward "a reigning House whose head and members are to her [Ireland] almost absolute strangers," expressed sympathy to the royal family for their personal loss. At the same time an article appeared in the *Contemporary Review* from Lord Lorne proposing four Irish parliaments, one for each of its provinces.[168]

The end of August saw a visit to the Dublin Horse Show by the duke of Edinburgh, while royal naval vessels were berthed at Kingstown. He was warmly received by cheering crowds in Dublin.[169] The Dublin Corporation did not make him an official address of welcome to the city and came in for some criticism as a result. William Meagher, the lord mayor, explained rather unconvincingly that this was because he had not been officially informed of the visit and because the duke had come while on active service as a naval officer. Meanwhile, the duke's ship had sailed on to Cork harbor, where he was officially greeted by the Liberal mayor of Cork, though the latter was later censured for his greeting by the Corporation of Cork.[170]

The Irish Party's *United Ireland* was scornful of the visit, with references to "A Guelph, A Guelph!," "The Dook and his Fleet," and "the great Admiral." It belittled his welcome in Dublin. "The few flunkeys who are always to be found in Dublin made themselves conspicuous by dogging his steps, lifting their hats and getting up here and there the ghost of a cheer." And as for his reception of the mayor of Cork and his associates on board his ship, "The Grand Llama kept his manners in his pocket along with the keys of the buffet cellar and neither compliments nor champagne rewarded the aquatic pilgrims."[171]

In September Spencer made one of his viceregal sorties to the southwest. He received a cool reception at Millstreet where banners proclaimed "God Prosper Irish Industries," "Faith and Fatherland," "God Save Ireland," and "Parnell for ever."[172] Few lords lieutenant had been as unpopular as Spencer. Ironically, the reason for this had to do with the perception

167. *FJ*, 11 March 1884.
168. *FJ*, 29 March 1884.
169. *FJ*, 29 August, 1 September 1884.
170. *FJ*, 13 September 1884.
171. *United Irishman*, 6, 13 September 1884.
172. *FJ*, 8 September 1884.

that, with a little more pressure, the Liberal government, which was relatively well disposed to nationalist Ireland, could be forced into the concession of home rule.

Spencer found himself put under political pressure from nationalists on a whole range of issues, many of them not within the normal ambit of politics. William O'Brien in *United Ireland* pursued a homophobic witch hunt against army officers and Dublin Castle officials that resulted in a series of libel and criminal trials through the second half of 1884. Politically, it was used as evidence of "the scandal of the Spencer system."[173] Of more importance was the case of Myles Joyce who was executed on 15 December 1882 for his part in the murder of a family of five at Maamtransa, County Galway. There was some doubt as to his guilt and, in an age in which the Irish were receiving very adverse publicity on account of the outrages of the Land War and dynamite attacks in Britain, his case was seized upon by nationalist politicians as an example of British iniquity against Ireland.

As lord lieutenant Spencer was principally blamed for the incident. At the end of October 1884 Irish MPs disrupted the Commons over the issue. Sir Charles Dilke recalled visiting Spencer in Dublin and going out for a walk with him. Spencer "was assailed by the majority of those we met with shouts of 'Who killed Myles Joyce?' while some varied the proceedings by calling 'Murderer!' after him."[174]

Queen Victoria recorded Spencer's views about all of this in her journal. "This shameful raking up of trials and asking for an enquiry was quite an impossibility and could not be granted."[175] She had taken an interest in the original Maamtrasna incident. A young child called Patrick Joyce had survived the attack and the queen had expressed a wish "to contribute something to him." Spencer reported to the queen that the child was "ignorant of the existence of God and evidently was little better than an untaught savage." With the help of the Catholic archbishop of Tuam, "a good and loyal man," Spencer arranged for the child to be admitted to the Artane Industrial School in Dublin where he even visited him. Spencer enjoyed his visit to Artane: "Your Majesty would have liked the hearty way which they sang the National Anthem."[176]

173. *FJ*, 5 November 1884.

174. S. Gwynn and G. M. Tuckwell, *The Life of the Rt Hon. Sir Charles W. Dilke*, 2 vols. (London: 1917), 2:138–39, quoted in Gordon, *The Red Earl*, 1:33.

175. RA QVJ, 14 October 1884.

176. RA D 34/158, 35/1, 2, Lord Spencer to Queen Victoria, 21 November 1882, 1, 11 January 1883.

In spite of this the *Freeman's Journal* concluded its summation of 1884 with a catalogue of accusations against Spencer. "The acts of a Government by Coercion in Ireland were incompatible with the professions of liberality and freedom made by the Lord Lieutenant's cabinet colleagues in England." It went on to highlight the case of Myles Joyce and "[t]he nameless scandals which revealed Dublin Castle officialdom as a polluted and putrid thing."[177] But Spencer thought he had a trump card up his sleeve: a visit from the Prince and Princess of Wales that would assuage Irish discontent.

❖

Parnell's *United Ireland* opened 1885 by publishing a cartoon of "Erin Presenting New Colours for 1885 to Her Soldiers." Erin took the form of a queen and her soldiers were Parnell and his colleagues.[178] Parnell himself, while not quite announcing that 1885 would be his equivalent of O'Connells's repeal year, began the year by intensifying his campaign for home rule with a major speech in Cork on 21 January calling for the restoration of Grattan's Parliament.[179] By holding up the late-eighteenth-century Irish parliament as an ideal without adverting to the very different circumstances of the late nineteenth century, he and other Irish nationalist politicians put themselves in the advantageous position of appearing to call for a defined constitutional arrangement while waiting on British politicians, who might be persuaded or coerced into agreeing with them, to fill in the details.

In Dublin, however, there was alarm in nationalist circles when the new lord mayor, John O'Connor, paid a courtesy visit to Spencer on 3 January. O'Connor was already a controversial figure. He had been selected by the nationalist caucus as its candidate for lord mayor by a narrow victory of twelve votes to ten over his opponent James Winstanley, whose campaign had been undermined by the revelation that he was a Freemason. Winstanley denied that he was an active Mason and claimed that he was the victim of anti-Protestant bias.[180]

O'Connor was an example of the new sort of council member. He was accused of being in politics to protect the vintners' trade and of having stood against a teetotaller because the latter favored Sunday closing.[181]

177. *FJ*, 31 December 1884.
179. *Nation*, 24 January 1885.
181. *FJ*, 30 June 1884.

178. *United Ireland*, 3 January 1885.
180. *FJ*, 28 June 1884.

When he was elected by the full council on 8 July speeches in his favor were lukewarm. One member admitted that O'Connor did not have the eloquence of a Gray or a Dawson but nonetheless had "a big generous Irish heart" and would maintain the level of hospitality at the Mansion House to "the average standard."[182]

At the new-style civic banquet on 1 January there was a toast to the queen. The next day O'Connor paid his courtesy call on the lord lieutenant at the Vice Regal Lodge. When he was criticized for doing this at a radical nationalist meeting on 12 January, his private secretary wrote to the papers defending him on the grounds that he had only been following the precedent of some of his immediate predecessors. It was a measure both of O'Connor's relatively low standing in public esteem and, more importantly, of how quickly the public mood was changing in an anti-British direction, that the defense of precedence was not enough. Spencer was "the most unpopular of unpopular Viceroys" because of "the hanging of an innocent man" and "the horrible and revolting disclosures of Dublin Castle."[183] The public mood disconcerted even the Irish Party. "It is only fair to Lord Mayor O'Connor to remember that he only followed in the footsteps of all his predecessors in paying a State visit to the Lord Lieutenant," pleaded *United Ireland*.[184]

On 11 February Edward Cardinal McCabe, Cullen's relatively brief successor in the see of Dublin, died. "The Cardinal was most loyal to Her Majesty and helpful to the Government," Spencer wrote to Ponsonby while asking that the queen send a message of sympathy to Nicholas Donnelly, the auxiliary bishop of the diocese.[185] The *Freeman's Journal* agreed. McCabe had been a supporter of Dublin Castle and an opponent of the "national cause."[186] The Dublin clergy had meanwhile elected the strongly nationalist William Walsh as vicar capitular, interim ruler of the diocese. Walsh was eventually to succeed as archbishop in spite of the disinclination of the pope to appoint him.

Donnelly was delighted to receive the message from the queen and read it at a meeting of the clergy of Dublin. Spencer told Granville what happened next:

182. *FJ,* 8 July 1884.   183. *FJ,* 16 January 1885.
184. *United Ireland,* 17 January 1885.
185. RA D 27/23, Lord Spencer to Sir Henry Ponsonby, 11 February 1885.
186. *FJ,* 19 February 1885.

He said that it will be for the Vicar Capitular to write to me to express to the Queen their thanks for the message. Upon his saying this there was a murmur throughout the assembly & it was pronounced as an impossible thing to do. It was finally agreed that the Bishop should convey by word of mouth to me the acknowledgement.[187]

Spencer had been working toward a royal visit since the autumn of the previous year, suggesting it to the Prince of Wales in October 1884.[188] His attempts to get the chancellor of the Exchequer, H. C. E. Childers, to agree to finance the visit failed. Spencer feared that if the money for the visit had to be voted by Parliament Irish MPs would vote against it.[189] Childers believed the queen should foot the bill, though he noted that "[s]he hates Ireland and everything to do with it."[190]

Spencer intensified his efforts in January 1885 to secure a visit, and framed his arguments in favor to the queen in terms of current events. A visit from the Prince of Wales would, the queen thought, be seen as "an attempt at conciliation in reply to the recent explosions in London."[191] "We cannot conciliate those who sympathise with them [the dynamiters]," argued Spencer, "but we may discourage them by showing that considerable numbers of Irishmen are loyal."[192]

At the end of January Spencer told Gladstone that the current spate of attacks on him was damaging the monarchy in Ireland. He wanted the lord lieutenancy replaced by a purely political secretaryship of state and was desperate for a royal visit because the Irish "are more easily moved to loyalty for the Queen and Royal family than the English or Scotch."[193] The queen agreed to the visit but with reluctance. She refused to countenance her son holding a levee, as it would undermine the position of the lord lieutenant.[194] The Prince of Wales successfully persuaded his mother oth-

---

187. Lord Spencer to Lord Granville, 19 February 1885, in Emmet Larkin, *The Roman Catholic Church and the Creation of the Modern Irish State, 1878–86* (Dublin: Gill and Macmillan, 1975), 255.

188. Gordon, *The Red Earl*, 1:31.

189. Lord Spencer to H. C. E. Childers, 26 October 1884, in Gordon, *The Red Earl*, vol. 1, no. 367, p. 277.

190. H. C. E. Childers to Lord Spencer, 28 October 1884, Spencer Papers, in Gordon, *The Red Earl*, vol. 1, no. 368, p. 278.

191. Lee, *Edward VII*, 1:236.

192. Lee, *Edward VII*, 1:236.

193. Lord Spencer to W. E. Gladstone, 26 January 1885, GP Add MSS 44312 ff 1–8, in Gordon, *The Red Earl*, vol. 1, no. 386, p. 291.

194. RA D 37/32, Sir Henry Ponsonby to Queen Victoria, 26 February 1885.

erwise on the grounds that the lord lieutenancy was now such a politicized office that Conservatives could not go to Dublin Castle while a Liberal was there whereas he would provide an apolitical occasion that would enable both sides to attend.[195]

The queen also refused to pay for the visit. The prince's private secretary wrote to Ponsonby that "if the visit does take place, he [the prince] should go to Ireland at the express wish of the Government . . . that he imagines neither the Queen nor the Cabinet can suppose that he expects to derive any personal pleasure from the visit."[196] Eventually Gladstone agreed to find £3,000 from the Special Service Fund.[197]

The visit of the Prince and Princess of Wales was announced at the end of February. The heir to the throne's visit to Dublin was linked with his work as a member of the Royal Commission on Housing for the Poor.[198] In the Commons Gladstone fended off a suggestion that the visit coincide with the dropping of coercion, an amnesty for prisoners, and the setting up of an investigation into miscarriages of justice.[199] Almost immediately after the announcement of the visit some American Fenians issued a probably not very serious death threat against the prince's life.[200]

In Ireland the *Freeman's Journal* hoped that if the visit was "clearly dissociated from politics" the royal couple would be received "with respect and cordiality."[201] But most nationalist leaders did think it was political, at least "political" in the sense of a hoped-for enthusiasm for royal visitors being used as an antidote to nationalism in Ireland and to the growing temptation to give in to nationalist demands in some quarters in England. As one correspondent to *United Ireland* put it:

They [the Castle authorities] do not believe that the doctrines of the Land and National Leagues are fixed principles in their [Irish people's] souls. . . . No but they do believe that the "fierce light which leads to the throne" will so dazzle

195. Gordon, *The Red Earl*, 1:32.

196. RA T 9/5, Francis Knolly to Sir Henry Ponsonby, 26 January 1885, in Philip Magnus, *King Edward the Seventh* (London: Murray, 1964), 188.

197. RA T 9/10, 13, W. E. Gladstone to the Prince of Wales, 3 February 1885; the Prince of Wales to W. E. Gladstone, 6 February 1885.

198. Edward VII, in *DNB*, Second Supplement, vol. 1 (London: Smith, Elder, 1912), 546–610.

199. 27 February 1885, *Parliamentary Debates*, 3d Series, vol. 294 (18 November 1884–3 March 1885), col. 1610.

200. Lee, *Edward VII*, 1:238.

201. *FJ*, 24 February 1885.

Irishmen that they, one and all, men, women and children, will fall down and worship the heirs to England's Crown and power.[202]

Within the next few weeks a nationalist consensus of opposition to the visit began to develop. The *Freeman's Journal*, however, stood apart from the consensus in its welcome for the visit and thus drew on itself the odium of *United Ireland*. Edmund Dwyer Gray, proprietor of the *Freeman's Journal* and a nationalist MP, even went so far as to tell the Prince of Wales privately, after a meeting of the Housing Commission on which they were both serving, that he was delighted at the visit and hoped the prince would "be satisfied with your reception."[203] As the visit approached, though, even the *Freeman's Journal* was to fall in behind the nationalist consensus, calling the visit political though still asserting that "[w]e cannot think that personally the Prince was any part of it."[204]

On 1 March at a meeting in the Phoenix Park to protest against William O'Brien's recent suspension from the Commons, O'Brien himself spoke, exploiting the crowd's racism against what he saw as Ireland's colonial treatment:

It won't do for them to insult and badger the representatives of the Irish people today and send over tomorrow their Prince and Princess of Wales (groans and cries of "they need not come here") to amuse us with their glass beads and trinkets as if we were a nation of negroes (groans). . . . [T]he days of Royal tomfoolery in Ireland are gone and gone for ever (great cheering).

At the same meeting, the lord mayor, having learned the lesson of two months before, promised not to fly his standard over the Mansion House during the royal visit.[205] Within days he had thought better of it and was writing to the papers that he intended no disrespect to the Prince of Wales, whose visit was part of his work on the Housing Commission.[206]

United Ireland alleged that O'Connor had written his letter at the behest of Michael Dwyer, secretary of the Vintners' Association, who had pointed out to him that the prince was a Freemason and Irish vintners needed the support of the English breweries, whose owners were also presumably Masons, to fend off the threat of Sunday closing. If this was true it was very ironic, as O'Connor had been elected on anti-Masonic grounds.

United Ireland then quoted from *Truth*, Henry Labouchère's radical jour-

---

202. *United Ireland*, 28 February 1885. 203. Lee, *Edward VII*, 1:238.
204. *FJ*, 9 April 1885. 205. *FJ*, 2 March 1885.
206. *FJ*, 5 March 1885.

nal, about the relationship between the visit and the English discourse about ruling Ireland. "The poor Irish are in the unpleasant position that unless they are downright rude they will be assumed to be contented. Now they are not contented and don't wish to be thought so." *United Ireland* went on to argue that "[u]p to the present the Nationalists had been disposed to let the Prince alone. They have been driven from that attitude by the persistent efforts [of men like O'Connor] to rekindle the embers of sycophancy in Ireland."[207]

On 11 March Dublin nationalist members of the Dublin Corporation heard read a letter from Parnell asking nationalists to be neutral about the visit and decided not to support the customary loyal address to the prince during his visit.[208] Two days later the Irish Party issued a public statement alleging that royal visits were always used for political purposes by both British political parties and that all Irish public bodies should be neutral on the visit.[209] On 16 March a formal meeting of the Dublin Corporation considered its options. Should there be a loyal address, a strongly nationalist address, or, as T. D. Sullivan proposed, simply no address at all? The Corporation eventually opted for Sullivan's proposal.[210] The Cork Corporation followed suit soon afterward. In both cities, however, citizens' committees, made up mostly of Tories, were soon established to draw up their own loyal welcomes.[211]

The nationalist Limerick Corporation refused to make an address but fell into a dispute with the Limerick Chamber of Commerce which took it upon itself to draw up a welcome to the prince in the name of the people of Limerick.[212] On 11 April *United Ireland* brought out a special edition in opposition to the royal visit, or "invasion," as it preferred to see it. The Prince of Wales was depicted in a cartoon in his Masonic apron. Page after page carried messages of opposition to the visit from around the country. "A plague on their royal visits," was the message from Killala, County Mayo, for example. The paper's greatest coup was a message from Thomas Croke, the nationalist archbishop of Cashel. He wrote that the royal visitors "can expect nothing from the oppressed people of Ireland but a dignified reserve and the clarity of their silence."[213]

At a meeting of the National League in Dublin on 7 April, the day of

207. *United Ireland*, reported in *FJ*, 7 March 1885.
208. *FJ*, 12 March 1885.   209. *FJ*, 14 March 1885.
210. *FJ*, 17 March 1885.   211. *FJ*, 17, 21 March 1885.
212. *FJ*, 7 April 1885.   213. *United Ireland*, 11 April 1885.

the arrival of the royal couple in Ireland, Tim Healy presented the Prince of Wales as an innocent tool of Spencer. "I presume he has come hither, to some extent as a kind of competitor for popular favour with Mr. Parnell (laughter)." Spencer wanted to use him "as a species of white wash brush for the dirty reeking walls of Dublin Castle." William O'Brien said the purpose of the visit was to cause dissent in nationalist ranks. William Redmond's speech had a sinister chill to it:

> In every house over which floated a flag they knew that they had an enemy (hear, hear). . . . The present was the occasion to draw a line between the Nationalists and the anti-Nationalists. . . . On the arrival of the Royal visitors at Kingstown it would be a good thing to note the people who became frantic with joy.[214]

Behind these speeches, though, was an evident anxiety that the visit might indeed prove successful and a determination that for their part nationalist leaders ought to do everything they could to make the visit an occasion for ideological polarization. The *Times* certainly thought this was the case. "The Separatists show an uneasy suspicion" that loyalty to the Crown among Irish Catholics "is more powerful than they are willing to allow."[215]

The Prince and Princess of Wales, with their son, Prince Albert Victor, arrived in Dublin on 8 April. After traveling to Dublin Castle, where they were to stay, they visited the cattle show at Ballsbridge. Some of the streets in Dublin were crowed six deep and large crowds turned out in the evening to see the city's illuminations, though competing crowds sang "God Save the Queen" and "God Save Ireland" at each other.[216] The next day the Princes of Wales held a well-attended levee but no Catholic bishops turned up at it. Spencer was disappointed as, following a much publicized incident in which the late and loyal Cardinal McCabe had been placed in a very inferior position at the Vice Regal dinner table, the lord lieutenant had recently revised the official protocol to give Catholic bishops increased precedence.[217] That day the prince and his son visited the Golden Lane tenements and the new artisans dwellings at the Coombe, fulfilling his role as a commissioner for housing. Spencer told the queen that "the people in the poorest district of Dublin received the Prince with open arms."[218] The

214. *FJ*, 8 April 1885.   215. Reported in *FJ*, 8 April 1885.
216. *FJ*, 9 April 1885.   217. *FJ*, 4 March, 10 April 1885.
218. RA D 37/34, Lord Spencer to Queen Victoria, 9 April 1885, in Gordon, *The Red Earl*, vol. 1, no. 395, p. 296.

princess visited Alexandra College and in the evening held a drawing room.[219]

On Friday, 10 April, the royal visitors received loyal addresses, laid the foundation stone of the Kildare Street national museum, and received honorary degrees from the Royal University, which had replaced the Queen's University in 1879. The next day the princess inaugurated the Alexandra Basin in the Dublin Docks and there were visits to Trinity College and to the Artane Industrial School. By this stage there was no doubt that the visit had become a great popular success in Dublin. As the royal carriage crossed what was now known as O'Connell Bridge on Sackville Street they received a "very enthusiastic" reception. On Sackville Street itself "cheer after cheer" was given.[220]

Yet the very success of the visit was finally to provoke the definitive antipathy toward monarchy of the nationalist elites and a decisive shift within the discourse of nationalism in its attitude toward the Crown. On Saturday, 11 April, despite the efforts of Irish nationalist newspapers such as the *Nation* to suggest that there had merely been "some degree of excitement amongst a small section of the people,"[221] the British press, most notably the *Times*, celebrated the success of the visit and did so in imprudently triumphalistic terms. The *Times* had initially been cautious. "We have no inclination to exaggerate the political significance of this enthusiastic reception" was its position on 9 April. Such caution had vanished two days later:

In vain has Mr. Parnell warned his followers not to recognise the Prince's visit. . . . Irishmen for once have dared to say what they have thought and they have probably learned with some surprise how very large a number of their countrymen are like-minded with themselves and how poor a show Mr. Parnell makes when he declares himself in the royal presence.[222]

The royal visit had been directly pitted against the authority of Parnell and the hold of Irish nationalism on its constituency. As the *Nation* put it, "the British press having sown the wind, the Prince of Wales is now compelled to reap the whirlwind."[223] The views of the *Times* were a godsend to nationalist leaders, as they provided a pretext for an intensified campaign of

---

219. *FJ*, 10 April 1885.   220. *FJ*, 13 April 1885.
221. *Nation*, 11 April 1885.   222. *Times*, 9, 11 April 1885.
223. *Nation*, 18 April 1885.

opposition to the visit. On Sunday, 12 April, ten mass nationalist demonstrations, addressed by leaders of the Irish Party, were held throughout the
country in opposition to the visit.

At Cork John Deasy told the crowd that the welcome the prince had received had been merely that of "a good many flunkeys." The real people of
Ireland had been pursuing a line of neutrality toward the visit but this had
been deliberately misrepresented in England as a political triumph for the
visit. At the Kilmallock meeting a speaker referred to the heir to the throne
as a foreign prince, at which someone in the crowd, not understanding that
it was the prince's Britishness that supposedly made him foreign, shouted
that he should go back to Germany. At the same meeting, Eugene Sheedy,
a radical nationalist priest, mirror imaging the new role of the monarchy as
the emblem of Britain's imperial greatness, said that the Crown was "the
symbol of Ireland's slavery."

Imperial comparisons were made at other meetings. It was only two
months since the news of the defeat and death of General Gordon at
Khartoum by the forces of the Sudanese leader, the Mahdi, an event that
fatally weakened Gladstone's administration. At the meeting at Fethard,
County Tipperary, Parnell was hailed as "the Irish Mahdi," with Spencer,
who was known as "Foxy Jack," rather than the Prince of Wales, in the role
of Gordon:

> The march through Ireland will be a greater failure than the march to Khartoum.
> We may not go the length of sending Foxy Jack per express to Paradiso with his
> head under his arm but we will chase him out of Ireland as we chased out Forster
> and Trevelyan.

At Dundalk William Redmond wished the British Empire in India grief in
its conflict with the Russians on the northwest frontier.[224]

Clearly nationalist leaders were enraged both by the popularity of the
visit—though they did not grant that it was popular—and by the construction that was being put on it in Britain. Clearly also the policy of
neutrality of the Irish Party had failed. It was only at the meeting at Kan-
turk, however, that William O'Brien took the obvious and logical step of
moving the policy forward to active opposition. He warned that as the royal party passed through Mallow the next day on its way to the south of

---

224. *FJ*, 13 April 1885. The present author's great great grandfather, James Murphy
(1805–1889) of Seafield House, Blackrock, County Louth, was one of those present on the
platform at the Dundalk meeting.

Ireland "we shall have an opportunity of letting the Prince of Wales know what Irishmen dare to say." He understood that unpleasantness to royalty was necessary if the ideology of British rule in Ireland was to be punctured:

I believe that if the Prince of Wales leaves Ireland without hearing the opinions of the people of Ireland readily and plainly expressed, we will have to bring this country to the verge of revolution again before we can convince Englishmen that there is anything seriously wrong with us.[225]

Monday, 11 April, began with the prince presenting colors to the Duke of Cornwall's Light Infantry at Dublin Castle. At 1:00 p.m. the Spencers left Dublin Castle for Kingsbridge Station and were the object of both cheering and hissing from the crowds. At 1:15 p.m. Lord Mayor O'Connor, playing the part of an opponent of the visit, arrived at the City Hall, adjoining Dublin Castle. He was hissed by some people in the crowd but shouted out from the balcony of the City Hall that "[h]e would telegraph to Mallow and Cork that he had been hissed by Orangemen and Freemasons, landlords and bailiffs." It was an ugly threat to retaliate by having things made unpleasant for the Waleses. When the royal couple themselves left the Castle they were cheered all the way to the train station, whence they set out for Ballyhooly, County Cork, where they were to stay with Lord and Lady Listowel at Convamore.

At 5:00 p.m. the royal train reached Mallow, where the Tory town commissioners were to present a loyal address. There was cheering from the group of people on the station platform but five hundred police and soldiers were employed in keeping back a large and hostile crowd led by William O'Brien and three other nationalist members of Parliament: Tim Harrington, John Deasy, and John O'Connor (not the lord mayor). The police, under Inspector Carr, charged the crowd and Harrington was injured. O'Brien, perhaps hoping for the kudos of an injury himself, shouted at Carr that he was a coward and a bully. That night those who had taken part in the demonstration moved on to Cork and held a meeting.[226] William O'Brien's triumphal verdict was that "[w]e have stuck a pin in the balloon that the English papers were inflating."[227]

The next day the prince and princess made a largely private visit by train to Lord Waterford at Curraghmore. There were ominous signs of

225. *FJ*, 13 April 1885. 226. *FJ*, 14 April 1885.
227. *United Ireland*, 18 April 1885.

what was to come in the display of black flags along much of the line. On 15 April the Waleses traveled to Cork City. The visit began off well enough, but when the royal couple reached the principal streets of the city, Patrick Street and Grand Parade, "hisses and groans mingled largely with the cheers." A visit to the Queen's College had to be canceled because the students hissed the royal couple and tore up a Union Jack outside the college. Onions and stones were thrown at the carriage at various points along the route.

At the Custom House Docks a military band greeted the couple with "God Save the Queen," but on the other side of the quay there was a counterdemonstration with the singing of "God Save Ireland." "On the one side were the loyalists, the military and the police and on the other masses of people who gave vent to the most extraordinary outbursts of groans, hisses and cries of 'God Save Ireland.'" The Prince and Princess of Wales departed by steamer. That evening John O'Connor publicly burned copies of several English newspapers before a large crowd in the city and told it that "[y]ou have made a new departure in the reception which the Prince is to receive in Ireland."[228]

Meanwhile Parnell had raised the question of the police treatment of the crowd at Mallow in the Commons with a series of admittedly rather pedantic enquiries concerning under whose authority the action had been taken. He alleged that it was on the instructions of a director of the railway company and with the cooperation of a drunken Inspector Carr but against the express orders of the local magistrate. The protests fizzled out when it later emerged that a delegation of the protesters had been offered a place on the platform but had tried to occupy the whole of it.[229]

The Waleses' visit to Killarney went off without too much difficulty. Spencer was their host in the home of the now impoverished Kenmare. The next few days were spent in placid sightseeing.[230] The return journey to Dublin on 20 April, however, was something of an ordeal. At Tralee the train was booed. At Listowel people held up banners with slogans calling on the prince to remember Mallow and Myles Joyce and to "Avoid Foxy Jack." There was a nationalist demonstration at Newcastle West and na-

228. *FJ* 16 April 1885; *United Ireland*, 18 April 1885.

229. 14, 16 April 1885, *Parliamentary Debates*, 3d Series, vol. 296 (20 March–16 April 1885), cols. 1623–24, 1636–38, 1856–60.

230. *FJ*, 20 April 1885.

tionalist protests on the way into Limerick, though the station itself was in the hands of the loyalist chamber of commerce.[231]

The royal couple returned to several more days of engagements in Dublin before trips to Belfast and Derry and thence back to Britain.[232] The prince's parting speech was much criticized by nationalists for its references to "attachment to the Crown and Constitution" and its criticisms "of those who seek to foment disloyalty amongst us." Back in England he announced that his visit had been "a labour of love."[233]

However, the visit that had begun so promisingly from the point of view of the monarchy had turned into an almost total disaster. If it had been a contest between the Prince of Wales and Parnell, the prince might have won the first round but Parnell, relying on his Irish lieutenants and without having to leave England where he effectively lived, had emerged as the winner of the bout. In his hour of victory the fiery William O'Brien paused to pity the Prince of Wales's plight: "I believe there is nobody who now more thoroughly realises than he does himself, that he has been placed in an utterly false position." But it was only a brief pause as O'Brien went on to tell the National League that the prince should have been "scuttling out of the country as quickly as he possibly can, just as his countrymen are scuttling from the Soudan before the Mahdi and from Afganistan before General Komaroff (laughter and applause)."[234]

Spencer reported on the visit to the queen, who was angered by what had happened at Mallow and Cork. His analysis was that the active opposition organized by nationalist leaders had been "arrived at at the last moment when the success of the visit to Dublin became known and when the English papers presumptively linked the Irish Party with complete effacement. . . . [T]he marks of Disapprobation shown in Cork were very distinct and offensive." However, "Had the Prince and Princess not gone to Cork it would have been an admission that loyalty was defeated and that the party of disorder were triumphant." He admitted that he had not imagined that the bad feeling would have been so pronounced," but hoped that the visit would "discredit the extreme party."[235]

The purpose of the visit had been to use royal popularity to assuage

231. *FJ*, 21 April 1885.   232. *FJ*, 24, 27, 28 April 1885.
233. *FJ*, 28 April, 4 May 1885.   234. *FJ*, 22 April 1885.
235. RA D 37/36, Lord Spencer to Queen Victoria, 17 April 1885, in Gordon, *The Red Earl*, vol. 1, no. 397, p. 297.

Irish nationalist discontent and shore up the union. In the first few days it had almost succeeded. The fact that the Irish Party had had to marshal all its resources in order to turn public opinion against the visit was a significant tribute to the continuing popularity of the monarchy in Ireland. Confronted with the ultimate failure of the visit, Spencer was faced with the choice either of accepting that nothing could be done to counteract Irish nationalism, a judgment that could only lead a Liberal politician to accept some form of home rule, or to redouble his efforts to win over the Irish, through contact with the royal family. Spencer chose the latter course. In this he had an ally in the Prince of Wales, who wrote to his mother from Ulster that more royal visits were needed to destroy "the influence, which undoubtedly exists, of those abominable agitators who wish to separate this country from Great Britain."[236]

Spencer went to visit Queen Victoria on 6 May to persuade her to agree to the establishment of an Irish royal residence, in the event of the abolition of lord lieutenancy, which he was pressing, unsuccessfully as it turned out, on the cabinet.[237] She remained unpersuaded. Even if the lord lieutenancy was abolished, retaining the Vice Regal Lodge would suffice for occasional visits from the members of her family.[238] Two days later she told him definitively that "[s]he does not think a royal residence in any part of Ireland will ever attract any of the Royal Family."[239] Spencer wrote in despair to Ponsonby that "I feel inclined to throw up the sponge and retire to my plough in Northamptonshire."[240]

Spencer's hopes for a royal residence were part of a larger scheme of governmental reform in Ireland that would reduce the power of Dublin Castle and come close to, but stop short of, home rule. He wanted to create a new system of local government and to establish a central board for primary education for Ireland. Chamberlain wanted the board also to have control over the poor law, sanitation, and public works. Gladstone himself

---

236. RA Z 455/22, the Prince of Wales to Queen Victoria, 26 April 1885, in Magnus, *Edward the Seventh*, 190.

237. RA D 37/40, 15, Lord Spencer to Queen Victoria, 6 May 1885 (quoted in Gordon, *The Red Earl*, vol. 1, no. 398, p. 299); Sir Henry Ponsonby to Queen Victoria, 15 May 1885.

238. RA D 37/43, Queen Victoria to Lord Spencer, 6 May 1885, in Gordon, *The Red Earl*, vol. 1, no. 399, p. 299.

239. RA D 37/40a, Queen Victoria to Lord Spencer, 8 May 1885.

240. RA D 37/44, Lord Spencer to Sir Henry Ponsonby, 11 May 1885, in Gordon, *The Red Earl*, vol. 1, no. 401, p. 300.

even wanted to give it power over the police. The cabinet agreed on the need for more land reform but disagreed on the extent to which coercion powers should be maintained.[241] Ponsonby warned the queen that "[t]he danger of such a board held in Dublin would be that they might become a sort of parliament."[242] It all turned out to be moot, however, as the government fell over the budget in early June, with Irish members joining the Tories to defeat Gladstone.

One of Gladstone's last acts was to secure an annuity for Queen Victoria's youngest daughter, Princess Beatrice, on her marriage, though he had to promise that there would be an investigation into the future of royal grants. Thirty-eight MPs led by Labouchère, and including some Irish members, voted against the measure. It gave them the opportunity to compose the coda for the recent royal visit to Ireland. William Redmond said that the visit of the Prince of Wales to Ireland had given the Irish people the impression "that Royalty is something we must take off our hats to and cheer, whether we like or not, on pain of having our heads broken by a policeman and being turned out of our railway stations." He went on to urge that it was time "this superstition which prompts the English people to feed and to pamper Royal personages were got rid of, when you see the streets of your capital filled with unfortunate wretches who are starving."

The continuing popularity of the monarchy with many people in Ireland, the promotion by the monarchy of Irish integration in the United Kingdom, and the fillip that Irish support for the monarchy gave to British beliefs that Ireland could be mollified without home rule, all created dangers for the Irish nationalist project. The 1885 visit thus brought to a head a growing anti-monarchical trend among Irish nationalists. Further, it forced nationalists for the first time into open displays of antipathy to the royal family.

Lord Spencer had gambled with the monarchy and had lost. The visit, far from strengthening the union, had damaged the position of monarchy in Ireland to such an extent that there was now a settled antipathy toward it among nationalist elites. There was now also the beginnings of a denial on the nationalist side that loyalty to the Crown was compatible with nationalism and the beginnings of an ideology of denial that any such pro-monarchical nationalists existed that was to push such persons to the mar-

241. RA D 37/52, W. E. Gladstone to Queen Victoria, 23 May 1885.
242. RA D 37/54, Sir Henry Ponsonby to Queen Victoria, 26 May 1885.

gins and reduce them to virtual silence and invisibility. Much of this was reflected eloquently in William O'Brien's speech during the Princess Beatrice debate:

[C]ertain recent events make it necessary for me also to protest against its being supposed that the Irish people entertain the same feelings as the English people, or participate in their enthusiasm about the Royal Family, or have, indeed, any feeling with regard to them except such loyalty as the strict letter of the law enforces. That, unquestionably is my definition of the loyalty of the Irish people towards England. . . . Royal personages are brought over to that country [Ireland] on a political campaign. . . . [Y]ou cannot expect the Irish people, while things of this sort are going on, to exhibit the same enthusiasm for the functions of the Royal Family, whom they never see except in the character of political agents, and whom they can neither hold aloof from without being misrepresented, or tell the truth to without having their heads broken.[243]

243. 14 May 1885, *Parliamentary Debates*, 3d Series, vol. 298 (8 May–7 July 1885), cols. 506–11.

CHAPTER SEVEN

"Unionist Vote-Catcher"

From the Jubilee of Union to the
Famine Queen, 1885–1901

Between the fall of Gladstone in June 1885 and the recall of Parliament in January 1886, following a general election in November 1885, Lord Salisbury briefly held power at the head of a minority Conservative government. Lord Carnarvon was appointed as lord lieutenant. He and the new Irish lord chancellor, Edward Gibson, created Lord Ashbourne, were given seats in cabinet, whereas the new chief secretary, Sir William Hart Dyke, was not.

Lord Spencer, whom the queen thought deserved "the greatest credit" for his work in Ireland,[1] departed Dublin with the crowd shouting "Foxy Jack" and "Myles Joyce" at him.[2] In spite of his stated ambition to do without coercion, Carnarvon was booed as well as cheered on his official entry into Dublin. For the first time the lord mayor and the Dublin Corporation refused to take part in the ceremony of welcome during which the mace and civic sword were placed at the lord lieutenant's feet and the city keys given into his hands.[3] In August Carnarvon visited points on the west coast from *H.M.S. Valorous* but was coolly received, except in Sligo where he was

1. Queen Victoria to Lord Salisbury, 18 July 1885, in Buckle, *Letters*, second series, 3:687.
2. *FJ*, 29 June 1885.
3. *FJ*, 8 July 1885.

greeted with an address from the Sligo Corporation.[4] He reported to the queen, however, that his reception had been "cordial ... [and] in some places enthusiastic." His assessment of the attachment of Irish people to the Crown and the United Kingdom, on the one hand, and to nationalism, on the other, acknowledged the existence of that plurality of allegiances that so concerned nationalist leaders. He wrote that "there still remains a very considerable sense of loyalty, which if circumstances favour, might be fanned into a much warmer flame." Nationalism was strong and yet "[t]his 'nationalism' in very many cases is distinctly united with the appearance of loyalty to Your Majesty, and in no case does it seem to be formally disjoined." Republicans were "an extremely small minority."[5]

In October at an election meeting in Wicklow Parnell called for the yielding of an independent parliament to Ireland, adducing the position of Canada in the British Empire and of Hungary in the Hapsburg Empire as examples of the benefits of this concession. He went on to assert that "under 85 years of Parliamentary connection with England Ireland has become intensely disloyal and intensely disaffected (applause)."[6] Salisbury interpreted this speech as a call for imperial federation, a plan to provide a new more equal structure for the relationship between colonies and Britain within the British Empire. He denied that Parnell's plan would be the answer to Ireland's problems and asserted that "[t]o maintain the integrity of the Empire must undoubtedly be our first policy with respect to Ireland."[7]

In spite of this, there were signs of a possible alliance between Parnell and the Tories throughout the autumn. In the middle of August the Ashbourne Land Purchase Act made five million pounds available for loans to enable tenants to buy their farms. Earlier that month Carnarvon had actually met Parnell in secret and discussed the issue of home rule, though when the meeting became public knowledge a year later they disagreed on the extent to which Carnarvon had actually expressed any support for home rule.[8] In any event, on 21 November Parnell called on Irish voters in Britain to vote for the Tories at the election.

Salisbury deliberately kept the queen in the dark about Carnarvon's meeting with Parnell, so fearful was he of her reaction to any temporizing

---

4. *FJ*, 21 August 1885.
5. RA D 37/82, Lord Carnarvon to Queen Victoria, 26 August 1885.
6. *FJ*, 6 October 1885.
7. *FJ*, 8 October 1885.
8. F. S. L. Lyons, *Charles Stewart Parnell* (London: Collins, 1977), 285–88.

with nationalism.[9] Toward the end of October the queen tested Carnarvon's views on concessions to Ireland by sending him a copy of a memorandum from Gladstone to her about the reforms the late Liberal government had contemplated. His comments on the central board scheme were equivocal and he managed to argue that, because it would be unicameral, it might be more damaging to the union than a home rule parliament with the constraint on a presumably nationalist popular assembly of a second chamber, representative of pro-union interests.[10] Talk of concessions to Irish nationalists continued in government circles in November. Salisbury told Ponsonby that he regretted that the queen had been kept updated about Carnarvon's developing views, which the cabinet did not share, and which Salisbury thought might lead to home rule and thence to a degree of independence that would "reduce the connection between England and Ireland to a personal union expressed in Her Majesty's Sovereignty. In every other respect the two kingdoms will be independent."[11]

The election in late November resulted in the return of 334 Liberals, 250 Tories, and 86 home rulers, all firmly pledged to support Parnell. The Tory government did not resign at once but awaited the return of Parliament in January. Meanwhile, it became clear that Gladstone was undergoing a conversion toward support for home rule, with the Tories in turn retreating into a hardened resistance to any move in that direction. Sensing the Liberal conversion, Irish Party MPs began to sound moderate. Tim Healy, for example, offered his support for the idea of a member of the royal family becoming resident in a home rule Ireland.[12]

Queen Victoria opened Parliament in person in January 1886 to show her support for Salisbury. The government's situation worsened, however, when it was announced that Carnarvon had resigned over his difference of views with the cabinet. "Lord Carnarvon's resignation now has done great harm, as well as his imprudent language," wrote the queen.[13]

The government contemplated the reintroduction of coercion, confirming the queen's view that force rather than concession was the correct poli-

9. Frank Hardie, *The Political Influence of the British Monarchy, 1868–1952* (London: B. T. Batsford, 1970), 17.

10. RA D 37/99, Lord Carnarvon to Queen Victoria, 26 October 1885.

11. Lord Salisbury to Sir Henry Ponsonby, 29 November 1885, in Ponsonby, *Henry Ponsonby*, 199–200.

12. Callanan, *Healy*, 139–40.

13. RA QVJ, 14 January 1886.

cy toward Ireland.[14] Gladstone moved to use his majority to bring down the government over a British agriculture vote, but the real reason was Ireland. The fact that several prominent Liberals, including Hartington and G. J. Goschen, supported the Tories in the vote was a sign that Gladstone could not command the confidence of all of his party in his pursuit of home rule.[15] The queen had written to Goschen urging him and Hartington not to support home rule.[16] She had also advocated the formation of, in her terms, a moderate government of Tories and Whigs, with Hartington as prime minister and Salisbury as foreign secretary, in order to keep Gladstone out of office.[17] Meanwhile, Ponsonby supported the notion of having Gladstone, Salisbury, and perhaps even Parnell meet to discuss a way forward for Ireland.[18]

"The Queen is miserable at the prospect of losing her Ministers," wrote Reginald Brett. "She thinks Gladstone's Government will be the worst ever constructed, even by him. She, finding it was useless to send for Hartington, wished Goschen to go down to Osborne to advise her, and to see if any course was possible except to send for Mr Gladstone."[19]

Gladstone, however, returned to office on 1 February. In due course Lord Aberdeen was appointed lord lieutenant and John Morley chief secretary. When she met Gladstone on the day of his appointment the queen thought him "almost fanatically" convinced "that he is almost sacrificing himself for Ireland." She warned Gladstone that his proposals for home rule would not work and would lead to civil war in Ireland. Clinging to a common English view of Irish politics, that Irish politicians had somehow bewitched an unwilling electorate, she dismissed the Irish parliamentarians as "low, disreputable men; who were elected by order of Parnell and did not genuinely represent the whole country."[20] On another occasion Pon-

14. Jenkins, *Gladstone*, 543. That month Ponsonby had been urging the value of a cross-party policy of concession to Ireland on the queen but he had not persuaded her (Hardie, *Political Influence*, 17; Ponsonby, *Henry Ponsonby*, 202–6).

15. Jenkins, *Gladstone*, 540–42.

16. Queen Victoria to G. J. Goschen, 20 December 1885, G. J. Goschen to Queen Victoria, 22 December 1885, in Buckle, *Letters*, second series, 3:713–16.

17. Hardie, *Political Influence*, 90.

18. Ponsonby, *Henry Ponsonby*, 202–5.

19. Maurice V. Brett, *Journals and Letters of Reginald Viscount Esher* (London: Ivor Nicholson and Watson, 1934), vol. 1 (1870–1903), p. 122.

20. RA QVJ, 1 February 1886, in Queen Victoria, *Letters of Queen Victoria*, ed. George Earle Buckle (London: Ivor Nicholson and Watson, 1934), third series, vol. 1 (1886–1890), p. 36.

sonby referred to the "'Irish representatives.' She jumped down my throat. 'They are not Irish representatives. They don't represent the Irish people and Mr Gladstone knows it.'"[21]

The queen lost no time in communicating her discussions with Gladstone to Salisbury, now leader of the opposition. She showed him Gladstone's secret memorandum on home rule. He had already entered the pantheon of most favored prime ministers, along with Melbourne and Disraeli. "I gave him an enamelled photograph of myself and promised him a bronze bust which was not quite ready. When I expressed a wish to have his likeness he offered to give me a copy of Watt's portrait of himself."[22]

Hartington, Goschen, Bright, and the dying Forster refused to join the cabinet. Chamberlain and Trevelyan, however, did, but resigned when Gladstone produced his draft home rule bill in March.[23] Meanwhile, E. J. Saunderson had founded the Ulster Unionist Party to fight against home rule in that part of Ireland where unionists, as they were now called, were in a majority. Lord Randolph Churchill encouraged the movement with a trip to Belfast in February, thus famously playing "the Orange card." However, when he asked his audience what Ireland's "great want" was, someone, surprisingly, called out "The Queen and peace." "Prosperity" was the answer Churchill had in mind.[24]

The queen had little time for arguments in favor of home rule, least of all the argument that with home rule the Crown would become the strongest link between Britain and Ireland.[25] Gladstone was still ardently trying to convert the queen, however, and his memoranda to her indicate how far his thinking had developed beyond his old justice-for-Ireland position and how reliant that thinking was on his experience of the spread of nationalism in Europe. He now believed that it was not enough that Ireland should have good laws but "that these laws should proceed from a congenial and native source, that they should be their own laws." The Austrians had made good laws for Italy, but the Italians had still wanted them to leave. After solving all Irish grievances "we [still] find ourselves face to face with Irish Nationality, and its demands."[26] Ponsonby also read the

21. Ponsonby, *Henry Ponsonby*, 209.
22. RA QVJ, memoranda, 5, 8 February 1886.
23. *FJ*, 15, 27 March 1886.
24. *FJ*, 23 February 1886.
25. Lee, *Queen Victoria*, 478.
26. RA D 38/31b, W. E. Gladstone, memorandum, 23 March 1886.

memorandum but told the queen he doubted whether Irish nationalist politicians would be satisfied with the limited home rule that Gladstone offered.[27] Three days after receiving her prime minister's memorandum Queen Victoria met Goschen. They discussed what a party of ex-Liberals opposed to home rule, under Hartington and Chamberlain, might be called. The queen suggested "Loyalists or Constitutionalists." In the event they were to be known as "Liberal Unionists."

On 8 April the home rule bill was introduced into Parliament. Six days later Salisbury, Goschen, and Hartington appeared on the same platform at the Haymarket in London to oppose the measure at a public meeting.[28] The queen had told Hartington that his actions were signs of "patriotism and loyalty."[29] Over the next weeks she acted as an intermediary between Salisbury for the Tories and Goschen for the Liberal Unionists. Though she had wanted Salisbury or Hartington to take power immediately, after the hoped-for defeat of Gladstone, in a coalition of Tories and Liberal Unionists, a consensus emerged that a general election would be better.[30] Salisbury was aware that no one in the wider world suspected the truth about the supposedly constitutionally neutral queen's vigorously partisan political campaign against home rule. He argued therefore that if the queen refused to allow a general election after a putative defeat of Gladstone her partisanship would be revealed and Irish and Radical MPs "will think, and say, that the Queen is keeping them from Home Rule."[31] Rumors of the queen's secret activities may have been leaking. Whatever the cause, Ponsonby felt it necessary to reassure Gladstone that rumors that the queen was prepared to refuse a dissolution were not true.[32]

Seeing Gladstone in early May, Queen Victoria thought him looking "ill and haggard." She urged extensive local government in Ireland rather than home rule. He told her the Irish would be less dangerous with a par-

27. RA D 38/32, Sir Henry Ponsonby to Queen Victoria, 24 March 1886.

28. *FJ*, 9, 16 April 1886.

29. RA D 44/11, Queen Victoria to Lord Hartington, 11 April 1886.

30. RA D 44/15, 19, 20, 22, Queen Victoria to G. J. Goschen, 25 April 1886; G. J. Goschen to Queen Victoria, 2 May 1886; Lord Salisbury to Queen Victoria, 6 May 1886; J. G. Goschen to Queen Victoria, 13 May 1886.

31. RA D 44/24, Lord Salisbury, memorandum on dissolution, 15 May 1886.

32. John Brooke and Mary Sorensen, eds., *The Prime Ministers' Papers: W. E. Gladstone, Vol. 4: Autobiographical Memoranda, 1868–1894* (London: Royal Commission on Historical Manuscripts, 1981), 80.

liament of their own. Later that day she wrote to him "with pain as she always *wishes to be able* to give her Prime Ministers her *full support* but it is impossible for her to do so, when the union of the Empire is in danger of disintegration and serious disturbance." She did, however, grant that Gladstone believed he was acting in the interests both of Ireland and of the empire.[33]

By the middle of May it looked as though there were enough Liberal dissidents to defeat home rule. Gladstone himself began to recognize this as early as 10 May.[34] He attacked Churchill in the Commons ten days later, comparing him to Smith O'Brien who had told the Commons of his intention to go to Ireland and levy war against the queen. Queen Victoria refused to acknowledge the force of such a comparison between Churchill and Smith O'Brien, for "the former . . . is only maintaining what is still the law of the United Kingdom, whereas the latter defied the law and declared war against the Queen for which he was prosecuted and condemned."[35]

In an effort to save the home rule measure, and in spite of the queen's disapproval of the expedient,[36] Gladstone announced on 27 May that if the bill passed its current second reading stage it would be withdrawn and reintroduced in an amended form in the autumn. However, on 8 June it was defeated by 341 to 311 votes, with Chamberlain and Hartington leading 93 Liberals against it.[37]

Gladstone asked the queen for a general election. After it he was left with only 193 Liberal supporters in the Commons. Seventy-seven Liberal Unionists were returned, together with 85 Nationalists and 316 Tories. This left the Tories as by far the largest party but still 20 seats short of an overall majority, albeit in a decidedly anti–home rule Commons.

Queen Victoria's only disappointment in the election was the defeat of her friend G. J. Goschen. She consulted him on whom she should invite to become prime minister. He advised her to summon Lord Salisbury and, through Goschen, she urged Hartington "in my name" to form a coalition

---

33. RA QVJ, 6 May 1886. RA D 38/65, Queen Victoria to W. E. Gladstone, 6 May 1886.

34. RA D 38/76, 77, W. E. Gladstone to Queen Victoria, 10 May 1886; Sir Henry Ponsonby to Queen Victoria, 12 May 1886.

35. RA D 38/85, 88, W. E. Gladstone to Queen Victoria, 20 May 1886; Queen Victoria to W. E. Gladstone, 22 May 1886.

36. RA D 38/97, Sir Henry Ponsonby to Queen Victoria, 28 May 1886.

37. *FJ*, 15, 28 May, 8 June 1886.

with the Tories, "without which there could be no permanent Gov^t."[38] Three months earlier she had agreed with Salisbury, with whom she was in constant contact during the home rule crisis, that this would be the best course.[39]

Meanwhile, in nationalist Dublin, the departing Lord Aberdeen was cheered by great crowds and hailed as the best lord lieutenant since Lord Fitzwilliam in the 1790s.[40] The public mood, though bitterly disappointed, had warmed considerably even in the six months since the civic banquet. With T. D. Sullivan as lord mayor, it had concluded with a toast to Ireland and the singing of his very own "God Save Ireland."[41] When Lady Aberdeen had later remonstrated with him about the lack of a toast to the queen, however, he had told her "she was right and said there were several extreme nationalists in the Council who would raise a riot if he did not avoid this. He hoped, however, to get rid of these men when he would return to the honoured custom."[42]

Lord Salisbury resumed office at the end of July. "I cannot help feeling very thankful," recorded the queen, though a few days later she was alarmed to hear from Salisbury that the Liberal Unionists were refusing to join the government, leaving open the possibility of a drift back towards Gladstone and "thus endangering the union."[43] As for the Grand Old Man himself, she told him she hoped "his sense of patriotism may make him feel that the kindest and wisest thing he can do for Ireland is to abstain from encouraging agitation by public speeches."[44]

Queen Victoria believed that she ought not to be a neutral constitutional umpire but instead an active participant in the government. The general view was different; when a selection of her letters from the period of the first home rule crisis was published in the early 1930s, it occasioned criticism. J. L. Hammond, whose 1938 *Gladstone and the Irish Nation* remains one of the few studies of the relationship between Ireland and a United Kingdom politician, wrote of the letters that they

38. RA QVJ, 6, 10, 13 July 1886.
39. RA D 44/6, Lord Salisbury to Queen Victoria, 7 April 1886.
40. *FJ,* 4 August 1886.
41. *FJ,* 17 February 1886.
42. RA D 38/141, Lord Aberdeen to Sir Henry Ponsonby, 20 August 1886.
43. RA QVJ, 20, 24 July 1886.
44. Queen Victoria to W. E. Gladstone, 31 July 1886, in Buckle, *Letters,* third series, 1:169.

show with what little imagination or sense of her constitutional duty the Queen acted from first to last in the final phases of the Irish question. . . . [I]f she had shown a trace of the wisdom and balance that she showed at the time of the Disestablishment of the Irish Church, she might have rendered an incalculable service to the Empire.[45]

The remarkable thing at the time was the fact that so little information on the queen's activities got beyond the political inner circle. In the mind of the Irish public she remained a pillar of constitutional neutrality, though her hostility to Gladstone was widely reported in both the British and the Irish press.[46] Referring to home rule, Charles Dawson said that "[w]hatever the other states of the realm might do he was sure that the Queen would not be an obstruction to ratifying the will of the people whenever that will be made known."[47]

In the course of an article for the queen's sixty-sixth birthday that managed to be critical of her heir's life-style and payments from the Civil List for "a locust army of German hangers-on," the *Freeman's Journal,* nonetheless, asserted that "[t]he Queen has been undeniably one of the most constitutional of Sovereigns."[48] A year later, during the height of her intrigues with Goschen and Salisbury, the same paper described her as "[a] constitutional ruler who has rigidly respected the liberties of the people from the first day of her long reign."[49]

Ironically, at the outset of Gladstone's last government and his second attempt at home rule in 1892, the queen's reputation for a constitutional propriety if anything sympathetic to Irish nationalism was enhanced by the publication of the biography of Archibald Tait who had been archbishop of Canterbury during the disestablishment of the Irish Church. Irish nationalist reviewers such as J. G. Swift MacNeill read the account of the queen's role in the affair as a good omen for the winning of home rule.[50]

45. J. L. Hammond, *Gladstone and the Irish Nation* (London: Longman, Green, 1938), 436.
46. *FJ,* 2 February 1886.
47. *FJ,* 5 December 1883.
48. *FJ,* 25 May 1885.
49. *FJ,* 12 May 1886. An article in the *Freeman's Journal* on 17 May 1897 highly critical of Queen Victoria's attitude to Ireland nonetheless evinces no knowledge of her political intrigues against home rule.
50. *FJ,* 10 September 1892.

The first home rule crisis had brought about something of an ideological realignment in the language of adherence to the Crown, with, if anything, a strengthening of the cohesion of notions of loyalty to the Crown and support for the union. As late as the 1870s Irish nationalists had been keen to assert their loyalty to the throne but to distinguish such loyalty from submission to the union. In 1871 John Martin had written to the *Times* that

I try to do my duty as an Irish subject, and I desire that the Queen should begin to do hers as sovereign of Ireland. That is what I understand by my loyalty to the Throne. But let no English commentator flatter himself that by loyalty to the Throne I mean allegiance and subjection to him and his countrymen.[51]

In 1877 the *Freeman's Journal* warned the duke of Marlborough on his arrival as lord lieutenant that the Irish people's loyalty was "regulated by the amount of protection they feel, and the sense that they have but a portion of that which is rightly theirs."[52]

For the opponents of home rule, loyalty to the Crown was coterminus with adherence to the union. Their rallying cry was the queen and constitution. This cleverly allowed them to continue to claim to be loyal to the Crown even when opposing the policy of government of the day and perhaps, when it came to it, laws passed by Parliament inimical to the union. It also automatically enabled them to refer to the supporters of home rule as being disloyal.[53] In 1883 Joseph Chamberlain in a speech that acknowledged the "undeniable tyranny and oppression" that had been visited on Ireland, nonetheless referred to "loyal Ulster" as opposed to "the three other provinces of Ireland."[54]

This was not a distinction, however, that nationalists were willing to accept at face value. When it became clear that Gladstone had changed his mind on home rule in December 1885, the *Freeman's Journal* deprecated press speculation on the fate of the "'loyal' minority" in a home rule Ireland. "If a proper system of Home Rule were adopted, the 'loyal' minority would immediately be merged in the loyal majority, for the whole population would become loyal."[55] At a meeting of the Dublin Corporation to draw up an address to Aberdeen on his departure, William Meagher praised Gladstone's support for home rule as "patriotic . . . because by carrying

51. *FJ*, 13 September 1871.   52. *FJ*, 11 January 1877.
53. Boyce, "Marginal Britons," 233.   54. *FJ*, 2 April 1883.
55. *FJ*, 18 December 1885.

out such a policy he would make this country one of the most loyal of her Majesty's vast dominions."[56]

Nationalists were also quick to point out the ambiguity in the unionists' slogan of queen and constitution. The *Freeman's Journal* claimed in 1888, for example, that the loyalty of unionists to the Crown was in the end relative and dependent on the Crown's support for the union. If the queen had ratified home rule "would she have committed thereby an act of treason to the Empire?" An analogous situation had been disestablishment when it was said that some elements of the pro-establishment side had threatened "to kick the Queen's Crown in the Boyne, if she acted as a Constitutional Monarch." The loyalty of unionists was thus principally to "a set of political dogmas" and only in a secondary sense to the monarchy as such. The position of unionists with regard to the Crown was thus not all that far from the position of nationalists. "If they are free to say their loyalty is conditional, then so are others to say that their loyalty also is conditional."[57]

In spite of such arguments, one of the outcomes of the first home rule crisis was the further adoption by opponents of the measure of the language of British patriotism and loyalty to the Crown. Supporters of home rule were casually referred to as disloyal by Conservatives. This was dangerous for the Liberal Party in Britain which now found itself portrayed as being in the camp of disloyalty. It was especially true during the queen's Golden Jubilee celebrations of 1887, which in Britain were hailed as a festival of the triumph of the union and the defeat of home rule.[58] Irish Nationalist leaders, however, pursuant to their policy of excluding the monarchy from nationalist self-identity, placed themselves in opposition to the jubilee.

❖

On 17 September 1886 the new Tory lord lieutenant, Lord Londonderry, made his formal entry into Dublin. The relationship between the new government and Irish nationalists was arctic at best. Londonderry was not greeted by the lord mayor and the Dublin Corporation. On 4 October,

56. *FJ*, 31 July 1886.
57. *FJ*, 4 February 1888.
58. Williams, *Contentious Crown*, 137: "While newspapers of both parties commended Victoria's constitutional conduct, they used the Jubilee as an occasion for political debate over the rights and wrongs of Home Rule."

however, the representatives of four Irish cities, Cork, Limerick, Waterford, and Clonmel, traveled to Gladstone's home at Hawarden Castle to confer the freedom of their municipalities on him.[59]

That autumn the Land War, led by Parnell's lieutenants, flared up again in what became known as the "plan of campaign" phase. Lord Salisbury's government responded with a new coercion measure. It gave the lord lieutenant wide permanent powers. Thus it was unlike previous coercion measures, which had always expired after a set period. This new bill caused a strong reaction in nationalist circles and was dubbed "the Jubilee Coercion Bill."[60] It was the first sign that the queen's jubilee would become a focus for the expression of Irish nationalist discontent.

The queen's jubilee was at the end of June 1887. At the beginning of May Irish Catholics demonstratively celebrated the fiftieth anniversary of the ordination of Pope Leo XIII.[61] The same day the Commons voted to approve the funds necessary for the queen's jubilee in June. The motion was opposed by British Radicals and Irish nationalists. The jubilee, which was to be celebrated in Britain as a half century of progress and prosperity, was for nationalists a half century of disaster. T. P. O'Connor told the house that during the queen's reign three and a half million people had been evicted in Ireland and one and a quarter million people had starved to death. Ought Irishmen therefore "to go to Westminster Abbey and to offer thanks to Providence for 1,250,000 of their countrymen having been starved to death in the course of Her Majesty's reign—starved to death by the legislation of parliament?" Arthur O'Connor went further: "I sincerely hope that before another century has passed this nation will be a Republic and not a Monarchy."[62] Two days later the queen on a visit to the Mile End Road in London was booed, according to Lord Salisbury, by "Socialists and the worst Irish."[63]

On 22 May the Commons attended a special jubilee thanksgiving service at St Margaret's Church, Westminster. Bishop Boyd-Carpenter of Rippon preached an anti-Gladstone and anti–home rule sermon. The Irish Party did not attend.[64]

59. *FJ,* 5 October 1886.   60. *FJ,* 28 March 1887.

61. *FJ,* 13 May 1887.

62. 12 May 1887, *Parliamentary Debates,* 3d Series, vol. 314 (26 April–13 May 1887), cols. 1770–92.

63. Weintraub, *Victoria,* 12.

64. Jeffrey L. Lant, *Insubstantial Pageant: Ceremony and Confusion at Queen Victoria's Court* (London: Hamish Hamilton, 1979), 56.

Throughout the early part of June there were concerns both in government circles and in the press that the principal jubilee service at Westminster Abbey on 21 June, which was to be attended by an array of crowned heads, might become the subject of an Irish terrorist attack. On 1 June the *Times* published an article entitled "The Dynamite Party, Past and Present." Over the next two weeks both the *Manchester Guardian* and the *Daily Telegraph* added to the sense of public tension by claiming that there was an Irish-American conspiracy against the jubilee.[65] The *Freeman's Journal* saw it all as a ruse to increase support for the passing of the coercion bill.[66]

On 20 June the abbey was thoroughly searched and nothing was found.[67] Next day the service passed off without incident. Justin McCarthy wrote to his friend Mrs Campbell Praed that evening that the "calamity such as some people seem to have feared and almost anticipated" had not happened.[68] In February 1888 several men were arrested and later convicted on dynamite charges. In some quarters this was taken as a sign that there had been substance to the stories of a bomb plot.[69]

The fact that Irish politicians were boycotting the jubilee service added to rumors that they were doing so to avoid getting caught up in an explosion.[70] The lord chamberlain, Lord Latham, had consulted the Irish chief secretary, A. J. Balfour, on who should be invited from Ireland. Balfour told him that "the Irish Mayors must be asked—just as if they were loyal subjects of Her Majesty—some may return insolent answers, but I see no harm in this, rather the reverse."[71] Almost all refused, with the mayor of Cork publishing his reply that "the Irish people were not prepared to dance in chains."[72] Those few who accepted, such as Thomas Harper of Wexford, had to endure the opprobrium of the nationalist leadership.[73]

Irish nationalist leaders made frequent tours of North America. The return of William O'Brien from one such coincided with the days immediately preceding the jubilee celebrations in London. His journey from Cork to Dublin on Sunday, 19 June, was the pretext for nationalism's countercelebrations to the jubilee. He received ovations at every stations on his train journey to Dublin from Cork, where he had landed, and he excoriated the "jubilee of fifty years of coercion rule in Ireland." In Dublin itself there

65. Lant, *Insubstantial Pageant*, 72, 74.   66. *FJ*, 17 June 1887.

67. Lant, *Insubstantial Pageant*, 73.   68. Lant, *Insubstantial Pageant*, 76.

69. Lant, *Insubstantial Pageant*, 75.   70. Lant, *Insubstantial Pageant*, 75.

71. Lant, *Insubstantial Pageant*, 77.

72. *Cork Examiner*, 24 May 1887, quoted in Lant, *Insubstantial Pageant*, 77.

73. *FJ*, 10 June 1887.

was a mass procession to Sackville Street, which the Dublin Corporation had been legally unable to rename O'Connell Street, and a reception for O'Brien by the lord mayor and nationalist members of the Dublin Corporation.[74]

Jubilee day was a quiet one in Dublin, though the Orange Lodge in Rutland Square was stoned. In Cork there was a minor riot when two shots were fired from the offices of the *Cork Constitution,* a Tory journal.[75] On the same day the *Freeman's Journal* promised that if Queen Victoria were to visit a home rule Ireland, "O'Connell-street would witness at last a demonstration to the Sovereign and the reigning family which is now reserved for the leaders of the people bravely struggling for their rights."[76] This view reflected what would become the official line of the nationalist leadership concerning the boycotting of royal occasions for much of the next three decades. Refusal to participate was a protest against the refusal to grant home rule. It was the line taken by *United Ireland:*

What a jubilee it might have been if the policy of justice and conciliation had triumphed. If Ireland's voice, loyal and free, loyal because free, swelled the great chorus, "God Save the Queen." . . . Ireland's place should have been beside England at the Queen's Throne. Our blood and brain have helped to build up that vast Empire that rejoiced at the Jubilee. Poverty, misery, slavery and famine have been our reward.[77]

In London the *Times* took the opportunity of jubilee day to counter the nationalist assertions that the queen's reign had brought nothing but disaster to Ireland. The famine had been caused by the fact that Ireland had been "a semi-savage community. . . . Such a community at once proceeds to breed up to the new level of subsistence and that is what the backward districts of Ireland did under the combined influence of ignorance, superstition, laziness, increase of food and the *pax Britannica.*" The reduction in the population of Ireland since the famine, "although doubtless accompanied in its earlier stages by much human suffering is essentially a healthy process of accommodation of population to resources," which had led to a rise in living standards. "That Ireland shares in this improvement on any terms she owes to her political connexion with Great Britain; that she has not shared in it more fully she owes to herself."

The British Parliament had done everything it could "for social amelio-

74. *FJ,* 20 June 1887.   75. *FJ,* 22 June 1887,
76. *FJ,* 21 June 1887.   77. *United Ireland,* 25 June 1887.

ration" in Ireland and by extending the franchise "has thrown political power in Ireland into the hands of the most ignorant and easily misled sections of the community," the result being the Irish Parliamentary Party. The greatest peril the Victorian age had faced was Irish home rule which had been an attempt "to drive a wedge into the very heart" of the British Empire. The defeat of home rule was the greatest "political triumph" of the age, one that would make the next half century as great as the one that had preceded it.[78]

For the last four days in June Dublin received a jubilee visit from Prince Albert Victor, known as Eddy, and Prince George. They were the grandsons of the queen and the sons of the Prince of Wales. Eddie was second in line to the throne. He was accused by the *Freeman's Journal* of looking bored and of smirking during the official ceremony of welcome. On the last day of the visit he received an honorary degree from Trinity College, an occasion rendered memorable by the irreverent behavior of the students who cheered and called "Give us a speech" at the prince. When the name of the lord chief justice, Sir Michael Morris, who was also to receive an honorary degree, was announced in Latin, someone cried "Ah, call him Mickey." Even Eddy laughed at that.[79]

United Ireland denounced the visit as "a mockery and an insult to the nation."[80] The pope had wanted the archbishop of Dublin, William Walsh, to greet the princes. He was relieved that the instruction to do so arrived too late to be acted upon. Had he done so, "the result would have been to drive our people from their attitude of respectful silence to one of hostile demonstration."[81]

The nationalist counter to the visit took the form of parody. In February 1888 two of the leading Liberal supporters of home rule, John Morley and Lord Ripon, were invited to visit Dublin and receive the freedom of the city. Their visit was a nationalist riposte both to the recent fêting of Hartington and Goschen by Dublin Tories and to the visit of the princes. Albeit subtly, the *Freeman's Journal* was not slow to make the latter comparison:

Two leading English Liberal statesmen will be welcomed with a popular demonstration, heretofore reserved for Irish patriots, and will be escorted by masses of

78. *Times,* 21 June 1887.   79. *FJ,* 28 June, 1 July 1887.

80. *United Ireland,* 2 July 1887.

81. Emmet Larkin, *The Roman Catholic Church and the Plan of Campaign, 1886–88* (Cork: Cork University Press, 1978), 106.

Irishmen in processional order through the streets of the capital city as National guests. The Marquess of Ripon and Mr Morley will arrive at Kingtown this evening and there, where Princes and Viceroys have so often heard the phrases of servile adulation and the peons of party triumph broken by the hisses and murmurs of a sullen people, the unmistakable sonorousness of a whole nation's greeting will first meet the ears of the lieutenants and colleagues of the grand old statesman, Gladstone, the friend of Ireland.[82]

Lord Londonderry regarded his tenure as lord lieutenant as a matter for which he deserved the highest degree of gratitude. Reporting to Salisbury that attendances at the viceregal levee and drawing room were up compared to those under the Liberal Spencer, he concluded that "[t]his has made me feel to some slight extent recompensed for the enormous sacrifice I made at your special request in July last by accepting the post of Viceroy here." Salisbury hastily arranged for the queen to write to Londonderry with her thanks for his efforts.[83]

The years 1887 and 1888 were difficult ones for the Irish administration. Even though coercion was accompanied by a new concessionary land act, the plan-of-campaign phase of the Land War was to continue until 1981. In August 1887 the National League was declared illegal. The news caused Queen Victoria to "[r]ejoice at [the] decision arrived at—and at [the] firm line taken."[84] Over the next two years T. D. Sullivan, John Dillon, the Redmond brothers, and William O'Brien were all to find themselves sentenced to terms of imprisonment. In September 1887 the police fired into a crowd at Mitchelstown, killing three.

By the spring of 1889 it became clear that Lord Londonderry was nearing the end of his term in office. His resignation was announced on 9 April.[85] There were calls for the existing lord lieutenancy to be abolished and replaced by a secretaryship of state and a member of the royal family living in Ireland.[86] In May Prince Albert Victor paid a visit to Belfast. He

---

82. *FJ*, 1 February 1888.

83. RA D 39/2, 3, Lord Londonderry to Lord Salisbury, 7 February 1887; Lord Salisbury to Queen Victoria, 11 February 1887.

84. RA D 39/25, Queen Victoria to Lord Salisbury, 19 August 1887.

85. *FJ*, 10 April 1889.

86. 11 April, 13 May 1889, *Parliamentary Debates*, 3d Series, vol. 335 (9 April–13 May 1889), cols. 253–54, 1862–63.

was one of those mentioned as royal resident. The *Freeman's Journal* hoped the prince would marry an Irish lady: "[G]oodness knows the country could furnish a prettier and better bred one than the German ring of poor and ugly cousins."[87]

On 29 May Salisbury appointed Lord Zetland as lord lieutenant. "One great man goes and another, equally great, takes his place," sniped the *Freeman's Journal*, which also joked that Salisbury had had to work his way through the alphabet of peers before he could get one to accept the position.[88] That same day as Zetland was appointed Salisbury had met a delegation of Irish unionists who urged the appointment of a royal prince. The coincidence of the two events looked like a rebuff for the unionists from their own prime minister.[89]

❖

In March 1887 the *Times* published a series of articles whose general title "Parnellism and Crime" spoke for itself. On 18 April it published a facsimile letter apparently linking Parnell with the Phoenix Park murders. The initial controversy over the allegations eventually died down but was rekindled in July 1888 when F. H. O'Donnell's attempt to sue the *Times* over the issue failed. Parnell demanded an official enquiry and the government, hoping to discredit Parnell, brought in a Special Commission Bill to enable it to take place. Salisbury told the queen he hoped the commission would "bring out the circumstances of the conspiracy in their fullest scope."[90] In the event, the investigation resulted in the vindication of Parnell when in February 1889 Richard Pigott was revealed as the forger of the letters on which the *Times*'s allegations had been based. In spite of the fact that Parnell's own evidence before the commission in May did not go so smoothly, he was now a hero in Liberal circles. Lord Spencer demonstratively shook him by the hand at a dinner of the 80 Club.[91]

The summer of 1889 was an anxious one for Queen Victoria with regard to her family. All her children had now married and received annuities from Parliament. Now it was the turn of her grandchildren, but her application to Parliament for grants for two of the Prince of Wales's children, Prince Albert Victor and Princess Louise, who was about to get married,

87. *FJ*, 22 May 1889.   88. *FJ*, 31 August, 7 October 1889.
89. *FJ*, 30 May 1889.
90. RA D 40/10, Lord Salisbury to Queen Victoria, 23 July 1888.
91. *FJ*, 9 March 1889.

ran into strong opposition from the radical wing of the Liberal party. The government agreed to the setting up of a select committee on the issue, under W. H. Smith, the Tory leader in the Commons. The membership of the committee included Gladstone and Liberal radicals such as John Morley and Henry Labouchère. Parnell and his close ally Thomas Sexton were also members.[92] As lord mayor of Dublin that year Sexton had proposed a toast to the queen at a Mansion House dinner, telling his audience that "none of us holds her Majesty acccountable for their [the ministers'] excesses."[93]

The government was anxious to obtain as great a degree of agreement as possible on the committee. In the event, Gladstone, ever the loyalist in spite of his troubles with the queen, managed to get general support from almost everyone on the committee apart from Labouchère for a proposal to increase the Prince of Wales's annuity by £9,000 so that he could support his children from his own resources.[94] In the Commons the English Radicals were dismayed at the support of Parnell and Sexton for the compromise. "I think that English Radicals," said one, "who have made great sacrifices in order to promote the cause of Home Rule, will regret that on this occasion, which is to them a very important, if not a vital, one, these hon. Gentlemen should have separated themselves from us."[95]

The more benevolent attitude of Parnell to the monarchy was a function of his continuing alliance with the Liberal Party. He had decided to support the measure at Gladstone's urging. He feared, though, and with some justification, that his own party would not be pleased with his decision and might not support it when it came to a vote in the Commons itself. Accordingly, he made himself scarce before the vote so that a meeting of the Irish Parliamentary Party could not take place. He appeared in the chamber at the time of the vote and told the members of his party to vote as they liked. But he then went on himself to vote in favor of the motion. The other members of the party felt they had no other option but to join him.[96] The Conservatives cheered the Irish members who followed them into the same lobby for the vote. "Go in and get your cheer: it will probably be the last Tory cheer you will every get," Labouchère told Justin Mc-

92. *FJ*, 5, 18 July 1889.   93. *FJ*, 24 April 1889.
94. *FJ*, 23, July 1889.
95. 25 July 1889, *Parliamentary Debates*, 3d Series, vol. 338 (10 July–31 July 1889), col. 1333.
96. *National Press*, 8 January 1892.

Carthy.[97] Joseph Biggar, the last Irish member through the lobby, "drew forth prolonged cheers and laughter from all quarters of the house."[98] The *Times* praised the Irish parliamentarians for being "apparently desirous of showing their loyalty to the Crown in a very effective way."[99]

In December 1889 Parnell was cited in the papers of the O'Shea divorce case. The case was heard in November 1890. Parnell's involvement with Mrs O'Shea led first to his abandonment by the British Liberal Party, then to his condemnation by the Catholic Church in Ireland, and finally to a split within the Irish Parliamentary Party in December 1890 that took ten years to heal. Over the next eight months Parnell desperately campaigned in Ireland in a series of by-elections in which his candidates were defeated. His health gone, he died on 6 October 1891.

When the initial news of Parnell and Mrs O'Shea broke, the queen was gleeful. She wrote to her daughter Vicky, now dowager empress of Germany, "Here the excitement is intense about Parnell and what the G.O.M. will do. In Ireland the feeling is very strong against Parnell on account of his proving himself such a liar and having perjured himself. It is satisfactory to see wickedness punished even in this world."[100] Parnell's death almost a year later coincided with that of W. H. Smith, a favorite of the queen: "He died from devotion to his work. . . . What a startling Event is Mr Parnell's death. But *what* a contrast! *He* was a really bad & worthless man who had to answer many lives lost in Ireland."[101]

At the same time as the Irish Party was imploding, Ireland itself seemed to become more amenable from the government's point of view. When Zetland finally made his state entry into Dublin on 16 December 1889 he reported to the queen that he had been impressed by the displays of loyalty he had received: "Altho' Lord Zetland is not prepared to state that there were absolutely no dissentient voices heard while passing through the

97. Callanan, *Healy*, 230, quoting Justin McCarthy and Mrs. Campbell Praed, *Our Book of Memories* (London: Chatton & Windus, 1912), 186–7.

98. *FJ*, 27 July 1889.

99. *Times*, 25 July 1889.

100. Queen Victoria to the Empress Frederick, 29 November 1890, in Agatha Ramm, *Beloved and Darling Child: Last Letters between Queen Victoria and Her Eldest Daughter, 1886–1901* (Stroud: Alan Sutton, 1990), 117.

101. Queen Victoria to Lord Salisbury, 8 October 1891, quoted in Viscount Chilston, *W. H. Smith* (Toronto: Univeristy of Toronto Press, 1965), 357–8.

streets of Dublin, he may inform Your Majesty that the crowd which was large was orderly and cordial."[102] He wrote to the queen after a visit to the southwest in May that "[a] remarkable change for the better is taking place. . . . At almost every village of any importance L[or]d Zetland drove through the people were assembled in large numbers and addresses of welcome were presented."[103]

For six months from May 1891 Prince Albert Victor, now duke of Clarence, was stationed with the 10th Hussars in Dublin. It was a low-key stay, with a visit to the Dublin Horse Show with Lord Zetland being about his only public appearance. Shortly before his departure Eddy was visited by his brother George. On the day of their departure for home they both visited Parnell's grave at Glasnevin cemetery. While in Dublin Prince George, the future King George V, contracted typhoid fever but recovered from it.[104] In early December Clarence became engaged to Princess Victoria Mary of Teck.[105]

As the duke of Clarence was the second in line to the throne, the question of whether the Dublin Corporation should present a loyal address on the occasion of his engagement arose. The *Freeman's Journal* pointed out that the custom of toasting the queen at civic banquets, abandoned in the early 1880s, had been resumed in the late 1880s as "[i]t was no longer felt to be good policy to refuse to drink the health of the Queen." The practice had been restored to enable Gladstone to counter the arguments of the enemies of home rule that the Irish were disloyal. It had "furnished Mr Gladstone with a powerful argument in favour of Home Rule." If the policy of loyalty justified the toasting of the queen, it also justified an address on the royal engagement, the paper argued.[106]

However, at its meeting on 11 January, the Corporation decided, as a protest against coercion, not to make a loyal address to the queen but to send a simple message of congratulations to Clarence.[107] On 14 January, however, the duke himself died of pneumonia. The Dublin Corporation met immediately and voted their condolences. In replying, the Prince of Wales, whose reputation had recently been damaged by the baccarat scandal, alluded vaguely to the possibility that his son might have been about

102. RA D 40/34, Lord Zetland to Queen Victoria, 17 December 1889.

103. Lord Zetland to Queen Victoria, 19 May 1891, in Buckle, *Letters* (London: John Murray, 1931), third series, vol. 2 (1891–1895), pp. 31–33.

104. *FJ*, 19 November 1891.   105. *FJ*, 8 December 1891.

106. *FJ*, 11 January 1892.   107. *FJ*, 12 January 1892.

to return to Ireland, though he did not make clear whether this was to be in the role of lord lieutenant or not: "Our dear son was very happy in Ireland and was about to return there had he not been stricken down by his fatal illness."[108]

In May Prince George was created duke of York. A year later he became engaged to his late brother's fiancée. They married on 6 July 1893. The Dublin Corporation, by then split between bitterly divided groupings of nationalists, voted against presenting a loyal address on the occasion, in spite of the ammunition that it gave to unionists at a time when Gladstone was once again endeavoring to secure home rule.[109] There was little public rejoicing in nationalist Ireland on the day of the wedding, though to the surprise of the lord lieutenant there was a fervent singing of "God Save the Queen" in Loughrea, County Galway, which "is one of our black spots."[110] The *Freeman's Journal* blamed the general lack of loyal demonstrations on the fact that in the name of the sovereign "the natural feelings and aspirations of the people have been rebuked as disloyal." It went on to assert that the truly disloyal were "those who identified the Crown with a political party and a sect, and thus cheated the Monarchy of its inheritance of Irish devotion."[111]

❖

There was a general election in July 1892 that returned a majority committed to the introduction of home rule for Ireland. "Ireland has recovered its quiet and prosperity so wonderfully that it is very wicked to try and upset everything again," was the queen's verdict on the resurrection of home rule.[112] By August the queen's worst fears were realized: Gladstone, "that dreadful old man," was once more in power.[113] Sir Henry Ponsonby's daughter, Betty Montgomery, was present when Gladstone met the queen on 15 August:

He was most obviously nervous; fumbling with his stick. Not so, the Queen. She hated having to receive him again as the Premier, but with the utmost *"savior faire"*

108. *FJ,* 19 January 1892.

109. *FJ,* 6 June 1893.

110. RA D 42/114, Lord Houghton to Sir Henry Ponsonby, 28 July 1893.

111. *FJ,* 7 July 1893.

112. Queen Victoria to the Empress Frederick, 22 June 1892, in Ramm, *Beloved and Darling Child,* 144–45.

113. Queen Victoria to Sir Henry Ponsonby, 26 July 1892, in Ponsonby, *Henry Ponsonby,* 217.

and *"grâce d'état"* she walked in, shook hands and added with a smile. "You and I, Mr Gladstone are slower than we used to be!"

Montgomery sat beside Gladstone at dinner:

He went on openly to a glorification of the policy he advocated for Ireland. I looked at the lovely Belfast linen table cloth, in which were woven the Rose, Thistle and Shamrock, with the motto, "Quis separabit?" just in front of us.

After dinner, the Queen came straight up to me and asked: "What did Mr Gladstone talk to you about?" "Home Rule, ma'am!" She shrugged her shoulders and said: "I know! . . . he always will!"[114]

Lord Houghton, later known as Lord Crewe, became lord lieutenant and received a "hearty welcome from the people"[115] on his formal entry into Dublin, though he himself thought it was "not of an enthusiastic character."[116] Several days later he refused to accept an address from the Dublin Chamber of Commerce on account of its unionist tone.[117] Unionists, and even the Irish lord chief justice, soon began to boycott his state functions at Dublin Castle.[118] The queen, however, had little sympathy with him and chose to take the boycott as a snub of the government's "political representative" rather than of her.[119]

Queen Victoria was quick to tell Gladstone that what the restored chief secretary, John Morley, had reported as being the "peace and order" of Ireland was "the result of six years of firm and just government."[120] Once more Gladstone set about trying to convince the queen via closely argued memoranda that he was right and she was wrong on home rule and that the people she listened to, who were almost all Conservatives and Unionists, were not necessarily representative of public opinion:

At the present juncture, the views of your Majesty's actual advisers, although now supported by a majority of the people . . . are hardly at all represented . . . in

114. Ponsonby, *Henry Ponsonby*, 399.   115. *FJ*, 4 October 1892.

116. RA D 41/10, Lord Houghton to Queen Victoria, 6 October 1892, in Buckle, *Letters*, third series, 2:165.

117. *FJ*, 8 October 1892.

118. RA D 41/57, 42/4, Lord Houghton to Sir Henry Ponsonby, 9 February 1893 (quoted in Ponsonby, *Henry Ponsonby*, p. 219); Lord Houghton to Queen Victoria, 17 March 1893.

119. Sir Henry Ponsonby to Lord Houghton, 13 February 1893, in Ponsonby, *Henry Ponsonby*, 226.

120. W. E. Gladstone to Queen Victoria, 29 September 1892; Queen Victoria to W. E. Gladstone, 3 October 1892, in Buckle, *Letters*, third series, 2:160–62.

the powerful social circles with which Your Majesty has ordinary personal intercourse.

He went on to try to give the queen a reason for supporting home rule.
He argued that home rule, as he proposed it, was a conservative measure
"as tending to the union of the three countries (whose moral union must
surely be allowed to be at the least very imperfect) and the stability of the
Imperial Throne and institutions." He also hinted that the recent radical-
ization of the Liberal Party was due to "the feverish atmosphere which
had been created by the prolongation and the fierceness of the Home Rule
controversy." If home rule was not granted now further radicalism might
be expected.[121] In reply, the queen wrote that she believed the Irish saw
home rule as "a stepping stone to separation" and she doubted whether
Irish nationalists would rule their country with "the proverbial 'fair play'
of an Englishman."[122]

On Christmas Eve 1892 there was an explosion at Dublin Castle in
which a policeman was killed. The retired Fenian, James Stephens, condemned it as the work of an enemy of home rule.[123] For Queen Victoria,
however, it was the result of the new government's leniency toward convicted prisoners.[124] At the end of January 1893 the queen indicated her assessment of the likely effects of home rule by insisting that Gladstone drop
the phrase "better Government" from the reference to home rule in the
queen's speech.[125]

The home rule bill was introduced into Parliament in February but the
queen was annoyed at the way in which the government brushed aside the
official protests of Ulster Unionists. The government argued that Ulster
Unionists had been threatening resistance to the will of Parliament.[126] Indeed, in the Lords there had been a clash between two former lords lieutenant. Spencer had accused Londonderry of encouraging resistance to
home rule "to the extent of the shedding of blood."[127] But to Queen Victoria the government's determination to push on with home rule while ig-

121. RA D 41/18, W. E. Gladstone, memorandum to Queen Victoria, 28 October 1892,
in Buckle, *Letters*, third series, 2:172–76.

122. RA D 41/25, Queen Victoria to W. E. Gladstone, 15 November 1892, in Buckle,
Letters, third series, 2:181–82.

123. *FJ*, 28 December 1892.

124. RA D 41/44, Queen Victoria to John Morley, 27 December 1892.

125. RA D 41/55a, W. E. Gladstone to Queen Victoria, 29 January 1892.

126. RA D 42/2a, A. West to Sir Henry Ponsonby, 14 March 1893.

127. *FJ*, 3 February 1893.

noring protests against it amounted to "trying to force this dangerous measure down the throats of all the really respectable and influential people in Ireland."[128] Gladstone was still hopeful of puncturing the queen's resistance even to the unlikely extent of commending a speech by John Redmond as "one of the best statements of the Irish cause Mr Gladstone has ever heard, and [which] would well repay perusal by any who desire to be acquainted with it."[129] Gladstone was impressed by the moderation of the once fiery Redmond. When the Commons voted its congratulations on the marriage of the Yorks, Redmond urged an amnesty for Irish political prisoners but did so "inoffensively."[130]

By May it was clear that the home rule bill would be passed by the Commons. However, because of the defection of the Whigs in 1886, less than a tenth of the members of the Lords supported the government. Thus there was a fatalistic acceptance among the supporters of home rule that the bill stood no chance of passing there. Rumors were reported in the newspapers that the queen had agreed with Salisbury that in the event of the defeat of the bill in the Lords and even against the wishes of the government there should be a general election.[131] She certainly took soundings in July with Lord Salisbury and the duke of Devonshire, as by then Hartington had become, via the duke of Argyll.[132] By early August Salisbury was definitely opposed to a forced election.[133]

The queen was also putting out feelers to Lord Rosebery, a half-hearted Liberal supporter of home rule, of whom she had hopes. She told him that until Gladstone had resumed office, "All was going on very well, and moderate measures of self-government could have been gradually resorted to, but not such a dangerous one, which, if passed, would inevitably cause great misery to Ireland, and most likely civil war."[134]

The Salisburys visited Ireland in June. Lady Salisbury reported to the queen of the *"horror* and *terror"* of home rule they had encountered.[135]

128. RA D 42/8, Queen Victoria to Lord Rosebery, 3 April 1893.

129. RA D 42/14, W. E. Gladstone to Queen Victoria, 13 April 1893.

130. W. E. Gladstone to Queen Victoria, 14 July 1893, in Buckle, *Letters,* third series, 2:281.

131. *FJ,* 22 May 1893.

132. RA QVJ, 11 July 1893, in Buckle, *Letters,* third series, 2:279.

133. RA D 44/50, Lord Salisbury, memorandum, 8 August 1893.

134. Queen Victoria to Lord Rosebery, 16 June 1893, in Buckle, *Letters,* third series, 2:262.

135. RA D 44/41, Lady Salisbury to Queen Victoria, 2 June 1893, in Buckle, *Letters,* third series, 2:258.

Meanwhile Houghton was reporting positively from his trip to the west of Ireland that "[l]oyalty is not . . . the monopoly of the north-east corner of Ulster."[136] Thomas Sexton claimed that the welcome given the lord lieutenant was "the most conclusive evidence of a spirit of loyalty to the Sovereign ever known in the history of that country."[137] The *Freeman's Journal* agreed that Houghton had been well received: "Hitherto the Viceroy has generally been the representative of all that Irishmen hate most and the character of the Queen's representative has been lost in that of the anti-Irish partisan. . . . But now that has changed and now they are glad to greet the Sovereign's representative."[138] In her reply to Houghton the queen took a different view. The quiet in Ireland was due to the work of the previous Tory government. "She is certain that the Irish people when uninfluenced by agitation and undisturbed by political change are as devoted to her as their countrymen in Great Britain."[139]

After his visit to the west of Ireland, where in Sligo his visit had been advertised as that of "the friend and representative of Mr. W. E. Glastone and his Home Rule Government,"[140] Houghton moved on to the south of Ireland. He ran into trouble for accepting an address from the Cork Corporation "from which every expression of loyalty to the Sovereign had been excluded by a direct vote" and which called for the release of political prisoners. This looked like partisan behavior when put beside his previous refusal to accept the pro-union address of the Dublin Chamber of Commerce.[141]

Toward the end of July there were disorderly scenes in the Commons over the home rule bill. The queen wrote to the prime minister:

In the midst of all this unseemly riot and the disgraceful conduct of many members the Queen wonders if Mr Gladstone does not feel that the Majority of the British Nation feel very strongly the way in which the small Irish majority is used to force through a measure so repugnant to their feelings and so frought with dangers to the constitution?[142]

---

136. RA D 42/62, Lord Houghton to Queen Victoria, 28 June 1893.

137. 11 July 1893, *Parliamentary Debates*, 4th Series, vol. 16 (26 June–18 July 1893), col. 1280.

138. *FJ*, 10 July 1893.

139. RA D 42/107, Queen Victoria to Lord Houghton, 19 July 1893.

140. 22 June 1893, *Parliamentary Debates*, 4th Series, vol. 13 (2 June–23 June 1893), cols. 1063–64.

141. 7 July 1893, *Parliamentary Debates*, 4th Series, vol. 16 (26 June–18 July 1893), col. 1680.

142. RA D 42/115, Queen Victoria to W. E. Gladstone, 29 July 1893.

Meanwhile a petition to the queen against home rule had been signed by over a hundred thousand Irishwomen. Its organizers were anxious to present it to the queen in person. However, constitutional propriety dictated that it be sent to the home secretary, H. H. Asquith, who was less enthusiastic about the petition, which came in "a huge coffin-like structure of walnut-wood with brass handles. . . . It would make not a bad settee for a smoking room."[143]

On 2 September 1893 the second home rule bill was passed by the Commons. It was sent to its fate in the Lords, where the queen noted that the government spokesmen sounded "apologetic . . . and half hearted."[144] On 8 September the bill was thrown out by the Lords by 419 votes to 41. "A crushing majority indeed," wrote the queen, "and what is more remarkable, the crowd outside cheered very much and cheered L[or]d Salisbury!"[145]

Gladstone resigned in late February 1894 and was succeeded as prime minister by Rosebery. Within days he had rescinded the Liberals' support for home rule and agreed with Lord Salisbury's Anglocentric view of the United Kingdom, which had no basis in law, that "as long as England refuses Home Rule, Home Rule can [not] be established in Ireland." Rosebery concurred: "England, as the predominant Member of the partnership of the Three Kingdoms, will have to be convinced of its justice and equity."[146] Though he soon modified this statement, it was clear that Liberal support for home rule was waning. In June 1895 the government lost a vote and resigned. A subsequent election confirmed Salisbury in power at the head of a government of Conservatives and Liberal Unionists. With A. J. Balfour succeeding Salisbury in 1902, the Tories were to remain in power for ten years and were in Ireland to pursue, with some success, a policy of conciliation variously known as "constructive conservatism" or "killing home rule with kindness."

At Westminster Irish parliamentarians now had so little influence that they could only hope to fight rather minor battles. One such was the pro-

143. RA D 43/7, 8, 10, H. H. Asquith to Sir Henry Ponsonby, 11 August 1893; Sir Henry Ponsonby to Queen Victoria, 12 August 1893; H. H. Asquith to Sir Henry Ponsonby, 14 August 1893.

144. RA QVJ, 6 September 1893.

145. RA QVJ, 9 September 1893, in Buckle, *Letters*, third series, 2:311.

146. 12 March 1894, *Parliamentary Debates*, 4th Series, vol. 22 (12 March–9 April 1894), cols. 22, 32.

posal to spend public money on a statue of Oliver Cromwell at Westminster. John Redmond told the Commons it would "give great offence" in Ireland.[147] In 1896 the discovery of a supposed Irish plot to assassinate the tsar, who was then visiting Queen Victoria at Balmoral, was alleged by some to be part of a secret British maneuver in its diplomatic relations with Russia and France.[148] In Ireland itself one of the highlights of the mid-1890s was the twenty-fifth anniversary of the ardently nationalist Thomas Croke's episcopacy in Cashel in July 1895. It was celebrated not only with religious services but with a procession, the presentation of addresses, and an elaborate banquet.[149] It was also marked by the erection of a special monument in January 1897.[150] An early clue to the countermonarchical significance of the event lay in its being called "A National Jubilee."[151]

Meanwhile Queen Victoria's own Diamond Jubilee was now on the horizon. Most of the mainstream nationalist groups hoped they could ignore it. Indeed, one of them contemplated supporting the candidature of Sir Robert Sexton, a Tory, as lord mayor of Dublin for the jubilee year as potentially less embarrassing than having a nationalist.[152] But just as the old Irish parliamentary leaders were beginning to look tired, new small groupings of radical nationalists and republicans were springing up. Their varying agendas focused not so much on Parliament as on the revival of the Irish language, the creation of an Irish literature in English, the improvement of rural life through agricultural cooperation, or the struggles of the proletariat. These were the years of the beginnings of such movements as the Anglo-Irish literary revival and Irish-Ireland.

The leaders of some of the groups that came under these and other rubrics often reveled in public controversy in ways no longer of interest to the now ageing Irish Parliamentary leadership, of whom they were often contemptuous or dismissive. A key element for all these groups was a new cultural element to the nationalism that they advocated. Ireland ought not

---

147. 17 June 1895, *Parliamentary Debates*, 4th Series, vol. 34 (22 May–24 June 1895), col. 1271.

148. Maud Gonne McBride, *A Servant of the Queen* (1938; Gerrard's Cross: Colin Smythe, 1994), 184–85; *FJ*, 14, 23 September and 6, 15 October 1896.

149. *FJ*, 19 July 1895.

150. *FJ*, 25 January 1897.

151. *FJ*, 27 March 1895.

152. *FJ*, 30 November 1896.

simply to have its own independent legislature but its own form of life, distinct from Britain and uniquely Gaelic, though how that might be construed remained problematic.

There were indeed some, such as Arthur Griffith, founder of the original Sinn Féin movement, who advocated at least in theory a continuing role for monarchy in a free Ireland, along the lines of the Hapsburg monarchy's role in a Hungary freed from Austrian domination. However, as a whole, the supporters of these movements were hostile to monarchy. Many were to want an independent Ireland to become a republic. Republicanism became an accepted and respectable political stance within nationalism, albeit a much less homogeneous nationalism than in the days of Parnell. Anti-monarchical agitation provided the more radical groups with a convenient platform for drawing attention to themselves and for drawing a distinction between them and the tired forms of traditional parliamentary nationalism.

✦

The Tory lord lieutenant, Lord Cadogan, was anxious to popularize the queen's Diamond Jubilee in Ireland. To this end he held a state banquet at Dublin Castle for two hundred and fifty people on 13 March 1897. He tried to present it as a representative gathering, but in fact most of the party was made up of members of Ireland's aristocracy and gentry, whose economic and political day was effectively done as rural society emerged from the Land War with the old system of tenants and landlords on its way to being replaced with smallholder ownership. Only about half a dozen nationalists turned up at Cadogan's banquet. The *Freeman's Journal* spoke of "the cold indifference of the Irish people to-day towards the Sovereign and her authority."[153]

For the first time a new note of personal dislike of Queen Victoria began to appear in the utterances even of mainstream nationalists. This was apparent at the meeting of the Dublin Corporation on 17 May which voted not to present an address on her jubilee.[154] On 28 May the Irish Parliamentary Party issued a manifesto calling on the Irish people not to take part in the jubilee celebrations.[155] Plans were already well under way for the largest scale countermonarchical riposte ever in the form of a whole

Personal dislike

153. *FJ*, 15 March 1897; also see *FJ*, 17 May 1897.
154. *FJ*, 18 May 1897.
155. *FJ*, 29 May 1897.

year of commemorations of the 1798 rebellion in 1898, a year that as it turned out would accelerate the new radical trend in nationalist politics. In June 1897 William Redmond explicitly linked the planned commemoration of 1798 with the Diamond Jubilee for the benefit of the Commons:

The record of the last sixty years being what it was for Ireland it would be a mockery for any Irishman to pretend to join in the [Diamond Jubilee] celebrations. In another year Irishmen would be celebrating the rebellion of 1798 when, driven by outrage and torture, they had taken up arms in self defence.[156]

The jubilee celebrations began in London on Sunday, 20 June, with a series of church services. They coincided with Decoration Day in nationalist Ireland, an occasion for laying flowers on the graves of dead, iconic nationalist leaders. The next day a letter appeared in the *Freeman's Journal* from the young, nationalist, radical Maud Gonne. She had been refused entry to two Protestant churches where some of the nationalist leaders were buried. "Are we no longer to be allowed to decorate with flowers the tombs of our dead because Victoria celebrates her Jubilee?" she asked. She ended her letter by reporting words she heard one man speak near St. Michans' Church: "'Please God we will drive the tyrants from our land, that will be the way to honour Robert Emmet.'—and I knew he echoed the Jubilee thoughts of the people of Ireland."[157]

On 21 June the Commons's loyal address was opposed by the Irish Parliamentary Party, under John Dillon, after an unsuccessful attempt to amend the address, by John Redmond, leader of that group of nationalists that had split away from the main party in support of Parnell.[158] But the Irish parliamentarians were no longer the awe-inspiring force they had once been. The *Times* noted that some Irish MPs had taken tickets for the stand on Speaker's Green to view the jubilee procession: "Convictions which cannot withstand the temptation of a reserved seat can scarcely be regarded as intrinsically formidable."[159] However, when Samuel Young, nationalist MP for Cavan, attended a garden party given by the queen for MPs on 5 July, he came in for severe criticism at home. The queen had been delighted to take the opportunity to meet some radical MPs. But when told that there were no nationalists to be presented to her she was reported as saying, "'Ah, that is a pity.'"[160]

156. *FJ*, 18 June 1897.   157. *FJ*, 21 June 1897.
158. *FJ*, 22 June 1897.   159. *Times*, 8 June 1897.
160. *FJ*, 5 July 1897.

On 22 June the formal Diamond Jubilee celebration took place at St Paul's Cathedral in London. The *Freeman's Journal* surveyed some of the main streets of Dublin for signs of jubilee decoration. On Grafton Street sixty-four out of one hundred and twenty-four buildings were decorated, on College Green it was sixteen out of thirty-seven, and on Dame Street nineteen out of eighty-two.[161]

The jubilee was met with indifference in nationalist Ireland, though there was a riot in Boyle, County Roscommon, where the local regiment had been demonstrative in its celebrations.[162] The principal protest against the jubilee in Dublin was organized by one of the new fringe radical groups, James Connolly's Irish Republican Socialist Party. Connolly had issued a manifesto attacking the "political and social order of which in these islands [the] Crown is but the symbol."[163]

On 21 June he held an anti-jubilee meeting in Foster Place which was addressed by Maud Gonne. She told those gathered that the queen's reign "had brought more ruin, misery and death" than any previous period. The meeting was twice attacked by students from Trinity College, wielding sticks and singing "God Save the Queen."[164] Now on the evening of Jubilee Day itself Connolly and Gonne took part in a more attention-grabbing demonstration. They organized a funeral procession through the streets of Dublin with a coffin marked "British Empire" and attendant slogans linking the queen's reign with Irish grievances: "The Record Reign," "Starved to Death," "Evicted," "Emigrated," "Executed." The procession was attended by several hundred demonstrators and there was a confrontation with police at College Green, where the statue of William III was draped with a green flag.[165]

In her memoirs, provocatively entitled *A Servant of the Queen*, the queen in question being Ireland, Gonne recalled that the coffin was thrown into the River Liffey with cries of "Here goes the coffin of the British Empire. To Hell with the British Empire!"[166] With Connolly now under arrest, Gonne and her admirer, the poet W. B. Yeats, repaired to the National Club in

161. *FJ*, 23 June 1897.

162. *FJ*, 24 June 1897.

163. Austen Morgan, *James Connolly: A Political Biography* (Manchester: Manchester University Press, 1988), 34.

164. *FJ*, 22 June 1897.

165. *FJ*, 23 June 1897.

166. Margaret Ward, *Maud Gonne: A Life* (London: Pandora, 1990), 46.

Rutland Square. Earlier in the evening at a meeting held in City Hall to discuss plans for the 1798 commemoration they had both made speeches. Yeats had denounced the British Empire as being built on "rapine and fraud" and called the 1798 commemoration "a jubilee of their own," while Gonne had announced that she would make a pilgrimage to the 1798 battle sites as a protest against the queen's jubilee.[167]

Not very democratically, Connolly had arranged with council workers to cut the power supply off to buildings whose owners had wanted to illuminate them for the jubilee. However, the power was still on at Rutland Square where, after the mock funeral, Gonne conducted an open-air slide show of scenes of evictions from a window in the National Club onto a specially erected large screen opposite.[168] A riot followed in which a seventy-eight-year-old woman who was passing by was injured and later died.[169]

The accounts of Yeats and Gonne differ as to what happened next. Gonne recorded that, in spite of Yeats's protests, she left the National Club to join the crowd rioting in the street.[170] Yeats, however, anxious to keep the object of his affection out of harm's way, maintained that he succeeded in detaining her against her will inside the club. "She was very indignant at my interference. I refused to let her leave the National Club. She showed magnificent courage through the whole thing. . . . She is now the idol of the mob & deserves to be."[171] After the exertions of the jubilee demonstrations Gonne went to Aix-les-Bains to recuperate.[172]

As after the 1887 jubilee, the Diamond Jubilee was followed by a royal appearance in Ireland. A visit of the duke and duchess of York was announced immediately after the jubilee but did not take place until the end of August. Cadogan said that it would be a semiprivate visit. However, the *Freeman's Journal* denounced the *Times* for suggesting that the Yorks would be

167. *FJ*, 23 June 1897.

168. Ward, *Gonne*, 45.

169. *FJ*, 26 June 1897.

170. Ward, *Gonne*, 47.

171. W. B. Yeats to William Sharp, 30 June 1987, in Warwick Gould, John Kelly, and Deirdre Toomy, *The Collected Letters of W. B. Yeats, Vol. 2: 1896–1900* (Oxford: Clarendon Press, 1997), 117.

172. R. F. Foster, *W. B. Yeats: A Life, Vol. 1: The Apprentice Mage* (Oxford: Oxford University Press, 1997), 181.

welcome in Ireland because nationalist politics was in decline: "Those party scribes who depict the Monarchy as a sort of Unionist vote-catcher render a poor service to the Monarchy."[173]

Public speculation continued throughout the summer. Would the queen accept a jubilee address from Dublin Tories?[174] Ought Irish prisoners, who had been convicted under coercion legislation, to be released as a jubilee gesture and in connection with the Yorks' visit?[175] And, now that a new generation of royals had entered the picture, should there be a royal residence in Ireland?[176]

As time for the visit approached, British newspapers played down the idea of its having a partisan political dimension. The *Times* referred tellingly to "the lesson of 1885." The *Freeman's Journal* repeatedly emphasized that there could be no loyalty to the Crown so long as home rule was denied.[177] On their entry into Dublin the duke seemed reserved and the duchess nervous.[178] However, in spite of a small protest by Connolly's party, the ten-day stay of the Yorks in Dublin, which took in visits to Leopardstown races and the Dublin Horse Show, was greeted with enthusiasm by the population.[179] Monarchy's capacity to engender public enthusiasm in nationalist Ireland was intact. After Dublin they visited Killarney, staying with Lord Kenmare, and then they went north to Newtownstewart, as guests of the duke of Abercorn at Barons Court, and to the Ards Peninsula, as guests of Lord Londonderry at Mount Stewart. They also visited Derry and Belfast and met the Catholic primate, Cardinal Logue, and other bishops.[180] The Yorks departed with every reason to feel satisfaction at their visit. Indeed, they returned for the races in April 1899.[181] Meanwhile, in nationalist Ireland, there was something of a minor scandal when it was revealed that the correspondent for their jubilee visit for the English *Daily Graphic*, who had reported it in the most effusive terms, was in fact the editor of a prominent Irish nationalist newspaper.[182]

173. *FJ,* 29 June 1897.   174. *FJ,* 5 July 1897.
175. *FJ,* 5 August 1897.   176. *FJ,* 24 July 1897.
177. *FJ,* 18, 19 August 1897.   178. *FJ,* 9 September 1897.
179. *FJ,* 24, 26 August 1897.

180. *FJ,* 30 August, 2, 4, 6, September 1897. The Yorks had been invited to open an exhibition in Belfast in 1894 but had refused on the grounds that it was not a national exhibition; see *FJ,* 8 November 1894.

181. *FJ,* 12 April 1899.   182. *United Ireland,* 16 October 1897.

In the light of the success of the visit, the speculation around a royal residence in Ireland and whether the lord lieutenancy might be abolished and York installed as an apolitical representative of the Crown increased. York himself was enthusiastic about the idea. The Prince of Wales also wished his son to reside in Ireland for part of the year but thought the lord lieutenancy ought to be abolished lest the duke and the lord lieutenant become rival symbols of loyalty to the Crown. The cabinet was in favor of a royal residence but against abolishing the lord lieutenancy.[183] But the plan foundered on the continuing objections of the queen to an Irish royal residence,[184] even though she acknowledged that "George and Mary have been wonderfully well received in Ireland."[185]

Public support for an Irish royal residence came from the National Union of Conservative Associations[186] and from the Irish Tourist Association.[187] The *Manchester Courier* reported that a site had even been found for the residence at Leopardstown.[188] Irish parliamentarians, hostile to the influence of monarchy in nationalist Ireland, objected to the idea of a royal residence. Michael Davitt, now an MP, wrote a strong attack against it in the *Westminster Gazette:*

Our aspirations are not to be satisfied by regal pageants and we believe that there is not and never has been a desire on the part of any member of the Royal family to take up a position in Ireland which must necessarily become one of a political character.[189]

He and Dillon denounced the project on the occasions on which it was raised in the Commons.[190]

※

183. Lee, *Edward VII*, 1:224.

184. RA D 39/43, Queen Victoria to Lord Cadogan, 3 September 1897, in Buckle, *Letters* (London: John Murray, 1932), third series, vol. 3 (1896–1901), p. 198.

185. Queen Victoria to the Empress Frederick, 11 September 897, in Ramm, *Beloved and Darling Child*, 207.

186. *FJ*, 18 November 1897.

187. 4 February 1897, *Parliamentary Debates*, 4th Series, vol. 45 (19 January–8 February 1897), col. 1311.

188. *FJ*, 28 September 1897.   189. *FJ*, 16 September 1897.

190. 2 August 1897, *Parliamentary Debates*, 4th Series, vol. 52 (31 July–6 August 1897), cols. 105–6. 10 March 1898, *Parliamentary Debates*, 4th Series, vol. 54 (25 February–15 March 1898), cols. 1249–50.

The last years of Queen Victoria's reign coincided with the Boer War (1899–1902). Britain's protracted campaign to extinguish the independence of the two Boer republics in southern Africa was deeply unpopular internationally. In Ireland it produced paradoxes. Both new and old nationalist elites denounced the war as an imperialistic adventure against two white, Christian nations that they saw as being in a rather similar position to Ireland vis-à-vis the British Empire. The new radical nationalist groups in particular now had a galvanizing issue to address.

Some four hundred Irishmen, including John MacBride, who was to marry Maud Gonne in 1903, volunteered for service with the Boers. But nothing illustrates the inadequacy of official nationalist discourse, of whatever variety, to encompass all the realities of Catholic nationalist Ireland more than the fact that more than seventy times that number, twenty-eight thousand Irishmen, fought with the British army against the Boers. Until the middle of World War I a career in the British army was considered a perfectly respectably option in Ireland. Paradoxically, the Irish contribution to Britain's Boer War effort, at a time when Britain was internationally reviled, boosted Irish popularity in Britain to an all-time high. It melted the hostility to Ireland of Queen Victoria, who had entered on a new period of activity in the service of her army's morale, and paved the way for her final visit to Ireland. For a brief moment in 1900 it appeared as if Ireland was a valued and normal part of the United Kingdom.

Dublin, however, was a politically truculent place at the onset of the war in 1899. Maud Gonne was currently under the influence of the anti-Semitic French right. Believing that the war was part of the same general Jewish conspiracy that had been behind the Dreyfus case, she established the "Boer Franco-Irish Committee" in October. On 17 December a brief riot followed its celebration of the early Boer victories of the war.[191] On 1 March 1900 there was another riot outside the Mansion House in Dublin after the British relief of Ladysmith between students from Trinity College, waving Union Jacks and cheering the queen and Generals Roberts and Buller, on the one hand, and a crowd cheering the Boers and their leader Kruger, on the other.[192] Four days later the Dublin Corporation passed a vote of sympathy with Kruger on the Boer loss.[193]

Meanwhile in Britain the standing of Irish soldiers was on the rise both

191. Anna MacBride White and A. Norman Jeffares, eds., *The Gonne-Yeats Letters, 1893–1938: "Always Your Friend"* (London: Hutchinson, 1992), 222–23.

192. *FJ,* 2 March 1900.   193. *FJ,* 6 March 1900.

with the public and with the queen. Arthur Dunn, bugler with the Dublin Fusiliers, had become an unlikely hero after surviving a futile advance on the enemy that he had mistakenly caused himself. He was introduced to Queen Victoria, who presented him with a silver bugle.[194] Irish soldiers took a prominent part in the relief of Ladysmith.[195] A telegram from the queen to Sir Redvers Buller in South Africa was published in which she wrote, "I have heard with the deepest concern of the heavy losses sustained by my brave Irish soldiers. I desire to express my sympathy and my admiration of the splendid fighting qualities they have exhibited throughout their trying operation."[196] Visiting military casualties at the Herbert Hospital in London some weeks later the queen noted "a great number of Irish soldiers. . . . Some were badly wounded."[197] The *Times* summed up the growing mood in Britain:

> The Irish regiments, faithful alike to their Queen and to the long-established and often-confirmed traditions of their valour and their loyalty, have done more to promote the Imperial interest of Ireland than could have been accomplished by legislators in a generation and have gilded everything Irish in a halo of romance which is not likely soon to disappear.[198]

Even Irish parliamentarians began to make political capital out of the new mood of martial admiration for Ireland. John Redmond, now the leader of the recently reunited Irish Party, in a speech sympathizing with the Boers, told the Commons that "I, as an Irishman, cannot help feeling a thrill of pride at the record of the heroism of the Irish lads from Mayo and Roscommon, who have suffered so terribly in this war."[199]

In early March it was felt that there should be a British gesture toward Ireland. In fact, three were made. One was the formation of a regiment of elite Irish guards. This had first been suggested as long ago as the Crimean War.[200] Now both the War Office and the queen were in agreement that such a regiment should be established.[201]

194. Weintraub, *Victoria*, 611–12.   195. Weintraub, *Victoria*, 615.

196. *FJ*, 1 March 1900.

197. RA QVJ, 22 March 1900, in Buckle, *Letters*, third series, 3:516.

198. *Times*, 17 March 1900.

199. 7 February 1900, *Parliamentary Debates*, 4th Series, vol. 78 (30 January–14 February 1900), col. 834.

200. 27 June 1855, *Parliamentary Debates*, 3d Series, vol. 139 (22 June–14 August 1855), cols. 1459–60.

201. Lord Lansdowne to Sir Arthur Bigge, 3 March 1900; Sir Arthur Bigge to Lord Lansdowne, 5 March 1900, in Buckle, *Letters*, third series, 3:498.

The second gesture concerned the wearing of shamrock by Irish soldiers. This had long been banned and had often been used by Irish MPs to attack the government in one of their minor wars. In 1897 one soldier had committed suicide when dismissed from the army for, among other things, wearing shamrock.[202] In 1898 William Redmond had been suspended from the Commons for protesting at a sailor's getting fourteen days' punishment for wearing shamrock.[203] Now it was not only legalized in the army but became the London fashion on St Patrick's day 1900 when it was widely worn by all sections of the metropolitan population. The *Freeman's Journal* registered the ambivalence of official Irish nationalism to this unaccustomed British approbation:

The truth is that the imagination and enthusiasm of the venerable Queen of England and of her people have been startled by Celtic valour. The spear with which the gallant Boer was struck down was forged in no English forge; it was unhappily purely Celtic in its make.[204]

On 10 January 1900 Prince Arthur, duke of Connaught, who had not been allowed to go to South Africa as he had wished, was installed as commander-in-chief in Ireland.[205] "I am very glad Arthur is going to Ireland," wrote the queen to her daughter Vicky, the Empress Frederick. "It is a good thing in every way I think."[206] On the same day as the duke's swearing-in the editor of a French satirical magazine was acquitted of a charge against public decency for printing a "gross" cartoon of Queen Victoria and President Paul Kruger.[207] It was the queen's custom in the spring of each year to spend some time on the French or Italian Riviera. Both because of continental hostility and the impropriety of the queen taking a holiday during a time of national crisis, it was agreed that the queen would not travel to the Continent in 1900. This left the way open for a third gesture to Ireland, a trip to Dublin instead.

The queen discussed the idea with Prince Arthur on 3 March. He was

202. 11 April 1897, *Parliamentary Debates*, 4th Series, vol. 68 (13 March–6 May 1897), cols. 277–80.

203. 4 April 1898, *Parliamentary Debates*, 4th Series, vol. 56 (4 April–29 April 1898), cols. 23–27.

204. *FJ*, 19 March 1900.

205. Frankland, *Connaught*, 214.

206. Queen Victoria to the Empress Frederick, 29 December 1899, in Ramm, *Beloved and Darling Child*, 242.

207. *FJ*, 11 January 1900.

to make most of the arrangements,[208] but the decision to go was to be hers alone. She wrote the Empress Frederick, "You will be startled when I tell you that I am going early next month to visit Ireland. It is entirely my own idea as was also my giving up going abroad. It will give great pleasure and do good."[209]

The visit was announced publicly on 7 March 1900, the same day as Lord Wolseley's order about shamrock in the army was published. The reaction among nationalist elites to the visit was initially uniformly hostile. The *Freeman's Journal*, now no longer under the control of the Gray family, recalled how during the early part of the queen's reign, "[a] State-aided famine decimated the people and made the land desolate." It doubted whether the queen would be greeted with "any transports of loyalty" and went on to lament that Irish soldiers had "been butchered wholescale to make a British victory in the Transvaal." Meanwhile the London press anticipated that a successful visit would damage Irish nationalism.[210]

On 8 March John Redmond welcomed the legalization of shamrock in the army. He went on to say that

our people will, moreover, treat with respect the visit which the venerable Sovereign proposes to make to their shores, well knowing that on this occasion no attempt will be made to give that visit a party significance, and that their chivalrous hospitality will be taken in no quarter to mean an abatement of their demand for their national rights, which they will continue to press until they are conceded.[211]

Gerald Balfour, the Irish chief secretary, told the queen that though Redmond's statement was less than most loyal subjects would say it was "more than might perhaps have been expected of one who, whatever his private views, poses in America and elsewhere as something very little better than a rebel."[212] It was certainly much more than some of Redmond's fellow Irish parliamentarians were prepared to countenance. It privately infuriated William O'Brien, whose United Irish League had not yet aligned itself with the Irish Parliamentary Party:

208. RA QVJ, 8 March 1900, in Buckle, *Letters*, third series, 3:497.

209. Queen Victoria to the Empress Frederick, 7 March 1900, in Ramm, *Beloved and Darling Child*, 247.

210. *FJ*, 9 March 1900.

211. 8 March 1900, *Parliamentary Debates*, 4th Series, vol. 80 (5 March–21 March 1900), col. 402.

212. Gerald Balfour to Queen Victoria, 8 March 1900, in Buckle, *Letters*, third series, 3:506.

Redmond's statement in the House of Commons last night revolutionises the whole situation. Unless we are to throw up the national cause altogether it is impossible for any nationalist to cooperate any longer with a gentleman who uses his situation as a leader to express his gratitude for the Shamrock . . . and puts in for a slavish reception for a lady who comes to typify all that is most hateful in English rule.[213]

The day after Redmond's speech the nationalist members of the Dublin Corporation, taking their cue from him, met in private at the Mansion House and voted by forty-three to three, in favor of presenting a loyal address to the queen. In other nationalist quarters, however, the response was very different. The Irish-Transvaal Committee, whose members included Griffith, Connolly, Yeats, and Gonne, sent Redmond a telegram challenging him "to come to Dublin and repeat in public the statement you made tonight in the name of the Irish people."[214] Anna Parnell wrote a public letter suggesting that people dip their shamrocks in ink. John O'Leary publicly dissociated himself from Redmond's remarks, and Tim Harrington, a veteran of Mallow in 1885 and a member of the Dublin Corporation who had not been present for the vote at the Mansion House, denounced the Corporation's decision.[215]

The next day William Redmond announced that if the Corporation agreed to a loyal address he would resign his membership of it.[216] A day later John Redmond, alarmed at the reaction to his statement and claiming that it had been misunderstood, stated that he too was against a loyal address.[217] However, the visit had caught official nationalism off guard and John Redmond's uncertain note had not helped.

The Corporation met on 14 March to vote on the address. As he read the text of the address at the meeting, the nationalist but pro-address lord mayor, Thomas Pile, was jeered with cries of "You read it like an Englishman." He was supported by a predecessor, J. M. Meade, who called those in the gallery "cheap republicans," and claimed that if home rule was granted "no one would have more pleasure in singing that Bill than the Queen, if she lived." When it came to the vote thirty were for the address and twenty-two against. The *Freeman's Journal* called it "a blow to the Na-

---

213. William O'Brien to Jerry McVeagh, 9 March 1900, in Joseph V. O'Brien, *William O'Brien and the Course of Irish Politics, 1881–1918* (Berkeley and Los Angeles: University of California Press, 1976), 120–21.

214. *FJ*, 10 March 1900.   215. *FJ*, 12 March 1900.
216. *FJ*, 13 March 1900.   217. *FJ*, 14 March 1900.

tionalist movement." Outside City Hall after the meeting Pile and Meade were booed and Harrington was cheered.[218]

Two days later Pile established a Mansion House committee to prepare for the visit. It received public support from noblemen such as Lords Powerscourt and Cavan, Dublin merchants like Maurice Dockrell, and from Nicholas Donnelly, the Catholic auxiliary bishop of Dublin. The Dublin Tory leader Sir Robert Sexton, who had established a citizens committee, the device used in the past to welcome royal visitors boycotted by the Corporation, also threw in his lot with the lord mayor.[219]

Next day was St Patrick's Day when the lord mayor's procession, which had once been held on New Year's Day, now took place. There was only one open carriage in the procession, that of some of the nationalist members of the Corporation who had voted against the address. They carried a Transvaal flag. The lord mayor's state coach, however, was stoned in Harcourt Street. Other Irish mayors had been invited but only two had appeared. D. J. Hegarty, mayor of Cork, was booed because he was one of only four members of the Cork Corporation to vote for an address. The lord mayor of Belfast got a better reception, with cries of "'He's against us, but he's honest.'"[220]

The other significant event of the day occurred at Thurles, where one of the numerous monuments to 1798 constructed in the wake of the 1898 commemoration was unveiled. John Dillon used his speech on the occasion to attack the royal visit:

But today we are invited to be grateful because the monarch of another race has sought to dip that emblem [the Shamrock] of our people in the blood that has been shed at the Tugela and on other battlefields in South Africa and to dye the green shamrock red in the rivers of Irish blood which have been shed in an unjust, a cruel and an unholy war.[221]

He then went on to give a deeply paradoxical analysis of the reasons for the queen's visit, illustrative of those very ambiguities in Ireland about the war and the monarchy, which anxious nationalist leaders pretended did not exist. The queen was coming for two reasons, Dillon argued. The first was because Ireland opposed the war. This reason acknowledged that at least in some quarters it was felt that the queen had sufficient influence in Ireland to change public opinion on the matter. The second reason was be-

218. *FJ,* 15 March 1900.   219. *FJ,* 17 March 1900.
220. *FJ,* 19 March 1900.   221. *FJ,* 19 March 1900.

cause the Irish were good soldiers and the queen wanted to recruit more of them for the war. This reason alluded to the existing Irish military contribution to the war, and thus of course implied that opposition to the war in Ireland was not so total in the first place as Dillon had been making out.[222]

Dillon ended his speech on a note of caution about protests against the queen which distinguished the Irish parliamentarians from the younger, more radical nationalists: "The Queen is a woman and an old woman and in Ireland these two facts would save her from insult."[223]

On 19 March a letter was published in the *Freeman's Journal* from J. H. Parnell, brother of Anna Parnell and the late Irish nationalist leader. He held the honorary position of city marshal of Dublin, whose job it was to present the city keys in the traditional ceremony of welcome to lords lieutenant and members of the royal family:

We have Royalty here; let us make the most of it for the welfare of the country. It is the brave Irish who began this change in English sentiment. Let us then do all we can to encourage the visit of her Majesty and of all foreigners to our rich and beautiful country.[224]

His letter was quickly followed by another from his sister critical of the visit and referring to "the famine queen."[225] What is of note about J. H. Parnell's letter, though, is not only its disagreement with most nationalist sentiment on the visit but its reference to the queen as a foreigner. This was a growing trend in public discourse and had been used previously by John O'Leary and others. It went further than the traditional use of "queen of England" by nationalists and even Dillon's recent "monarch of another race" reference, though at a United Irish League meeting in Killarney on 8 April William O'Brien was to adopt the custom, referring to Queen Victoria as "the foreign queen."[226]

The next prominent person to enter the public debate was W. B. Yeats. He also gave two reasons for the queen's visit: recruitment to the army and "National hatred; hatred of our individual National life." Noting that Queen Victoria planned to set out for her trip to Ireland on 2 April and that this was the centenary anniversary of the introduction of the Act of Union into the British Parliament, he called for a meeting in the Rotunda

222. *FJ*, 19 March 1900.
224. *FJ*, 19 March 1900.
226. *FJ*, 9 April 1900.

223. *FJ*, 19 March 1900.
225. *FJ*, 20 March 1900.

on that day to protest the union, with John O'Leary in the chair and all Irish MPs present. He concluded with a rather revisionist account of the Diamond Jubilee: "If the people are left to organise their own protest as they did on Jubilee night, there will be broken glass and batoned crowds."[227]

Irish parliamentarians were not going to be told what to do and did not act on the suggestion, though Tim Harrington did get the Dublin Corporation to pass a resolution against the Act of Union as being "obtained by fraud and shameful corruption."[228] On the day of the queen's entry into Dublin it was revealed that James Egan, a former Fenian prisoner and now Dublin's civic sword bearer, had resigned his position rather than take part in the welcome. Yeats warned that welcoming the queen was to support the British Empire in an unjust war against the Boers: "Whoever stands by the road way cheering for Queen Victoria, cheers for that Empire, dishonours Ireland and condones a crime."[229]

Maud Gonne's major attack on the visit took the form of her "Famine Queen" article in Arthur Griffith's *United Irishman*, causing most of the copies of the paper to be seized by the police on publication day.[230] Ramsey Colles, editor of the *Irish Figaro*, likened Gonne to Herodotus, "the father of lies." In retaliation, Griffith attacked Colles in his office and was sent to prison for two weeks when he refused to be bound over to keep the peace. Colles went on to accuse Gonne of being in receipt of a government pension of £300 granted to her late father, a British army officer. He had to apologize when sued for libel but during the case Gonne and Griffith found themselves mauled in the witness box.[231]

According to Gonne's "Famine Queen" article, the queen, whose soul was "vile and selfish," hated Ireland, a country "whose inhabitants are the victims of the criminal policy of her reign, the survivors of sixty years of organised famine." She contrasted the fate of "poor Irish emigrant girls, whose very innocence makes them an easy prey" with "this woman, whose bourgeois virtue is so boasted, and in whose name their homes were de-

227. *FJ*, 20 March 1900. Toward the end of the nineteenth century it became common practice for the building once known as the Rotundo to be called the Rotunda.

228. *FJ*, 31 March 1900.

229. *FJ*, 4 April 1900.

230. *FJ*, 7 April 1900.

231. Donal P. McCracken, *The Irish Pro-Boers 1877–1902* (Johannesburg: Perskor, 1989), 83, 86.

stroyed." The article comes to a climax with the queen, transformed into a mythic hybrid of a ghoul and witch confronting a defiant, personified Ireland. The English were afraid of losing the Boer War.

In their terror they turn to Victoria, their Queen. She has succeeded in amassing more gold than any of her subjects, she has always been ready to cover with her royal mantle the crimes and turpitudes of her Empire and now, trembling on the brink of the grave, she rises once more to their call. . . . Taking the Shamrock in her withered hand, she dares to ask Ireland for soldiers—for soldiers to fight for the exterminators of their race. Ireland's reply, "Queen, return to your own land. . . . See! Your recruiting agents return alone and unsuccessful from my green hills and plains, because once more hope has revived and it will be in the ranks of your enemies that my children will find employment and honour."[232]

The old royal yacht *Victoria and Albert,* one of the few remaining paddle boats still in operation, arrived in Kingstown harbor on the afternoon of 3 April. The queen came ashore the next day at 11:30 a.m. She received an ecstatic welcome. Driving through the cheering crowds toward Dublin she noticed that there was "scarcely a policeman or soldier" to be seen. She passed under inscriptions over the road reading, "Blest for ever is she who relied on Erin's honour and Erin's pride"[233] and "In her a thousand virtues closed as Mother, Wife and Queen." At Leeson Street Bridge a special gate was erected for the formal entry into the capital. Athlone Pursuivant, a heraldic officer, went through a ritual with the lord mayor, requesting and gaining entry for the queen into the city. As the queen drove through Dublin on her way to the Vice Regal Lodge she noted that "[e]ven the Nationalists in front of the City Hall seemed to forget their politics and cheered and waved their hats."[234]

Frederick Ponsonby, who was accompanying the queen, was amazed by the warmth of her reception in Dublin:

Although I had seen many visits of this kind, nothing had ever approached the enthusiasm and even frenzy displayed by the people of Dublin. There were, however, two places where I heard ugly sounds like booing, but they only seemed like a sort

232. Elizabeth Coxhead, *Daughters of Erin: Five Women of the Irish Renaissance* (London: Secker and Warburg, 1965), 45–46.

233. Based on the final two lines of Thomas Moore's "Rich and Rare Were the Gems She Wore."

234. RA QVJ, 4 April 1900.

of bagpipe drone to the highly-pitched sound of cheering. One of these was the office of some Nationalist newspaper, and the other a house on the Quay.[235]

Arriving at Vice Regal Lodge Queen Victoria was in for a shock as news reached her of an assassination attempt on the Prince and Princess of Wales in Brussels by a pro-Boer anarchist. That evening police prevented the Irish-Transvaal Committee from holding a torch-lit procession.[236] In spite of this Dublin must have seemed a safer place for the queen to be than some others. The *Times* certainly thought so:

> The hearty and generous welcome, unbroken by any discordant voices, which the Queen received yesterday on entering her Irish capital stands out all the more conspicuously in view of the dastardly attempt on the life of the Prince of Wales at the Northern Station in Brussels. . . . They [the Irish people] will rejoice that political passion does not take the brutal form of Continental Anarchism.[237]

The queen's welcome presented nationalist elites with a hermeneutical difficulty. Resistant to the notion that monarchical enthusiasm could be compatible with nationalist identity, they had to resort to the sort of convoluted reasoning of the *Freeman's Journal* in its report of the queen's arrival: "Whenever the welcome was demonstrative it was partisan, when it was national it was restrained with the bounds that courtesy demanded." However, almost immediately, it went on to admit that it had indeed been Irish nationalists who had given the queen her warm welcome. This forced it to adopt a second means of trying to explain the welcome away: "It is a weakness of the Irish character . . . that the nation is ever prone to trust too readily to friendly professions, to forget and forgive at the first vague hint of repentance and atonement."[238]

The queen was frail and in the last year of her life. The visit was essentially a private one, so the three weeks of her visit were relatively quiet ones, though she was attentive to correspondence concerning the South African war. Almost every afternoon she went out for a three-hour drive of around twenty miles. The people always cheered; as the royal carriage approached a village, Frederick Ponsonby would cause his horse to make a noise to alert Princess Beatrice to wake up her mother to wave at the peo-

235. Frederick Ponsonby, *Recollections of Three Reigns* (London: Eyre and Spottiswood, 1951), 63.

236. *FJ*, 5 April 1900.   237. *Times*, 5 April 1900.

238. *FJ*, 5 April 1900.

ple. Ponsonby noted that the people were adept at distinguishing between the head of state and the government. In one village he heard a woman call, "God Save the Queen" and another, mistakenly pointing at him, shouting "And down with the Minister in Attendance."[239]

Royal engagements had been arranged, but for the most part they were carried out by the other members of the royal family who were accompanying the queen. However, Queen Victoria undertook a number of engagements herself. At the Royal Hospital in Kilmainham an old soldier who had fought in the Afghan war of 1839 presented her with a nosegay and "[a]ll the old men cheered." At Dublin Castle, not now being very mobile, she was carried upstairs to the state drawing room, where Gottlieb's orchestra performed two pieces and Lady Limerick played the piano. On the way back to the Vice Regal Lodge "the people were very enthusiastic as they always are here."[240]

On 21 April there was a great military review in the Phoenix Park conducted by Prince Arthur and attended by his mother. "We then drove home amidst such tremendous cheering as I have never heard."[241] The queen visited the Meath and Mater Hospitals and the Masonic School and drove "through endless streets full of enthusiastic people."[242] The Adelaide Hospital was "situated in the very poorest part of the town. The street in which it stands is a very narrow one and the people literally thronged around the carriage, giving me the most enthusiastic welcome, as indeed I receive everywhere."[243]

In a significant gesture to the Catholic middle classes, Queen Victoria also visited Ireland's three leading Catholic boarding schools. Two of them were girls' schools, Loreto Convent, Rathfarnham, where the college orchestra, which including six Irish harps, played "God Save the Queen," and the Sacred Heart Convent, housed in what had once been the Mount Anville home of William Dargan.[244] Castleknock College was a school for boys, who on account of their warm welcome of the queen were invited to visit the Channel Fleet then moored at Kingstown.[245] The then lord chief justice of England, Lord Russell of Killowen, was a past pupil of Castleknock. He had monitored the case of the miscarriage of justice concern-

239. Frederick Ponsonby, *Recollections*, 64.   240. RA QVJ, 14 April 1900.
241. RA QVJ, 21 April 1900.   242. RA QVJ, 24 April 1900.
243. RA QVJ, 17 April 1900.   244. RA QVJ, 20, 17 April 1900.
245. RA QVJ, 22 April 1900; *FJ*, 23, 26 April 1900, in James H. Murphy, ed., *Nos Autem: Castleknock College and Its Contribution* (Dublin: Gill and Macmillan, 1996), 99–100.

ing Captain Dreyfus, whom Maud Gonne's friends so hated, for the British government and written Queen Victoria reports on it.

Archbishop Walsh of Dublin made himself scarce during the visit, but the queen, who in old age had once more become favorable to Catholicism, made friends with the archbishop of Armagh, Cardinal Logue, who dined with her on 19 April. The queen thought Logue "pleasing in manner, though hardly in looks."[246] Frederick Ponsonby wrote that "[t]he Queen went out of her way to make herself agreeable, while the Cardinal was quite captivated by her."[247] Queen Victoria was also charmed to meet a Sister of Charity, "a nice little thing, who does my washing, and she kissed my hand."[248]

Ironically, religion, inasmuch as the monarch was a Protestant and most of her Irish subjects Catholics, had never been much of a public issue for the monarchy in Ireland. But denominational barriers were becoming more and more pronounced and the issue entered into the arrangements for the queen's most significant public engagement during her visit. The queen's stay in Ireland had been criticized for its alleged military agenda. The organizers of the visit managed brilliantly to wrong foot those who made such a criticism by focusing the visit on children. On Saturday, 7 April, Lady Arnott organized a children's gathering in the Phoneix Park to see the queen. Five days later the queen met a thousand more children who had been unable to make it to the main gathering.[249] Just before she left Queen Victoria gave £5 each to two girls who had presented her with shamrock. Shamrock poured into the Vice Regal Lodge from all quarters thereafter.[250]

The official figure given for those who attended the main children's gathering was fifty-two thousand. The *Freeman's Journal* said it was twenty-one thousand, but admitted that "[t]he number was far in excess of that anticipated."[251] Even though there were a number of Catholic ladies as well as Protestants on the organizing committee, there was opposition to the gathering in some Catholic quarters on the grounds that the children had been promised refreshments. Receiving food from a Protestant revived memories of "souperism," the practice whereby Catholics were allegedly given food during the famine on condition that they converted to Protestantism.[252]

---

246. RA QVJ, 19 April 1900.
247. Frederick Ponsonby, *Recollections*, 63.
248. RA QVJ, 16 April 1900.
249. *FJ*, 13 April 1900.
250. Frederick Ponsonby, *Recollections*, 65.
251. *FJ*, 9 April 1900.
252. M. J. F. McCarthy, *Five Years in Ireland, 1895–1900* (London: Simpkin, Marshall, Hamilton, Kent, 1901), 486, 535.

More vocal opposition came from Maud Gonne, who announced that she was going to hold a counter-Patriotic Children's Treat for those "who had the courage to refuse to assist at the Queen's Show in the Phoenix Park."[253] Initially planned as a pilgrimage to Wolf Tone's grave at Bodenstown, it was scaled down to a much more modest picnic, which took place at Clonturk Park, just north of the city center, to which some accounts claimed as many as twenty to thirty thousand children marched on 1 July.[254]

Queen Victoria was thoroughly pleased with her visit to Ireland. "I left the Vice Regal Lodge with regret, having spent a very pleasant time there, though a somewhat tiring one." Her yacht left from Dublin's North Wall:

I felt quite sorry that all was over and that this eventful visit which created so much interest and excitement had, like everything in this world, come to an end, though I own I am very tired and long for rest and quiet. I can never forget the really wild enthusiasm and affectionate loyalty displayed by all in Ireland and shall ever retain a most grateful remembrance of this warm hearted and sympathetic people. Even when I used to go round the grounds in my pony chair and the people outside caught sight of me, they would at once cheer and sing "God Save the Queen."[255]

The visit had been an enormous success from the point of view of monarchy. Even the *Freeman's Journal* had to grudgingly admit that this was the case, though it did so by emphasizing that the queen was an old lady:

But nobody who moved among the crowds could fail to discover that undernote of indifferent curiosity, mixed, perhaps, here and there with some admiration for the pluck of the little old lady who after thirty-nine years' absence and in the extremity of old age conquered her repugnance towards Ireland in order to put in a stroke for her Army, her Empire and her Throne. The Queen seemed to reciprocate the civility of the popular attitude.[256]

Somehow it was easier to deal with a British monarch if she could be presented in the guise not of an adult but of a guileless, childlike young

253. *FJ*, 17 April 1900.

254. McCracken, *Irish Pro-Boers*, 86. See too Senia Paseta, "Nationalist Responses to Two Royal Visits to Ireland, 1900 and 1903," *Irish Historical Studies* 31 (1998–99): 494. The figure of thirty thousand originated in a speculation several weeks before the event in the *United Irishman* about how many might possibly attend.

255. RA QVJ, 26 April 1900.

256. *FJ*, 27 April 1900.

woman, as Queen Victoria had been seen during her earlier trips to Ireland, or of a harmless, childlike old woman, as she was now seen. As she lay dying early the next year, the same newspaper depicted her as an "aged lady [who] had hoped to end her reign in peace" but who had been "deliberately deceived" about the Boer War and forced to visit Ireland.[257] It was reminiscent of O'Connell's claims that she had been deceived about Ireland by Peel's government. Queen Victoria thus ended her life, as far as this strand of Irish discourse was concerned, as an innocent but deceived old woman, having once been an innocent but deceived young woman. When she died, the Dublin Corporation, in spite of the protests of the newly elected lord mayor, Tim Harrington, voted its condolences.[258]

At the end of the 1900 visit the council of the Royal Dublin Society proposed a statue of Queen Victoria for the city. It was emphasized that this would be a personal tribute to the queen and not a glorification of the Crown. John Hughes was the sculptor; the statue that he produced was designed to be as acceptable as possible to Irish nationalist sensibilities. The queen was depicted as an old woman and the surrounding figures celebrated the heroism of Irish soldiers in the Boer War. It was unveiled in 1908 on Leinster Lawn in front of Leinster House, which was to become the seat of the independent Irish parliament. It was removed in 1948 to make way for a monument to some of the founders of the new state and in 1987 donated to Sydney, where it now stands.[259] The statue of Prince Albert still survives on Leinster Lawn.

257. *FJ*, 19 January 1901.
258. *FJ*, 24 January 1901.
259. Judith Hill, *Irish Public Sculpture: A History* (Dublin: Four Courts, 1998), 141–42, 146.

Conclusion

Ireland, Coburg, and Windsor in
the Twentieth Century

The relationship between nationalism and monarchy in nineteenth-century Ireland was one of increasing hostility on the part of the former toward the latter. But it was a hostility based on fear: fear of the undoubted popularity of monarchy among large sections of the Irish Catholic nationalist population and fear of the uses to which that popularity might be put. Nationalist leaders were concerned that royal visits might dampen the backing for calls for self-government and that the enthusiasm with which royal visitors were received would be used to bolster the British will to rule in Ireland, by seeming to provide evidence that the nationalist Irish, in spite of their leaders, were loyal both to the monarchy and, by extension, to the constitution. Indeed, it was the combination of the monarchy's popularity and alignment with the union constitution that made it such a perceived threat, though nationalist leaders could never acknowledge the true nature of that threat. The popularity of the monarchy was an embarrassment and had to be denied. Instead, the hostility to monarchy that nationalist elites enforced on the population was shrouded in an ideology in which the monarchy bore the blame for the actions of British politicians in Ireland, in a way that mirrored the valorization of monarchy in Britain itself for the perceived successes of the nineteenth century.

Queen Victoria visited Ireland on four occasions. In 1849, 1853, 1861, and

1900 she was met with a popular enthusiasm that surpassed all expectations and generally abashed hostile, nationalist opinion. In considering Queen Victoria's posthumous reputation in Ireland, though, it is ironic to note that the very success of her 1900 visit ensured a deepening personal hatred of her among many staunch nationalists for whom loyalty to the monarchy was now incompatible with Irish national identity and who were disconcerted by the continuing capacity of monarchy to capture public acclaim in Ireland. Their opposition to her needed a focus that disguised its real cause, and they found it in the "famine queen" slogan.

The Irish association of Queen Victoria with blame for the famine went back at least as far as her Golden Jubilee, when in England she became the symbol for British imperial success. The jubilee, for example, had been celebrated at the Church of the Holy Innocents, on 37th Street, New York City, with a requiem mass for those who had died in the famine, complete with catafalque surrounded by six candles.[1] The famine queen myth also came to be associated with the allegation that Queen Victoria, as a sign of her supposed indifference to Irish suffering, had given only £5 for famine relief. It is uncertain when or how this story arose, but it may be associated with a real incident during the mid-1890s when the queen gave £5 to Mary Donnelly whose family was swallowed up in the Kerry mudslide. *United Ireland* drew attention to the incident and used it to criticize the amount of Irish taxpayers' money the queen was receiving for her upkeep.[2]

The famine queen caricature sees Queen Victoria as being somehow directly responsible not only for the famine but also for the entire canon of nationalist grievances during her reign. The famine queen largely displaced the hostile memory of those British politicians, such as Lord Clarendon, the "starvation Viceroy,"[3] and Lord John Russell, the "Attorney General of Starvation,"[4] who at the time of the famine had been the real objects of nationalist ire in a way in which the queen had not been. In 1848, for example, the *Freeman's Journal* had commended another paper for drawing "the line of demarcation between the starvation ministry and the Queen."[5]

The early-twentieth-century antipathy to Queen Victoria was particularly strong among radical nationalist women of English or Anglo-Irish

1. *New York Times*, 22 June 1887.
2. *United Ireland*, 23 January 1897; *FJ*, 16 May 1897.
3. *FJ*, 4 April 1850.
4. *FJ*, 29 May 1878.
5. *FJ*, 12 July 1848.

background. It was their efforts in particular that resulted in her lasting vilification in nationalist mythology as the famine queen. Prominent among the promoters of the slogan were Maud Gonne and Anna Parnell. The latter's poem on the death of Queen Victoria is a good example of their efforts:

> Not four more years have passed to-day
> And now the Queen, the Famine Queen,
> Herself has passed away,
> And that dread form will never more be seen,
> In pomp of fancied glory and of pride,
> Or humbled, scored, defeated as she died;
> For by God's will she was amongst the first to fall
> Beneath those mills of His that grind so wondrous small.[6]

The famine queen passed quickly into the common parlance of nationalist mythology. As late as 1995, for example, the discovery of a statue of the queen at University College, formerly Queen's College, Cork, where it had been buried several decades earlier, enabled the myth to have another outing in the letters columns of Irish newspapers from correspondents hostile to the statue being put on public display.[7]

Nor did Queen Victoria's reputation concerning Ireland fare much better in English discourse. This was for very different reasons, though out of a similar overestimation of the power of monarchy as that which had caused nationalist antipathy. In England, Queen Victoria became the scapegoat for the failure of British policy in Ireland. The tone was set within a few years of her death by the *Dictionary of National Biography* in its discussion of the success of her 1900 visit:

But it brought into broad relief the neglect of Ireland that preceded it, and it emphasised the errors of feeling and judgment which made her almost a complete stranger to her Irish subjects in their own land during the rest of her long reign.[8]

6. Anna Parnell, "22nd January 1901," in Jane McL Côté, *Fanny and Anna Parnell* (Dublin: Gill and Macmillan, 1991), 262. In addition, the autumn of 1900 saw the production in Dublin of W. B. Yeats and Lady Gregory's *Cathleen ni Houlihan*, with Maud Gonne in the title role. It was a play whose regal embodiment of Ireland was rightly read by its audience as a riposte to the late Queen Victoria. See Terence Brown, *The Life of W. B. Yeats* (Dublin: Gill and Macmillan, 1999), 135–36.

7. See Luke Gibbons, *Transformations in Irish Culture* (Cork: Cork University Press, 1996), 71–72.

8. *DNB*, 22 (Supplement):1368.

In the 1930s Frank Hardie castigated the failure to build on the success of her 1849 visit as "the greatest mistake of her life" and reported that "[i]t has been said that Queen Victoria lost Ireland for England."[9] In the early 1950s when it was clear that the British Empire was in its twilight years, Algernon Cecil wrote:

[I]f Victoria had brought herself to cross the Irish Sea year by year, or even rather less often, she would have won the hearts of her Irish subjects . . . and, as he [Lord Salisbury] saw, more than Eire hung upon the result. "If Ireland goes," he once told his daughter, from whom I had the story, "India will go fifty years later." Ireland went, and India, to all intents and purposes, not so much as fifty years later.[10]

The queen's supposed neglect of Ireland had ludicrously now become the cause of the breakup of the entire British Empire. This was a line of argument that at once obviously overestimated the influence of the monarchy and underestimated Irish nationalism. It was part of the discourse that had sustained the British will to continue to rule in Ireland and enabled members of the political establishment to believe that nationalist grievances were superficial and that Ireland could become a contented part of the United Kingdom—if only it was only given justice or received enough royal attention.

In this view, Queen Victoria was responsible for fatally damaging the union of Britain and Ireland through her neglect of the latter. The monarchy had injured the constitution. But the truth was quite the reverse. It was the monarchy in Ireland that was fatally damaged by its zealous commitment to a very problematic constitution.

The death of Queen Victoria in 1901 found the relationship between monarchy and nationalism in the context of the union in a very different position from what it had been at the beginning of her reign. The union between Britain and the whole of Ireland itself had two more decades to run and the issues that had beset Queen Victoria concerning Ireland had also to be tackled by her son Edward VII, who reigned until 1910, and her grandson George V, who reigned until 1935. What follows here is a sketch

9. Hardie, *Political Influence*, 18, 177.

10. Algernon Cecil, *Queen Victoria and Her Prime Ministers* (London: Eyre, Spottiswood, 1953), 83.

of the relationship between Irish nationalism and the British monarchy in the period of the late union and indeed since then.

Edward VII's reign turned out to be in all kinds of ways a much more successful one than his mother had ever thought possible. This was true in Ireland as much as anywhere else, where his bonhomie and love of racing stood him in good stead. It was also not generally known that he was adamantly opposed to home rule. Indeed, quite the contrary for "[b]y the tongue of rumour he was accredited with a sympathetic appreciation of the popular demand."[11] Immediately upon his accession he considered making his son George lord lieutenant in Ireland but was dissuaded by the government.[12] Over the years of his reign the idea of sending over George or the duke of Connaught[13] to Ireland as lord lieutenant continued to be discussed but it did not lead to any change in the existing viceregal system or the pattern of occasional royal visits.

Religion became a more prominent issue between the king and Ireland for two very different reasons. The first had to do with the rituals of accession. Because there had not been a new monarch for nearly sixty-four years, there had been no revision of the procedures that marked the new reign. On 14 February 1901 the king appeared in Parliament therefore to make a declaration repudiating transubstantiation and other Catholic doctrines as superstitious and idolatrous, as required by unrevised precedent.[14] John Redmond described the oath as "wantonly insulting" and went on to warn that "as long as the Oath is in existence and His Majesty swears that Catholics are idolatrous I for one will oppose His Majesty's salary."[15] Irish MPs went on to vote against the new king's civil list.[16]

Conversely, there were constant stories that Edward VII was well disposed to Catholicism and indeed that he might soon convert to Catholicism himself. This was little more than a recrudescence of the very old Catholic fantasy of converting a new monarch, a fantasy that had been prevalent in the early years of the reign of Queen Victoria. Nonetheless, it caused anxiety in certain Protestant circles. A story that the king had at-

11. *FJ*, 7 May 1910.

12. Lee, *Edward VII*, 2:161–62; Magnus, *Edward the Seventh*, 291–92.

13. Frankland, *Connaught*, 258.

14. Magnus, *Edward the Seventh*, 292.

15. 18 February 1901, *Parliamentary Debates*, 4th Series, vol. 89 (23 January–27 February 1901), col. 320.

16. Magnus, *Edward the Seventh*, 289.

tended mass while visiting the Austrian spa at Marienbad provoked an attack on him in one Irish, anti-Catholic journal: "This is what the Oxford Movement has done for England in the course of half a century, and for that portion of the British nation whose Christianity is veneered Paganism, Edward the Seventh is undoubtedly a fitting ruler."[17]

King Edward planned to visit Ireland in the spring of 1902. However, to the intense disappointment of Cadogan, who resigned as lord lieutenant shortly thereafter, the king canceled the visit when Irish MPs cheered a Boer victory in the Commons.[18] It was announced that this had been done on the advice of the government. In Ireland the move was misread as the government fearing the "visit of a frank and open-minded Sovereign to an Ireland disloyal and disaffected to the Government of which he is the Constitutional head."[19] The king's popularity increased to a degree and something of the same sense of a pro-Irish monarch being restrained by an anti-Irish British government as had been present in O'Connell's depiction of Queen Victoria under Peel's government descended on the incident.

The king's coronation was set for June 1902 but had to be postponed due to serious illness. To the *Freeman's Journal,* the king was someone who had only made the accession declaration under protest, who had supported an honorable peace with the Boers, who had been anxious to visit Ireland after his accession, and who had supported Gladstone's home rule measure. Most of this was incorrect. However, believing it, the paper went on to say that Ireland was sympathetic to the king in his illness: "[S]he breathes the prayer today, 'God Save the King.'"[20]

Recovered from illness, the king was crowned in August. James Connolly denounced the coronation as "a piece of Royalist and Capitalist propaganda."[21] The Irish Party stayed away from the coronation and held a meeting in City Hall in Dublin instead. "In Ireland Edward VII is not a Constitutional Monarch," John Redmond told those assembled. "Why there is no race in the world, which, by instinct, is more inclined to sentiments of loyalty than the Irish. Why do not these English statesmen give

---

17. Thomas Connellan ed., *The Catholic* (Dublin: October 1904), 151–52. I am grateful to Dr. Patrick Maume for this reference.

18. Lee, *Edward VII,* 2:164–65.

19. *FJ,* 13 March 1902.

20. *FJ,* 25 June 1902.

21. Morgan, *Connolly,* 35.

us something to be loyal to?"[22] In 1902 this line of argument, that Ireland would be loyal to the Crown if only home rule was granted, was a rather old-fashioned one.

A visit from King Edward and Queen Alexandra eventually took place in July 1903. Dublin's lord mayor, Tim Harrington, who had protested against the Prince of Wales in Mallow in 1885 and opposed the 1900 address to Queen Victoria, actually proposed a loyal address for this visit. However, after heated controversy the Dublin Corporation eventually decided not to make an address.[23] Griffith and Gonne were active and vociferous in opposing the address and the visit. Gonne hung a black petticoat from her window in Coulson Avenue and went on to defend her house from the police intent on removing it.[24] One of the groups with which Gonne was associated in her opposition to the visit was the People's Protection Committee. It later became the National Council, which in September 1907 merged with the Sinn Féin League to become the original Sinn Féin Party, from which almost all the postindependence Irish nationalist political parties descend.[25]

Current events favored the success of the visit. The Wyndham land act was passing through its final stages in Parliament and there were hopes that the sixty-year controversy concerning higher education in Ireland might at last be resolved. It was rumored that the king had said, "I shall come to Ireland with an Education Bill in one hand and a Land Bill in the other."[26] His frankly undeserved reputation for being favorable to Irish nationalism was thus enhanced. It was doubly enhanced by his tactful reaction to the news of the death of Pope Leo XIII just as he arrived in Dublin. The king at once sent his condolences to Cardinal Logue. "In thus recognising the constituted authorities of the Church in Ireland and making them the channel of his condolences, his Majesty has given proof of his knowledge of Irish conditions and his careful attention to the details of State procedures."[27] Even Archbishop Walsh attended a levee.[28] When the king and

22. *FJ,* 11 August 1902.

23. *FJ,* 14 July 1903; Lee, *Edward VII,* 2:166.

24. Margaret Ward, *Maud Gonne: Ireland's Joan of Arc* (London: Pandora, 1990), 82–83.

25. Leon O'Bróin, *Revolutionary Underground: The Story of the Irish Republican Brotherhood, 1858–1924* (Dublin: Gill and Macmillan, 1976), 126.

26. Lee, *Edward VII,* 2:167.

27. *FJ,* 22 July 1903.

28. *DNB,* 1 (2d Supplement):599.

queen visited Maynooth, the clerical students good-humoredly displayed a picture of the king's Derby winner, Persimmon.[29]

Yeats wrote sarcastically to the papers saying he expected the sporting columns would in future include tips from the archbishops of Armagh and Dublin.[30] The novelist George Moore declared that he was so shocked by the lack of patriotism of the Irish Catholic clergy in welcoming the king that he was going to join the Church of Ireland instead.[31] As he and everyone else knew, it was a rather perverse decision, given the even greater attachment of most members of the Church of Ireland to the Crown. Therein, indeed, lay the very attraction of the move for him.

The king and queen were very warmly welcomed to Dublin by the crowds and spent several days carrying out engagements. The French journal *Courier du Soir* recorded the "astonishing loyalty" shown to the royal couple.[32] King Edward and Queen Alexandra then went to Belfast, where they unveiled a statue to Queen Victoria and opened the Royal Victoria Hospital.[33] From Belfast they moved on to Derry and then sailed down the West Coast in the royal yacht, stopping in Connemara and taking the train on to Kerry. Finally they went to Cork, where they were greeted by the lord mayor. Eighteeen years after their last disastrous visit they received "a popular ovation" in the city.[34] When the king left Queenstown for Cowes, he heard the people call "Come back!"[35]

There was delight in government circles about the success of the visit, a delight reminiscent of that for Queen Victoria's visit in 1849. The prime minister, A. J. Balfour, hailed it as the beginning of "a happier era." He told the king, "No such event has occurred in the history of the Monarchy: a history which so far as Ireland is concerned has been but little diversified by any gleam of brightness."[36] Sir Horace Plunkett told Lord Knollys that the people feel Edward "prides himself on being the ruler of Ireland."[37]

29. Lee, *Edward VII*, 2:168.

30. George Moore, *Hail and Farewell* (Gerrard's Cross: Colin Smythe, 1985), 727.

31. Moore, *Hail and Farewell*, 457.

32. *FJ*, 29 July 1903.

33. *Belfast Newsletter*, 28 July 1903.

34. *FJ*, 3 August 1903.

35. Wyndham, *Life and Letters*, 2:460, quoted in Lee, *Edward VII*, 2:168.

36. A. J. Balfour to King Edward VII, 3 September 1903, quoted in Lee, *Edward VII*, 2:169.

37. Sir Horace Plunkett to Lord Knollys, 30 November 1903, quoted in Lee, *Edward VII*, 2:170.

Whatever the popular reception, there was in fact little real cause for rejoicing for the monarchy from the visit as far as official nationalism was concerned. Edward VII as king was personally liked in a way in which Queen Victoria had not been since the early 1860s. The perception that she had a repugnance for Ireland bolstered visceral Irish anti-monarchism. The king's visit therefore showed that anti-monarchism was a reality among certain important sections of the nationalist community even when personal dislike was absent. It was the *Belfast Newsletter* that pointed out that beneath the apparent warmth of the nationalist welcome of the king lay a continuing anti-monarchism. Referring to the members of the Dublin Corporation and their decision not to offer a loyal address it noted that

[t]hey professed to be willing to receive the King and Queen courteously, but they drew a distinction between the courtesy due to a distinguished visitor and the loyalty which subjects owe their Sovereign. Their action amounts to a denial that Edward VII is King of Ireland and the denial is not based upon any doubt as to the right of succession but on the assertion that Ireland ought to be entirely independent of Great Britain.[38]

❖

There were several more royal visits to Ireland during the first decade of the twentieth century. In April 1904 the king and queen attended the races in Dublin and visited some great country houses in the southeast of the country. Their only real official engagement was the laying of the foundation stone of the new College of Science in Dublin.[39] The same evening the royal couple received an ovation when they attended the theater.[40] The *Freeman's Journal* complained that there had been no progress on university education and that after the 1903 visit honors had been given in a plainly partisan fashion to those councils that had broken nationalist ranks and welcomed the king officially.[41]

Early in 1905 Prince George, now Prince of Wales, visited Connemara and held a levee and drawing room in Dublin Castle.[42] In July 1907 the king and queen paid their final visit to Dublin for two days to see the International Exhibition and to go to the races. The visit was marred by the discovery, just before the king's arrival, that the admittedly very valuable insignia of the grand master of the Order of St. Patrick, which were rather

38. *Belfast Newsletter,* 22 July 1903.   39. *FJ,* 29 April 1904.
40. Lee, *Edward VII,* 2:172.   41. *FJ,* 26 April 1904.
42. *FJ,* 21 January 1905.

grandly known as the "Irish crown jewels," were missing from their safe in Dublin Castle.[43] The king was furious but the jewels were never recovered and the mystery of what happened to them was never satisfactorily solved. Sir Arthur Vicars, Ulster king at arms, was dismissed after an official investigation found he had not ensured that the jewels were properly secured.[44]

The Liberals were back in power and Lord Aberdeen, whose wife had taken an abiding interest in the promotion of Irish industry over the years, had returned as lord lieutenant for a second and very extended time. The 1907 royal visit was at his invitation, but because he did not invite the king and queen to stay at the Vice Regal Lodge they stayed overnight on the royal yacht.[45] This time the *Freeman's Journal* praised the king's "undisguised and unpretentious" friendliness toward Ireland but wished that "the golden link of the Crown" was the only bond of union between Britain and Ireland.[46] When King Edward VII died in May 1910 a votive mass was celebrated for him at the Catholic Pro-Cathedral in Dublin attended by Archbishop Walsh.[47] One minor nationalist newspaper went so far as to say that the late king "was the first British sovereign to begin the work of reconciling the races which centuries of misgovernment and misunderstanding had well-night made impossible."[48]

King George V and Queen Mary were crowned on 22 June 1911. Once more the Irish Party boycotted the coronation but John Redmond sounded almost apologetic in his statements about the matter, wishing the king well and welcoming his forthcoming visit to Ireland.[49] The king and queen visited Dublin for five days in early July with their daughter Princess Mary and their eldest son, David. The latter was to be installed as Prince of Wales immediately afterward and was to reign briefly as Edward VIII before abdicating in 1936 and assuming the title of duke of Windsor.

The royal visitors were warmly received by the crowds in Dublin.[50] The most vociferous opposition to the visit came from groups of radical na-

43. *FJ*, 8 July 1907.

44. See Elizabeth Longford, *Darling Loosy: Letters of Princess Louise, 1856–1939* (London: Weidenfeld and Nicolson, 1991), 54.

45. *FJ*, 11, 12 July 1907.

46. *FJ*, 11 July 1907.

47. *FJ*, 21 May 1910.

48. *Nationalist and Leinster Times*, 14 May 1910, quoted in Lee, *Edward VII*, 2:720.

49. Denis Gwynn, *The Life of John Redmond* (London: George G. Harrap, 1932), 188–89.

50. *Times*, 10 July 1911.

tionalist women, again largely of Anglo-Irish background. At a meeting in Foster Place on 4 July Countess Markievicz, who was a member of the Gore-Booth family, and Helena Molony burned a Union Jack. Markievicz denounced those members of the Corporation who had accepted honors with all the contempt of an aristocrat toward those in trade. To her they were "Sir Fishmonger Pile, Sir Standard-bake O'Downes and Sir Wood-bine O'Farrell."[51]

The Parliament Act of 1911 reduced the veto of the Lords to a power to delay legislation. A willing Liberal government promoted a new home rule bill, but the problem of the refusal of Ulster Unionists to countenance home rule remained and led to heightened tensions. George V saw part of his role as constitutional monarch as being to work toward national consensus. His Buckingham Palace conference of July 1914 failed to resolve the Ulster impasse but was significant if only because the inclusion of Irish nationalists indicated an acknowledgment of the legitimacy of their aspirations within the union context.[52]

The matter remained unresolved by the outbreak of the World War I. Tens of thousands of nationalist Irishmen volunteered for service in the British army with John Redmond's blessing, believing that home rule would be the postwar prize. His brother William, who had been so strongly anti-monarchical in the 1880s, died on active service in 1917. When John Redmond himself died the next year, King George sent an official representative to his funeral.[53]

By the end of the war all was changed. The British monarchy was renamed, and was now no longer the house of Saxe-Coburg and Gotha, after Prince Albert, but in a new anti-German age, the house of Windsor. Ireland too was changed. The Irish Party was swept away at the 1918 elections by Sinn Féin, now pledged to the immediate achivement of an independent Irish republic. It was the beneficiary of the disaffection from Britain that resulted from the attempt to impose military conscription on Ireland in 1918 and from the sympathy and support that accrued to the cause of those republicans and socialists who had initiated an apparently futile rebellion in Ireland in 1916 and whose leaders had been executed for their

51. *FJ*, 5 July 1911.
52. *FJ*, 25 July 1914.
53. Gwynn, *Redmond*, 594.

pains. Inasmuch as they had hopes for success, they lay with a German intervention on their behalf. In order to assure that support, Patrick Pearse and Joseph Plunkett, two of the principal leaders of the rebellion, had discussed the possibility of installing a German prince, specifically Prince Joachim, as king of Ireland. The move would have had the further advantage, they thought, that the new king, not being an English speaker, might be well disposed to learn and thus promote the use of the Irish language, which they favored.[54] Even discussing the possibility of a new sort of kingship, however, indicated a pragmatic attitude toward republicanism.

In 1919 Sinn Féin established its own parliament, the Dáil, and several years of effective war followed between its forces, the Irish Republican Army, and the forces of the Crown. The Dáil met appropriately in Dublin's Mansion House, given the role of the lord mayor and the Corporation as Ireland's nationalism's partial parliament in the nineteenth century. Britain pushed on with its own solution for Ireland and established a provincial parliament for what would become Northern Ireland, the Ulster Unionist heartland in six of the northeastern counties. George V's call for conciliation throughout Ireland in his speech at the opening of that parliament[55] paved the way first for a truce between Crown and republican forces in July 1921 and then for the Anglo-Irish Treaty of December of that year which resulted in the independence from Britain of the rest of the island.

The treaty led to a split in the Dáil and to the brief but bloody Civil War, in what was now known as the Irish Free State, from 1922 to 1923. The central issue rested not so much on the partition of Ireland but on the failure to win a republic. This was most forcefully apparent in Britain's successful insistence on the retention of the monarchy and on the introduction of a new oath of allegiance to the Free State Constitution and of fidelity to the British monarch as head of the Commonwealth for Irish parliamentarians. In fact, Ireland had achieved the high degree of independence of a dominion within the British Commonwealth. The Crown was to be represented by a governor general who would act on the advice of the Irish government. Tim Healy, once the singer of Jacobite songs in the Commons, was installed as first holder of the office. The role of the

---

54. Desmond Fitzgerald, *Memoirs of Desmond Fitzgerald, 1913–1916* (London: Routledge and Kegan Paul, 1968), 141.

55. *FJ*, 23 June 1921.

Crown was thus purely formal in order "to comfort English opinion and to deceive it as to the status of the new polity but it actually succeeded in deceiving much of Sinn Féin and the IRA who saw, or claimed they saw, a puppet state being erected on Irish soil."[56]

The objections raised in the Dáil debates to the continuing role of the Crown reflected such concerns. Erskine Childers, an opponent of the treaty, feared that the governor general would have the power to control the Irish government in the interests of Britain. Mary MacSwiney, sister of the lord mayor of Cork who had died on hunger strike in prison during "the Troubles," worried that the governor general's circle would be a source of social corruption. Markievicz anticipated that the governor general would be English and would inhibit the spread of Gaelic culture and the Irish language. He would undermine the morality of the new state and advocate "immorality and divorce laws," thus imperilling the purity of young Irish women. Most bizarrely she warned that the king's daughter, Princess Mary, would be married off to the pro-treaty leader, Michael Collins, and that he would be installed as the first governor general.[57]

The Civil War that resulted from the treaty split was won by the pro-treaty side, which also commanded a majority in the Dáil. Throughout the 1920s Irish politicians helped to shape the direction of the Imperial conferences that resulted in the 1931 Statue of Westminster, an effective recognition of the independence of dominions. In 1932 Éamon de Valera, leader of the anti-treaty group, came to power through the ballot box. He set about undermining the remaining position of the Crown in the Irish Free State by appointing a nonentity to the post of governor general and then, under the guise of the 1936 abdication crisis, reducing the role of the Crown to external relations only.[58] His new constitution established a presidency but still left the slimmest of links with the Crown and Commonwealth. It was not until 1949 and under a different government that Ireland was finally declared a republic and left the Commonwealth.

The office of president of Ireland has almost no political or constitutional power and lacks a specific ceremonial or social role, though its hold-

56. Tom Garvin, *1922: The Birth of Irish Democracy* (Dublin: Gill and Macmillan, 1996), 52.

57. Brendan Sexton, *Ireland and the Crown, 1922–1936: The Governor-Generalship of the Irish Free State* (Dublin: Irish Academic Press, 1989), 49–50.

58. Sexton, *Ireland and Crown*, 165. Superficially at least De Valera's notion of the Crown acting for Ireland in its external relations bears some resemblance to the old idea of the Crown as a "golden link" between Britain and Ireland.

ers have often been sedulous in supporting the work of charities and community groups and in promoting Ireland abroad. It was designed to be the antithesis to the monarchy that it superceded.[59] Only in the early 1990s did it enjoy a significant public profile, but this was because the election of Mary Robinson as president symbolized a particular change toward liberalism in the political culture of the state.

From 1968 Northern Ireland began to descend into internal conflict between those in favor of continuing that province's union with Great Britain and those in favor of joining with an Irish state. Significantly, the issue of the monarchy was that which distinguished linguistically between those on either side prepared to use violent and constitutional means to secure their ends. "Unionists" and "nationalists" were terms given to those who were generally unwilling to resort to violence, whereas "loyalists" and "republicans" were terms given to those who were. In 1979 the British monarchy suffered its first and only casualty from the Irish conflict with the murder of Lord Mountbatten, uncle of the husband of Queen Elizabeth II, by the IRA at his County Sligo holiday home.

The fascination of many Irish people with monarchy continued. In 1981 a party of two hundred Welsh speakers who had come to Dublin to escape the wedding of Prince Charles and Lady Diana Spencer, a relation of the Red Earl, "expressed amazement that most of the pubs they visited were dominated by television sets showing the wedding."[60] When Princess Diana died sixteen years later flags were flown at half mast on Irish government buildings and numerous bouquets of flowers were laid outside the British embassy in Dublin.[61]

The lack of a visit from a British monarch to the independent Irish state was rightly taken as a sign of the absence of normalization of relations between the United Kingdom and Ireland. The problematic issue was that of Northern Ireland, whose right to dissent from union with the rest of the island the south was reluctant to recognize until the end of the twentieth century. In the last decades of that century the troubles in

59. Dr. Douglas Hyde became the first president in 1938, under de Valera's new constitution. However, until the Republic of Ireland Act came into force in 1949, King George VI continued to have a role to play in Irish diplomatic accreditation, though little attention was ever drawn to it. Arguably, he, and not the president, was the Irish head of state until 1949.

60. *Irish Times,* 30 July 1981.

61. *Irish Times,* 4 September 1997.

Northern Ireland caused successive British and Irish governments to work closely together and to agree on ways forward for Northern Ireland. Having spent two decades trying to defeat terrorism, the governments changed tack in the 1990s and attempted to win terrorism over to the constitutional path.

Both Irish presidents of the 1990s, Mary Robinson and Mary McAleese, met the reigning British monarch, Queen Elizabeth II, and there were reciprocal, low-key visits by members of the British royal family to the Republic of Ireland such as those of Prince Charles in 1995 and of his father, the duke of Edinburgh, in 1998. Ironically, at the close of the century, the danger for large-scale, formal, royal visits to the Republic of Ireland continued to lie not in the possibility that royal visitors might not be well received by the Irish people but that they might be too well received. The possibility remained that the recrudescence of old, royal enthusiasms in the south could still engender old nationalist fears, especially in the north.

Chronology

24 May 1819	Birth of the future Queen Victoria.
29 January 1820	George IV succeeds George III.
22 June 1821	Duke of York resigns as grand master of the Orange Order.
12 August– 3 September 1821	George IV visits Dublin.
4 November 1822	Lord Lieutenant Wellesley bans Orange ceremony at statue of William III.
9 May 1823	Daniel O'Connell founds Catholic Association.
31 March 1825	Catholic Association and Orange Order suppressed.
18 May 1825	Catholic relief bill defeated in the Lords.
13 July 1825	New Catholic Association established.
5 January 1827	Duke of York dies.
April 1828	Corporation Act repealed and Test Act modified.
5 July 1828	O'Connell is elected MP for County Clare.
14 August 1828	Orange "Brunswick Constitution Club of Ireland" formed.
13 April 1829	"Catholic emancipation" passed.
26 June 1830	William IV succeeds George IV.
14 August 1833	Irish Church Temporalities Act.
4 February 1834	William IV's speech on repeal.
March 1835	Lichfield House Compact.
4 August 1835	Duke of Cumberland is revealed as grand master of Orange Order.
20 June 1837	Accession of Queen Victoria.
28 June 1837	O'Connell's forms "Friends of the Queen" to fight the general election.
18 July 1837	Lord John Russell publicly writes to Lord Lieutenant Mulgrave concerning the queen's support for the Whigs' Irish policy.
21 February 1838	O'Connell is presented to the queen.

28 June 1838	Coronation of Queen Victoria.
8–10 May 1839	"The Bedchamber Plot."
23 May 1839	O'Connell holds Dublin demonstration to thank the queen for keeping Sir Robert Peel out of office.
5 July 1839	Lady Flora Hastings dies.
23 November 1839	Victoria is engaged to Albert.
5 December 1839	O'Connell welcomes the engagement.
27 January 1840	O'Connell supports annuity for Prince Albert.
10 February 1840	Marriage of Victoria and Albert.
15 April 1840	Foundation of Repeal Association.
10 June 1840	First assassination attempt on Queen Victoria.
13 June 1840	O'Connell writes a letter to the Irish people on the subject. Throughout July meetings of Irish townspeoples and Catholic clergy send addresses to the queen.
21 November 1840	Princess Victoria born.
1 November 1841	O'Connell becomes lord mayor of Dublin.
9 November 1841	Prince of Wales, future Edward VII, born.
9 April 1842	O'Connell presents address to Queen Victoria on the birth of the Prince of Wales; controversy occurs when O'Connell is not given the customary baronetcy.
30 May 1842	Second assassination attempt on Queen Victoria.
29 June 1842	O'Connell presents address to Queen Victoria on her escape.
3 July 1842	Third assassination attempt on Queen Victoria.
9 May 1843	Peel tells Commons that the queen opposes repeal.
11 May 1843	O'Connell refuses to believe it.
22–26 May 1843	Controversy erupts over dismissal of pro-repeal magistrates by Irish lord chancellor Sugden.
24 August 1843	Queen's prorogation speech defends the union and criticizes repeal agitation.
29 August 1843	O'Connell attacks the speech but distinguishes it from the queen.
1 October 1843	Mullaghmast "monster" meeting.
7 October 1843	Banning of Clontarf monster meeting.
9 October 1843	O'Connell refuses to believe the queen was responsible for the ban.
10 October 1843	O'Connell and others arrested.
14 January 1844	Trial of O'Connell begins.
10 February 1844	O'Connell convicted of "conspiracy."
9 May 1844	Parliamentary debate on proposal to abolish the Irish lord lieutenancy.
30 May 1844	O'Connell imprisoned.

4 September 1844	O'Connell's conviction reversed by Lords.
17 December 1844	Appointment of three Catholic bishops to the Charitable Bequests' Board.
7 April 1845	Lords debate imminent visit of queen to Ireland.
28 April 1845	O'Connell opposes a visit.
21 May 1845	Dublin lord mayor invites queen to Ireland.
30 May 1845	O'Connell's national levee criticized as a parody of royalty.
8 June 1845	O'Connell's progress through Cork.
30 June 1845	Maynooth College Act passed.
9 September 1845	Potato blight first noted; beginning of the famine.
13 December 1845	Dublin Corporation memorial to Queen Victoria on famine.
26 June 1846	Corn laws repealed.
13 January 1847	First Queen's Letter appealing for funds for the Irish famine.
15 May 1847	Death of O'Connell.
15 March 1848	At a meeting of the Irish Confederation T. F. Meagher proposes that a delegation be sent to Queen Victoria asking her to summon an Irish parliament.
20 March 1848	Petition of Dublin trades and citizens to the queen on repeal of the union.
21 March 1848	Charges of sedition to be pressed against W. S. O'Brien, T. F. Meagher, and J. Mitchel.
23 March 1848	Mitchel tells Confederation he opposes a petition to the queen and supports a republic.
22 April 1848	Crown and Government Security Act.
13 May 1848	Mitchel is arrested, and later tried and sentenced to transportation.
16 May 1848	Failure of trials of O'Brien and Meagher.
8 July 1848	Arrest of John Martin and Charles Gavan Duffy.
25 July 1848	Habeas corpus suspended.
29 July 1848	Smith O'Brien's rising in County Tipperary.
September and October 1848	Trials and death sentences for those involved in Tipperary rising.
19 May 1849	Fourth assassination attempt on Queen Victoria.
5 June 1849	Death sentences of W. S. O'Brien and others commuted to transportation.
12 July 1849	Dolly's Brae killings.
2–11 August 1849	First visit of Queen Victoria to Ireland.
17 May 1850	Lord John Russell introduces a bill to abolish the lord lieutenancy.
10 March 1851	Dublin Corporation petitions the queen against abolition.
27 June 1850	Fifth assassination attempt on Queen Victoria.

29 July 1851	Ecclesiastical Titles Act.
12 May 1853	Opening of the Dublin Exhibition.
29 August– 3 September 1853	Second visit of Queen Victoria to Ireland.
7 July 1857	Moves in Commons to abolish the lord lieutenancy.
17 March 1858	James Stephens founds Irish Republican Brotherhood in Dublin.
April 1858	Prince of Wales visits Ireland.
26 June 1858	Prince Alfred visits Ireland.
Summer 1958	Cardinal Wiseman tours Ireland.
17 March 1859	Prince of Wales visits Irish College in Rome.
20 March 1860	Prince Albert is embarrassed by the publication of von Humboldt's letter.
16 August– 12 September 1860	Prince of Wales visits Canada and the United States.
15 January 1861	Terence Bellew MacManus dies.
16 March 1861	Duchess of Kent dies.
29 June 1861	Prince of Wales arrives in Ireland for military training.
22–29 August 1861	Third visit of Queen Victoria to Ireland.
10 November 1861	Funeral of Terence Bellew McManus.
14 December 1861	Albert's death and Victoria's retirement.
20 July 1852	Catholic University ceremony held in Drumcondra.
22 September 1862	John Gray begins collection for O'Connell monument.
29 September 1862	Plan to place Albert statue in Stephen's Green begins debate on its opening.
February 1863	Controversy in Dublin Corporation over a loyal address on Prince of Wales's wedding.
10 March 1863	Marriage of Prince and Princess of Wales.
8 January 1864	Prince Albert Victor born.
13 January 1864	Dublin Corporation controversy over address on birth of Prince Albert Victor; finally agreed on 1 February.
8 February 1864	Opposition to College Green site for Albert statue.
15 February 1864	A. M. Sullivan proposes College Green site for Grattan statue.
22, 29 February 1864	A. M. Sullivan organizes Rotundo meetings against Albert statue in College Green.
2 May 1864	Dublin Corporation begins to turn against the Albert statue proposal for College Green.
17 May 1864	It is revealed that Queen Victoria has already approved the College Green site.
8–12 May 1865	Prince of Wales visits Ireland to open the Dublin Exhibition.
3 June 1865	Prince George born.

26 July 1865	Dublin Corporation's loyal address on the birth of Prince George.
18 December 1865	Leinster Lawn approved as site for Albert statue.
17 February 1866	Habeas corpus suspended to deal with Fenians.
20 August 1866	Reception held for newly elevated Cardinal Cullen in Dublin.
11 February 1867	Chester Castle raid.
12 February 1867	Fenians muster in County Kerry.
5–6 March 1867	Fenians skirmish in Dublin mountains and also in Munster.
24 May 1867	Memorial to reprieve death sentence on T. F. Burke is rejected by the lord lieutenant.
27 May 1868	Clemency for Burke is granted.
20 June 1867	Clan na Gael founded in New York to unite Fenians.
13 September 1867	Queen renames Irish police Royal Irish Constabulary in gratitude for their work against Fenians.
11 September 1867	Colonel Thomas Kelly and Captain Deasy arrested in Manchester.
18 September 1867	Freeing of Kelly and Deasy results in the death of Sergeant Brett.
1 November 1867	Five men found guilty of the murder of Brett.
21–22 November 1867	Clerkenwell demonstration and delegation to Windsor Castle.
23 November 1867	Three "Manchester martyrs" hanged (two others reprieved).
13 December 1867	Clerkenwell jail explosion.
December 1867	Government fears for the queen's life.
12 March 1868	Assassination attempt on Prince Alfred in Australia.
3 April 1868	Commons approves Gladstone's disestablishment resolutions.
15–24 April 1868	Prince and Princess of Wales make ceremonial visit to Dublin.
4 May 1868	Disraeli announces the delay in his resignation.
7 May 1868	The Commons asks the queen not to make any more Irish Church appointments.
14 May 1868	Dublin Corporation address to the queen on Prince Alfred.
24 August 1868	False reports of a Fenian assassination plot against Queen Victoria at Lucerne.
5 March 1869	Amnesty petitioners meet the queen.
5 April–4 May 1869	Prince Arthur visits Ireland.
27 April 1869	Daniel O'Sullivan, mayor of Cork, insults the royal family.
12 May 1869	O'Sullivan resigns in face of a bill of pains and penalties.
26 July 1869	Disestablishment becomes law.
28 June 1869	Amnesty Association launched.
17 May 1870	Isaac Butt founds the Home Government Association.
19 May 1870	Publication of alleged letter of Prince of Wales to Prince Alfred in India, favorable to Ireland.
25 May 1870	Prince Arthur at St. John's, Canada, during Fenian skirmish.

1 August 1870	Gladstone's first land act.
14 March 1871	Irish ladies' amnesty petition on the occasion of the royal wedding.
21 March 1871	Marriage of Princess Louise to Lord Lorne.
24 March 1871	Dublin Corporation address on the wedding.
31 July 1871	Twenty-eight Irish MPs vote against Prince Arthur's annuity.
31 July–7 August 1871	Prince of Wales and other members of royal family visit Dublin.
6 August 1871	Fenian amnesty meeting in Phoenix Park broken up by police.
August 1871	French republicans visit Ireland.
3 September 1871	Amnesty meeting in Phoenix Park draws up petition to the queen.
23 October 1871	Butt denounces Home Secretary Bruce's reply to the amnesty petition in the name of the queen.
27 February 1872	Thanksgiving for recovery of Prince of Wales.
29 February 1872	Sixth assassination attempt on Queen Victoria.
4–8 June 1872	Prince Alfred visits Dublin.
9 June 1872	Attempt to blow up the Dublin Albert statue.
8 January 1873	Home Rule Confederation of Great Britain founded.
2 November 1873	Queen Victoria receives communion at Crathie Church.
18–21 November 1873	Home Rule League founded.
26 May 1874	Prince Arthur becomes duke of Connaught.
29 June 1875	Attack on the Albert statue in Dublin.
7 July 1875	Joseph Biggar objects in the Commons to money for the Prince of Wales's Indian trip.
5–6 August 1875	O'Connell centenary.
March 1876	Irish Parliamentary Party opposition to the Royal Titles Bill is muted, in the hope of a Fenian amnesty.
24 July 1876	Dublin Corporation address to the queen on the return of the Prince of Wales from India in April.
9 October 1876– 17 May 1878	Prince Arthur, duke of Connaught, stationed in Ireland on military service.
1 January 1877	Queen Victoria is proclaimed "Empress of India."
7 July 1877	Emperor and empress of Brazil visit Ireland.
31 July 1877	Beginnings of obstructionism by Irish MPs in Parliament.
28 August 1877	C. S. Parnell becomes president of Home Rule Confederation of Great Britain.
17 October– 12 November 1877	Gladstone visits Ireland.
4 January 1878	Last Fenian prisoners released.
2 April 1878	Lord Leitrim murdered.
1 May 1878	Prince Arthur engaged to Princess Louise of Prussia.

24–27 October 1878	John Devoy suggests "new departure" to Parnellites.
25 July 1878	Commons approves marriage annuity for Prince Arthur, duke of Connaught.
20 November 1878	Lord mayor of Dublin proposes Irish marriage gift to Prince Arthur.
14 December 1878	Death of Princess Alice; Dublin Corporation telegrams sympathy.
20 December 1878	Cork mayor's meeting for gift to duke of Connaught fails.
26 December 1878	Queen Victoria's public letter of thanks for condolences.
26 January 1879	Irish Republican Brotherhood Supreme Council rejects "New Departure" at a meeting in Paris.
22 February–23 March 1879	Empress Elizabeth of Austria-Hungary visits Ireland.
10 March 1879	Dublin lord mayor presents first part of wedding gift to the duke of Connaught.
13 March 1879	Marriage of duke and duchess of Connaught.
20 April 1879	Irishtown meeting launches land agitation.
5 May 1879	Isaac Butt dies.
16 August 1879	National Land League of Mayo founded.
8 September 1879	Prince Leopold visits Irish north coast.
21 October 1879	Irish National Land League founded.
27 October 1879	Presentation of silver service to the Connaughts.
19 December 1879	Duchess of Marlborough's Irish Relief Fund launched.
26 December 1879	Queen gives £500 to duchess of Marlborough's fund.
2 January–11 March 1880	Parnell's American tour.
2 January 1880	Mansion House Relief Committee set up.
20 January 1880	Lord Mayor Gray presides at meeting of MPs, causing Lord Lieutenant Marlborough to boycott the civic banquet.
4 February–7 March 1880	Empress Elizabeth makes second visit to Ireland.
9 March 1880	Publication of pre-election letter from Beaconsfield to Marlborough critical of the loyalty of supporters of home rule.
18 March 1880	Home Rule Party manifesto for the election, at which Gladstone is returned to power.
9–11 April 1880	Prince Alfred visits Galway and Dublin.
22 April 1880	U.S. relief ship *Constellation* arrives in Queenstown; Prince Alfred helps distribute its supplies.
4 May 1880	Commander Potter of the *Constellation* is made a freeman of Dublin.
17 May 1880	Parnell as chairman of Irish Parliamentary Party.

19 September 1880	Parnell calls for what was to be known as boycotting.
29 September 1880	Lord Mountmorres murdered.
24 October 1880	Ladies' Land League founded.
2 November 1880	Parnell and others charged with conspiracy to prevent payment of rent.
January 1881	Explosions in Britain.
23 January 1881	Collapse of Parnell trial.
24 January 1881	Introduction of coercion legislation.
3 February 1881	Michael Davitt arrested.
2 March 1881	Protection of Person and Property Act.
21 March 1881	Peace Preservation Act for Ireland.
22 August 1881	Gladstone's second land act.
15 September 1881	Dublin Corporation to coordinate the 1882 National Industrial Exhibition.
15–17 September 1881	Land League Conference in Dublin agrees with Parnell to "test the act."
2 October 1881	Parnell speaks of links with Crown in Cork.
7 October 1881	Gladstone replies in Leeds.
9 October 1881	Parnell replies to Gladstone.
13 October 1881	Parnell, and later others, arrested.
18 October 1881	"No Rent Manifesto" issued.
20 October 1881	Land League outlawed.
9 December 1881	Disarray at Exhibition General Committee over role of the queen.
22 December 1881	Belfast committee withdraws and project collapses.
25 January 1882	Dublin lord mayor forms a limited company to organize an exhibition along nationalist lines.
2 March 1882	Seventh assassination attempt on Queen Victoria.
6 March 1882	Dublin Corporation passes motion of sympathy with Queen Victoria.
23 March 1882	42 Irish MPs oppose marraige annuity to Prince Leopold.
2 May 1882	Parnell and others released under "Kilmainham Treaty."
2 May 1882	Chief Secretary W. E. Forster resigns in protest.
6 May 1882	Lord Frederick Cavendish and T. H. Burke murdered.
23 June 1882	T. M. Healy sings Jacobite song in the Commons.
18 August 1882	Prevention of Crime Act.
8 August 1882	Maamtrasna murders.
15 August 1882	Dublin O'Connell monument unveiled, 1782 centennial celebrated, and National Industrial Exhibition opened.
18 August 1882	Arrears Act.

17 October 1882	Foundation of Irish National League.
1 January 1883	New-style Dublin civic banquet without lord lieutenant.
15 March 1883	Explosion at Local Government Board, Whitehall, and attempt to bomb the *Times* offices.
7 April 1883	Discovery of dynamite in London.
9 April 1883	Explosives Act.
3 July 1883	Opening of Cork Exhibition.
14–21 July 1883	Controversy over knighthoods rather than baronetcies for eminent Irish doctors.
30 October 1883	Explosion on underground close to Charing Cross Station.
3 November 1883	High security for duke and duchess of Connaught at Charing Cross Station.
29 January 1884	Some Tories boycott Lord Lieutenant Spencer's levee.
26 February 1884	Explosion at Victoria Station.
29 February 1884	Attacks on Paddington and Charing Cross Stations.
10 March 1884	John Redmond denies he called on people to cheer the queen while in Australia.
28 March 1884	Security at Chester for Prince of Wales's visit to Aintree.
30 May 1884	Explosions at St. James's Square and at Scotland Yard.
28–31 August 1884	Prince Alfred visits Dublin, where he is not officially welcomed, and later Cork, where after welcoming him the mayor is criticized.
1 October 1884	Pact between bishops and Irish Parliamentary Party whereby the latter agree to press Catholic claims in education.
3 January 1885	Dublin lord mayor John O'Connor visits lord lieutenant, causing controversy.
24 January 1885	Explosions at Westminster Hall, the House of Commons, and the Tower of London.
1 March 1885	At a Phoenix Park meeting William O'Brien attacks the forthcoming royal visit to Ireland.
3 March 1885	The National League criticizes the visit.
9 March 1885	Dublin Chamber of Commerce establishes a citizens' committee to welcome the Prince and Princess of Wales.
11 March 1885	Dublin nationalist councillors decide against a loyal address.
13 March 1885	Irish Party calls the visit political and ask nationalists not to do anything to damage national demands.
16 March 1885	Dublin Corporation votes not to welcome the royal visit.
20 March 1885	Cork Corporation votes similarly.
7–26 April 1885	Prince and Princess of Wales visit Ireland.
7 April 1885	T. M. Healy, William O'Brien, and William Redmond attack the visit at a meeting of the National League.

11 April 1885	London *Times* sees the visit as a political victory.
12 April 1885	Ten "monster" meetings of the National League call for respectful neutrality over the visit.
13 April 1885	Protests at Mallow Station against royal visit.
15 April 1885	Protests in Cork.
14 May 1885	Annuity for Princess Beatrice opposed by several Irish MPs.
14 August 1885	"Ashbourne" Land Purchase Act.
5 October 1885	Parnell's Wicklow speech proposes Austria-Hungary solution.
7 October 1885	Salisbury's reply at Newport.
21 November 1885	Parnell calls on Irish in Britain to vote Conservative at forthcoming election, at which Gladstone is returned to power.
8 April 1886	Gladstone introduces home rule measure into Parliament.
16 April 1886	Gladstone introduces the Irish Land Sale and Purchase Bill.
8 June 1886	Home rule bill defeated.
23 October 1886	"Plan of Campaign."
18 December 1886	"Plan of Campaign" declared illegal.
7, 10, 14 March 1887	"Parnellism and Crime" articles.
28 March 1887	Criminal Law Amendment Bill introduced.
18 April 1887	*Times* publishes facsimile letter linking Parnell with Phoenix Park murders.
12 May 1887	Irish MPs oppose jubilee estimates bill.
12 May 1887	Duke of connaught leave bill opposed by some Irish MPs.
12 May 1887	Pope Leo XIII's jubilee.
14 May 1887	Queen booed by Irish on Mile End Road, London.
22 May 1887	Jubilee service at St. Margaret's, Westminster.
23 May 1887	Dublin Corporation decides not to attend the jubilee.
24 May 1887	Cork mayor refuses to attend jubilee.
9 June 1887	Wexford protests at mayor's acceptance of jubilee invitation.
19 June 1887	Triumphal progress of William O'Brien from Cork to Dublin.
21 June 1887	New York protest against Queen Victoria.
21 June 1887	Queen Victoria's Golden Jubilee.
27–30 June 1887	Princes Albert Victor and George visit Dublin.
23 August 1887	Land act.
9 September 1887	Three die at Mitchelstown.
1 December 1887	Dublin Unionist banquet for Hartington and Goschen.
31 January–2 Feburary 1888	Reception in Dublin for Ripon and Morley.
20 April 1888	Papal rescript condemns "Plan of Campaign."

24 December 1888	Land Purchase Act.
20–22 February 1889	Richard Pigott exposed as forger by special commission investigating Parnellism and crime.
21–23 May 1889	Prince Albert Victor visits Belfast.
4, 9 July 1889	Commons sets up select committee to consider Queen Victoria's request for annuities for her grandchildren.
17–23 July 1889	Parnell supports Gladstone's compromise over the annuities.
24 December 1889	O'Shea divorce filed, citing Parnell.
15, 17 November 1890	O'Shea divorce hearing.
25 November 1890	Parnell reelected as chairman of Irish Party.
28 November 1890	Parnell denounces Liberal alliance.
1–6 December 1890	Parnell ousted as Irish Parliamentary Party leader.
3 December 1890	Irish bishops' standing committee condemns Parnell.
3 February 1891	Failure of Irish Parliamentary Party reconciliation.
28 February 1891	Parnell's republican remarks in Meath.
3 April 1891	Parnell loses North Sligo election.
May 1891	Prince Albert Victor begins six months military service in Dublin.
25 June 1891	Parnell marries Katherine O'Shea.
7 July 1891	Parnell loses Carlow election.
5 August 1891	Land Purchase Act.
6 October 1891	Parnell dies.
31 October 1891	Princes Albert Victor and George visit Parnell's grave on the day of their return to England.
14 November 1891	Prince George gets typhoid after his visit to his brother in Dublin.
7 December 1891	Betrothal of Prince Albert Victor, duke of Clarence, to Princess May of Teck.
11 January 1892	Dublin Corporation refuses to make a loyal address but does agree to send a message on the betrothal of Prince Albert Victor, duke of Clarence.
14 January 1892	Death of Prince Albert Victor; Corporation sends condolences.
September 1892	Publication of Tait biography reassures nationalists about Queen Victoria.
7 October 1892	Lord Lieutenant Houghton refuses to receive address from Tory Dublin Chamber of Commerce.
24 December 1892	Explosion at Dublin Castle kills a policeman.
13 February 1893	Gladstone introduces home rule bill.
3 May 1893	Prince George, duke of York, and Princess May betrothed.
5 June 1893	Dublin Corporation declines to make a loyal address.
6 July 1893	Marriage of duke and duchess of York.

14 July 1893	John Redmond urges an amnesty on occasion of Commons' congratulations to the Yorks.
8 September 1893	Home rule bill defeated in the Lords.
12 March 1894	Rosebery agrees with Salisbury that England may veto home rule.
19 July 1895	Archbishop Croke's "National Jubilee."
24 January 1897	Jubilee Cross for Croke in Cashel.
13 March 1897	Lord Lieutenant Cadogan's Dublin Castle dinner for the queen's Diamond Jubilee.
17 May 1897	Dublin Corporation decides against a jubilee address.
28 May 1897	Manifesto of Irish Party against the jubilee.
17 June 1897	William Redmond criticizes the jubilee in the Commons.
20 June 1897	Maud Gonne protests her exclusion from precincts of nationalist tombs. Demonstration in Bodenstown.
21 June 1897	Commons address on jubilee opposed by Irish MPs. Maud Gonne addresses a Dublin meeting against the jubilee.
22 June 1897	St. Paul's Cathedral Diamond Jubilee service. Maud Gonne and James Connolly protest in Dublin.
3 July 1897	One Irish MP attends a Windsor garden party.
18 August– 9 September 1897	Duke and duchess of York visit Ireland.
15 September 1897	Michael Davitt disparages the royal visit.
10–22 April 1899	Duke and duchess of York visit Ireland.
3–5 July 1899	Duke and duchess of Connaught visit Ireland.
17 December 1899	Boer victory meeting in Dublin leads to a riot.
10 January 1900	The duke of Connaught becomes Irish commander-in-chief until 1902.
30 January 1900	Reunion of Irish Party under John Redmond.
1 March 1900	Pro-war Trinity College students attack Dublin Mansion House.
7 March 1900	Irish soldiers allowed to wear the shamrock.
8 March 1900	John Redmond makes a statement about the shamrock and the queen's visit in the Commons. Irish Transvaal Committee sends him a critical telegram.
9 March 1900	Private meeting of Dublin councillors agree to present an address to Queen Victoria.
9 March 1900	Sir Robert Sexton forms a citizens committee to greet the queen. It adjourns on 12 March in anticipation of a Corporation welcome.
12 March 1900	Letters critical of the visit and a Corporation address published from Anna Parnell, Tim Harrington, and William Redmond.
14 March 1900	Letter published from John Redmond saying his statement was misunderstood and that he is against an address.

16 March 1900	Lord Mayor Pile chairs Mansion House meeting about greeting the queen. The citizens's committee joins it.
17 March 1900	Disruption of lord mayor's procession in Dublin.
17 March 1900	Pro-Irish enthusiasm in London.
17 March 1900	Father Kavanagh and John Dillon attack the visit at Thurles.
19 March 1900	J. H. Parnell disagrees with his sister over the visit; she replies on 20 March.
20 March 1900	W. B. Yeats suggests a Rotunda meeting to mark the centenary of the union.
4–26 April 1900	Queen Victoria makes her fourth (and last) visit to Ireland.
4 April 1900	Police prevent nationalist demonstration.
4 April 1900	Anarchist assassination attempt on the Prince and Princess of Wales in Brussels.
4 April 1900	W. B. Yeats publishes his second letter against the visit.
4 April 1900	Police break up Dublin demonstration.
5 April 1900	Irish Guards formed.
7 April 1900	Maud Gonne publishes "The Famine Queen."
7 April 1900	Phoenix Park children's gathering.
8 April 1900	William O'Brien attacks the royal visit.
22 April 1900	Queen Victoria visits Castleknock College.
26 April 1900	Honors awarded in connection with the royal visit.
26 April 1900	James Egan, Dublin swordbearer, who refused to meet the queen, made freeman of Limerick.
1 July 1900	Gonne's Patriotic Children's Treat held at Clonturk Park, Dublin.
22 January 1901	Queen Victoria dies.
23 January 1901	Dublin Corporation passes resolution of condolences.
February 1901	Accession oath controversy.
2 February 1901	Queen Victoria's funeral. Forced closings in Ireland on mourning day.
7 March 1902	Irish MPs cheer Boer victory in the Commons.
13 March 1902	Edward VII postpones his visit to Ireland.
17 April 1902	John Redmond says Irish MPs will not attend the coronation.
31 May 1902	Boer War ends.
24 June 1902	Coronation postponed due to the king's illness.
10 August 1902	Coronation of Edward VII. The Irish Party protests at Dublin City Hall.
21 July–1 August 1903	King Edward and Queen Alexandra visit Ireland.
14 August 1903	"Wyndham" Land Act.
24 September 1903	George Moore converts to Protestantism.

26 April– 4 May 1904	King and queen visit Ireland for a second time. Maud Gonne, Arthur Griffith, and others form the National Guard to oppose the visit.
24 January– 4 February 1905	George, Prince of Wales, visits Ireland.
6 July 1907	Theft of "Irish crown jewels" discovered.
10–11 July 1907	King and queen visit Dublin Exhibition.
6 May 1910	Death of Edward VII and accession of George V.
7 May 1910	William Redmond asks Asquith to alter the oath of accession.
20 May 1910	Edward VII's funeral. Votive mass in Dublin Pro-Cathedral.
22 June 1911	Coronation of George V. Dublin demonstration addressed by Major MacBride and Countess Markiewicz.
4, 5 July 1911	Dublin Corporation fails to agree on an address to the king.
4 July 1911	Countess Markievicz and Helena Moloney burn British flags.
8–12 July 1911	King George and Queen Mary visit Ireland.
18 August 1911	Parliament bill passed.
11 April 1912	Home rule bill introduced.
16 January 1913	Home rule bill passed by Commons.
21 March 1914	Curragh mutiny.
24–5 April 1914	Larne gun running.
26 July 1914	Howth gun running and Bachelor's Walk shootings, which wound thirty-seven.
21–24 July 1914	Buckingham Palace Conference.
4 August 1914	World War I begins.
18 September 1914	Enacted Government of Ireland Act suspended for the duration of the war.
24–9 April 1916	Easter Rising.
18 April 1918	Irish Conscription Act.
21 January 1919	Dáil meets at Mansion House in Dublin.
December 1920	Government of Ireland Act.
22 June 1921	King George opens Northern Ireland parliament.
11 July 1921	Truce agreed between Irish and British forces.
6 December 1921	Anglo-Irish Treaty.
7 January 1922	Dáil ratifies the treaty.
14 April 1922	Anti-treaty forces seize the Four Courts in Dublin.
25 October 1922	Irish Constitution passed and T. M. Healy becomes governor general.
27 April 1923	End of Civil War.
11 December 1931	Statute of Westminster.

11 December 1936	Abdication of King Edward VIII.
11 December 1936	Constitution (Amendment No 27) Act removes the Crown and governor general from the Consitution. Executive Authority (External Relations) Act allows king to act for Ireland in external affairs only.
13 May 1937	Dublin statue of George II destroyed in an explosion the day after the coronation of King George VI.
14 June 1937	New Irish Constitution, establishing a presidency, is approved.
18 April 1949	Ireland becomes a republic and leaves the Commonwealth.
27 August 1979	Murder of Lord Mountbatten.
29 July 1981	Wedding of Prince and Princess of Wales.
27 May 1993	President Mary Robinson visits Queen Elizabeth II in London.
31 May–1 June 1995	Prince of Wales visits Ireland.
31 August 1997	Death of Diana, Princess of Wales.
10 April 1998	Good Friday Agreement.
10 November 1998	Duke of Edinburgh visits Dublin.
11 November 1998	President Mary McAleese and Queen Elizabeth II at Messines Ridge memorial.
12 December 1999	President McAleese visits Queen Elizabeth II in London.

Interaction Between Monarchy and Nationalism

Royal Event	Nationalist Reaction
20 June 1837 Queen Victoria's accession.	June 1837 O'Connell's Friends of the Queen, an anti-Tory electoral alliance and part of O'Connell's attempt to wrest "loyalty" from Toryism and for nationalism.
28 June 1838 Coronation.	Celebrations.
8–10 May 1839 Bedchamber Crisis.	25 May 1838 O'Connell's Dublin demonstration of thanks.
23 November 1839 Victoria's engagement to Albert.	5 December 1839 At Bandon, O'Connell's hyperbolic welcome for the engagement.
19 February 1840 Victoria and Albert marry.	Celebrations in Dublin. Orange riots in Derry.
10 June 1840 Oxford assassination attempt.	June 1840 O'Connell's letter on the subject leads to countrywide meetings.
2 November 1840 Birth of Princess Victoria.	Celebrations.
9 November 1841 Birth of Prince of Wales.	• O'Connell welcomes the birth. • Controversy when O'Connell as lord mayor is not offered the customary baronetcy on the birth of a princely heir.
9 May 1843 Peel tells Parliament that Victoria opposes repeal.	11 May 1843 O'Connell tells a meeting he does not believe it.
24 August 1843 Queen's prorogation speech defends the union.	29 August 1843 O'Connell attacks the speech but distinguishes it from the queen.

(table continues)

Royal Event	Nationalist Reaction
7 October 1843 Banning of Clontarf meeting.	9 October 1843 O'Connell denies that the queen was responsible for the banning.
7 April 1845 Royal visit to Ireland discussed.	• 28 April O'Connell contrives to oppose it, recognizing the failure of his "loyalty" policy. • 21 May Lord mayor of Dublin petitions the queen to visit but receives a noncommittal reply. • 30 May, 8 June O'Connell's "national levees" in Dublin and Cork parody royalty.
2–11 August 1849 Victoria and Albert visit Ireland.	• Enthusiastic welcome by populace in Dublin. • Controversy over public illuminations in Dublin and amnesty for 1848 convicts in Cork. • Abortive plan by a small group to kidnap the queen.
17 May 1850 Government bill to abolish lord lieutenancy.	10 March 1851 Dublin Corporation presents petition to queen, who gives a noncommittal reply.
29 August to 3 September 1853 Victoria and Albert visit the Dargan Exhibition in Dublin.	Enthusiastic welcome by populace of Dublin.
April 1858 Visit by Prince of Wales.	Summer 1858 Cardinal Wiseman's triumphant tour of Ireland.
26 June 1858 Very brief visit by Prince Alfred to Limerick.	Mayor takes him to view the statue of O'Connell.
17 March 1859 Prince of Wales calls on Irish College, Rome.	Paul Cullen takes him to nearby church to view a statue of O'Connell.
September 1860 Prince of Wales refuses Orange welcomes in Canada.	His decision is welcomed in Ireland.
22–29 August 1861 Victoria and Albert visit Dublin (driving through the principal streets), the Curragh, and Kerry.	• The royal visitors are enthusiastically received. • 10 November 1861 T. B. McManus funeral. Patrick Lavelle contrasts patriotic exile McManus with Castle supporters. • 20 July 1862 Catholic University ceremony in Drumdondra.
10 March 1863 Marriage of Prince and Princess of Wales.	• Disturbances in Dublin and Cork. • Dublin Corporation presents addresses to queen and Prince of Wales.
8 January 1864 Birth of Prince Albert Victor.	Controversy in Dublin Corporation over an address; agreed eventually.

Royal Event	Nationalist Reaction
17 May 1864 Revelation that queen has approved College Green site for Albert statue.	18 December 1865 Intense private negotiations lead to Albert committee choosing Leinster Lawn instead—as the Dublin Corporation is now unwilling to allow College Green to be used.
8–12 May 1865 Prince of Wales opens Dublin Exhibition.	20 August 1866 Reception for new cardinal Cullen in Dublin.
3 June 1865 Birth of Prince George.	26 July 1865 Dublin Corporation present a loyal address.
27 May 1867 Clemency for Thomas Burke who had been sentenced to death.	Clemency interpreted as compassion on the part of the queen.
12 March 1868 Assassination attempt on Prince Alfred in Australia.	14 May 1868 Dublin lord mayor presents queen with an address.
15–24 April 1868 Ceremonial visit by Prince and Princess of Wales to Dublin.	• Enthusiastic reception of royal visitors. • Beginning of amnesty movement.
5 March 1869 Amnesty petitioners meet the queen.	Amnesty petitioners think she is sympathetic.
5 April–4 May 1869 Visit by Prince Arthur.	27 April 1869 At a banquet for released Fenians, Mayor O'Sullivan of Cork expresses approval of assassination of princes. A Commons bill to disbar him from office forces him to resign.
21 March 1871 Marriage of Princess Louise to Lord Lorne. Rumors of queen's Presbyterianism.	• 14 March 1871 Irish ladies present amnesty petition. • 24 March 1871 Dublin Corporation presents a loyal address.
31 July 1871 Prince Arthur annuity vote.	28 Irish MPs vote against it.
31 July–7 August 1871 Prince of Wales, Prince Arthur, and the Lornes visit Dublin Agricultural Exhibition.	• 6 August 1871 Amnesty meeting in Phoenix Park broken up by police. • August 1871 French republicans under Count de Flavigny feted by A. M. Sullivan.
23 October 1871 Receipt of reply in the name of an ill queen by Home Secretary Bruce to amnesty petition.	Bruce's reply denounced by Isaac Butt.
4–8 June 1872 Prince Alfred opens Dublin exhibition and views partially complete Albert statue.	9 June 1875 Attack on the Albert statue.

(table continues)

Royal Event	Nationalist Reaction
7 July 1875 Commons debates money for Prince of Wales's Indian trip.	Opposed by Joseph Biggar.
March 1876 Royal titles bill.	Muted opposition from Irish MPs in hopes of Fenian amnesty.
11 May 1876 Return of Prince of Wales from successful tour of India.	24 July 1876 Dublin Corporation presents address to queen, after some oppposition on account of the Prince of Wale's apparent anti-Catholicism in Malta.
13 March 1879 Marriage of Prince Arthur, duke of Connaught, to Louise of Prussia.	• 25 July 1878 Commons approves marriage grant. • 20 November 1878 Dublin lord mayor proposes marriage gift for Connaughts. • 20 December 1878 Cork mayor's meeting for Connaughts gift fails. • 10 March 1879 Dublin lord mayor presents first part of gift to Prince Arthur. • 27 October 1879 Presentation of silver service to Connaughts.
14 December 1878 Death of Princess Alice.	Dublin Corporation telegrams sympathies to queen.
9 January 1879 Report that Queen Victoria has tried to dissuade Empress Elizabeth from visiting Ireland.	• March 1879 Controversy over the empress's rudeness in Dublin following her visit to Ireland, 22 February–23 March. • 4 February–7 March 1880 Empress Elizabeth's second visit. • 26 January 1881 Parnell and Irish MPs advise the empress that it is safe to return again, to Queen Victoria's anger.
22 April 1880 Prince Alfred, duke of Edinburgh, helps with U.S. relief ship.	4 May 1880 Freedom of Dublin given to captain of the U.S. ship.
2 March 1882 Assassination attempt on queen.	6 March 1882 Dublin Corporation congratulates queen on her escape.
23 March 1882 Prince Leopold's annuity vote.	Irish MPs vote against it.
28–31 August 1884 Visit by Prince Alfred to Dublin Horse Show. He is later warmly greeted by Cork mayor.	• 1 September Dublin lord mayor explains why there was no greeting for him. • 12 September Cork mayor reprimanded for his greeting.

Royal Event	Nationalist Reaction
• 7–26 April 1885 Visit by Prince and Princess of Wales.	• 1 March William O'Brien attacks royal visit at Phoenix Park meeting. • 3 March National League criticism.
• 11 April *Times* proclaims the visit a triumph and a defeat for Parnell.	• 13 March Irish Party asks people to be neutral about the visit. • 16 March Dublin Corporation vote not to take part in it. • 20 March Cork Corporation vote similarly. • 12 April Ten monster meetings call for neutrality toward the visit. • 13 April O'Brien and others insult the Prince and Princess of Wales at Mallow. • 15 April Insults for royal couple at Cork.
14 May 1885 Commons debate over annuity for Princess Beatrice.	Opposed by several Irish Party MPs.
12 May 1887 Duke of Connaught leave bill.	Opposed by Irish Party MPs.
12 May 1887 Jubilee estimates.	Opposed by some Irish MPs.
14 May 1887 Victoria's visit to East End of London.	She is insulted by Irish residents.
22 May 1887 Commons jubilee service.	Boycotted by Irish Party MPs.
21 June 1887 Golden Jubilee.	• 23 May Dublin Corporation refuses to attend. • 24 May Cork mayor rejects invitation. • 9 June Wexford protests at mayor's acceptance of invitation. • 19 June: Triumphal progress of William O'Brien from Cork to Dublin on his return from North America. • 21 June: New York rally against Queen Victoria.
• 27–30 June 1887 Postjubilee visit of Princes Albert Victor and George to Dublin.	31 January–2 February 1888 Ripon and Morley receive enthusiastic reception in Dublin and freedom of the city.
• 1 December 1887 Dublin Unionist banquet for Hartington and Goschen.	
July 1889 Commons controversy over money for next generation of royal family.	Under Gladstone's urging, Parnell gets Irish Party to support compromise arrangements.

(table continues)

Royal Event	Nationalist Reaction
7 December 1891 Betrothal of Prince Albert Victor, duke of Clarence, to Princess Mary of Teck.	11 January 1892 Dublin Corporation disputes over an address.
14 January 1892 Death of Prince Albert Victor, duke of Clarence.	Dublin Corporation sends condolences.
3 May 1893 Betrothal of Princess Mary of Teck and Prince George, duke of York.	• 5 June 1893 Defeat of Dublin Corporation motion for loyal addresses. • 14 July 1893 Commons congratulations on prince's engagement: Redmond urges amnesty.
1897 Jubilee (general).	• 19 July 1895 "National" Jubilee for Archbishop Croke. • 14 January 1897 Jubilee Cross for Croke at Cashel. • 1898 Anniversary celebrations for 1798.

1897 Jubilee (specific).	• 17 May Dublin Corporation vote against an address.
	• 28 May Irish Party manifesto against the jubilee.
	• 17 June William Redmond criticizes jubilee in Commons.
	• 20 June Demonstration at Bodenstown.
	   • Maud Gonne protests the banning of visits to tombs of Irish patriots.
	• 21 June Commons jubilee address opposed by Irish Party.
	   • Gonne addresses Dublin anti-jubilee meeting.
	• 22 June Gonne and Connolly protest in Dublin.
	• 3 July One Irish Party MP attends Windsor garden party.

18 August–9 September 1897 Visit by the duke and duchess of York; English press see it as a success.	15 September 1897 Michael Davitt denies it was a success.
4–26 April 1900 Visit by Queen Victoria to Dublin.	• The visit is enthusiastically received.
• 7 March Irish soldiers to be allowed to wear shamrock.	• 1 March Pro-war Trinity College students attack Mansion House.

Royal Event	Nationalist Reaction
• 17 March British enthusiasm for Ireland in London.	• 8 March John Redmond welcomes the visit in the Commons but later, under criticism, changes his position.
• 4 April Arrival of queen.	• Criticism of Dublin lord mayor for agreeing to greet the queen.
• 5 April Formation of Irish Guards.	• 20 March Yeats suggests a protest on 2 April, centenary of passing of the union.
• 7 April Thousands of children see the queen in the Phoenix Park.	• 4 April Police break up nationalist demonstration.
• 26 April Honors awarded in connection with the queen's visit.	• 7 April Seizure of *United Irishman* because of Gonne's "Famine Queen" article. • 8 April William O'Brien attacks the visit at United Irish League rally in Killarney. • 26 April James Egan, Dublin swordbearer, who refused to greet queen, made freeman of Limerick. • 1 July Gonne holds a patriotic treat for children opposed to the Phoenix Park rally.
22 January 1901 Death of queen.	23 January Dublin Corporation votes condolences.
13 March 1902 Edward VII's visit to Ireland postponed.	Because Irish Party MPs cheered Boer victory in Commons on 7 March.
10 August 1902 Coronation.	Irish Party protests in Dublin.
21 July to 1 August 1903 Visit of Edward VII.	• Enthusiastically received. • 24 September George Moore converts to Protestantism because Irish Catholic clergy received King Edward!
26 April to 4 May 1904 Visit of Edward VII.	Gonne and Griffith form National Guard to oppose the visit; in 1908 it merges with Sinn Féin League to become Sinn Féin.
20 May 1910 Funeral of Edward VII.	Votive mass in Dublin's Pro-Cathedral.
22 June 1911 Coronation of George V.	Major MacBride and Countess Markiwicz protest in Dublin.
8–12 July 1911 Visit of George V.	5 July Dublin Corporation fails to agree on an address.
22 June 1921 George V opens Stormont parliament.	Helps to open negotiations between British Government and Sinn Féin.

Bibliography

ARCHIVES

Britain

Royal Archives: Windsor Castle
Queen Victoria Papers
Queen Victoria Journals

Ireland

National Archives Ireland
Chief Secretary's Office Registered Papers
National Library of Ireland
General Sir Thomas Larcom papers

NEWSPAPERS AND JOURNALS

Australia

Melbourne Argus

Britain

Contemporary Review	*Nineteenth Century*
Court Circular	*Observer*
Daily Express	*Pall Mall Gazette*
Daily Telegraph	*Pilot*
Globe	*Punch*
Illustrated London News	*Reynolds's Newspaper*
London Gazette	*Spectator*
London Review	*Star*
Manchester Courier	*Times*
Manchester Guardian	*Truth*
Morning Herald	*Weekly Register*
Morning Post	*Westminster Gazette*

France

Courier du Soir
Gazette de France

Ireland

Belfast Newsletter	*Irish Figaro*
Belfast Weekly Vindicator	*Irishman*
Catholic	*Irish Monthly*
Cork Constitution	*Irish People*
Cork Examiner	*Irish Times*
Daily Express	*Munster News*
Dublin Evening Mail	*Nation*
Dublin Evening Packet	*Nationalist and Leinster Times*
Dublin Evening Post	*National Press*
Dublin Gazette	*Morning News*
Dublin Mercantile Advertiser and Weekly Prices Current	*Press*
Dublin University Magazine	*Saunder's News-Letter*
Dublin Weekly Register	*Southern Reporter*
Evening Herald	*United Ireland*
Freeman's Journal	*United Irishman* (John Mitchel)
Irish Daily Independent	*United Irishman* (Arthur Griffith)
Irish Felon	*Weekly Freeman's Journal*
	Weekly News

United States of America

Celtic Monthly
New York Herald
New York Times

PUBLISHED PAPERS

Aspinall, A., ed. *Letters of George IV, 1812–30.* 3 vols. Cambridge: Cambridge University Press, 1938.

———, ed. *The Diary of Henry Hobhouse, 1820–1827.* London: Home and Van Thal, 1947.

Bahlman, Dudley W. R., ed. *The Diary of Sir Edward Walter Hamilton, 1885–1906.* 2 vols. Oxford: Clarendon Press, 1972.

Bolitho, Hector, ed. *The Prince Consort and His Brother: Two Hundred New Letters.* New York: Appleton Century, 1934.

———, ed. *Letters of Queen Victoria from the Archives of the House of Brandenburg-Prussia.* New Haven, Conn.: Yale University Press, 1938.

———, ed. *Further Letters of Queen Victorian from the Archives of the House of Brandenburg-Prussia.* London: Thornton, Butterworth, 1938.

Brett, Maurice V., ed. *Journals and Letters of Reginald Viscount Esher, Vol. 1: (1870–1903).* London: Ivor Nicholson and Watson, 1934.

Brooke, John, and Mary Sorensen, eds. *The Prime Ministers' Papers: W. E. Gladstone.* 4 vols. London: Royal Commission on Historical Manuscripts, 1971–1981.

Chichester Samuel Parkinson Fortesque, Baron Carlingford. *Lord Carlingford's Journal.* Edited by A. B. Cooke and J. A. Vincent. Oxford: Oxford University Press, 1971.

Collier, E. C. F. *A Victorian Diarist: Extracts from the Journals of Mary, Lady Monkswell, 1875–1895.* London: John Murray, 1944.

———. *A Victorian Diarist: Later Extracts from the Journals of Mary, Lady Monkswell, 1895–1909.* London: John Murray, 1946.

Connell, Brian. *Regina v. Palmerston: The Correspondence between Queen Victoria and Her Foreign and Prime Minister, 1837–1865.* London: Evans Brothers, 1962.

Cusack, M. F., ed. *The Speeches and Public Letters of the Liberator.* 2 vols. Dublin: McGlashan and Gill, 1875.

Dean of Windsor and Hector Bolitho, eds. *Letters of Lady Augusta Stanley: A Young Lady at Court, 1849–1863.* New York: George H. Doran, 1927.

Dowden, Wilfred S. *The Letters of Thomas Moore.* Oxford: Clarendon Press, 1994.

Esher, Viscount. [*The Training of a Sovereign.*] *The Girlhood of Queen Victoria: A Selection of Queen Victoria's Diaries, 1832–1840.* London: John Muray, 1912.

Fitzpatrick, W. J., ed. *The Correspondence of Daniel O'Connell the Liberator.* 2 vols. 1875; Dublin: John Murray, 1888.

Foot, M. R. D., and H. G. C. Matthew. *The Gladstone Diaries.* 14 vols. Oxford: Clarendon Press, 1968–1994.

Fulford, Roger, ed. *Dearest Child: Private Correspondence of Queen Victoria and the Princess Royal, 1858–61.* 1964; London: Evans, 1977.

———, ed. *Dearest Mama: Private Correspondence of Queen Victoria and the Crown Princess of Prussia, 1861–64.* 1968; London: Evans, 1977.

———, ed. *Your Dear Letter: Private Correspondence of Queen Victoria and the Crown Princess of Prussia, 1865–71.* London: Evans, 1971.

———, ed. *Darling Child: Private Correspondence of Queen Victoria and the Crown Princess of Prussia, 1871–78.* London: Evans, 1976.

———, ed. *Beloved Mamma: Private Correspondence of Queen Victoria and the German Crown Princess, 1878–85.* London: Evans, 1981.

Gooch, G. P. *The Later Correspondence of Lord John Russell, 1840–1878.* 2 vols. London: Longmans Green, 1925.

Gordon, Peter. *The Red Earl. Papers of the Fifth Earl Spencer, Vol. 1: 1835–1885.* Northampton: Northampton Records Society, 1981.

———. *The Red Earl. Papers of the Fifth Earl Spencer, Vol. 2: 1885–1910.* Northampton: Northampton Records Society, 1986.

Greville, Charles. *The Greville Memoirs, Part 1: A Journal of the Reigns of King George IV and King William IV.* 3 vols. London: Longmans, Green, 1874.

———. *The Greville Memoirs, Part 2: A Journal of the Reign of Queen Victoria from 1837 to 1852.* 3 vols. Edited by Henry Reeve. London: Longmans, Green, 1885.

———. *The Greville Memoirs, Part 3: A Journal of the Reign of Queen Victoria from 1852 to 1860.* 2 vols. Edited by Henry Reeve. London: Longmans, Green, 1887.

———. *The Greville Memoirs: A Journal of the Reigns of King George IV, King William IV, and Queen Victoria.* 8 vols. Edited by Henry Reeve. London: Longmans Green, 1896.

———. *The Letters of Charles Greville and Henry Reeve, 1836–65.* Edited by A. H. Johnson. London: Unwin, 1924.

———. *The Greville Diary.* 2 vols. Edited by Philip Whitwell Wilson. London: Heineman, 1927.

————. *The Greville Memoirs, 1814–60.* 7 vols. Edited by Lytton Strachey and Roger Fulford. London: Macmillan, 1938.

Gould, Warwick, John Kelly, and Deirdre Toomey, eds. *The Collected Letters of W. B. Yeats, Vol. 2: 1896–1900.* Oxford: Clarendon Press, 1996.

Hansard's Parliamentary Debates. 3d Series (1830–1891). 4th Series (1892–1908).

Hibbert, Christopher, ed. *Queen Victoria in Her Letters and Journals: A Selection by Christopher Hibbert.* London: John Murray, 1984.

Hutton, A. W., and H. J. Cohen, eds. *The Speeches and Public Addresses of the Rt Hon. W. E. Gladstone, MP.* 10 vols. London: Methuen, 1894.

Jagow, Kurt, ed. *Letters of the Prince Consort, 1831–1861.* Translated by E. T. S. Dugdale. London: John Murray, 1938.

Jennings, Louis, ed. *The Croker Papers: The Correspondence and Papers of the Late Right Honourable John Wilson Croker.* 3 vols. London: John Murray, 1884.

Johnson, Nancy E., ed. *The Diary of Gathorne Hardy, Later Lord Cranbrook, Political Selections 1866–92.* Oxford: Clarendon Press, 1981.

Kapp, Friedrich, trans. *Letters of Alexander von Humboldt to Varnhagen von Ense from 1827 to 1858.* 1859; London: Trübner & Co., 1860.

Kelly, John, and Eric Domville, eds. *The Collected Letters of W. B. Yeats, Vol. 1: 1865–189).* Oxford: Clarendon Press, 1986.

Kelly, John, and Ronald Schuchard, eds. *The Collected Letters of W. B. Yeats, Vol. 3: 1901–1904.* Oxford: Clarendon Press, 1994.

Kennedy, A. L., ed. *My Dear Duchess: Social and Political Letters to the Duchess of Manchester, 1858–1868.* London: John Murray, 1956.

Laurence, D., ed. *Collected Letters of Bernard Shaw.* 3 vols. New York: Viking, 1985.

Lytton, Lady. *Notebooks of a Spinster Lady, 1878–1903.* New York: Cassell, 1919.

Longford, Elizabeth. *Darling Loosy: Letters to Princess Louise, 1856–1939.* London: Weidenfeld and Nicolson, 1991.

MacBride White, Anna, and A. Norman Jeffares, eds. *The Gonne-Yeats Letters, 1893–1938: "Always Your Friend."* London: Hutchinson, 1992.

Mallet, Marie. *Life with Queen Victoria: Marie Mallet's Letters from Court, 1887–1901.* Edited by Victor Mallet. London: John Murray, 1968.

O'Connell, John, ed. *The Life and Speeches of Daniel O'Connell.* 2 vols. Dublin: James Duffy, 1846.

————, ed. *The Select Speeches of Daniel O'Connell.* 2 vols. Dublin, 1854.

O'Connell, Maurice R., ed. *The Correspondence of Daniel O'Connell.* 8 vols. Dublin: Blackwater, 1972–1980.

Pethica, James, ed. *Lady Gregory's Diaries, 1892–1902.* Gerrards Cross: Colin Smythe, 1996.

Ponsonby, Frederick. *The Letters of the Empress Frederick.* London: Macmillan, 1929.

Powell, Anthony, ed. *The Barnard Letters, 1778–1824.* 2 vols. London: Duckworth, 1928.

Ramm, Agatha, ed. *Political Correspondence of Mr Gladstone and Lord Granville, 1876–1886.* 2 vols. Oxford: Oxford University Press, 1962.

————. *Beloved and Darling Child: Last Letters between Queen Victoria and Her Eldest Daughter, 1886–1901.* Stroud: Alan Sutton, 1990.

Robinson, Lionel G., ed. *Letters of Dorothea, Princess Lieven during Her Residence in London, 1812–34.* London: Longmans & Co., 1902.

Sanders, Lloyd C. *Lord Melbourne's Papers.* London: Longmans, Green, 1889.

Stoney, Benita, and Heinrich C. Weltzien, eds. *My Mistress the Queen: The Letters of Frieda Arnold, Dresser to Queen Victoria, 1854–9.* Translated by Sheila de Bellaigue. London: Weidenfeld and Nicolson, 1994.

Victoria, Queen. *Letters of Queen Victoria, First Series, 1837–1861.* 3 vols. Edited by A. C. Benson and Viscount Esher. London: John Murray, 1907.

———. *Letters of Queen Victoria, Second Series, 1862–1885.* 3 vols. Edited by George Earle Buckle. London: John Murray, 1926, 1926, 1928.

———. *Letters of Queen Victoria, Third Series, 1886–1901.* 3 vols. Edited by George Earle Buckle. London: John Murray, 1930, 1931, 1932.

Vincent, John, ed. *Disraeli, Derby, and the Conservative Party: Journals and Memoirs of Edward Henry, Lord Stanley, 1849–1869.* Hassocks: Harvester, 1978.

———, ed. *The Crawford Papers: The Journals of David Lindsay, Twenty-Seventh Earl of Crawford and Tenth Earl of Balcarres, 1871–1940.* Manchester: Manchester University Press, 1984.

Weintraub, Stanley, ed. *Bernard Shaw Diaries.* University Park: University of Pennsylvania Press, 1986.

Wellington, A., ed. *Despatches, Correspondence, and Memoranda of Arthur Duke of Wellington.* 8 vols. Edited by Sidney Owen. London, 1867–1880.

Wiebe, M. G., and J. A. W. Gunn, eds. *Benjamin Disraeli, Letters.* Vol. 3, *1838–1841*; Vol. 4, *1842–1847*; Vol. 5, *1848–1851.* Toronto and Buffalo: University of Toronto Press, 1987, 1989, 1993.

Zetland, Marquis of. *Letters of Disraeli to Lady Chesterfield and Lady Bradford.* 2 vols. London: Benn, 1929.

BOOKS AND ARTICLES

Aalen, F. H. A., and Kevin Whelan, eds. *Dublin City and County: From Prehistory to Present.* Dublin: Geography Publications, 1992.

Albert, Harold A. *Queen Victoria's Sister.* London: Robert Hale, 1967.

Alter, Peter. "Symbols of Irish Nationalism." *Studia Hibernica* 14 (1974): 104–23.

Altick, Richard D. *The English Common Reader: A Social History of the Mass Reading Public, 1800–1900.* Chicago: University of Chicago Press, 1957.

———. *Victorian People and Ideas.* London: Dent, 1974.

Anderson, Benedict. *Imagined Communities: Reflections on the Origin and Spread of Nationalism.* 1981. London: Verso, 1983.

Arnstein, Walter L. "Queen Victoria's Speeches from the Throne: A New Look." In Alan O'Day, ed., *Government and Institutions in the Post-1832 United Kingdom* (Lewiston, N.Y.: Edward Mellen, 1995), 127–53.

———. "Queen Victoria's Other Island." In William Roger Louis, ed., *More Adventures with Britannia: Personalities, Politics, and Culture in Britain* (Austin: University of Texas Press, 1999), 45–66.

Ashdown, Dulcie. *Queen Victoria's Family.* London: Hale, 1975.

———. *Victoria and the Coburgs.* London: Hale, 1981.

Aspinall, A. *Lord Brougham and the Whig Party.* Manchester: Manchester University Press, 1927.

———. *Politics and the Press c. 1780–1850.* London: Home and Van Thal, 1949.

Auchincloss, Louis. *Persons of Consequence: Queen Victoria and Her Circle.* London: Weidenfeld and Nicolson, 1979.

Bagehot, Walter. *The English Constitution.* 1867; London: Fontana, 1979.

Baker, Sybil E. "Orange and Green: Belfast, 1832–1912." In H. J. Dyos and M. Wolff, eds., *The Victorian City: Images and Realities,* 2 vols. (London: Kegan Paul, 1973), 2:789–814.

Banks, Marcus. *Ethnicity: Anthropological Constructions.* London: Routledge, 1996.

Bardon, Jonathan. *A History of Ulster.* Belfast: Blackstaff, 1992.

Bartlett, Thomas. *The Fall and Rise of the Irish Nation: The Catholic Question, 1690–1830.* Dublin: Gill and Macmillan, 1992.

Beckett, J. V. *The Aristocracy in England, 1660–1914.* Oxford: Blackwell, 1986.

Bell, Robert. *A Description of the Conditions and Manners of the Peasantry of Ireland.* London, 1804.

Bendix, Reinhard. *Kings or People: Power and the Mandate to Rule.* London: University of California Press, 1978.

Bew, Paul. *C. S. Parnell.* Dublin: Gill and Macmillan, 1980.

———. *John Redmond.* Dundalk: Dundalgan Press, 1996.

Biggs-Davison, John, and George Chowdharay-Best. *The Cross of St Patrick: The Catholic Unionist Tradition in Ireland.* Abbotsbrook: Kensal, 1984.

Blake, Robert. *Disraeli.* London: Oxford University Press, 1969.

Bolitho, Hector. *Victoria the Widow and Her Son.* London: Cobden-Sanderson, 1934.

Bourne, K. *Palmerston: The Early Years, 1784–1841.* London: Allen Lane, 1982.

Boyce, D. G. "The Marginal Britons: The Irish." In Robert Colls and Philip Dodd, eds., *Englishness: Politics and Culture, 1880–1920* (London: Croom Helm, 1986), 230–53.

———. *Nineteenth-Century Ireland: The Search for Stability.* Dublin: Gill and Macmillan, 1990.

———. *Nationalism in Ireland.* 3d ed. London: Routledge, 1995.

Boyce, D. G., Robert Eccleshall, and Vincent Geoghegan, eds. *Political Thought in Ireland since the Seventeenth Century.* London: Routledge, 1993.

Bradshaw, Brendan, and Peter Roberts. *British Consciousness and Identity: The Making of Britain, 1533–1707.* Cambridge: Cambridge University Press, 1998.

Brent, Richard. *Liberal Anglican Politics: Whiggery, Religion, and Reform, 1830–1841.* Oxford: Clarendon Press, 1987.

[Brougham, Lord]. *Letter to the Queen on the State of the Monarchy by a Friend of the People.* London: Simpkin, Marshall, 1839.

Broughton, Lord. [John Hobhouse]. *Recollections of a Long Life, with Additional Extracts from His Private Diaries.* 6 vols. Edited by Lady Dorchester. London: John Murray, 1909–1911.

Brown, Terence. *The Life of W. B. Yeats.* Dublin: Gill and Macmillan, 1999.

Brynn, Edward. *Crown and Castle: British Rule in Ireland, 1800–1830.* Dublin: O'Brien, 1978.

Buckland, Patrick. *Irish Unionism, Vol. 1: The Anglo-Irish and the New Ireland, 1885–1922.* Dublin: Gill and Macmillan, 1972.

———. *Irish Unionism, Vol. 2: Ulster Unionism and the Origins of Northern Ireland, 1886–1922.* Dublin: Gill and Macmillan, 1973.

Buckle, G. E., and W. F. Monypenny. *The Life of Benjamin Disraeli, Earl of Beaconsfield.* London: John Murray, 1929.

Bulwer, H. L., and E. W. Ashley. *The Life of Henry John Temple, Viscount Palmerston, with Selections from His Correspondence.* 5 vols. London: Richard Bentley, 1870–1876.

Burke, S. Hubert. *Ireland Sixty Years Ago.* London: John Hodges, 1885.

[Butt, Isaac.] "Ireland under Lord Clarendon." *Dublin University Magazine* 39 (1853): 377–83.

———. *Home Government for Ireland. Irish Federalism: Its Meaning, Its Objects, and Its Hopes.* 1870. Dublin: Irish Home Rule League, 1874.

———. *Ireland's Appeal for Amnesty.* Glasgow: Cameron and Ferguson, 1870.

Byron, Lord. *The Poetical Works of Lord Byron.* London: John Murray, 1876.

Callanan, Frank. *T. M. Healy.* Cork: Cork University Press, 1996.

Cannadine, David. *Lord and Landlords: The Aristocracy and the Towns, 1774–1967.* Leicester: Leicester University Press, 1980.

———. "The Context, Performance, and Meaning of Ritual: The British Monarchy and the 'Invention of Tradition,' c 1820–1977." In Eric Hobsbaum and Terence Ranger, eds., *The Invention of Tradition* (Cambridge: Cambridge University Press, 1983), 101–64.

———. *The Decline and Fall of the British Aristocracy, 1880–1980.* New Haven and London: Yale University Press, 1990.

Cannon, John, and Ralph Griffiths, eds. *Oxford Illustrated History of the British Monarchy.* Oxford: Oxford University Press, 1988.

Carlyle, Thomas. *Reminiscences of My Irish Journey in 1849.* London: Sampson Low, Marston, Searle and Rivington, 1882.

Cecil, Algernon. *Queen Victoria and Her Prime Ministers.* London: Eyre and Spottiswoode, 1953.

Chadwick, H. M. *The Nationalities of Europe and the Growth of National Ideologies.* Cambridge: Cambridge University Press, 1945.

Chilston, Viscount. *W. H. Smith.* London: Routledge and Kegan Paul, 1965.

Churchill, Jennie. *Reminiscences of Lady Randolph Churchill.* New York: Century, 1908.

Clark, J. C. D. *English Society, 1688–1832: Ideology, Social Structure, and Political Practice during the Ancien Regime.* Cambridge: Cambridge University Press, 1985.

Cloncurry, Valentine Baron. *Personal Recollections of the Life and Times, with Extracts from the Correspondence of, Valentine Lord Cloncurry.* Dublin: James McGlashan, 1849.

Colley, Linda. "The Apotheosis of George III: Loyalty, Royalty, and the British Nation, 1760–1820." *Past and Present* 102 (1984): 94–129.

———. *Britons: Forging the Nation, 1707–1837.* New Haven, Conn.: Yale University Press, 1992.

———. "Britishness and Otherness: An Argument." In Michael O'Dea and Kevin Whelan, eds., *Nations and Nationalism: France, Britain, Ireland, and the Eighteenth-Century Context,* Studies in Voltaire and the Eighteenth Century Vol. 335 (Oxford: Voltaire Foundation, 1995), 61–77.

Conacher, James. *The Aberdeen Coalition, 1852–55: A Study in Mid-Nineteenth-Century Party Politics.* Cambridge: Cambridge University Press, 1968.

———. *The Peelites and the Party System, 1846–52.* Newton Abbot: David and Charles, 1972.

Comerford, R. V. *Charles J. Kickham: A Study in Irish Nationalism and Literature.* Dublin: Wolfhound, 1979.

———. *The Fenians in Context.* Dublin: Wolfhound, 1985.

———. "Patriotism as Pastime: The Appeal of Fenianism in the Mid-1860s." In *Reactions to Irish Nationalism, 1865–1914* (Dublin: Gill and Macmillan, 1987), 21–32.

Cookson, J. *Lord Liverpool's Administration, 1815–1822.* Edinburgh: Scottish Academic Press, 1975.

Corish, Patrick J. *Maynooth College, 1795–1995.* Dublin: Gill and Macmillan, 1995.

Côté, Jane McL. *Fanny and Anna Parnell.* Dublin: Gill and Macmillan, 1991.

Cowper, K. C. C. *Earl Cowper, K.G.: A Memoir.* Privately printed, 1913.

Coxhead, Elizabeth. *Daughters of Erin: Five Women of the Irish Renaissance.* London: Secker and Warburg, 1965.

[Croker, J. W.] "Lord Clarendon and the Orange Institution." *Quarterly Review* 86 (December 1849): 228–94.

Crosby, T. L. *Sir Robert Peel's Administration, 1841–46.* Newton Abbot: David and Charles, 1976.

Cullen, L. M. *Princes and Pirates: The Dublin Chamber of Commerce, 1783–1983.* Dublin: Dublin Chamber of Commerce, 1983.

Cunningham, Hugh. "The Language of Patriotism." *History Workshop* 12 (Autumn 1981): 23–4.

————. "The Conservative Party and Patriotism." In Robert Colls and Philip Dodd, eds., *Englishness, Politics, and Culture, 1880–1920* (London: Croom Helm, 1986), 283–307.

Curtin, Nancy J. *The United Irishmen: Popular Politics in Ulster and Dublin, 1791–98.* Oxford: Clarendon Press, 1994.

[D'Alton, John]. *Visit of Her Most Gracious Majesty Queen Victoria and His Royal Highness Prince Albert to Ireland, August 1849.* Dublin, 1849 [not published].

Daly, Mary E. *Dublin the Deposed Capital: A Social and Economic History, 1860–1914.* Cork: Cork University Press, 1985.

————. *The Famine in Ireland.* Dundalk: Dun Dealgan, 1986.

Daunt, W. J. O'Neill. *Eight-Five Years of Irish History, 1800–1885.* 2 vols. London: Ward and Downey, 1886.

Davidson, R. T., and William Benham. *Life of Archibald Campbell Tait, Archbishop of Canterbury.* 2 vols. London and New York: Macmillan, 1891.

Davies, Alun C. "Ireland's Crystal Palace, 1853." In J. M. Goldstrom and L. A. Clarkson, eds., *Irish Population, Economy, and Society: Essays in Honour of the Late K. H. Connell* (Oxford: Clarendon Press, 1981), 249–70.

Davies, John. "Victoria and Victorian Wales." In Geraint H. Jenkins and J. Beverley Smith, eds., *Politics and Society in Wales, 1840–1922. Essays in Honour of I. G. Jones* (Cardiff: University of Wales Press, 1988), 7–28.

Davies, Norman. *The Isles: A History.* London: Macmillan, 1999.

Davis, Richard. *The Young Ireland Movement.* Dublin: Gill and Macmillan, 1987.

————. *Revolutionary Imperialist: William Smith O'Brien.* Dublin: Lilliput, 1998.

Denieffe, Joseph. *A Personal Narrative of the Irish Revolutionary Brotherhood, Giving a Faithful Report of the Principal Events from 1855 to 1867, Written at the Request of Friends.* New York: Gael, 1906.

Dennis, Barbara, and David Skilton, eds. *Reform and Intellectual Debate in Victorian England.* London: Croom Helm, 1987.

De Vere White, Terence. *Kevin O'Higgins.* Tralee: Anvil, 1965.

Devine, T. M., and D. Dickson, eds. *Ireland and Scotland, 1600–1850: Parallels and Contrasts in Economic and Social Developments.* Edinburgh: John Donald, 1983.

Devine, T. M., and Rosalind Mitchison, eds. *People and Society in Scotland, Vol. 1: 1760–1830.* Edinburgh: John Donald, 1988.

Devoy, John. *Recollections of an Irish Rebel.* New York: Young, 1929.

Dickson, David, Dáire Keogh, and Kevin Whelan, eds. *The United Irishmen: Republicanism, Radicalism, and Rebellion.* Dublin: Lilliput, 1993.

Dickson, Tony, and James H. Treble, eds. *People and Society in Scotland, Vol. 3: 1914–1990.* Edinburgh: John Donald, 1992.

Duff, David. *The Life of HRH Princess Louise Duchess of Argyll.* Bath: Cedric Chivers, 1940.

Duffy, Charles Gavan. *Spirit of the Nation.* Dublin: James Duffy, 1843.

———. *Young Ireland: A Fragment of Irish History, 1840–50.* 3 vols. 1880; London: Unwin, 1896.

———. *A Bird's Eye View of Irish History.* Dublin: Duffy, 1882.

———. *Four Years of Irish History, 1845–49.* London: Cassell, Petter, Galpin, 1883.

———. *The League of the North and the South: An Episode in Irish History, 1850–54.* London: Chapman and Hall, 1886.

———. *Thomas Davis.* London: Kegan, Paul, Trench, Trübner, 1890.

———. *Conversations with Carlyle.* London: Sampson Low, Marston, 1892.

———. *My Life in Two Hemispheres.* 2 vols. 1898; Shannon: Irish University Press, 1969.

Elliott, Marianne. *Wolfe Tone: Prophet of Irish Independence.* New Haven, Conn.: Yale University Press, 1989.

Epton, Nina. *Victoria and Her Daughters.* London: Weidenfeld and Nicolson, 1971.

Fitzgerald, Desmond. *Memoirs of Desmond Fitzgerald, 1913–1916.* London: Routledge and Kegan Paul, 1968.

Fitzroy, Almeric. *Memoirs of Sir Almeric Fitzroy.* London: Hutchinson, 1925.

Foley, Tadhg, and Seán Ryder. *Ideology and Ireland in the Nineteenth Century.* Dublin: Four Courts, 1998.

Foster, R. F. *Modern Ireland, 1600–1972.* London: Penguin Books, 1988.

———. *W. B. Yeats: A Life, Vol. 1: The Apprentice Mage.* Oxford: Oxford University Press, 1997.

Frankland, Noble. *Witness of a Century: The Life and Times of Prince Arthur, Duke of Connaught, 1850–1942.* London: Shepheard, Walwyn, 1993.

Fraser, Flora. *The Unruly Queen: The Life of Queen Caroline.* London: Macmillan, 1996.

Fraser, W. H., and R. J. Morris, eds. *People and Society in Scotland, Vol. 2: 1830–1914.* Edinburgh: John Donald, 1990.

Fulford, Roger. *The Royal Dukes.* London: Duckworth, 1933.

———. *The Prince Consort.* London: Macmillan, 1949.

Gailey, Andrew. *The Death of Kindness: The Experience of Constructive Unionism, 1890–1905.* Cork: Cork University Press, 1987.

Galloway, Peter. *The Most Illustrious Order: The Order of St Patrick and Its Knights.* London: Unicorn, 1999.

Garvin, Tom. *The Evolution of Irish Nationalist Politics.* Dublin: Gill and Macmillan, 1981.

———. *1922: The Birth of Irish Democracy.* Dublin: Gill and Macmillan, 1996.

Gash, Norman. *Sir Robert Peel: The Life of Sir Robert Peel after 1830.* London: Longman, 1972.

———. *Aristocracy and People in Britain, 1815–65,* vol. 8 of *The New History of England.* London: Edward Arnold, 1979.

Gellner, Ernest. *Nations and Nationalism.* Ithaca, N.Y.: Cornell University Press, 1983.

Gibbons, Luke. *Transformations in Irish Culture.* Cork: Cork University Press, 1996.

Gillen, Mollie. *The Prince and His Lady.* London: Sidwick and Jackson, 1970.

———. *Royal Duke.* London: Sidgwick, Jackson, 1976.

Gonne, Maud. "Reine de la Disette." Republished as "The Famine Queen." *United Irishman*, 7 April 1900.

———. *A Servant of the Queen: Reminiscences.* 1938; Gerrards Cross: Colin Smythe, 1994.

Gray, Peter. *The Irish Famine.* London: Thames and Hudson, n.d.

———. *Famine, Land, and Politics: British Government and Irish Society, 1843–50.* Dublin: Irish Academic Press, 1999.

Grey, Charles. *The Early Years of His Royal Highness the Prince Consort.* London: Smith, Elder, 1867.

Greville, Charles. *Past and Present Policy of England towards Ireland.* London: Moxon, 1845.

Grogan, Geraldine F. *The Noblest Agitator: Daniel O'Connell and the German Catholic Movement, 1830–50.* Dublin: Veritas, 1991.

Guedalla, Philip. *The Queen and Mr Gladstone.* London: Hodder and Stoughton, 1933.

Gwynn, Denis. *The Life of John Redmond.* London: George G. Harrap, 1932.

Gwynn, S., and G. M. Tuckwell. *The Life of the Rt Hon. Sir Charles W. Dilke.* 2 vols. London: John Murray, 1917.

Halévy, Élie. *A History of the English People in the Nineteenth Century, Vol. 4: Victorian Years, 1841–95.* London: Ernest, Benn, 1961.

Hamer, D. A. *John Morley: Liberal Intellectual in Politics.* Oxford: Clarendon Press, 1968.

Hammond, J. L. *Gladstone and the Irish Nation.* London: Longmans, 1938.

Hanlon, H. J. *Industry and Ascendance in Britain, 1865–1914,* vol. 9 of *The New History of England.* London: Edward Arnold, 1979.

Harcourt, Freda. "The Queen, the Sultan of Turkey, and the Viceroy: A Victorian State Occasion." *London Journal* 5, no. 1 (May 1979): 35–56.

———. "Gladstone, Monarchism, and the New Imperialism, 1868–74." *Journal of Imperial and Commonwealth History* 14, no. 1 (October 1985): 20–51.

Hardie, Frank. *The Political Influence of Queen Victoria, 1861–1901.* Oxford: Oxford University Press, 1935.

———. *The Political Influence of the British Monarch, 1868–1952.* London: B. T. Batsford, 1970.

Harkness, D. W. *The Restless Dominion: The Irish Free State and the British Commonwealth of Nations, 1921–31.* London: Macmillan, 1969.

Healy, T. M. *Loyalty Plus Murder.* Dublin: M. H. Gill, 1884.

Heyck, Thomas William. *The Dimensions of British Radicalism: The Case of Ireland, 1874–95.* Urbana: University of Illinois Press, 1974.

———. *The Transformation of Intellectual Life in Victorian England.* London: Croom Helm, 1982.

Hibbert, Christopher. *George IV, Vol. 1: Prince of Wales, 1762–1811.* London: Longmans, 1972.

———. *George IV, Vol. 2: Regent and King, 1811–30.* London: Allen Lane, 1973.

Hill, Jacqueline. "National Festivals, the State, and 'Protestant Ascendancy' in Ireland, 1790–1829." *Irish Historical Studies* 24 (1984–1985): 30–51.

———. *From Patriots to Unionists: Dublin Civic Politics and Irish Protestant Patriotism, 1660–1840.* Oxford: Clarendon Press, 1997.

Hill, Judith. *Irish Public Sculpture: A History.* Dublin: Four Courts, 1998.

———. "Ideology and Cultural Production: Nationalism and the Public Monument in Mid Nineteenth-Century Ireland." In Tadhg Foley and Seán Ryder, eds., *Ideology and Ireland in the Nineteenth Century* (Dublin: Four Courts, 1998), 55–68.

Holland, B. *The Life of Spencer Compton, Eighth Duke of Devonshire.* 2 vols. London: Longmans, 1911.

Homans, Margaret. *Royal Representations: Queen Victoria and British Culture, 1837–1876.* Chicago: University of Chicago Press, 1998.

Homans, Margaret, and Adrienne Munich, eds. *Remaking Queen Victoria.* Cambridge Studies in Nineteenth-Century Literature and Culture. Cambridge: Cambridge University Press, 1997.

Hoppen, K. T. *Elections, Politics, and Society in Ireland, 1832–1885.* Oxford: Clarendon Press, 1984.

———. *Ireland since 1800: Conflict and Conformity.* London: Longman, 1989.

Hough, Richard. *Edward and Alexandra: Their Private and Public Lives.* London: Hodder and Stoughton, 1992.

Howes, Frances. *Henry Brougham.* New York: St. Martin's Press, 1958.

Hudson, Katherine. *A Royal Conflict.* London: Hodder and Stoughton, 1979.

Hutchinson, John, and Anthony D. Smith, eds. *Nationalism.* Oxford: Oxford University Press, 1994.

Jackson, Alvin. *The Ulster Party: Irish Unionists in the House of Commons, 1884–1911.* Oxford: Clarendon Press, 1989.

James, Louis, ed. *Print and the People, 1819–1851.* London: Allen Lane, 1978.

James, Robert Rhodes. *The British Revolution: British Politics, 1880–1939, Vol. 1: From Gladstone to Asquith, 1880–1914.* London: Hamilton, 1976.

———. *Albert Prince Consort.* London: Hamilton, 1983.

Jeffrey, Keith, ed. *"An Irish Empire?" Aspects of Ireland and the British Empire.* Manchester: Manchester University Press, 1996.

Jenkins, Roy. *Gladstone.* London: Macmillan, 1995.

Joyce, James. *A Portrait of the Artist as a Young Man.* 1916; London: Penguin Books, 1992.

Kearney, Hugh. *The British Isles: A History of Four Nations.* Cambridge: Cambridge University Press, 1989.

Kelleher, Margaret. *The Feminization of Famine: Expressions of the Inexpressible?* Cork: Cork University Press, 1997.

Kelleher, Margaret, and James H. Murphy, eds. *Gender Perspectives in Nineteenth-Century Ireland: Public and Private Spheres.* Dublin: Irish Academic Press, 1997.

Kerr, Donal. *Peel, Priests, and Politics: Sir Robert Peel's Administration and the Roman Catholic Church in Ireland, 1841–46.* Oxford: Clarendon Press, 1982.

———. *"A Nation of Beggars"? Priests, People, and Politics in Famine Ireland, 1846–1852.* Oxford: Clarendon Press, 1994.

Kinealy, Christine. *This Great Calamity: The Irish Famine, 1845–52.* Dublin: Gill and Macmillan, 1994.

The King of the Emerald Island. London: Roake and Varty, n.d.

Kiste, John van der, and Bee Jordoon. *Dearest Affie: Alfred, Duke of Edinburgh, Queen Victoria's Second Son, 1844–1900.* Gloucester: Alan Sutton, 1984.

Kuhn, William M. "Ceremony and Politics: The British Monarchy, 1871–72." *Journal of British Studies* 26, no. 2 (April 1987): 133–62.

Lant, Jeffrey L. "The Jubilee and the Nationalists." *Irish Times,* 10 June 1977.

————. *Insubstantial Pageant: Ceremony and Confusion at Queen Victoria's Court.* London: Hamish Hamilton, 1979.

Larkin, Emmet. *The Roman Catholic Church and the Creation of the Modern Irish State, 1878–1886.* Dublin: Gill and Macmillan, 1975.

————. *The Roman Catholic Church and the Plan of Campaign, 1886–1888.* Cork: Cork University Press, 1978.

————. *The Roman Catholic Church in Ireland and the Fall of Parnell, 1888–1891.* Liverpool: Liverpool University Press, 1979.

————. *The Making of the Roman Catholic Church in Ireland, 1850–1860.* Chapel Hill: University of North Carolina Press, 1980.

————. *The Consolidation of the Roman Catholic Church in Ireland, 1860–1870.* Dublin: Gill and Macmillan, 1987.

————. *The Roman Catholic Church and the Home Rule Movement in Ireland, 1870–1874.* Dublin: Gill and Macmillan, 1990.

————. *The Roman Catholic Church and the Emergence of the Modern Irish Political System, 1874–1878.* Dublin: Four Courts, 1996.

Lee, Sidney. *Queen Victoria: A Biography.* London: Smith, Elder, 1902.

————, ed. *Dictionary of National Biography, 2d Supplement: 1901–1911.* 3 vols. London: Smith Elder, 1912.

————. *King Edward VII: A Biography.* 2 vols. London: Macmillan, 1927.

Leighton, C. D. A. *Catholicism in a Protestant Kingdom.* London: Macmillan, 1994.

Levy, John, ed. *A Full and Revised Report of the Three Days' Discussion in the Corporation of Dublin on the Repeal of the Union.* Dublin, 1843.

Litvack, Leon. "Exhibiting Ireland, 1851–3: Colonial Mimicry in London, Cork, and Dublin." In Leon Litvack and Glenn Hooper, eds., *Ireland in the Nineteenth Century: Regional Identity* (Dublin: Four Courts, 2000), 15–57.

Longford, Elizabeth. *Victoria RI.* 1964. London: Pan, 1966.

Loughlin, James. *Ulster Unionism and British National Identity since 1885.* London: Pinter, 1995.

————. "'Imagining Ulster': The North of Ireland and British National Identity, 1880–1921." In S. J. Connolly, ed., *Kingdoms United? Great Britain and Ireland since 1500.* (Dublin: Four Courts, 1998), 109–22.

Lyons, F. S. L. *John Dillon: A Biography.* London: Routledge and Kegan Paul, 1968.

————. *Charles Stewart Parnell.* London: Collins, 1977.

Lyons, F. S. L., and R. A. J. Hawkins, eds. *Ireland under the Union.* Oxford: Clarendon Press, 1980.

McCaffrey, Lawrence J. *Daniel O'Connell and the Repeal Year.* Lexington: University of Kentucky Press, 1966.

McCarthy, Justin. *Reminiscences.* London: Chatto and Windus, 1899.

————. *The Story of an Irishman.* London: Chatto and Windus, 1904.

————. *Irish Recollections.* London: Hodder and Stoughton, 1911.

McCarthy, Justin, and Mrs. Campbell [R. M.] Praed. *Our Book of Memories.* London: Chatto and Windus, 1912.

McCarthy, M. J. F. *Five Years in Ireland, 1895–1900.* London: Simpkin, Hamilton, Kent, 1901.

McCracken, Donal. *The Irish Pro-Boers, 1877–1902.* Johannesburg: Perskor, 1989.

McDonagh, Oliver. "The Last Bill of Pains and Penalties: The Case of Daniel O'Sullivan, 1869." *Irish Historical Studies* 19 (1974–1975): 136–55.

———. *O'Connell: The Life of Daniel O'Connell, 1775–1847.* London: Weidenfeld and Nicholson, 1991.

McDowell, R. B. *The Irish Administration, 1801–1914.* London: Routledge and Kegan Paul, 1964.

MacHale, Thomas, ed. *Correspondence between the Most Reverend Dr MacHale, Archbishop of Tuam, and the Most Reverend Dr Murray, Archbishop of Dublin, Relative to an Address to Be Presented to Her Majesty Queen Victoria, on the Occasion of Her Visit to Ireland in 1849.* Dublin: M.H. Gill, 1885.

MacKenzie, J. M., ed. *Imperialism and Popular Culture.* Manchester: Manchester University Press, 1986.

———. *Propaganda and Empire: The Manipulation of British Public Opinion, 1880–1960.* Manchester: Manchester University Press, 1984.

McIntyre, W. David. *The Commonwealth of Nations: Origins and Impact, 1869–1971.* Minneapolis: University of Minnesota Press, 1977.

Madden, D. O. *Ireland and Its Rulers since 1829.* London: Newby, 1844.

Magnus, Philip. *Gladstone: A Biography.* London: Murray, 1954.

———. *King Edward the Seventh.* London: Murray, 1964.

Mandler, Peter. *Aristocratic Government in the Age of Reform: Whigs and Liberals, 1830–1852.* Oxford: Clarendon Press, 1990.

Marlow, Joyce. *The Oak and the Ivy: An Intimate Biography of William and Catherine Gladstone.* Garden City, N.Y.: Doubleday, 1977.

Marples, Morris. *Wicked Uncles in Love.* London: Michael Joseph, 1972.

Martin, John. *The Quarrel between Ireland and England.* Dublin: Home Rule Association, 1872.

Martin, Kingsley. *The Magic of Monarchy.* London: T. Nelson, 1937.

———. *The Crown and the Establishment.* London: Hutchinson, 1962.

Martin, Theodore. *The Life of His Royal Highness The Prince Consort.* 5 vols. London: Smith, Elder, 1875–1880.

Maume, Patrick. *The Long Gestation: Irish Nationalist Life, 1891–1918.* Dublin: Gill and Macmillan, 1999.

Maxwell, H. E. *The Life and Letters of George William Frederick, Fourth Earl of Clarendon.* 2 vols. London: Edward Arnold, 1913.

May, Thomas Erskine. *The Constitutional History of England: Since the Accession of George the Third.* 3 vols. Edited and continued until 1911 by Francis Holland. London: Longman, Green, 1912.

Maye, Brian. *Arthur Griffith.* Dublin: Griffith College, 1997.

Miller, David W. *Queen's Rebels: Ulster Loyalism in Historical Perspective.* Dublin: Gill and Macmillan, 1978.

Miller, Kerby A. *Emigrants and Exiles: Ireland and the Irish Exodus to North America.* Oxford: Oxford University Press, 1985.

Milligan, Alice L. *A Royal Democrat: A Sensational Irish Novel.* 1890; Dublin: M. H. Gill, 1892.

Mitchel, John. *The Last Conquest of Ireland (Perhaps).* London: Burns Oates and Washbourne, n.d.

———. *Jail Journal.* 1854. Dublin: Gill, 1913.

———. *The History of Ireland from the Treaty of Limerick to the Present Time: Being a Continuation of the History of the Abbé MacGeoghegan.* Glasgow: Camerson, Ferguson, 1869.

Montesquieu, Charles-Louis de Secondat, Baron de. *Spirit of Laws.* 1748. London: University of California Press, 1977.

Monypenny, W. F., and G. E. Buckele. *The Life of Benjamin Disraeli, Earl of Beaconsfield.* 6 vols. London: John Murray, 1910–1920.

Moody, T. W. *Davitt and the Irish Revolution, 1846–82.* 1982. Oxford: Clarendon Press, 1984.

Moore, David C. *The Politics of Deference: A Study of the Mid-Nineteenth-Century English Political System.* Hassocks: Harvester, 1976.

Moore, George. *Hail and Farewell.* 1911; Gerrards Cross: Colin Smythe, 1985.

Morash, Chris. *The Hungry Voice: The Poetry of the Irish Famine.* Dublin: Irish Academic Press, 1989.

Morley, John. *The Life of William Ewart Gladstone.* 3 vols. London: Macmillan, 1903.

Morgan, Austen. *James Connolly: A Political Biography.* Manchester: Manchester University Press, 1988.

Morris, R. J. "Scotland, 1830–1914: The Making of a Nation within a Nation." In W. H. Fraser and R. J. Morris, eds., *People and Society in Scotland, Vol. 2: 1830–1914.* Edinburgh: John Donald, 1990.

Mulholland, Rosa. *Marcella Grace.* Edited by James H. Murphy. 1886. Washington, D.C.: Maunsel, 2000.

Murphy, James H. "The Role of Vincentian Parish Missions in the 'Irish Counter-Reformation' of the Mid-Nineteenth Century." *Irish Historical Studies* 24 (1984–1985): 152–71.

———. "The Wild Geese." *Irish Review* 16 (1994): 23–28.

———, ed. *Nos Autem: Castleknock College and Its Contribution.* Dublin: Gill and Macmillan, 1996.

———. *Catholic Fiction and Social Reality in Ireland, 1872–1922.* Westport, Conn.: Greenwood Press, 1997.

Murphy, John A. *The College: A History of Queen's/University College Cork.* Cork: Cork University Press, 1995.

Nairn, Tom. "The Glamour of Backwardness." *Times Higher Education Supplement,* 11 January 1985, p. 13.

———. *The Enchanted Glass: Britain and Its Monarchy.* London: Radius, 1988.

Neal, Frank. *Sectarian Violence: The Liverpool Experience, 1819–1814.* Manchester: Manchester University Press, 1987.

Nevill, Barry St. John. *Life at the Court of Queen Victoria, 1861–1901.* Exeter: Webb and Bower, 1984.

Nowlan, Kevin B. *Charles Gavan Duffy and the Repeal Movement.* Dublin: National University of Ireland Press, 1963.

———. *The Politics of Repeal: A Study in the Relations between Great Britain and Ireland, 1841–50.* London: Routledge and Keegan Paul, 1965.

O'Brien, Joseph V. *William O'Brien and the Course of Irish Politics, 1881–1918.* Berkeley and Los Angeles: University of California Press, 1976.

O'Brien, R. B. *Fifty Years of Concessions to Ireland.* 2 vols. London: Sampson Low, Marston, Searle and Rivington, 1883–1885.

————. *Thomas Drummond, Under-secretary in Ireland, 1835–40: Life and Letters.* London: Kegan, Paul, Trench, 1889.

————. *The Life of Charles Stewart Parnell, 1846–91.* 2 vols. London: Smith Elder, 1898.

O'Brien, William. *Recollections.* London: Macmillan, 1905.

————. *Evening Memories.* Dublin: Maunsel, 1920.

O'Brien, William, and Desmond Ryan, eds. *Devoy's Postbag.* 2 vols. Dublin: Fallon, 1948–1953.

O'Brien, William Patrick. *The Great Famine in Ireland and a Retrospect of the Fifty Years 1845–92.* London: Downey, 1896.

O'Bróin, Leon. *Revolutionary Underground: The Story of the Irish Republican Brotherhood, 1858–1924.* Dublin: Gill and Macmillan, 1976.

Ó Buachalla, Breandán. "*James Our True King:* The Ideology of Irish Royalism in the Seventeenth Century." In D. G. Boyce, Robert Eccleshall, and Vincent Geoghegan, eds., *Political Thought in Ireland since the Seventeenth Century* (London: Routledge, 1993), 1–35.

————. "Irish Jacobitism and Irish Nationalism: The Literary Evidence." In Michael O'Dea and Kevin Whelan, eds., *Nations and Nationalism: France, Britain, Ireland, and the Eighteenth-Century Context,* Studies in Voltaire and the Eighteenth Century Vol. 335 (Oxford: Voltaire Foundation, 1995), 103–116.

————. *Aisling Ghéar.* Baile Átha Cliath: An Clóchomhar, 1996.

O'Casey, Sean. *Drums under the Windows.* New York: Macmillan, 1956.

O'Connell, Daniel. *A Memoir on Ireland Native and Saxon, 1172–1660.* Vol. 1. London: C. Dolman, 1843.

O'Connell, John. *The Repeal Dictionary, Part 1 (From A to M).* Dublin: J. Browne, 1845.

O'Day, Alan. *The English Face of Irish Nationalism: Parnellite Involvement in British Politics, 1880–86.* Dublin: Gill and Macmillan, 1977.

————. *Irish Home Rule, 1867–1921.* Manchester: Manchester University Press, 1998.

O'Day, Alan, and John Stevenson, eds. *Irish Historical Documents since 1800.* Dublin: Gill and Macmillan, 1991.

O'Donovan Rossa, Jeremiah. *Rossa's Recollections, 1838 to 1898.* New York, 1896.

O'Farrell, Fergus. *Daniel O'Connell.* Dublin: Gill and Macmillan, 1981.

O'Farrell, P. *England and Ireland since 1800.* Oxford: Oxford University Press, 1975.

————. *The Irish in Australia.* Kensington: New South Wales University Press, 1987.

Ó Gráda, Cormac. *The Great Irish Famine.* Dublin: Gill and Macmillan, 1989.

O'Keeffe, C. M. "Queen Victoria and Mr Parnell." *Celtic Monthly,* June 1880, pp. 518–22.

O'Leary, John. *Recollections of Fenians and Fenianism.* 2 vols. London: Downey, 1898.

O'Mahony, C. *The Viceroys of Ireland.* London: John Long, 1912.

Orangeman, An. *An Address to the Duke of Sussex.* London: 1813.

O'Reilly, B. *John MacHale, Archbishop of Tuam: His Life, Times, and Correspondence.* 2 vols. New York, 1890.

O'Rourke, J. *The History of the Great Irish Famine of 1847 with Notices of Earlier Irish Famines.* Dublin: James Duffy, 1902.

O'Sullivan, Niamh. "The Iron Cage of Femininity: Visual Representation of Women in the 1880s Land Agitation." In Tadhg Foley and Seán Ryder, eds., *Ideology and Ireland in the Nineteenth Century* (Dublin: Four Courts, 1998), 181–96.

Ó Tuathaigh, M. A. G. *Thomas Drummond and the Government of Ireland, 1835–41.* Dublin: National University of Ireland Press, 1977.

Owens, Gary. "Nationalism without Words: Symbolism and Ritual Behaviour in the Repeal 'Monster Meetings' of 1843–5." In James S. Donnelly Jr. and Kirby A. Miller, eds., *Irish Popular Culture, 1650–1850* (Dublin: Irish Academic Press, 1998), 242–69.

Paget, Walburga. *Scenes and Memoirs.* London: Smith, Elder, 1912.

———. *Embassies of Other Days.* London: Hutchinson, 1923.

Parker, C. S., ed. *Sir Robert Peel from His Private Papers.* 3 vols. London: John Murray, 1891–1899.

———. *The Life and Letters of Sir James Graham.* 2 vols. London: John Murray, 1907.

Parnell, Anna. "How They Do in the House of Commons: Notes from the Ladies' Cage." *Celtic Monthly,* May 1880, pp. 469–72; June 1880, pp. 537–41; July 1880, pp. 17–21.

Paseta, Senia. "Nationalist Responses to Two Royal Visits to Ireland, 1900 and 1903." *Irish Historical Studies* 31 (1998–1999): 488–504.

Peatling, G. K. *From Unionism to Liberal Commonwealth: The Transformation of British Public Opinion towards Irish Self-Government, 1865–1925.* Dublin: Irish Academic Press, 2000.

Peel, Robert, Sir. *Memoirs by Sir Robert Peel.* 3 vols. Edited by Lord Mahon and Edward Cardwell. London: John Murray, 1856–1857. Vol. 1, *The Roman Catholic Question, 1828–9.* Vol. 2, *The New Government, 1834–5.* Vol. 3, *The Corn Laws, 1845–6.*

———. *Memoirs by Sir Robert Peel.* 2 vols. Edited by Earl Stanhope and Edward Cardwell. London: John Murray, 1857–1858.

Philpin, C. H. E. *Nationalism and Popular Protest in Ireland.* Cambridge: Cambridge University Press, 1987.

Ponsonby, Arthur. *Henry Ponsonby, Queen Victoria's Private Secretary, His Life from His Letters.* London: Macmillan, 1942.

Ponsonby, Frederick. *Side Lights on Queen Victoria.* London: Macmillan & Co., 1930.

———. *Recollections of Three Reigns.* London: Eyre and Spottiswoode, 1952.

Ponsonby, Mary. *Mary Ponsonby: A Memoir, Some Letters, and a Journal.* Edited by Magdalen Ponsonby. London: John Murray, 1927.

Prest, John. *Lord John Russell.* London: Macmillan, 1972.

Reactions to Irish Nationalism, 1865–1914. Introduction by Alan O'Day. Dublin: Gill and Macmillan, 1987.

Redmond-Howard, L. G. *John Redmond.* London: Hurst and Blacket, 1910.

Reid, T. Wemyss. *Life of the Rt. Hon. W. E. Forster.* 2 vols. London: Chapman, Hall, 1888.

Richardson, Joanna. *George IV: A Portrait.* London: Sidgwick and Jackson, 1966.

Robbins, Keith. *The Eclipse of a Great Power: Modern Britain, 1870–1975.* London: Longman, 1983.

Roberts, Andrew. *Salisbury: Victorian Titan.* London: Weidenfeld and Nicolson, 1999.

Robson, R. *Ideas and Institutions of Victorian Britain.* London: Bell, 1967.

Royal Commission on Historical Manuscripts. *Guide to Sources for British History, Based on the National Register of Archives, Vol. 1: Papers of British Cabinet Ministers, 1782–1900.* London: H.M.S.O., 1989.

———. *Guide to Sources for British History, Based on the National Register of Archives, Vol. 7: Papers of British Politicians, 1782–1900.* London: H.M.S.O., 1989.

Rubenstein, W. D. *Men of Property: The Very Wealthy in Britain since the Industrial Revolution.* London: Croom, 1981.

Russell, J., First Earl. *Recollections and Suggestions, 1813–73.* London, 1875.

Rutherford, John. *The Secret History of the Fenian Conspiracy.* 2 vols. London: Kegan, Paul, 1877.

Ryan, Mark. *Fenian Memoirs.* Dublin: M. H. Gill, 1945.

Saris, A. Jamie. "Imagining Ireland in the Great Exhibition of 1853." In Leon Litvack and Glenn Hooper, eds., *Ireland in the Nineteenth Century: Regional Identity* (Dublin: Four Courts, 2000), 66–86.

St. Aubyn, Giles. *Queen Victoria: A Portrait.* New York: Sinclair and Stevenson, 1991.

Samuel, Raphael. *Patriotism: The Making and Unmaking of British National Identity.* 3 vols. Vol. 1, *History and Politics.* Vol. 2, *Minorities and Outsiders.* Vol. 3, *National Fictions.* London: Routledge, 1989.

[Savry, M. W.] "Lord Clarendon's Administration." *Edinburgh Review* 93 (1851): 208–303.

Senior, H. *Orangeism in Ireland and Britain, 1795–1836.* London: Routledge and Kegan Paul, 1966.

Sexton, Brendan. *Ireland and the Crown, 1922–1936: The Governor-Generalship of the Irish Free State.* Dublin: Irish Academic Press, 1989.

Shannon, Richard. *Gladstone: Heroic Minister, 1865–1898.* London: Allen Lane, 1999.

Short, K. R. M. *The Dynamite War: Irish-American Bombers in Victorian Britain.* Dublin: Gill and Macmillan, 1979.

Sillard, P. A. *The Life and Letters of John Martin.* Dublin: James Duffy, 1901.

Sinclair, Andrew. *Death by Fame: A Life of Elizabeth, Empress of Austria.* London: Constable, 1998.

Sitwell, Edith. *Victoria of England.* Boston: Houghton Mifflin, 1936.

Smith, Anthony D. *Nationalist Movements.* London: Macmillan, 1976.

———. *Nationalism in the Twentieth Century.* Oxford: Martin Robertson, 1979.

———. *National Identity.* London: Penguin, 1991.

Stein, Richard L. *Victoria's Year: English Literature and Culture, 1837–38.* New York: Oxford University Press, 1987.

Stephen, Leslie, and Sidney Lee, eds. *Dictionary of National Biography.* 22 vols. London: Smith Elder, 1908–1909.

Stewart, Robert. *Henry Brougham, 1778–1868.* London: Bodley Head, 1885.

Stockmar, F. von. *The Memoirs of Baron Stockmar.* 2 vols. London: Longmans Green, 1873.

Stone, Laurence, and Jeanne C. Fantier Stone. *An Open Elite? England, 1540–1880.* Oxford: Clarendon Press, 1984.

Strachey, Lytton. *Queen Victoria.* London: Chatto and Windus, 1921.

Sullivan, A. M. *The Story of Ireland.* Dublin: A. M. Sullivan, 1867.

———. *The Trials of Messrs A. M. Sullivan, John Martin, J. J. Lalor, etc.* Dublin: Alley, 1868.

———. *New Ireland.* 2 vols. London: Sampson Low, Marston, Searle and Rivington, 1877.

Sullivan, T. D. *A. M. Sullivan: A Memoir.* Dublin: T. D. Sullivan, 1885.

Swift, Roger. "The Outcast Irish in the British Victorian City: Problems and Perspectives." *Irish Historical Studies* 25 (1986–1987): 264–76.

Swift, Roger, and Sheridan Gilley, eds. *The Irish in Britain, 1815–1939.* London: Pinter, 1989.

———. *The Irish in Victorian Britain: The Local Dimension.* Dublin: Four Courts, 1999.

Taylor, Miles. *The Decline of British Radicalism, 1847–1860.* Oxford: Clarendon Press, 1995.

Thompson, Dorothy. *Queen Victoria, Gender, and Power.* London: Virago, 1990.

Thompson, F. M. L. *English Landed Society in the Nineteenth Century.* London: Routledge and Kegan Paul, 1963.

Tingsten, Herbert. *Victoria and the Victorians.* London: George Allen and Unwin, 1972.

Touhill, Blanche M. *William Smith O'Brien and His Revolutionary Companions in Penal Exile.* Columbia: University of Missouri Press, 1987.

Trainor, Luke. *British Imperialism and Australian Nationalism.* Cambridge: Cambridge University Press, 1994.

Travers, Pauric. "Our Fenian Dead: Glasnevin Cemetery and the Genesis of the Republican Funeral." In James Kelly and Uáitéar MacGearailt, eds., *Dublin and Dubliners* (Dublin: Helicom, 1990), 52–72.

Villiers, G. J. T. H. *A Vanished Victorian, Being the Life of George Villiers, Fourth Earl of Clarendon.* London: Eyre & Spottiswoode, 1938.

Vincent, John. *Gladstone and Ireland.* Oxford: Oxford University Press, 1978.

Waldron, Jarlath. *Maamtrasna: The Murders and the Mystery.* Dublin: Edmund Burke, 1992.

Walpole, Spencer. *The Life of Lord John Russell.* 2 vols. London: Longmans Green, 1889.

Ward, J. T. *Sir James Graham.* London: Macmillan, 1967.

Ward, Margaret. *Maud Gonne: A Life.* London: Pandora, 1990.

Weintraub, Stanley. *Victoria.* 1987. London: John Murray, 1996.

———. "Victoria and Ireland: A Tale of Too Little and Too Late." In Birgit Bramsbäck and Martin Croghan, eds., *Anglo-Irish and Irish Literature: Aspects of Language and Culture* (Uppsala: Uppsala University Press, 1988), 213–220.

———. *Albert Uncrowned King.* London: John Murray, 1997.

Werly, J. M. "The Irish in Manchester." *Irish Historican Studies* 18 (1972–1973): 345–58.

Whatley, Christopher A. "Royal Day, People's Day: The Monarch's Birthday in Scotland, c. 1660–1860." In Roger Mason and Norman MacDougall, eds., *People and Power in Scotland: Essays in Honour of C. T. Smout* (Edinburgh: John Donald, 1992), 170–88. Whyte, J. H. *The Independent Irish Party, 1850–59.* Oxford: Oxford University Press, 1958.

———. *The Tenant League and Irish Politics in the Eighteen-Fifties.* Dundalk: Dundalgan, 1972.

Wickham Legg, L. G., ed. *Dictionary of National Biography (1931–1940).* London: Oxford University Press, 1949.

Wickham Legg, L. G., and E. T. Williams, eds. *Dictionary of National Biography (1941–1950).* London: Oxford University Press, 1959.

Williams, Richard. *The Contentious Crown: Public Discussion of the British Monarchy in the Reign of Queen Victoria.* Brookfield, Vt: Ashgate, 1997.

Wilson, John. *CB: The Life of Sir Henry Campbell-Bannerman.* New York: St. Martin's Press, 1973.

Woodham Smith, Cecil. *The Great Hunger: Ireland, 1845–1849.* London: Penguin Books, 1962.

———. *Queen Victoria: Her Life and Times.* London: Hamish Hamilton, 1972.

Wright, D. G. *Democracy and Reform, 1815–85.* Harlow: Longmans, 1970.

Wyndham, George. *Life and Letters of George Wynham.* Edited by J. W. Mackail and G. P. Wyndham. London: Hutchinson, 1925.

Ziegler, Philip. *William IV.* London: Harper, Row, 1971.

———. *Melbourne.* London: Collins, 1976.

Index

Abject Loyalty: Nationalism and Monarchy in Ireland During the Reign of Queen Victoria
was designed and composed in Centaur by Kachergis Book Design, Pittsboro,
North Carolina, and printed on 60-pound Glatfelter Natural Smooth
and bound by Sheridan Books, Ann Arbor, Michigan.